Hellenistic Land Battles
300–167 BCE

ALSO BY FRED EUGENE RAY, JR.
AND FROM McFARLAND

*Greek and Macedonian Land Battles of the
4th Century B.C.: A History and Analysis
of 187 Engagements* (2012)

*Land Battles in 5th Century B.C. Greece:
A History and Analysis of 173 Engagements*
(2009; paperback 2011)

BY PAUL M. BARDUNIAS AND
FRED EUGENE RAY, JR.
AND FROM McFARLAND

*Hoplites at War: A Comprehensive
Analysis of Heavy Infantry Combat
in the Greek World, 750–100 BCE* (2016)

Hellenistic Land Battles 300–167 BCE

A History and Analysis of 130 Engagements

FRED EUGENE RAY, JR.

McFarland & Company, Inc., Publishers
Jefferson, North Carolina

LIBRARY OF CONGRESS CATALOGUING-IN-PUBLICATION DATA

Names: Ray, Fred Eugene, Jr., 1949– author.
Title: Hellenistic land battles 300-167 BCE : a history and analysis of 130 engagements / Fred Eugene Ray, Jr.
Description: Jefferson, North Carolina : McFarland & Company, Inc., Publishers, 2020 | Includes bibliographical references and index.
Identifiers: LCCN 2020038128 | ISBN 9781476682563 (paperback : acid free paper) ∞
ISBN 9781476640907 (ebook)
Subjects: LCSH: Greece—History, Military—To 146 B.C. | Military art and science—Greece—History—To 1500. | Soldiers—Greece—History—To 1500. | Greece—History—281-146 B.C. | Battles—Greece—History. | Armies—Greece.
Classification: LCC U33 .R3945 2020 | DDC 355.4/738—dc23
LC record available at https://lccn.loc.gov/2020038128

BRITISH LIBRARY CATALOGUING DATA ARE AVAILABLE

ISBN (print) 978-1-4766-8256-3
ISBN (ebook) 978-1-4766-4090-7

© 2020 Fred Eugene Ray, Jr. All rights reserved

No part of this book may be reproduced or transmitted in any form or by any means, electronic or mechanical, including photocopying or recording, or by any information storage and retrieval system, without permission in writing from the publisher.

Front cover image: Pyrrhus of Epirus repulsed from Sparta © 2020 duncan1890/iStock

Printed in the United States of America

McFarland & Company, Inc., Publishers
Box 611, Jefferson, North Carolina 28640
www.mcfarlandpub.com

For those precious patriots who have sacrificed so very much on our nation's battlefields, and for the many honorable allies who have stood with such great bravery at their side.

Table of Contents

Preface   1

Introduction   3

1. Instruments of War: Last of the Successors (300–281 BCE)   5
   Grecian Warfare to the 3rd Century   5
   New Contenders and Old Successors   10

2. Phalanx Versus Legion: Sicilian Tyrants and Pyrrhic Wars (280–275 BCE)   21
   Feuding Greeks and Carthage   21
   Roman Warfare to the 3rd Century   24
   Pyrrhus in the West   28

3. Gauls, Pyrrhus, Carthage and Rome: Gallic Invasions, Last of Pyrrhus and the First Punic/Mercenary War (279–237 BCE)   40
   Gauls and Greeks   40
   Pyrrhus and Greece   49
   The First Punic/Mercenary War   54

4. Sundered Realms: Achaean, Illyrian, Anatolian, Cleomenean and Syrian Wars (245–217 BCE)   67
   Achaean League and Illyrian Actions   67
   Anatolia in Turmoil   71
   Cleomenean War   74
   Aratus' Last Battle, Molon's Revolt and the Fourth Syrian War   82

5. Phalanx Triumphant: The Second Punic War, Phase 1 (c. 236–211 BCE)   88
   Carthaginian Operations, 237–219   88
   Northern Italy, 218–216   90
   Italy, Sardinia and Iberia, 215–211   102

6. The Road to Zama: The Second Punic War, Phase 2 (210–202 BCE)   112
   Italy and Iberia, 210–205   112
   Northern Italy and Africa, 204–202   121

7. Twilight of the Phalanx: Antiochus III, Philopoemen and the First/Second Macedonian Wars (214–196 BCE)   131
   Seleucia's Frontiers   131
   The First Macedonian War and Philopoemen's Reforms   135
   The Second Macedonian War   139

8. An End to the Greek Way of War: Seleucia in Decline and the Fall
    of Macedonia (195–167 BCE)   148
    The Wars Against Nabis and Antiochus 148
    The Third Macedonian War 159
    Hybridization of Hellenistic Warfare 166

Conclusions   169
    Combat Formations—Revolution or Evolution? 169
    Hoplites, Sarissaphoroi, Theurophoroi and Legionaries 171
    Macedonian Cavalry Decline? 173
    Phalanx or Legion? 174
    Final Thoughts 176

Appendix 1: Roman Defeats at Allia (390 BCE) and Caudium (321 BCE)   179

Appendix 2: Hellenistic Land Battles/Keys to Victory (300–167 BCE)   182

Appendix 3: Legion Versus Phlanx (280–168 BCE)   186

Chapter Notes   187

Bibliography   219

Index   225

Preface

The catalogue of described battles herein called "Hellenistic" employs that term not only in the sense of them falling within a 134-year span of the wider temporal era so named (323–30 BCE), but also in each involving at least one army that embraced Grecian martial culture. Actions fought by Carthage, a barbarian nation whose military had for the most part adopted the Greek way of war, are therefore included, while those waged by Rome against non–Hellenistic foes are not due to Roman warfare having by the subject period broken sharply from its Hellenic roots. The passage of time has obscured the facts of these engagements as a great deal of the closest-to-contemporary written record has been lost, most related physical artifacts have turned to rust or dust, and even some of the very ground in dispute has been profoundly altered by both man and nature over the course of better than two millennia. The complete account of all significant combats in the targeted era needed to best illuminate its battlefield realities thus regularly requires some key elements to be extensively reconstructed. That process is unavoidably speculative yet can be highly informative when approached with caution and awareness of its innate limitations.

Given that broad national and cultural parameters hold fairly constant across large sets of engagements (a given nation's favored tactical methodology throughout the mid–3rd century for example), the unique factors that guide reconstruction of any particular action are most often reduced to topography and manpower. Fortunately, the sort of mutual consent to engage that was highly characteristic of ancient pitched combat usually favored selection of reasonably flat and open battlegrounds and our sources generally report any features contrary to that even when sparing of other data. And elsewhere, either clues within surviving narratives or modern studies of still-intact terrain can provide adequate topographic information. Manpower therefore tends to be the ingredient most frequently missing from what is needed to properly assess the credibility of historical sources, bridge any critical gaps in them, and logically project as likely and complete a course of events on the field of engagement as possible.

It is essential in devising an optimum battle evaluation that inputs on manpower be exacting as to troop types/armaments and numbers. Most of the time, our preserved literature provides these items for the more famous and best-described actions. However, for by far the greater number of engagements, this crucial data must be deduced in part or whole using any and all indirect sources that can be brought to bear. Most useful among these are: (1) casualty figures, (2) other musters for a subject army under similar circumstances, (3) better documented analogs involving comparable armies and situations, (4) known tactical/marching orders applied to the terrain limitations at hand, and (5) fighting-age strength by class/weaponry per a state's norms for mustering and estimated population.

Specific approaches for determining such "best guesses" at manpower are noted for all of the following reconstructions so that readers can make their own judgments as to each's relative probability.

Provision of historical/strategic contexts for the combat narratives presented here has been a high priority, calling for those that fall within the same campaign to be grouped together. As a result, though engagements are generally arranged in chronological order, there is considerable overlap on occasion to accommodate simultaneous fighting in unrelated theaters. This occurs most extensively in Chapters 5 and 6 that deal with the Second Punic War, covering that long struggle complete and separate from time-parallel actions elsewhere in the Hellenistic world whose descriptions resume in Chapter 7. All dates in the text and attached illustrations are BCE unless noted to the contrary. Transliteration of the Greek alphabet has always been problematic and the approach taken here is to use Romanized or Anglicized forms where likely to be more familiar to readers of English, and any foreign terms introduced are italicized on their initial appearance. Measurements employ the metric system with maps and other figures embedded near the first related text. There are extensive footnotes with supporting information in the form of literature citations as well as supplementary discussions (sometimes lengthy) that would otherwise unduly interrupt the primary narrative.

Any attempt to tell the story of long-ago Grecian battle begins with ancient authors like Herodotus, Thucydides, Xenophon, and Diodorus, whose preserved writings so vitally inform us today. Most influential for this particular study is the work of Polybius, who was contemporary with the latest portion of the subject period, and the extant texts of Plutarch, Livy, and Appian. Likewise, the contributions of modern investigators have been essential, as attested by how often those most relied upon are cited herein. I would also like to extend my thanks to Anton Khatsanovich, whose artistry has greatly enhanced my own crude illustrations. Finally, I am especially indebted to my friend and colleague Paul Bardunias, for not only saving me from errors of fact but also providing sage philosophical guidance toward making this and many a past effort more productive and genuine.

Introduction

Militaries within the Mediterranean core of western Hellenistic civilization were dominated at the dawn of the 3rd century BCE by various forms of the combat formation known as a phalanx. Based upon a rectangle of armored infantrymen equipped with spear and/or pike closely aligned in modest files and expansive ranks with attached auxiliaries both mounted and on foot, this method of fighting had been modified and locally adapted as it spread from 8th century roots in mainland Greece via copy and conquest to become the reigning standard for pitched battle from the Atlantic shore above the Pillars of Hercules to the broad plains in the shadow of India's lofty Hindu Kush. The lone exception to this approach for making war among the era's major powers was in central Italy at the rising city-state of Rome. Responding to challenges from barbarian rivals, the Romans had abandoned their own long-used phalanx in favor of a less dense and more flexible formation better suited to the rugged terrain on which they found themselves forced to operate. This alternate combat methodology would by 160 BCE come to almost completely eclipse phalanx-based warfare as Roman armies embarked on a campaign of territorial expansion, engulfing one competing Hellenistic state after another and driving those remaining to adopt elements of this new fighting technique in an ultimately futile effort to avoid absorption into Rome's growing empire.

Yet, inevitable as the triumph of Roman warfare might appear today, that was not at all obvious at the time. Many conflicts around the Hellenistic world down well into the 2nd century continued to be resolved solely by phalanx-based armies. And Rome was not very successful in initially challenging that long preeminent way of war. Indeed, its citizens twice had to fall back on the defensive in fear that foes might reach the city's gates in 280 and 218 after the phalanxes of Pyrrhus and Hannibal inflicted costly defeats upon their legions at Heraclea and Cannae respectively. Nor was the first Roman campaign overseas a success, ultimately meeting disaster at Tunes in 255 against a phalanx of Carthaginian and Greek heavy infantry under the brilliant Spartan mercenary Xanthippus. The fact is that even some of the most celebrated of legionary victories against Hellenistic arrays, as per that at Cynoscephalae in 197, were closely run affairs that might well have gone the other way.

The full story of pitched combat over the pivotal span from 300 to 167 BCE (when the last wholly Grecian phalanx might have engaged) is a multifaceted tale of innovative tactics devised by some of antiquity's greatest generals in leading eclectic mixes of men and arms to serve grand strategies both gloriously victorious and spectacularly failed. Gravely under-documented, the picture we have of this important segment of our martial past is less a stark photo than a complex and badly faded tapestry woven with many a loose strand deserving of serious investigation. And a best-possible enquiry into such challenging topics not only calls for analyses of famed actions frequently waged under exceptional conditions, but also the vast majority of smaller and much lesser known contests that can often be more reflective of the focus period's actual day-to-day battlefield truths. And it's toward that admittedly ambitious goal that the following detailed evaluations in context for all 130 significant engagements of the subject era's Hellenistic armies are humbly dedicated.

1. Instruments of War
Last of the Successors (300–281 BCE)

The late 4th century saw Macedonia's Alexander III (the Great) conquer the kingdom of Persia, adding it to inherited holdings at the southeastern edge of Europe in creating an empire stretching across parts of three continents. The instrument of that mighty feat was a large and powerful army that Alexander's father, Philip II, had crafted by creatively modifying the then dominant heavy infantry system of his Greek neighbors to the south. This martial juggernaut was professional, well-drilled, and battle-hardened and would grow deadlier still under the son. Coming to the throne very young, Alexander proved extremely ambitious and headstrong, attributes that led at times to recklessness in his operations and tactics. Yet, he was also a truly brilliant battlefield improviser, usually able to escape any predicament engendered by his inherent impetuosity. His men admired him for that rare genius, as well as for a highly charismatic personality and tremendous bravery in always leading from the front. Thus, when Alexander died in 323, those left holding his realm ("the Successors" as they came to be known) invoked his image if not always his tactics in seeking power for themselves.[1]

Incessant bouts of violence spawned by fraternal contests among the Successors would leave Alexander's Macedonian kingdom shattered for good by century's end. Ruling detached domains in Europe, Africa, and Asia, the survivors went their own ways. But though their political world was fragmented, these various royal warlords shared much militarily, all deriving their combat approaches from common prototypes. Still, there were some differences among them; these notably included subtle variations in how closely each hewed to tactics identified with Philip as opposed to alternatives developed by his heir. Personal history undoubtedly played a role in this, with a commander's past relationship to father and/or son exerting a unique effect. Moreover, each man had to acknowledge factors distinct to his own military situation and adjust material as well as tactics along diverse lines toward addressing that separate reality. Therefore, despite the Successor armies of the early 3rd century being unanimous in having a strong generic resemblance to those of both Philip and Alexander, a combination of chance history and practical adaptation rendered them at least modestly differing instruments of war.

Grecian Warfare to the 3rd Century

The tactical roots of Hellenistic warfare in the 3rd century go far back in time to the initial rise of linear battle formations among the Greeks. This is reflected in the poetry of

Homer, which dates from as early as the 8th century and portrays individual contests between aristocratic heroes set amid descriptions of wider action sounding very much like the sort of combat associated with the close-order arrays called phalanxes well documented by historians of the 5th and 4th centuries. More certainly dated and nearly as old (7th century), we also have verse from poets extolling martial virtues closely identified with phalanx fighting.[2] This innovation in tactics seems to have been an inevitable product of Greeks banding together into either a city-state (*polis*) or tribal/regional federation (*koinon*). Such collectives allowed pooling of resources toward more effectively pursuing grander military operations of either an aggressive or protective nature on behalf of these communities in contrast to past small-scale raiding for short-term material gain by lesser clans/tribes.

Perhaps largely motivated by the need for more crops to feed rapidly expanding populations, these new states came increasingly to apply their martial efforts toward either acquiring or defending marginal tracts of arable land. And to wage such border wars in an optimal manner, they established militias incorporating as much of the adult male population as could afford to take part at its own expense, usually according full citizenship exclusively to those so participating. Whereas Grecian warfare had previously revolved around a few warriors of high social status in possession of expensive armor and horses/chariots, these larger, revised armies were much more egalitarian by necessity. Their cores now consisted of spear-armed infantrymen called hoplites (*hoplitai* from *hopla*, weapons/arms, and thus "men-at-arms"[3]), causing this socio-military development to sometimes be labeled a "hoplite revolution." These men were among the more prosperous in their societies, having adequate wealth to acquire somewhat costly equipment; yet, they could muster in an order-of-magnitude greater numbers than the richer, horse-borne aristocrats of old.[4] Prestigious individuals among the latter continued to largely make up any given state's leadership; however, their role as a class on the field of battle now devolved to that of mounted auxiliaries. They thus joined foot-skirmishers too poor to afford armor in screening both ahead of the phalanx and off its flanks.

Though early Greek hoplites often carried two spears, one for throwing and the other for thrusting, they eventually became pure hand-to-hand (shock) fighters. Their primary weapon was a one-handed spear (*enchos* or *doru/dory*) around 2.5m in length. The hoplite dory was optimally designed solely for close combat, with its considerable reach allowing for at least the first two ranks of a tightly filed array to strike a directly opposed foe. It had a leaf-like steel point and a butt spike (*styrax* or *sauroter*, often of the valuable copper-tin alloy bronze). The latter joined with forward tapering of the wooden shaft to help shift the weapon's point of balance rearward so that, when held by a leather sleeve wrapped around that spot, the dory's business end would extend as far forward as possible for maximum range. Secondary armament beyond the spear consisted of either a steel straight-sword (*xiphos*) that was sharp on both edges or a downward curving saber (*makhaira* or *kopis*) sharp on its lower edge (and sometimes back-tip).

The most important piece of a hoplite's protective gear was a large (approximately 1m across) shield called an *aspis* (*aspides* plural). This was made of wood, its outer surface covered (often completely, but at least around the edge) with a thin (less than 0.5mm thick) layer of bronze that easily polished to a mirror-like finish. This device was distinctly round and concave (bowing outward) with an offset rim-reinforcement and was suspended from a sleeve (*porpax*) at center for the left-forearm and hand-grip (*antilabe*) near the perimeter.[5] That arrangement meant that the aspis' holder gained protection from its right half while the left covered the man standing alongside, which marked this device as being best suited for use in dense, linear formations. Other defensive equipment included a bronze helmet (*kranos*), a cuirass (*thorax*, initially bronze and later of lighter-weight leather or stiffened linen) for the torso, a banded kilt (*pteruges*) with strips of leather or layered linen to guard the upper thighs, and snap-on greaves (*knemides*) of bronze to ward from knee to foot. Most of this tackle (a hoplite's *panoplia* or panoply) was optional and there was a tendency over time for individuals to discard chosen items toward reducing cost and providing greater comfort. But the spear and shield always remained vital to standard Greek battle arrays.

The dominant combat formation of the ancient Greeks was the classical phalanx, which is sometimes distinguished from the later Macedonian phalanx (see below) as being "Doric" due to its presumed development among speakers of the Dorian Greek dialect in the Peloponnese of southwestern Greece. It perhaps originated there at Argos, hence common identification of the formation's characteristic aspis shield as "Argive"[6]; however, there is also evidence at Corinth and Sparta for its early employment. The truth is that the dawn of phalanx warfare is shrouded in great uncertainty and no small amount of controversy. The view considered most likely here is that it probably grew organically from warriors self-organizing in a "bottom-up" fashion.[7] This would have begun as a simple matter of missilemen lacking much in the way of protective gear sensibly sheltering behind better-supplied mates with shields and armor. As the number of such well-appointed combatants grew with the advent of larger and more inclusive communities, they would have eventually come together into tight, linear arrays as an equally practical way to fight foes straight ahead while comrades alongside shielded them from lateral strikes. With the count of heavy infantrymen continuing to swell, they came to span entire battle-fronts, and filing then let a second rank join the shock action even as those deeper in the array supplied both reserves and pushing potential toward getting all available strength into the fray.

The prototypical phalanx might thus have been an entirely self-organized phenomenon, with refinement of hoplite panoplies progressing logically from there toward creating an optimum warrior to service the formation. When fully developed, a classical phalanx's hoplites deployed shield-rim to shield-rim in ranks up to hundreds of men wide and usually filed in increments of four (four, eight, twelve, sixteen, etc.).[8] This formation was extremely powerful along its front, where scores to many hundreds of long spears could strike out from behind a mobile barrier of closely spaced shields. Its primary weaknesses lay first in a limited ability to cross uneven ground and still maintain the close order vital to its design; therefore, effective phalanx deployment was confined to relatively level surfaces. The phalanx's other major weakness stemmed from having all offensive potential focused forward, rendering flanks incapable of counter-attack. And even purely defensive efforts on those ends of the line were partially compromised. This was due to the hoplite aspis' suspension system, which for all its strengths, only covered the left side of a man standing on that flank and not the flank of one stationed along the right. It was thus necessary to ward the formation at each lateral extreme by placing it up against a buttress, usually a terrain feature, or providing a guard of light infantry and/or cavalry in the absence of such a physical anchor.

Regardless of any debatable details of the classical phalanx's possible bottom-up evolution, it's certain that the more sophisticated applications of that formation were imposed top-down by army leaders. Their options for this were, however, severely limited in most cases during the early centuries of phalanx warfare due to the non-professional nature of the troops involved. These were draftees that rarely if ever drilled as units. That rendered the typical militia formation incapable of executing anything beyond the most rudimentary of pre-engagement maneuvers, perhaps consisting in most instances of merely forming up in a reasonable semblance of rank and file before advancing at the enemy on signal (usually via *salpinx* horn). Once in contact with their foes, these hoplites (with their generals alongside and serving as little more than private soldiers in the ranks) would forge ahead single-mindedly against those immediately in front, with the sound and fury of close combat all about preventing awareness of what was going on even a few meters from where they stood. What followed, whether victory and pursuit or defeat and flight, was then much more a matter of instinct than any kind of imposed command and control. Still, some innate behaviors were consistent enough that leadership could take advantage of them, with what is generally called "rightward drift" being by far the most exploitable of those actions.

Thucydides has given us a detailed description of the way phalanxes tended to fade toward the right while marching into battle as each man instinctively sought protection from the shield next to him on that side.[9] Their right wing would thus often shift far enough beyond the left end of an opposing array that it could fold about that flank if unanchored to simultaneously strike from front, side, and even behind. That would usually trigger a rolling rout that tore the victimized formation apart as panic spread rightward to send men running for the rear lest they be closed about from multiple quarters. This ever-present threat led to the common practice of an army's best troops taking station on the right. There, in addition to braving an absence of shield protection along that flank, they could exploit this natural phenomenon of drift. The next most capable men would then stand far left to counter any similar ploy on the enemy's part, while the weakest soldiers held the phalanx's least demanding post at center.

It would take ancient Greece's most astute warriors at Sparta to refine and further weaponize this natural bent toward rightward drift into a studied tactic of much greater effectiveness known as *cyclosis*. That called not only for placing the finest fighters far right within their phalanxes, but also for those elites to deliberately exaggerate their shift toward the right and then envelop the enemy left flank with well-practiced precision. The intense peace-time drill that made this possible was unique to the Spartans, who were alone among the Greeks in fielding a professional army, doing so by means of a singular caste system in which serfs supported the state's hoplites as they pursued the full-time study of war. Several other poleis eventually followed Sparta's lead to some extent, enhancing their militias by forming contingents of picked men (*epilektoi*) trained at state expense.

State-of-the-art warfare in the mid–4th century Greek world was therefore a matter of classical phalanxes engaging in shock combat, their lengths divided into an attack segment on the right wing and a defensive segment on the left.[10] However, as alluded to above, Philip II of Macedonia now contributed a major innovation to the Grecian military toolbox by devising a formation variant with more specialized components. His nation did not have a tradition of phalanx warfare, depending instead on crowds of lightly armed foot-soldiers and aristocratic horsemen who uniquely employed lances as shock fighters. However, Philip as a boy had been a hostage at Thebes, where he came to appreciate the value of hoplite warfare such that he sought a chance to introduce it at home. That opportunity arose when the Macedonian throne became his upon the battlefield death of his older brother in 359. That autumn through the following spring, the young king raised a force of hoplites, probably drawing upon both a small royal bodyguard already in existence and Greek mercenaries fortuitously returning at just that moment from contingents disbanded by imperial decree in Persia.[11] These would form the right/strike wing of his new phalanx. But it was across the rest of his array where Philip now became a true pioneer of the ancient art of war.

With no more spearmen of his own on hand and lacking sufficient funds to contract an adequate force of additional hirelings to fill out the center and left of his formation, Philip stocked those ranks with locals outfitted inexpensively with a small shield (*pelte*) and long (3.5–4m), two-hand pike (*sarissa*) in lieu of the costly hoplite panoply. He then likely supplemented these men with a modest number of similarly equipped troops culled from among the mercenaries recently dismissed from Persian service. The Athenian general Iphicrates had devised the latter years earlier toward increasing the size of the phalanx he was leading in Egypt under contract to Persia, thereby transforming a surplus of light infantry into low-cost substitutes for hoplites in short supply.[12] Iphicrates had then gone on to serve in Thrace, where he aided Philip's father and was taken into the Macedonian royal family in reward. It was thus from this adopted brother that Philip got the idea for his own land's foot-skirmishers to take up the sarissa in quickly raising a large force of "hoplites on-the-cheap." And the chance repatriation of some of Iphicrates' own converted troopers then provided him with a team of experienced professionals to both slightly boost manpower within his budget and (perhaps of rather greater import) provide trainers/role models for his newly formed native pikemen.

But beyond simply providing an economical solution to Philip's shortage of heavy infantry, his corps of pikemen (*phalangitai* or phalangites) performed a specialized function within the phalanx and did so more effectively than the traditional hoplites they were designed to replace. The left/defensive wings of phalanxes were normally charged with holding their ground long enough for right/strike wings to carry their side of the battleground and secure a victory. Yet they had to do this despite often being badly out-classed by a foe's best troops posted on his opposing right wing and aided by rightward drift. The result was that these defensive arrays frequently failed too soon and triggered an outright defeat or gave way more or less in synch with the enemy's corresponding left to set up simultaneous right-wing successes that then either led to a reengagement or rendered the battle mutually costly and indecisive. However, Philip's phalangites, though not ideally equipped to project offensive force into a spear-armed front,[13] were vastly more adept at defending against the same compared to traditional hoplites. This was because a line of pikemen plying 3.5–4m long sarissai presented a daunting barrier of overlapping weapons at least three rows deep. Getting close enough to reach Philip's leading rank of phalangites with a spear of only some 2.5m in length was thus an extremely difficult task and, at the very best, would easily consume enough time to ensure his right wing had an excellent opportunity to carry its side of the field.

As for that Macedonian right/attack wing, though this was manned by hoplites (*hypaspitai* or hypaspists[14]) with gear essentially identical to that utilized by their counterparts in a classical Greek phalanx, Philip made innovations here as well toward instilling greater specialization and effectiveness. The first of these was to field a hoplite contingent of the highest possible quality, doing so by putting its men on a professional basis that allowed for extensive training both as individuals and in formation.[15] He then took advantage of his nation's singular brand of shock-capable cavalrymen to post those heavy troopers next to his elite hoplites, where they could use a lance (*xyston*) in direct support toward turning an enemy's left wing instead of merely contributing to a missile-armed flank screen as was typical for other horsemen of the era. And, finally, Philip sought to guarantee that the light infantry attached to his cavalry would perform to an equally high standard by hiring crack mercenaries for that role and mixing them in among the riders for optimum effect.[16]

Undergoing some minor tweaks in the ensuing years,[17] this new-style Macedonian phalanx rolled over Philip's foes to make him master of nearly all of Greece in the wake of a grand triumph over a last, large coalition phalanx of hoplites at the battle of Chaeronea in 338. Alexander inherited this deadly combat system upon his father's assassination two years later and skillfully put it to further use in greatly expanding the Macedonian empire. His applications of the formation differed from those of his sire mostly in having significantly greater reliance on mounted action. But, rather than fundamental change in the phalanx's design, this was more a consequence of having to fight cavalry-rich enemies across the wide plains of Asia as opposed to the classical phalanxes within restricting mountain valleys that had formed Philip's primary opposition. And the Successors that took up the Macedonian phalanx in the closing years of the 4th century followed this same pattern of adaptation to differing terrains and foes. The most notable development here was an increasing frequency of Macedonian-type phalanxes battling each other during conflicts between rival Successor kingdoms, which led to compensating for the relative ineffectiveness of hoplites against a hedge of sarissai by replacing them with elite pikemen on the attack wing better suited to fighting their own kind.[18] This was largely confined to Asia, where pike-armed phalanxes tended to keep each other in check as mounted contingents sought decisions off their flanks. In Europe, however, tactics and related deployments seem to have trended closer to those that had served Philip so well in the past, reflecting both more confined terrain and continued threats from opposing heavy spearmen.

The 3rd century thus opened with Grecian armies utilizing a variety of at least modestly differing combat systems. These included both classical phalanxes completely manned by hoplite spearmen as well as Macedonian phalanxes that varied regionally from something resembling Philip II's seminal design with hoplites and shock-horsemen on a strike-wing supported by pikemen elsewhere to much more pike-dependent arrays relying heavily upon attached cavalry for an offensive component. One useful way of looking at these linear battle formations in action regardless of the specifics of individual design has recently been proposed by Bardunias.[19] He classifies engagements according to the tactical scheme being practiced as specifically composed for any given combat setting, defining a trio of distinctive fighting modes: (1) *bludgeon*: advancing directly into line-versus-line shock combat; (2) *bastion*: holding in rearward reserve to support auxiliaries fighting forward; (3) *barricade*: standing as a screen for auxiliaries firing missiles from behind the last rank. Such assessments of how a Hellenistic army actually fought provide valuable insights into its other aspects as well.

New Contenders and Old Successors

The battle of Ipsus in 301 had taken the life of Antigonus Monophthalmos (One-eyed), the most senior of Alexander the Great's surviving commanders and the last with any realistic ambitions to control that conqueror's entire domain. But though Antigonus had lost his bid to gain the succession, his son Demetrius and son-in-law Pyrrhus had managed to survive the debacle, riding away with a modest collection of other escapees to fight another day. These young men (thirty-three and eighteen respectively) would go on to play prominent roles in the subsequent history of the Hellenistic world, both as famed generals and as kings over portions of the now broken empire that lay within Alexander's Macedonian homeland. Also surviving were four of Alexander's original Successors. These included the battle's victors: Cassander, Seleucus (I, Nikator/Conqueror) and Lysimachus. In the aftermath of Ipsus, Cassander solidified his control over Macedonia and most of Greece,

Seleucus took over the eastern provinces of Alexander's Asian conquests, and Lysimachus secured his hold on territories straddling the Hellespont in Thrace and Asia Minor (Mysia, Lydia, Phrygia, Ionia). And there was also Ptolemy I, who had not participated at Ipsus, but benefited nonetheless in that his rule from Egypt now stretched east as far as southern Syria (Coele Syria), which Seleucus seems to have been willing to effectively concede for convenience's sake.

Mantinea IV and Sparta I (294)

Demetrius was only thirteen when Alexander died and had no direct experience of the man's military methods. Therefore, though he clearly admired and tried to copy legendary aspects of Alexander's heroic leadership style (with disastrous results on occasion due to a lack of that role model's great talent for impromptu maneuvering), much of the nuts-and-bolts of his tactical training must have come from his parent. And Antigonus would certainly have hewn much closer to Philip on this than to Alexander, having already been a seasoned commander in his late 40s on the day the latter came to the throne in 336 (he had at that point seen more campaign seasons under the father than the son had seen birthdays). It's also notable that, even among Philip's officers, Antigonus likely stood out as something of an "old school" type. His early background and first known command under Alexander, which consisted of 7,000 allied hoplites, combine to provide indications of significant expertise in (and likely leanings toward) the classical tactics of those traditional Greek heavy infantrymen.[20] Antigonus and his son had obviously come to modify the older precepts of Greek and Macedonian warfare in the closing years of the 4th century, adapting them to campaign across the broad plains of their own Asian realm versus the narrow valleys that had hosted most of Philip's battles. Still, a thread of conservatism must surely have run through both men's martial fundamentals.

The early battle record of Demetrius was checkered. His first independent command at Gaza in 312 had ended in a very costly defeat after the twenty-two-year-old ignored sound advice not to attack a powerful and well-led enemy force and chose instead to make an ambitious cavalry charge in the manner of his idol, Alexander.[21] He appeared to redeem that catastrophe shortly thereafter by outmaneuvering and capturing a large opposing army, and in 306 scored notable victories in actual combat on both land and sea at Cyprian Salamis.[22] He then went on to capture Athens by siege (gaining the epithet Poliorcetes or Besieger); however, much the same sort of glory-seeking that had been so damaging at Gaza resurfaced when he elected to follow an initially successful cavalry foray with an extended and fatally incautious pursuit that utterly doomed his father and their army at Ipsus.

It seems to have been a chastened and rather less rash Demetrius that sought to recover his fortunes as the 3rd century began. Having lost all save a few naval bases along the coast of Asia Minor, on Cyprus, and at Corinth, he blockaded an Athens that had broken from him, starving it into submission in 295. Demetrius next moved into the Peloponnese toward establishing a new empire on the Greek mainland. Leaving a garrison in Athens in the summer of 294, he marched by way of allied Corinth to attack the Spartan king Archidamus IV, who met him along the northern entry to Laconia in eastern Arcadia near Mantinea. Our lone source[23] doesn't offer any detail on the composition of the armies involved, but they must have been relatively small compared to the huge hosts that contested the initial Successor Wars in Asia. Sparta was now greatly reduced in strength from its early 4th century hegemonic peak and might not have been able to field much more than 1,200

Greece, 3rd–2nd centuries BCE.

full citizens (*spartiatoi* or spartiates) equipped as hoplites.[24] This suggests that, even with an equal addition of lesser status citizenry (representing families demoted for financial reasons from the spartiate class plus associated residents or *perioeci*) and a couple of thousand local allies, Archidamus would probably have had only around 4,500 heavy spearmen available. These would likely have been supported by some 1,000 foot-skirmishers and a token force of a few hundred horsemen from this generally cavalry-poor region of Greece.

Estimates of Demetrius' strength range from an improbable 24,000 (theoretical capacity of his fleet[25]) to a more realistic figure based upon the decision by Archidamus to openly engage.[26] Frederick the Great observed that having a third or more greater manpower was of significant advantage in battle, and this practical reality was arguably just as true for combat between the linear formations of ancient times as for the similar arrays with very limited firearms capability of Frederick's day.[27] Such a fundamental concept is likely to have been well known and honored by those from Sparta's famously battle-savvy culture with its better than three centuries worth of applied combat experience. In the absence of a tactical force multiplier,[28] it is thus unlikely that Archidamus willingly deployed for open battle against a continent of heavy foot that was a third or more larger than his own. We might therefore project Demetrius fielding something like an 8,000-man army that had around 6,000 heavy-armed (perhaps all hoplites due to loss of any native Macedonian input and with maybe a third of them Corinthians added along the route of march), 1,500 light foot, and 500 horsemen.

Archidamus must have formed up across Demetrius' line of advance down the long valley hosting Mantinea, almost surely at a narrow point near the city where similar engagements had taken place in the past. Yet though this was restricted ground at only some 2,400m wide,[29] it would have been impossible for Archidamus to stretch his modest hoplite force completely across it at anything approaching an adequate depth of file. The sole realistic option was to file four-deep (the practical minimum for an effective array) across most of his front and a little deeper (likely six shields) on the right wing, thus forming a static line measuring 1,000m in width. To advance against this defensive set-up without extreme risk of introducing dangerous chaos into his formation's coherence, Demetrius then had to form up at least six shields deep across a similar expanse. The Spartan king was thus able to avoid any dangerous initial overlaps of his flank(s); nevertheless, he could only hope that his men's superior prowess and/or endurance would be sufficient to overcome the enemy's larger numbers. This was by no means an impossible premise. Phalanx battles often turned on a single wing, where a mere portion of an array could break its immediate opposition and then fold in to take the remainder of the enemy line at side/rear to forge a total victory. And just such targeted triumphs by undermanned Spartan phalanxes were legendary.[30]

It's probable then that Archidamus and the cream of Sparta's spearmen stood a firm six shields deep on the right wing of his otherwise thinner phalanx as Demetrius' formation moved into them all along the front to initiate a short but sharp spear fight. We have no details of this action in the scant surviving literature, but it's clear from their deployment for another battle shortly thereafter that Archidamus and most of his fellow Spartans withdrew with little or no pursuit from what is otherwise described as a rout. This strongly suggests that his more adequately filed and most capable men held their own on the right yet were unable to achieve the desired break-through there before their less skilled partners on the left succumbed to pressure from the enemy's best troops in half-again deeper array. Based on norms for such classical phalanx engagements, both the victors and Spartans probably suffered well less than 5 percent killed, while the latter's allies took steep losses in the range of 10–15 percent.

Archidamus and his Spartans retreated into their homeland and prepared to make a last stand. Shorn now of allied contingents, whose survivors must have fled for home, their host would have been quite small. Though having taken no more than light damage at Mantinea, they could at best have deployed a bit less than 3,000 hoplites; indeed, achieving even this only by calling up the polis' entire old-age and youth reserve, which numbered about a quarter the size of their prime-age field force.[31] With a few hundred foot-skirmishers warding rough ground on either flank of what must have been the best available chokepoint, Sparta's hoplites likely could have done no better than stand four to eight-deep in fixed position as the enemy closed to deliver a final blow.[32] Demetrius would have been able to array eight to sixteen shields deep in taking advantage of an overwhelming (2-to-1) edge in heavy-armed manpower that in all likelihood let him punch with some dispatch through an undoubtedly game but near-hopelessly overmatched foe. The Spartans lost 200 slain in the fight, giving a valiant account of themselves before yielding to suffer only modest post-battle pursuit.[33]

Archidamus and the bulk of his native army had come away from a pair of defeats with lives intact, but now saw their homeland on the verge of being conquered for the first time in its storied history. However, wider events intervened to save them. First, Demetrius' rivals chose that moment to take advantage of his having concentrated his strength in Greece by attacking his holdings in the east. Lysimachus, king of Thrace, took much of his Asian territory and Ptolemy I, king of Egypt, the whole of Cyprus except for the city of Salamis, where Demetrius' family held out under siege. But it was events on yet a third front that led Demetrius to withdraw from Sparta before completing its final reduction. Antipater had wrested the Macedonian throne from his younger brother Alexander V in 295, causing the latter to call for aid from Demetrius and others. Though Demetrius had elected to launch his Spartan campaign rather than respond immediately to this plea, he thought better of that option now considering his reverses elsewhere and finally redirected his efforts toward Macedonia. As it turned out, the initial crisis there had already been resolved; however, Demetrius was able to exploit lingering political turbulence in the kingdom to seize its crown for himself.

Getae Territory (c. 294–292)

Lysimachus was plagued by raids into the northern reaches of Thrace by the Getae, a particularly fierce and powerful Thracian tribe.[34] This warrior nation had faced Alexander back in 335 at a reported strength of around 10,000 javelin-armed infantrymen and 4,000 in skilled, light cavalry.[35] And though that might be more a tally of nominal tribal strength than what could muster for any given engagement, an 80 percent or even 60 percent deployment of such numbers would still have presented a daunting challenge. Nevertheless, Lysimachus elected to lead a punitive expedition against the Getae. We have no information on the make-up of his invasion force, but it would probably have numbered 10,000 strong in foot and at least 2,000 in horsemen given any proper consideration of the pending opposition. Lysimachus had likely contributed some 6,000–8,000 mercenary hoplites to the effort four years earlier at Ipsus,[36] and that seems reasonable both in terms of raw numbers and most appropriate troop type (called upon to operate in terrain unsuitable for pikemen) for the heavy-armed element here, with loyal Thracian javelineers providing the remainder of the infantry and all mounted troops.

Lysimachus marched north into Getae territory, perhaps crossing over the Hister (Danube) River to menace the tribe's heartland in bringing them to battle. We have no tactical details in the surviving literature on the ensuing engagement, being restricted to an account of attendant circumstances from Pausanius, a lone stratagem from Polyaenus, and a couple of somewhat confusing fragments from Diodorus (most of whose work for this period having been lost). The best interpretation seems to be that a faux Getae defector led the Macedonian on an exhausting march bereft of food and water that culminated in an ambush on terrain unsuitable for his phalanx. Forced into a desperate, fighting withdrawal, Lysimachus' main column became separated from a unit under his oldest son, Agathocles, who then met defeat in isolation and was captured. As for Lysimachus, he was apparently able to skirmish his way out of the immediate trap under cover of his own exceptionally robust light infantry. However, short on supplies in hostile territory with many a wounded man and his heir in enemy hands, he had little practical choice but to negotiate terms. The resulting non-aggression pact forced upon him gave a daughter in political marriage to the Getae chieftain and sent him home defeated in return for his son and what was probably the better part of his army.[37]

Pindos Pass (290)

Demetrius' fellow escapee from Ipsus in 301, his wife's brother Pyrrhus, had sheltered with Antigonus a year earlier after being ousted from Epirus in east-central Greece. However, after his sister's passing in 298, Pyrrhus' position changed, leaving him stranded in Egypt at the court of Ptolemy I, where he had been sent as a hostage to promote Demetrius' interests. He formed a cooperative relationship with Ptolemy (marrying his step-daughter), who then used his considerable resources in 297 to restore the young man to his homeland. And after eliminating a rival with whom he was forced to initially share power, Pyrrhus in 295 seized sole control of the Epiriote tribal union as hereditary chief of his own Molossians, the land's most populous and prosperous ethnic group. He then successfully set about boosting the nation's economy and continuing at an even faster pace to restore its martial might. And the latter's potential was indeed considerable, reflecting a military system directly rooted in the proven tactical concepts of no less a genius than Macedonia's Philip II.

Pyrrhus' uncle, Alexander of Epirus, was the younger brother of Philip's wife Olympia (mother of the more famous Alexander) and had taken shelter with his brother-in-law during a lengthy period of exile (355–341). Having observed (and likely served within) Philip's new style phalanx throughout most of its years of Greek conquest, Alexander had undoubtedly lost no time in reforming his own army along identical professional lines once Philip returned him to power as warlord over Epirus' tribal coalition. Honing this advanced military machine over the course of seven years, he had then taken it to Italy in support of the Grecian polis of Tarentum's war against local tribesmen. That adventure saw Alexander have considerable opening success only to lose his life in 332. But at least the core of his Philippian military survived and its residual elements now passed into Pyrrhus' skilled and eager hands to be upgraded and brought back to full potency. And it wasn't long before he had an opportunity to put that freshly reinvigorated force to good use, responding to Alexander V's plea for help in regaining the Macedonian throne in 295, and able to do so even faster than his former brother-in-law, Demetrius, who was still entangled in the Peloponnese.[38]

Resolving the situation in Macedonia, Pyrrhus claimed the western portions of its holdings for himself. He then came into conflict with Demetrius, who had usurped Alexander's crown and promptly embarked on a campaign of aggression both to the south (conquering Thessaly) and east (striking into Thrace). In 290, he finally turned west toward Pyrrhus, invading the younger man's Aetolian allies on the way toward Epirus itself. Hoping to face his opponents while they were yet divided, Demetrius met frustration when the Aetolians refused combat and fled instead into the nearby Pindos Mountains. This led him to march the flower of his army into eastern Epirus, leaving his general Pantouches behind to keep the Aetolians pinned in their highlands and unable to come to Pyrrhus' aid. However, that Epirote worthy was not simply standing on the defensive at home but was moving instead to join his allies in their own land. With their armies taking different routes, Demetrius and Pyrrhus bypassed each other and the latter found himself confronting a much weaker foe than expected in Pantouches with his modest rear-guard, who must have been holding watch on the plain just below the most likely pass that the Aetolians might use to make a sally out of their Pindos range refuges.

Compositions of the opposing forces here are speculative. An estimate for that of Pantouches can be based upon his assignment as well as past practice in a similar situation. Having to counter an Aetolian muster perhaps 9,000–12,000 strong with a fair-sized minority of heavy infantry,[39] Pantouches must have received a substantial portion of mercenary hoplites to core his command.[40] These would have had support from a strong contingent of foot-skirmishers and at least a modest number of mounted troops. Given a reasonable estimate of around 10,000 men in all,[41] something like 6,000 hoplites, 3,000 light infantrymen, and 1,000 horsemen of all types seems most likely. This would have been much like the holding force of 10,000 foot and 1,000 horse that Demetrius left behind as rearguard under similar circumstances after his recent conquest in Thessaly, when he had also turned his main effort against another target.[42] As for Pyrrhus, the army employed during his later Italian campaign in combination with the known ethnic make-up of his realm's population and probable similarity of its armament to that of Philip II suggests a likely order of battle. The expedition to Italy appears to have included some 16,000 Epirotes in total,[43] which fits with both an early 4th century indication of overall Epiriote potential as well as a modern evaluation of Pyrrhus' strength just a year prior to the action here.[44] As such, had the armament he led against Pantouches resembled Philip's past deployments, we might assume it had at least 14,000 foot-soldiers in the form of 3,000 hoplites, 9,000 pikemen, and 2,000 skirmishers plus 1,000 horsemen both heavy and light.

Our lone source on what happened on the battlefield is short on tactical details, mostly relating a thrilling tale of heroic combat between the two army leaders before the issue was finally settled in a general engagement.[45] Pyrrhus and Pantouches meeting in a personal duel certainly smacks of romantic fiction; however, the circumstances at hand would seem to favor an opening clash of cavalry in which such an encounter was at least possible. Caught on the plain by an enemy force clearly larger in size as well as stronger in heavy foot, the experienced Macedonian commander[46] must have ordered his infantry into the nearby pass, where it could hope to anchor against enclosing uplands as a ward against envelopment; and to cover the withdrawal, he would have sortied his cavalry and supporting foot-skirmishers against Epirote counterparts rushing to cut it off. The ensuing mounted action saw Pantouches go down wounded, whether by the hand of Pyrrhus or another, but not before buying sufficient time for his phalanx to take a defensive position within the mouth of the pass, behind which he and his surviving horsemen and light infantry then retired.

Pyrrhus now advanced with the Epirote heavy array, using its pikemen at center and left to fix the facing hoplites while smashing into the Macedonian left with his own spearmen in files having a depth advantage of half again if the foregoing manpower estimates are accurate.[47] Ultimately, the Epirote right wing speared and/or pushed ahead and "forced through and cut to pieces the phalanx of the Macedonians"[48] on its left wing. With their skirmishers pursuing those fleeing from and near that turned flank, Pyrrhus' hoplites began to wheel against what remained of the enemy formation. Pantouches saw this and, with the only escape route behind leading into unfamiliar territory filled with Aetolian hostiles, he took advantage of this brief lull as the enemy reformed to sensibly surrender along with some 5,000 of his men.[49]

When Demetrius learned of this reversal, he abandoned Epirus and pulled back into Macedonia lest the combined forces of Pyrrhus and the Aetolians now come against him. Pyrrhus returned home to a hero's welcome, having pressured a greatly feared invader into retreat and delivered a morale-boosting victory of epic proportions with minimal losses to his own men (perhaps 100 or so killed among his cavalry and hoplite contingents).[50] Glorying in his success, the Epirotes gave their young warlord the epithet "Eagle" to honor his soaring skill in battle. Pyrrhus was thus brimming with confidence when he led a pillaging expedition into Macedonian territory the next year. He had heard that Demetrius was seriously ill; however, when challenged by surprisingly robust resistance, he showed himself rather less bold (risk-prone?) than his famed cousin by refusing engagement, though enemy action during the ensuing withdrawal did deal him some damage. Still, that act of caution would pay dividends just a year later, when he returned with the strength so husbanded to meet Demetrius at last, only to have Macedonia's army drive the older man away in a revolt that put Pyrrhus on the throne in his stead. But this triumph proved limited in that he had to split rule with Lysimachus, Successor king of Thrace and much of Asia Minor.

Cyrrhestica (284)

Demetrius had fled from Macedonia in 288, and his former conquest Athens soon rejected him as well; however, he still retained military assets at Corinth, including a considerable fleet. He struck out from there against Athens in 286, but after proving unable to retake the city, diverted his attention toward recovering his lost holdings in Asia Minor. Thus, the next year, he left his son Antigonus (II Gonatus) in Greece with a holding force and descended with his ships on Ionia to disembark a mercenary host. Being generally successful at first, Demetrius was ultimately out-maneuvered by a small army under Lysimachus' son, Agathocles, and elected to abandon Ionia and flee into Cilicia. With Agathocles' skirmishers nipping at their heels, his men first took casualties in a difficult river crossing and then endured a forced march marked by extreme exhaustion as well as starvation. Plutarch reports that fallen marchers and desertions during this trial had cost Demetrios 8,000 men by the time he set up winter quarters at the city of Tarsus.[51] From here, he got the better of some lesser Seleucid contingents in a series of skirmishes that left him in control of the passes into Syria. But then an outbreak of disease took a further toll on his men, triggering more desertions. In assessing Plutarch's account of these events, it's clear that his figure of 8,000 cannot possibly be accurate for Demetrius' losses on the march or even after adding in the later deserters and victims of pestilence. Considering that his original landing party ran a mere 11,000 foot-soldiers with a modest attachment of cavalry,[52] this is more likely a preserved tradition on the force Demetrius retained in the aftermath of the ordeals above.[53] Yet even that less dire take would mean that his army suffered reduction by a quarter or more depending upon how much reinforcement had joined during the preceding Ionian campaign.

Damaged by his latest misfortunes and coming under pressure from Seleucus to leave Cilicia, Demetrius feigned a withdrawal toward Ionia, but instead instituted a surprise countermarch through the Amanus Mountains onto the Syrian plain in Cyrrhestica. Stopping close to where Seleucus was encamped near the local capital of Cyrrhos, he then

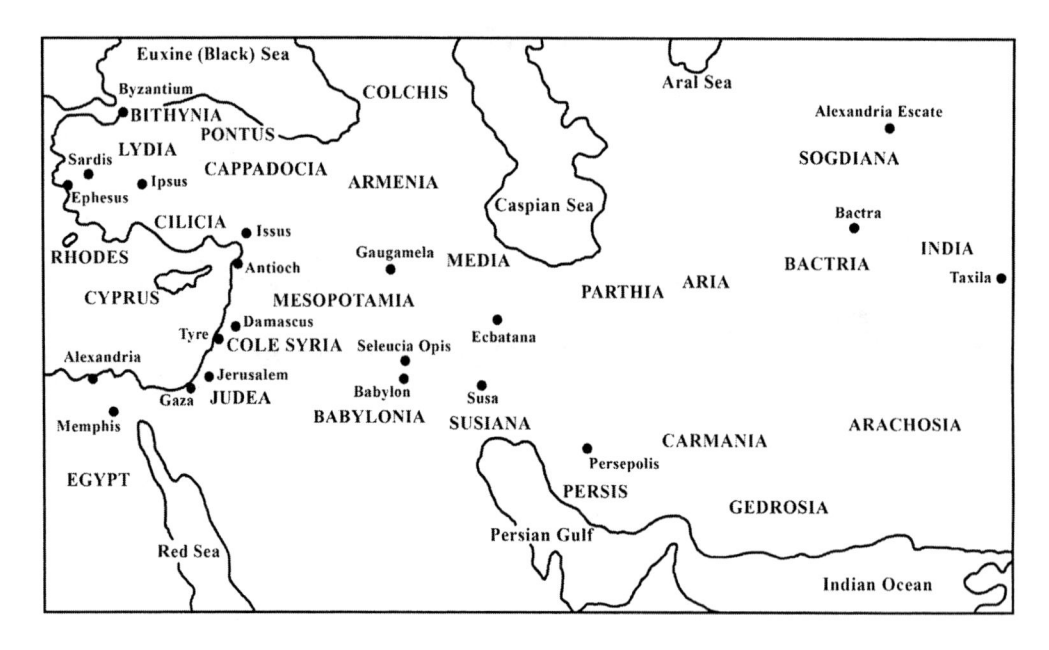

Grecian Near East, 3rd–2nd centuries BCE.

sought to execute a pre-dawn sneak attack. This stratagem had a low probability for success, with such maneuvering in the pitch dark of ancient times ending badly much more often than not; yet, the likelihood of besting a significantly larger armament in open combat must have looked near to nil. Advancing stealthily on the enemy position, Lysimachus anticipated that he could catch Seleucus and most of his army still abed. However, his movements were detected and, finding the opposition alert, he fell back toward the west.

Composition of Lysimachus' depleted armament is extremely speculative, but it's unlikely that he had more than 6,000 or so remaining in hired hoplites along with some 2,000 light infantrymen and a small cavalry contingent. The army in pursuit might have had as many as 2,000 hypaspist hoplites[54] and 6,000 phalangites drawn from Macedonian military settlements in Seleucid territory plus another 18,000 ethnically Asian pikemen (*pantodapoi* outfitted in Macedonian style). These heavy infantry contingents would have been supported by a substantial body of horsemen (there were at least 12,000 realm-wide, but the number here could well have been a third or less of that) and perhaps twice as many foot-skirmishers.[55] And to further unbalance the odds, Seleucus had a corps of war-elephants as well.

A conventional phalanx action out on the plain would have been suicidal for Demetrius. There was no way that he could hope to protect his flanks from rapid envelopment given his foe's decided advantage in overall manpower and, especially, foot skirmishers and mounted troops including those imposing elephants. The obvious tactic of choice in these circumstances would be to withdraw toward broken ground where his flanks could be anchored next to terrain features that would take Seleucus' cavalry, pachyderms, and light infantry out of the equation as well as limit how many of his heavy-armed could be effectively brought to bear. Victory would then not necessarily go to the side fielding the larger army, but quite possibly to that having the more capable heavy infantry as personified by his own veteran mercenaries. Bar-Kochva[56] has convincingly proposed that he took up position on this basis in one of the stream canyons present along his route of retreat.

These offered chokepoints from 500m to 750m across that he could completely span with a soundly filed phalanx. Perhaps having scouted just such a site during his earlier advance as a sensible precaution, Demetrius took up a defensive position there, probably arraying his sparse hoplite force of around 6,000 between rough ground on either flank at a strong depth of twelve shields.

The tactical challenge facing Seleucus at Cyrrhestica was analogous to that before Pyrrhus six years earlier in the Pindos Pass: a well-anchored force of hoplites immune to light-armed envelopment and stoutly resistant to a frontal assault from the sort of pikemen that made up the bulk of his own armament. And he seemed at first to seek the same solution, forming up his phalanx across the limited space available and closing to engage with most of the right third of his line (perhaps along a 125m front) composed of his own hoplites at a matching twelve-shields and all the Macedonian phalangites plus one division (3,000) of his pantodapoi filed sixteen-deep over the remainder. His cavalry, elephants, light infantry, and most of the pantodapoi plus a contingent of his best hypaspists remained behind.

Seleucus' phalanx closed into action and his pikemen effectively handled their spear-armed opponents, drawing some blood, but mostly just fixing them impotently in place as the melee evolved. Meanwhile, though, the hypaspists were faring poorly against opponents better experienced in fighting with dory and aspis and inspired by their commander, Demetrius, leading them in person. However, the Seleucid ruler had already put a countering stratagem into action. Having the advantage of local men on his side familiar with the area, he was aware of an alternative path around his foe's position and had sent a small force to negotiate it as soon as battle was engaged. This detachment (eight elephants, some light infantry, and the crack team of perhaps 500 hypaspists that had been retained at the rear), skirted the enemy's flank and suddenly emerged in back of Demetrius and his hoplites just as they were on the verge of turning the tide on that wing. At this critical juncture, Seleucus showed himself at the mercenaries' front, urging them to abandon his rival and surrender with honor to go into Seleucid service. Already disgruntled by their recent hardships and with fearsome elephants and elite spearmen menacing their rear, Demetrius' hirelings laid down their arms and gave him over as a prisoner.[57] Held thereafter in relatively luxurious custody, the fallen warlord and former Macedonian king would eventually drink himself to death.

Corupedium (281)

After the death of Ptolemy I in 283/82, Lysimachus and Seleucus I were all that remained of Alexander the Great's original successors. Though now in their twilight years,[58] both men remained vigorous and ambitious. This led in Lysimachus' case to the assassination of his heir Agathocles, who was brought into suspicion of having premature designs on the throne.[59] He followed this up with a campaign against the murdered man's supporters, causing those surviving his pogrom to take refuge with Agathocles' widow at the court of Seleucus. These exiles convinced their host that the time was ripe for him to capture Lysimachus' Asian territory since much of it was now in revolt. Seleucus seized the opportunity, knowing that his old comrade was not only suffering desertions and rebellions, but that the loyalty of many still standing by him might be quite tenuous as well. Yet, if Lysimachus saw these same problems, they certainly didn't slow his response. He quickly mounted an expedition to address Seleucus' threat and crossed the Hellespont, marching into Lydia.

There, he went into action against his last fellow Successor at Corupedium (Plains of Corus or Cyrus) to the west of Sardis.[60]

The site of this confrontation appears to have been just beyond the river Phyrgius/Hylus within a wide valley that stretched eastward between two lengthy mountain fronts. Mutual consent from such battle-savvy veterans to risk a decisive combat on the open ground of so broad a lowland strongly suggests that their armies were reasonably well matched. We can only guess at the battle orders based upon past deployments from the regions involved. As such, Lysimachus should have had a powerful contingent in tow from the Macedonian homeland despite recent defections and must have added troops from those portions of his Asian territories along or near his line of march (Mysia, Phrygia, and Lydia[61]). An educated guess at troop types would run above 25,000 in heavy infantry (perhaps 3,000 hypaspists, 9,000 Macedonian phalangites, and 15,000 pantodapoi),[62] some 3,000 horsemen (1,200 Macedonian heavy lancers and the rest Thracian and Asian javelineers), and 6,000 foot-skirmishers (Thracian and Asian missilemen at roughly one per cavalryman and per ten hoplites/pikemen).

Seleucus likely was able to match the opposing line-infantry (maybe 3,000 hypaspists alternatively equipped with pikes, 12,000 Macedonian colonist phalangites, and 12,000 pantodapoi)[63] and had 4,000 in cavalry (1,000 lance-armed heavy guardsmen and the rest Asian javelineers), elephants (strength unknown, but probably modest),[64] as well as 7,000–8,000 in light foot. The last would have consisted of those supporting the cavalry at a strength equal to the number of horsemen present, a team of missilemen for each elephant, and the remainder to skirmish ahead of the phalanx upon first approach and then protect its flanks.

The ensuing engagement must have been a typical phalanx clash as had often played out in the late 4th century across similar open settings upon lowland Asia Minor. This would have seen the heavy infantry arrays stalemating each other (if they came into contact at all) while mounted contingents determined the battle's outcome off one or both flanks. It's likely that the two kings accompanied their best mounted troops beyond their respective right wings, with Seleucus having strengthened the cavalry on either end of his line with a leavening of elephants supported by their attached foot skirmishers. Regardless, it was Seleucus that gained victory in the end as one among his horsemen or elephant teams brought Lysimachus down with a javelin.[65] But Seleucus would not long enjoy his success. Advancing on Macedonia in the company of Ptolemy Keraunos (son of Ptolemy I and connected to the Macedonian crown by marriage), the latter murdered the old man and followed this crime with a successful wooing of the late Lysimachus' army that gained him control of Macedon. Thus, with the deaths of Lysimachus and Seleucus I in 281, the long (42-year) era of the initial Successors to Alexander the Great finally came to a fittingly violent end.

2. Phalanx Versus Legion

*Sicilian Tyrants and Pyrrhic Wars
(280–275 BCE)*

As conflicts between Alexander's successors played out to re-shape national boundaries across the eastern Mediterranean region, important events were unfolding to the west as well. Prime among these for the future of the Hellenistic kingdoms was the rise of Republican Rome. That once minor city-state had come to dominate central Italy by the beginning of the 3rd century and would soon turn its ambitious eyes upon Magna Graecia (Greater Greece) in the south. Greek colonies there had long battled each other and nearby highland tribes for control over the rich resources of the Italian peninsula's lower end. As a result, those various hostile parties now constituted a disorganized patchwork of authorities ripe for conquest by the sort of unified force that the Romans could bring to bear. And much the same applied to the large island of Sicily. Barely separated from the toe of Italy by a narrow strait, this was a wealthy land whose native tribesmen had largely been driven into its interior by the efforts of Phoenician (Punic) trading centers in the far west and, especially, land-hungry agrarian colonists from Greece living along the mid-to-eastern coasts. Warfare had roiled Sicily for the last two centuries; some in the form of clashes between Grecian and Punic interests contesting island-wide control, but most pitting Greek against Greek.

Feuding Greeks and Carthage

Sicily had enjoyed a good deal of democratic governance in the past both at and under the sponsorship elsewhere of its largest and most powerful polis, Syracuse. However, one of the more characteristic aspects of Sicilian politics over that period was a marked propensity for spawning dictators (*tyrannoi* or tyrants); and, ironically, some of the most notable of these held sway at Syracuse itself, and often for extended periods. One such long-running Syracusan despot, Agathocles, was in place to begin the 3rd century, but fell to an assassin in 289 and was replaced after a turbulent year by Hicetas. That dictator ruled for eight years before going to war with another of his kind. This was Phintias, who had gained control of the south-central coastal city of Acragas (Agrigentum) just after Agathocles' death and declared himself king. Syracuse and Acragas were the greatest rivals among Sicily's Grecian colonies and, considering a report that both sides had ravaged the intervening region with multiple raids and that Syracuse subsequently made a move toward attaching Punic-aligned territory as well, it was likely a land dispute initiated by Hicetas that now set them to fighting.

Hyblaeus R. (c. 280)

The contesting forces met on the Hyblaeus River plain just below Hybla Heraea (near the modern city of Ragusa), which lay inland to the east of Acragas and southwest of Syracuse. Both armies would have been based around large contingents of mercenary hoplites (standard mainstay of all Sicilian tyrannies) with a supplement of citizen spearmen. A high-end projection of Syracusan potential runs in the vicinity of 17,000 hoplites (perhaps 11,000–12,000 mercenaries and 5,000–6,000 militiamen) with support from 4,500–6,000 foot-skirmishers and 1,000–1,500 horsemen.[1] As for Acragas, the last unblooded army that had sortied from that city (in 307) boasted something over 10,000 foot-soldiers (including maybe 8,000 hoplites) and 1,000 horsemen.[2] However, the indicated open engagement at a relatively neutral site at some distance between the two warring poleis strongly suggests mutually optimistic assessments of the chances for success by the opposing commanders as an indication of reasonably well-matched forces. This could reflect that Acragas had significantly greater manpower than a generation earlier. Alternatively (and perhaps rather more likely[3]), Syracuse's strength might have dropped over that same period to reach a rough equilibrium with its foe.

Regardless of whether Acragas had risen, Syracuse had fallen, or some combination of those scenarios applied, the confrontation at Hyblaeus River seems likely to have been a fairly even contest in terms of manpower that ultimately saw Syracuse's phalanx carry the day. Given Phintias' survival at what normally would have been a post on or near his right wing, there's a good chance that crack mercenary spearmen on the Syracusan right routed opposing militia to seal the victory, thus allowing the enemy tyrant to flee unharmed from the opposite end of the field. Hicetas must have heavily pursued the Acraganians to inflict significant damage against very light losses of his own. That removed any fear that those badly savaged foes might rally to again menace his southwestern flank, setting him free to move against Punic-associated land to the northwest of Syracuse.

Carthaginian Warfare and Terias R. (c. 280)

Punic interests on Sicily were sponsored by Carthage, a powerful colony of Phoenicia on the northern coast of Africa within a brief sail of its outposts in the island's far west. The Carthaginian war machine closely resembled that of contemporary Greece. Based upon concepts adopted by its founders from original neighbors in Caria and Ionia and in later years through contact with Greek colonies around the Mediterranean, the Carthaginian military had by no later than the 5th century become highly Hellenized in both equipment and tactics. It thus fielded hoplite phalanxes of the classical type, whose spearmen consisted of city residents as well as Liby-Phoenicians from its surrounding regions (analogous to Grecian perioeci), citizens residing in overseas colonies, and Libyan conscripts. These troops appear to have been organized into 3,000-man divisions, which might have had sub-units of 500 men each.[4] Such "African" heavy infantrymen wore open-face helmets and Greek-style body armor, carrying hoplon aspides and thrusting spears like the dory (though shorter at 2m than the Grecian norm of 2.5m).[5] And like their Greek prototypes, Punic phalanxes deployed their best troops on the right wing, indicating that the same sort of battle mechanics applied.[6]

Carthage's way of war differed some from that of Greece in its lighter equipped elements. Foot-skirmishers were conscripted African subjects or foreign mercenaries as

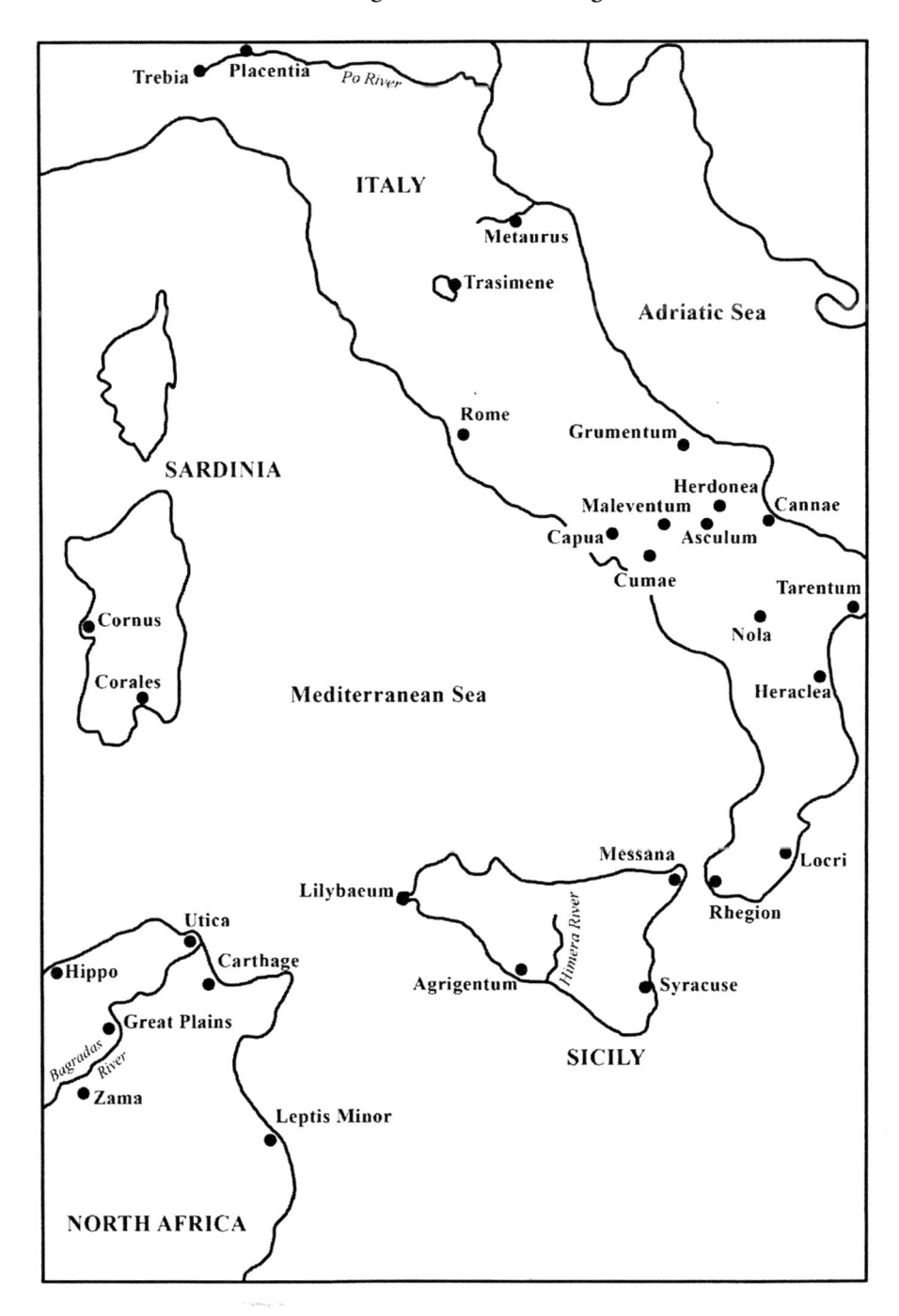

Central Mediterranean, 3rd–2nd centuries BCE.

opposed to the poorer citizenry and mostly Grecian hirelings in contemporary mainland Greek armies. These skirmishers were also present in larger proportion, often making up around a third of the infantry in Carthaginian hosts. Most of them were unarmored spearmen (*longchophorai*, carriers of the *longche*, a throwable light spear) or javelineers, with lesser contributions from archers (seemingly rare) and slingers (especially Balearic islanders). These light footmen carried small shields of various designs. Cavalry was usually present at 10–20 percent of the infantry count, often a bit more generous than was common for Grecian armies, with the level for any given campaign affected by travel conditions (deployments requiring marine transport or exceptional marches being smaller). These horsemen, like all in their era, rode without saddles or stirrups. They were mostly African at the dawn of the 3rd century, being either heavier Carthaginian/Liby-Phoenician riders (with lance, torso armor, and small, round shield[7]) or lighter North Africans (Libyans, Moors, and Numidians with small shields and javelins). Chariots were used down to the mid–4th century but had been phased out by 300. And the elephants famously deployed in later campaigns were yet to be adopted, not coming into the Carthaginian mix of arms until after being encountered with Pyrrhus (see below).

Hicetas' northern advance came to a halt inland of Catana at Terias River. It's unknown what kind of opposition he ran into there, but it must have been substantial relative to his own strength, which was probably toward the lower end of the range proposed for his battle against Phintias. A force adequate to meet that sort of threat would have been on the order of three Carthaginian heavy divisions (maybe 8,000 spearmen at parade strength accompanied by around 4,000 foot-skirmishers and less than 1,000 in cavalry) or their equivalent in some combination of Punic garrison troops and regional allies opposed to Syracuse's domination.[8] Of course, if Hicetas had a larger host than the above suggested minimum, then it would have taken a proportionally more massive Punic deployment to achieve what must have been a reasonably even balance of forces. It's debatable whether a much larger counter-force could have been fielded strictly from resources already in place on Sicily; however, Carthage might have responded with reinforcements via an amphibious landing given sufficient notice. And it's not unreasonable that such a call for help would quickly have gone out from its clients as soon as Acragas' defeat painted them as next in line for attack.

Whatever one makes of the foregoing manpower estimates, it seems that the Syracusans went down to defeat with heavy losses.[9] And, given Hicetas' escape this time around, it might well have been yet another case of a victor's superior right wing being decisive as so often happened when classical phalanxes came to grips. In retrospect, we can see this action along with the previous one at Hyblaeus River as mere extensions into the 3rd century of the infighting pattern among Greek warlords and Carthaginians that had long wracked Sicily. But while these sorts of conflicts were to continue for a few decades yet, a new threat of unprecedented scope was brewing at Rome on the Italian mainland.

Roman Warfare to the 3rd Century

Roman warfare in its earliest discernable form seems to have been a process of spear-armed warbands raiding each other and their neighbors with an aim to acquire portable wealth such as cattle, trade goods, and slaves.[10] This sort of rapaciousness was no doubt still dominant at the dawn of the 5th century, but the tactical means for its execution appear to have evolved. Rome's military system, like that at Carthage, was now organized around phalanx formations in the classical/Doric style. The Romans and other Latin communities in central Italy probably copied this combat scheme indirectly, taking it from their Etruscan neighbors, with whom they had long fought both alongside and against. The Etruscans had in turn gained the methodology via a voluminous, long-running trading relationship with the numerous Greek city-states that dominated southern Italy as well as in context of a marked Etruscan leaning toward all-embracing adoption of cultural imports.[11]

The Roman phalanx was manned by hoplites drawn from the ranks of powerful clans. These were mostly sited outside the city proper and had long made up semi-private armies operating under hereditary warlords.[12] The latter constituted an aristocratic elite that dominated Rome's leadership, doing so initially as royalty and later as elected officials. Just as in the case of his Greek counterpart, a Roman hoplite had to provide his own equipment,[13] including a thrusting spear (*hasta*), a sword (*gladius*) of the xiphos type, an aspis-like shield (*clipeus*), helmet (*galea*, usually of an open-faced variety), torso armor (*lorica*), and greaves (*ocreae*). It has been estimated that Rome could field 4,000 such heavy infantrymen in the early 5th century, with the count rising to 6,000 by century's end.[14]

Roman hoplites could have retained some archaic elements of the phalanx such as use of a second, throwing spear. We have one 5th century depiction of a clipeus-bearing warrior, either Latin or Etruscan, carrying two spears, one of which has a smaller head and is almost certainly meant to be thrown; and some early 5th century sculptures show use of auxiliary thigh and arm protection that had died out in Greece nearly a century earlier, perhaps reflecting a continued need to ward such projectiles.[15] Rome's phalanx drew support from small numbers of foot-skirmishers (*rorarii*) and horsemen (*equites*). The latter used a spear (*palta*, much like the hoplite hasta[16]), as did the skirmishers, with the footmen applying it to close-in fighting and as a missile of last resort during retreat. The rorarii eventually took up the javelin as well; however, there is little archaeological evidence supporting significant use of that weapon among Latin warriors of the subject period, who perhaps preferred the sturdier hasta as being more effective in shock combat and against cavalry.[17] Rome's light infantrymen do not appear to have carried a shield until very late in the 3rd century (a sturdy, round device with central handgrip called the *parma* is first mentioned in 211). That short-coming, maybe due to financial limitations, led earlier iterations of Roman skirmishers to fare poorly against better equipped Greek and Carthaginian counterparts as well as shield-bearing tribal warriors.

It is important to note that a major local variation in Rome's phalanx from Grecian prototypes appears to have been in how it created file depths. Based upon the projected size of Rome's hoplite levy and better documented evidence for later marching and filing practices, it has been reasonably proposed that Roman formation depths were probably built upon multiples of three rather than the four-man units prevalent in Greece.[18] This suggests a minimum file of three for a stationary formation standing purely on the defensive, with the first two ranks ranging out to strike at the enemy while the third stood ready to move up in replacement of any forward fighter that went down. Deeper phalanxes had higher practical maneuverability and could advance onto the attack; and the minimum for amateur soldiers to achieve this, six shields in depth, is widely believed to have been the most frequent battlefield deployment for Rome's draftee phalanxes, terrain restrictions and enemy deployments permitting.

Examining Roman phalanxes through the lens of Bardunias' three combat modes yields insights into the tactical challenges that they commonly expected to encounter. Composition of Rome's phalanx-based armies suggests that they must have opened most engagements in bastion mode with horsemen and light infantry skirmishing to the fore. However, the relative paucity of those arms usually rendered this no more than a brief preliminary phase. The prime goal of Roman tactics was for a bludgeon of hoplites to close as quickly as possible into shock action and resolve the contest. This made sense

2. Phalanx Versus Legion

in context of most threats coming from Etruscans or fellow Latins, both those peoples fielding shock-focused militaries very like to Rome's own,[19] or from lighter-equipped foes forced to hold fixed positions along approaches to their communities, crops, or other stationary assets. As to Bardunias' third phalanx mode, the formation of a barricading screen, the shortage of Roman missilemen would have rendered that exceedingly rare prior to the second decade of the 3rd century.

A key turning point in the trajectory of Rome's martial evolution came in 390 (387 per Greek chronologies) at the battle of the Allia.[20] This saw its phalanx, hurriedly reinforced by a call-up of reserves and other citizens, go down to costly defeat (see Appendix 1) against a levy of the Gallic Senones tribe. The victors followed this by marching on Rome and entered the city unopposed to put those few defenders remaining under siege on the Capitoline Hill. The Gauls finally left only after extracting a huge ransom in gold. The Romans were profoundly shaken by this disaster and began to significantly reformulate their military toward better meeting any future threat of a similar nature.

Consensus opinion at Rome seems to have been that the beating taken at Allia was largely due to inadequate numbers. This led to more than doubling manpower by tapping previously undrafted elements in the urban population and drawing subject former enemies into the citizen body.[21] A few among this influx of new recruits were well enough off to acquire costly hoplite panoplies; most, however, could only afford cheaper arms.[22] Something like half of the latter appear to have become shock-capable, acquiring a helmet, some body armor, and adding a *scutum* shield to their spear and sword. The large, oval scutum had a central hand grip and let these men engage hand-to-hand as a sort of "medium" infantry.[23] The remaining new recruits could manage no more than skirmisher gear and greatly boosted the count of light foot. Campaigning strength thus went from two levies (*legions*, one per consul) to four, with each boasting 3,000 heavy foot supported by perhaps 1,200 light-armed in bringing the nominal combatant total to 17,400 after adding a retained force of 600 horsemen.

The Roman phalanx now had some 1,800 clipeus-bearing hoplites per legion but required an adjustment in tactics to properly incorporate its many new scutum-carrying spearmen (*hastati*). Operating as a backing bastion for these more mobile soldiers fighting at the fore surely increased in both duration and importance; indeed, the hastati must have successfully resolved some actions without their hoplite bludgeon ever having to engage. Nevertheless, phalanxes continued as the prime arbiters of battlefield success, coming up to settle any issue still in doubt after the hastati had their say. Livy appears to have outlined just such a sequence in an engagement against Latin foes in 340 near Mount Vesuvius, where the hastati withdrew short of victory and their phalanx of hoplites then carried the fight.[24] Elsewhere, the foot-skirmishers might have replaced their lighter missiles with a heavier, Celtic-style javelin; all the same, though, there is still no sign that Roman arrays of this period were ever sufficiently secure in their capability with projectiles of any sort to deploy their heavy foot solely as a fronting barrier for missilemen.

The exact timing of this military expansion is unclear. Explicit evidence via Livy for a four-legion army doesn't appear until 311. Yet the markedly scanty nature of our sources for the preceding period reduces that to no more than a latest possible date. A distinct aspect of Roman mobilizations seems to be that they rarely reflected the city's full potential. Rome always seems to have had a great capacity to raise additional troops in any major crisis as well as an extraordinary ability to replace casualties and throw fresh armies into the field even after a highly devastating defeat as at Allia. This makes it possible that a larger host might have come into being earlier, perhaps before the late 340s when Livy infers that there were two consular levies of two legions each.[25]

The next pivot point in the evolution of the Roman army came at the battle of Caudium (aka the Caudine Forks)[26] in a war against the Samnite tribal federation, which occupied a mountainous region of south-central Italy below Latium. Samnite armies used armored infantry that carried scutum-style shields and tended to open combat with a barrage of javelins before charging into close-ordered spear fights.[27] Unlike the monolithic phalanx of Rome, whose hoplites required cover from the clipeus of a line-mate on their right and risked fatal loss of that vital protection should ranks open while moving over uneven ground, Samnite arrays were composed of a network of small units (*manipuli* or "handfuls"). Combined with the more independent design of the scutum, this methodology let the Samnites traverse rough terrain while maintaining a coherent formation. Its main weakness was that front-fighters had to be constantly aware of their broader environment and athletically shift shields about to get the same warding from different attack angles that was passively inherent within an intact phalanx. Therefore, when Samnites engaged well-ordered Roman hoplites, who could also employ slightly longer spears (2.5m or a bit more versus the 2m or so traditionally paired with a scutum[28]) under that same veil of mutual protection, the tribesmen would generally have to pay a steeper price in blood than they might reasonably hope to draw in return.

The natural impact of this contrast in tactical systems was that Rome could normally expect good results when catching its foes exposed on the plain but faced a daunting task if engaging in rugged uplands. The hastati, equipped much like the enemy even if not possessed of the same manipular organization, might ameliorate this to some extent. However, their relatively small numbers inevitably ceded resolution of any sizeable or extended action onto their more plentiful hoplite brethren. And the evolving nature of the Samnite fight eventually made those heavier spearmen's prospects quite problematic. While the early years of this war (326–322) saw the Romans do well, that very success led them onto the operational offensive. That meant waging campaigns ever farther into the Samnites' territory, where those foes could defend ground both familiar and highly favorable to their own way of war. Such was the situation in 321, when an army from Rome under its two consuls mounted an invasion of western Samnium.[29] The Samnites sprang an ambush that trapped the intruding force marching through a narrow valley near Caudium, with the ensuing battle (see Appendix 1) leading to a humiliating surrender. This cost the Romans all their arms and armor, and even some clothing in that Livy described the consuls as emerging "pretty much half-naked."

There was a five-year truce with the Samnites following Caudium. And it was most likely during this interval and in full consequence of that humbling event that the Romans reformed their way of war by mimicking the victorious barbarians' manipular combat system.[30] They thus discarded the phalanx for a more flexible array based upon three tranches of armored infantry (*acies triplex*) assisted by a leading screen of skirmishers. One major enabler of this radical change was the unprecedented price exacted by the recent surrender. All battlefield failures naturally came at a certain cost of material: gear stripped from the dead/captured, items tossed in flight, etc. But Caudium took an unprecedented toll in that the Roman army lost every piece of equipment it had taken into the field. Weapons, armor, mounts—everything was gone. Yet, bad as this was, it had a unique ancillary benefit in that Rome would incur no additional expense to significantly alter and improve its mix of replacement arms.[31] Moreover, the cease-fire terms also provided a lengthy period of relative peace in which to drill and instill any changes in tactics that new gear might require.

The result of this odd confluence of disaster and opportunity was the emergence at the truce's end of a different kind of Roman army. This featured a heavy-armed formation that retained the hastati six-deep at its fore; however, these modestly protected spear-bearers now added a heavy javelin to their panoply and would eventually go solely with that weapon in addition to a sword. The back of the formation also had something of a familiar look, being composed of heavy spearmen. These were "triarii," who stood a mere three-deep as a bulwark of last resort with little potential left to ply their former attack role. To compensate, the triarii substituted the scutum for the clipeus toward gaining just a little more flexibility applicable to offensive operations. The light infantry seems now to have been divided into those screening ahead of the hastati (leves) and those standing at the rear (rorarii), with the latter tasked to fire missiles from behind should the triarii form a fronting barrier.

But it was a new style of infantrymen that now completed the heavy-armed acies triplex. Positioned as its middle tranche between the hastati and triarii, these were "principes," who resembled the original hastati in plying a scutum, short spear, and secondary sword but had heavier armor. As per the latest version of the hastati, they would come to append a heavy javelin as well and were likewise destined to ultimately give up their spears and rely solely on swords for close-in fighting.[32] Filed six-deep, the principes were (as their title implies) meant to be the formation's main offensive element.

Though most of the troop types within this new tactical system were familiar from past practice, internal division of these plus the principes into small, semi-independent components (manipuli or maniples) gave them an improved capacity to maneuver over the kind of rugged surfaces that had previously compromised phalanx operations.[33] And that would be vital to prospects against the Samnites as well as other hill-country tribesmen. The reformed host featured four legions, each having 1,200 hastati, 1,200 principes, and 600 triarii plus 1,200 light foot (300 leves and 900 rorarii) as well as 600 horsemen attached to the entire army in a body (these eventually rising to 1,200 and divided among the legions at 300 apiece).[34] Generally accompanying these Roman legions into the field were a matching number of allied legions (*alae sociorum* or allied wings) that were probably very similar in size and armament save for usually having a larger mounted contingent of 900 horsemen.[35] Rome resumed its quarrel with Samnium in 316 and gained a successful temporary conclusion (304) before bringing the Samnites into subject alliance (293). All was going well; however, Rome's military challenges would soon take an ironic turn, flipping upside-down to send the city's legions farther afield onto open plains rather than the rugged uplands foreseen in their manipular redesign. And in battling across those distant flats, they would face Hellenistic phalanxes able to exploit many of the same tactical advantages that similar Roman arrays had forfeited a generation past.

Pyrrhus in the West

The sharing arrangement between Lysimachus and Pyrrhus for control of Macedonia collapsed after four years, and the Epiriote warlord had to fall back upon his homeland. Pyrrhus eventually found himself stymied, facing a difficult challenge should he wish to recover Macedonia, which had fallen to Ptolemy Keraunos after Lysimachus' death. And the same applied in southern and eastern Greece, where Demetrius' son

Antigonus Gonatas had gained wide sway. He thus came to fix on an opportunity that had arisen in the south of Italy. The leading polis there of Tarentum (Taras) was warring with Rome due to its intrusion into the affairs of Magna Graecia in the guise of aiding an effort against local barbarians. The Romans had installed garrisons in the region and, fearful of foreign domination, the Tarentines responded by first attacking a flotilla from Rome that was in violation of treaty restrictions and then capturing the closest garrison at Thurii. Subsequent negotiations on reparations for these acts went badly and Tarentum turned to Pyrrhus for help, much as it had to his uncle half a century earlier. Approached perhaps twice on this matter, Pyrrhus finally agreed to lead the effort against Rome, though doing so largely for ambitious motives of his own rather than due to any great concern for the plight of his new Italian allies.

Heraclea (280)

Pyrrhus mounted a powerful expedition to Italy in 280, sending a 3,000-man advance force of Epirotes and then sailing for Tarentum with 20,000 in regular infantry along with 2,500 specialist missilemen (2,000 archers and 500 slingers), 3,000 in cavalry, and 20 elephants.[36] This host included troops lent to him for a period of two years by Ptolemy, who was no doubt happy to have a potential rival for the throne abroad and far from his border. The Macedonians consisted of 5,000 infantrymen and probably 500 horsemen.[37] Breaking down these gross figures for Pyrrhus' army into their most likely components suggests that his infantry might have included 14,000 Epirotes (Molossians, Thesprotians, Chaosians, and Ambraciots). These were perhaps 12,000 heavy-armed (3,000 spearmen, including an Ambraciot regiment and select guard or *agema* of Chaosians,[38] with 9,000 phalangites) plus 2,000 javelineers. He also had 3,000 Greek mercenaries (from Aetolia, Acarnania, and Athamania) in the probable form of 1,000 Acarnanian hoplites along with 2,000 skirmishers in addition to the specialist hirelings with bow and sling. The 5,000-man Macedonian contingent of foot was probably a phalanx division in Philip II's style of 3,000 pikemen, 1,000 hypaspist spearmen, and 1,000 skirmishers. Pyrrhus' mounted troops would have counted 2,000 Epirotes, perhaps 1,000–1,500 heavy lancers (including a unit of guards that was probably Molossian) and 500–1,000 javelinmen plus the elephants and Ptolemy's 500 riders (Thessalian lights).[39]

Despite a storm, Pyrrhus reached Tarentum in anticipation of joining promised Italiote (Italian Greek) and sympathetic barbarian allies. Unfortunately, most of them had either received insufficient notice to mobilize or were blocked by Roman forces already in the field. This limited reinforcement to what was on hand at Tarentum itself. That probably amounted to 10,000 men per the tally for Pyrrhus' combined allied support later in the campaign (see *Asculum* below). We are told that the Tarentines were armed in Macedonian fashion,[40] likely a holdover from their somewhat successful three-year association with Alexander of Epirus and his Philippian phalanx.[41] An estimate of Tarentine manpower might thus be 6,000 in phalangite militia supported by 2,000 Italiote mercenary hoplites, 1,000 hired foot-skirmishers, and 1,000 in native cavalry with small shields and javelins.[42]

The Romans reacted strongly to the intervention of Pyrrhus, sending one consul to suppress any possible local threat to their rear while the other, Laevinus, marched out to confront the Epirote warlord. While our sources don't give any figures for Laevinus' force, Plutarch takes care to describe it as "a great army," and subsequent casualties indicate a strength of at least six legions/alae sociorum totaling almost 29,000 men.[43] The consul was

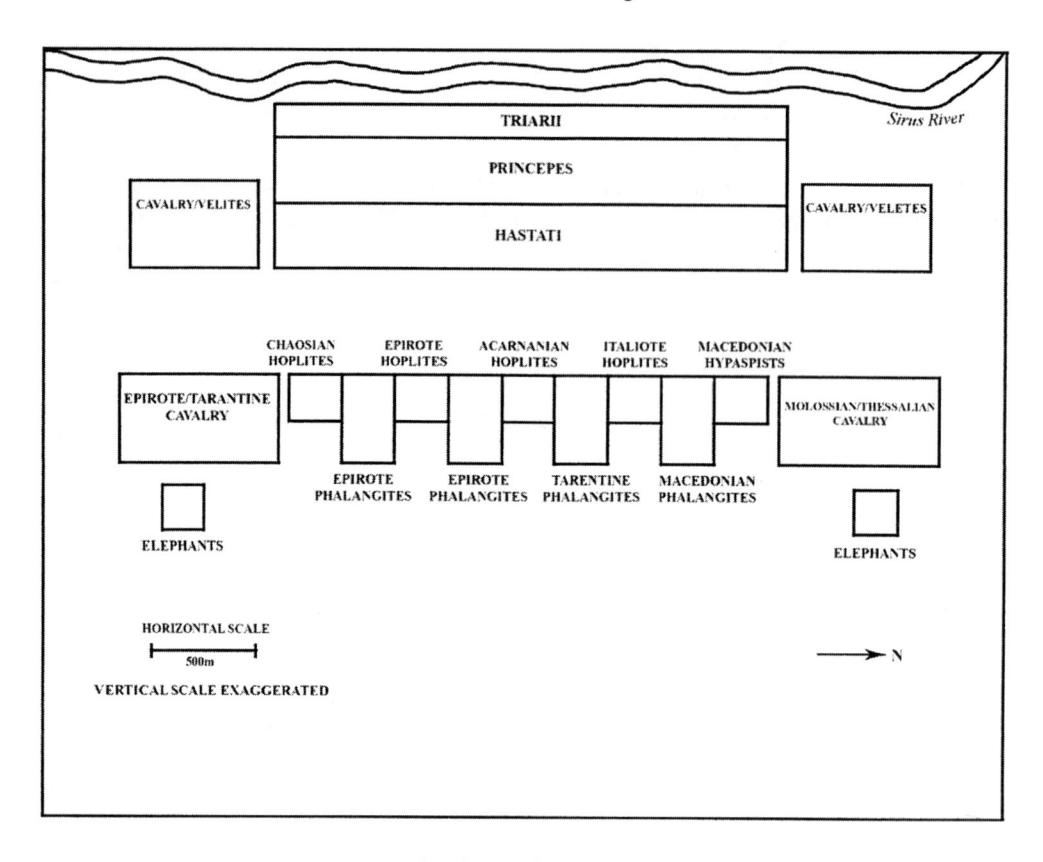

Battle of Heraclea, 280 BCE.

intent on defeating Pyrrhus before most of his allies could join him; he, therefore, went on the operational offensive, likely stopping briefly at Roman garrisoned Rhegium near the toe of the Italian boot before advancing toward Tarentum. Pyrrhus elected to engage in open combat and met the Roman thrust about halfway to Thurii, setting up camp on the plain between Heraclea on the coast and Pandosia inland at a site just short of the Sirus River and its hilly drainage area beyond

We know from Plutarch[44] that Pyrrhus had 3,000 cavalrymen on hand (most likely his Molossian guard of 500 plus 1,000 other Epirotes for a total of 1,500 heavies, the 500 Thessalians lent by Ptolemy, and 1,000 light horse from Tarentum); unfortunately, we have no listing of his infantry. However, we are told that Pyrrhus' army was somewhat smaller than that of Laevinus and included only men that he had either brought from Greece or gained in Tarentum.[45] Applying this toward a best guess at Pyrrhus' battle order suggests that he might have had 12,000 phalangites (6,000 Epirotes, 3,000 Macedonians, and 3,000 Tarentines), 5,000 hoplites (1,000 each of Chaosians, Ambraciots, Acarnanian mercenaries, Macedonians, and Italiote mercenaries), and 5,000 or so in light infantry (including the 2,500 archers and slingers) for 25,000 combatants in all. The garrisons left back at Tarentum and recently established elsewhere would thus have contained units of Epirote and Tarentine pikemen, hoplites (both Epirote and mercenary), foot-skirmishers, and Epirote light cavalry; most if not all of them perhaps a bit under-manned after having been drawn down to bring the contingents taking the field with Pyrrhus up to full establishment strength.[46]

Pyrrhus appears to have been willing to postpone action until additional allied support could arrive; however, he was obviously aware that the enemy had every intention of attacking before that could happen. He therefore posted some light-armed troops along his side of the Sirus as a tripwire alert should the Romans further take the initiative and attempt to ford and engage. And that was indeed what happened. Laevinus tried to get his vanguard over the flow, but it was rebuffed by Pyrrhus' pickets. Undeterred, the consul then sent some of his horsemen out of sight at a distance to make a crossing while he demonstrated along the riverside as a diversion.[47] This ploy succeeded, and the Roman riders cleared the blocking force with a surprise assault that let Laevinus begin transferring his infantry onto the far bank. But well-warned, Pyrrhus was forming up his battle formation as well, and he led a charge on the Roman cavalry screen with a full mounted force and supporting skirmishers to buy time for his infantry to align and possibly even to catch his foes so disorganized in their crossing as to be preemptively routed. The latter was not to be, however, as the Romans had forded in effective order and were ready to fight. Pyrrhus was thus soon facing a sound infantry array and withdrew, leading his horsemen back to take post off the wings of his now fully formed phalanx.

The Epirote warlord had clearly put his brief time in Italy to good use, gathering intelligence from Tarentine and Italiote mercenary partners on the fighting style and ability of his prospective opponents. He therefore introduced an innovation to Epirus' Macedonian-style combat formation that would allow it to perform better against Roman swordsmen. This called for alternating contingents of pikemen and spearmen all along the line, rather than simply confining the hoplites to a single strike-wing as had been past practice.[48] That would allow his majority sarissa-armed troops to not only fend off the attacks of their short-weapon wielding foes, against which they were nearly invulnerable (see below), but also provide solid bulwarks alongside the interspersed spear contingents. Well-warded thus from a turning on either flank, these hoplites could then more securely take advantage of their superior arms-reach and strike frequency (see below) to bleed the enemy. In addition to creating this interspersed "compound" phalanx, Pyrrhus also apparently held his elephants in reserve toward getting maximum effect out of their modest number through well-timed commitment against any vulnerable area the Romans might expose during the battle.[49]

Once Pyrrhus' horseman had taken flank-station (likely with the Molossians and Thessalians right and the other Epirotes and Tarentines left), he threw his phalanx at the enemy. We might assume from prevailing Greek/Macedonian norms that his formation's alternating pattern was designed as much as possible to keep troops familiar with each other in community, while placing the most reliable men rightmost and the next best on the left wing. If so, a reasonable guess at Pyrrhus' right-to-left deployment in round numbers might be: 1,000 Macedonian hypaspists, 3,000 Macedonian phalangites, 1,000 Italiote mercenary hoplites, 3,000 Tarentine phalangites, 1,000 Acarnanian mercenary hoplites, 3,000 Epirote phalangites, 1,000 Epirote hoplites, 3,000 Epirote phalangites, and 1,000 Chaosian hoplites. These 17,000 heavy infantrymen would have been filed shallow toward matching a slightly larger and more spread out foe, letting them stretch across some 2,250m in a repeating sequence of 250m-wide segments that presented either an overlapping pike-hedge or a bank bristling with spears.[50] Across the way, Laevinus and his legionaries spanned a roughly similar frontage with their hastati to the fore and the foot-skirmishers and horsemen now divided off each wing.[51]

The battle lines merged into a close combat that is sadly not much documented in our surviving sources beyond a good deal of individual heroics taking place around the person of Pyrrhus himself during the mounted fight that emerged off what must have been his right wing. But what we are told regarding the high casualties on both sides and that a significant number of the Roman dead were still facing forward when they fell[52] gives strong evidence for a long and unusually lethal infantry action. The hastati followed in turn by the principes must have brought down a few men in Pyrrhus' phalangite contingents with their javelins; then, however, they faced the seemingly near-impossible task of working their way past eight or so pike-points to bring their swords into play.[53] Reasonably wary in using their scutum shields to deflect the somewhat ponderous thrusts of their enemy's long weapons, the legionaries probably took relatively modest harm, yet could inflict precious little damage on their foes at the same time. This all suggests that most of the serious blood-letting along the infantry battle-line took place where sword challenged spear.

The brief Roman barrages of javelins likely had but small effect along those parts of Pyrrhus' front manned by his spearmen. This shower was, after all, considerably less dense and deadly than past mass-flights of arrows weathered by such well-armored/shielded troops—something dismissed on one famous occasion as merely allowing them to fight in the shade.[54] But once closed into shock contact, the Romans here had a much better opportunity to deal harm to the opposition than their comrades had that were facing pikemen. Cutting at spear-shafts and barging behind their shields, they undoubtedly got close enough to wield their swords to good effect. Yet even in these portions of the fight, material advantage lay with the Greeks. They were spaced at half the width of the legionaries and their longer weapons not only gave them greater reach, but also permitted at least the first two ranks to engage an opposing front-fighter. This translated into an effective four-against-one edge in favor of Pyrrhus' hoplites along a little over half the battlefront. Therefore, while the Romans significantly damaged their spear-armed opponents, they suffered even heavier losses in return.

With Pyrrhus' far-flanks protected by cavalry plus foot-skirmishers and his heavy infantry well-aligned, the Romans were forced into a frontal assault in which their manipular flexibility counted for little beyond an ability here and there to pull back from the enemy's weaponry. These dynamics between legion and phalanx tended to favor a lengthy and bloody stalemate for as long as the Greek formation could avoid envelopment and retain close order. The only real path to a Roman victory under such circumstances lay in eliminating enough of the thinly-filed spearmen to cut through one or more of their contingents. That would punch at least one broad hole in the Pyrrhic line to fatally compromise its cohesion. Hampered by the wide spacing needed to swing a sword and the literal short-comings of that weapon's range, this was a difficult proposition; still, even at an unfavorable rate of attrition, the greater depth of Rome's formation might get the job done given sufficient time. As it turned out, however, Pyrrhus was not about to allow his foes that key commodity. Perhaps fully conscious of the risks in a further extended engagement, he finally committed his reserve force of elephants.[55]

The elephants with attached slingers and archers had most likely been sitting behind Pyrrhus' cavalry on either flank,[56] and they now charged out to confront the Roman horse to devastating effect. Apparently fitted with small "towers" on their backs containing two javelineers,[57] these beasts threw Rome's riders into disarray, though much more with their mere presence than through any damage done by the handful of men atop them or from direct attacks with trunk, tusks, and feet. Not only did they frighten the Roman horsemen, but, critically, they panicked their mounts, which were shaken even more by the smell of these creatures than by their strange appearance. Seeing the enemy riders on his right milling about in disorder, Pyrrhus sent in the Thessalian cavalry and put them to rout. This let him take the nearby legionaries in flank, which sent fear-fueled chaos spreading through their ranks until all were in flight. Pyrrhus' horsemen and foot-skirmishers savaged this retreat, doing serious damage despite pursuit being truncated after an elephant was badly wounded.[58]

The most reliable casualty figures for the battle indicate that Pyrrhus lost something less than 4,000 men (around 15 percent) while killing 7,000 Romans (24 percent) and capturing 2,000 or so more, many of those being upper class cavalrymen.[59] It was a truly punishing fight. Rome's losses were indicative of an unusually severe defeat, while those of Pyrrhus helped spawn the term "Pyrrhic victory" for success gained at extraordinary cost. His 15 percent killed was much more characteristic of a well-beaten army in this era than a victorious one.[60] Moreover, Pyrrhus' horsemen had been heavily engaged throughout with their spear-armed Roman counterparts, and even had their casualties merely been proportional to the cavalry's percentage of army manpower (12 percent) they would have totaled some 300 killed among the Epiriotes alone. Clearly, such raw numbers were disturbing enough, but they went farther to upset the warlord in that many of the dead were not only valuable officers, but close companions as well.

Setting aside any personal grief, Pyrrhus was determined not to let his army's sacrifices lay fallow; thus, he possessed the abandoned enemy camp and advanced toward Rome, wasting the countryside and coming within 60km of the city before calling a halt. Despite his tardy allies from local tribes finally arriving after the battle, it seems unlikely that Pyrrhus intended to assault Rome with an army depleted by heavy losses and harboring many a wounded man. This threatening feint toward the enemy capital must have been designed to pressure his foes into coming to terms. And though that didn't happen, additional Italiotes and barbarian tribes were sufficiently impressed to now join his cause, while Campanians forming the garrison at Rhegium broke from Rome and allied with Mamertine ex-mercenaries across the way in Sicily to commit acts of piracy.

Asculum (279)

As Pyrrhus retired into winter quarters, Rome rushed to replace its losses and, possibly, raise new legions as well. And when the Epiriote leader took the field again in the spring of 279, a pair of new consuls marched out with a host consisting of perhaps ten legions, including four alae sociorum.[61] They camped outside Asculum in the foothills bordering Apulia's coastal plain and looked there to apply the costly lessons of Heraclea. Legionary swordsmen on that flat and open battlefield had been at severe disadvantage against a phalanx able to stall their frontal assault and turn a flank with superior light foot and mounted forces. The current bivouac was in ruggedly friendly terrain that would serve proof against a similar attack. However, another descent onto perilously level ground remained likely if they were to aggressively counter the enemy—something much desired to reassure shaken allies and neutral parties alike as to their strength and commitment to prevent further pillaging. They therefore took position above forested, river-bordered, and marshy ground well suited for anchoring one end of their line against mounted envelopment should it be necessary to advance onto the plain.

Camped on opposite sides of the river, the contending armies observed each other for some time. What then ensued was a double-phased engagement that unfolded over the course of two days.[62] The first phase probably involved only skirmishers (each side could field more than 12,000), whose bloody sparring had by the next afternoon left Pyrrhus in possession of the area along the waterway. The threat of missile fire from that vantage point forced the Romans to deploy significantly distant from their planned anchor, shifting to where a descent would find them engaging in the very sort of level and open-ended setting they had been trying to avoid. Yet, reluctant or not, the consuls ultimately elected to accept that disadvantage and issued orders to close into combat.

Pyrrhus commanded a well-reinforced army more than twice that fielded at Heraclea. Based on Dionysius' description of his deployments[63] and taking into account initial manpower adjusted for casualties and likely replacements/reinforcements,[64] the infantry assignments from right to left in round numbers might have been: Macedonian hypaspists (700–750), Macedonian pikemen (2,800–2,900), Italiote mercenary hoplites (2,000), Epirote pikemen (2,800–2,900), Epirote hoplites (700–750), Tarentine pikemen (6,000), Bruttian and Lucanian spearmen (10,000), Chaosian hoplites (700–750), Epirote pikemen (2,800–2,900), Acarnanian hoplites (700–750), and Samnite spearmen (10,000)—a total of almost 41,000 in heavy infantry (some 15,000 pikemen, 6,000 hoplites, and 20,000 theurophoros spearmen[65]). Just above 12,000 light footmen (about half from Greece) would then bring all classes of infantry up to some 53,000. These troops likely spanned an interval of 4,000m.[66] Cavalry probably ran around 7,500-strong (2,500 Epirotes and Thessalians, 1,000 Tarentines, and 4,000 Italian tribesmen). Pyrrhus split his allied light horse between the wings, placing elephant teams behind them and forming a central rear-reserve with his Epirote cavalry, which he led in person.

The Roman army likely consisted of ten legions (six of citizens and four alae sociorum), which would have counted 12,000 hastati, 12,000 principes, and 6,000 triarii for 30,000 in heavy infantry to which we can add 12,000 light foot and a cavalry force of 5,400 in bringing the total number of combatants to a little over 47,000 without counting armed baggage handlers.[67] The heavy foot would have been spaced at 2m/man and filed fifteen-deep in covering the same frontage as Pyrrhus. Cavalry and skirmishers were spread off each wing and a unique central reserve was set up in the rear as a counter to the opposition's elephants. The latter consisted of missilemen manning 300 ox-drawn wagons specially outfitted with a variety of devices meant to injure the enemy beasts. Some of these vehicles had cranes that could hurl grappling hooks, while others had long poles terminated by either an iron trident, a sword-like spike, or a scythe that could be swung out in attack. Many of the wagon-poles were also equipped with pitch-soaked grapnels to be set ablaze as a defensive measure.

The engagement that ensued once the Romans descended onto the plain seems to have been similar in most essentials to the previous action at Heraclea. This saw legionaries "not having the advantages of retreat or falling on as they pleased … obliged to fight on plain ground," with this coming against a foe standing in "a close and well-ordered body."[68] The dynamics that had played out at Heraclea applied once again in contests of different arms along the battle-front: Roman javelins having little to modest impact depending on target type and swords being most effective against spearmen. Unlike in that earlier combat, however, Pyrrhus could deploy his hoplites here at a depth that much reduced the risk of a localized breakthrough that would compromise his entire phalanx. His contingents of Greek pikemen and spearmen were thus comparably secure as they stalled and bled their short-weaponed foes along most of the battle-front. But the warlord's need to employ barbarian theurophoroi elsewhere in matching his enemy's formation width had created a new vulnerability. These tribesmen were opponents with whom the Romans were well familiar as the sort of men they had overcome many times in the past, and they put that experience to deadly use.

Knocking short spears aside and closing at a considerable price in blood within sword-reach of scutum/theuros-bearing foes lacking the mutual protections of a tight line of aspides, Rome's legionaries spread havoc among the front-fighters of Pyrrhus' tribal allies. The Samnites were up to that challenge and held firm on their wing, but the Lucanians and Bruttians in the interior of the line seem to have been less savvy about this kind of vicious shock fighting and eventually began to waver on their right, putting the Tarentine pikemen deployed along that side at hazard of being taken in flank. Pyrrhus observed this rapidly rising threat from directly behind and took decisive action. Releasing the elephants along both flanks to enter the fray, he sent most of his cavalry reserve into action. And just as at Heraclea, this critically timed and massive charge of beasts and mounted men swept all before it, chasing off the screening elements on at least one Roman flank (most probably the left) to clear a decisive strike there that soon had the battered legions in full retreat.

Dionysius asserts in some detail that the legionaries opposing the Lucanian and Bruttian contingent completed their penetration and the fleeing barbarians then took the neighboring Tarentines along with them. This may or may not be historically accurate,[69] but even if the Romans did score that localized success, it must have come just as the larger battle slipped away elsewhere. As for the anti-elephant wagons, those finished the day stranded and unused when their oxen went down under missile fire. Fortunately for the Romans, wooded uplands close to hand, rapid fall of night, and a refuge nearby at their camp all limited losses to pursuit. Nor did Pyrrhus' army suffer unduly. Our most reliable casualty figures from contemporary sources indicate (per Hieronymus) 6,000 Romans slain (13 percent) against (per Pyrrhus' own memoirs) 3,550 for their foes (6 percent), with the latter clearly falling largely among the allied contingents. Such losses were quite steep at a time when a battle's victor might reasonably expect to walk away with only 2–3 percent killed and those defeated maybe no more than two to three times that cost. Still, Asculum's casualties sit well within normal ranges in this era for winner and loser alike and don't by any stretch qualify it as a "Pyrrhic" victory akin to Heraclea.[70] The relatively modest losses indicated here versus those in that earlier battle must reflect a briefer combat. Engaging well past noon and breaking off before twilight on a short, spring day simply failed to provide enough time to kill all that many men even before darkness ended pursuit.

Not having capitulated after their first horrendous defeat against Pyrrhus, it is not surprising that the Romans continued to stand firm against him after this less costly second set-back. That left Pyrrhus facing the unsavory prospect of a grinding war of attrition in Italy against a stubborn and resilient foe. Moreover, he was set to lose more manpower when Ptolemy's Macedonians and Thessalian horse departed upon expiration of their contract. He therefore began to ponder diverting his ambitions either back to Greece or toward a newly arisen opportunity on Sicily to aid that island's Greeks against their old nemesis Carthage. Pyrrhus found the latter option more tempting in the end and crossed over to fight the Carthaginians. In doing so, he left behind a modest garrison[71] to aid his Italian allies in fending off any future resurgence by the still potent forces of Rome.

Maleventum (275)

Pyrrhus landed on Sicily in the fall of 278 and marched to Syracuse at the head of what might have been 11,000 foot-soldiers, 3,000 cavalrymen, and his elephants.[72] The Carthaginians had been besieging Syracuse, but withdrew despite having a considerable force on hand, perhaps not being prepared for a pitched battle. Carthage then waged a purely defensive war, forcing the Epirote warlord to work his way across Sicily in a dreary campaign of reducing one Punic-aligned site after another. Finally, all that remained was well-fortified Lilybaeum on a promontory at the western tip of the triangular island. Investing this last stronghold, Pyrrhus rejected a Punic offer to cede all Sicily save Lilybaeum, apparently being keen to purge Carthage entirely from the land as a prelude to invading North Africa. However, Lilybaeum proved able to sustain itself with seaborne supply and repelled multiple costly assaults until he was forced to give up the siege as winter approached. Retiring to the east, Pyrrhus then engaged the Mamertine allies of Carthage occupying Messana, who had been raising havoc in his rear during the Lilybaeum operation.[73] It's unlikely that this was a single battle despite Plutarch calling it an "open fight," since the Mamertines were badly outnumbered. More likely, Pyrrhus drove those former mercenaries back inside their walls through a series of small actions.

The Epiriote warlord had by this point worn out his welcome with the various Sicilian tyrants that had first called for his help. Their opposition seems as much as anything to have been motivated by self-interest, having become more fearful of Pyrrhus' dominance than of the now seriously weakened Carthaginians. And this erosion of support for their foe led the Africans to take the field for the first time in open counterattacks. As with the Mamertine fight, these must have been skirmishes well below the level of pitched battle; and similarly, they seem to have gone Pyrrhus' way. Still, they combined with the rising hostility among local Greeks to persuade him into abandoning Sicily. He therefore returned to Italy, coming ashore near Rhegium with 20,000 foot-soldiers and 3,000 horsemen plus the elephants.[74]

Heading to Tarentum, Pyrrhus came under attack from 1,000 Mamertines that had crossed to Italy earlier in support of Rome. Striking in irregular fashion, these spearmen contested his passage through some mountainous narrows and threatened to cut off the tail of his line of march. Pyrrhus responded and dispersed the Mamertines, but not before he had lost two precious elephants stationed among his rearguard.[75] Upon reaching Tarentum, the warlord set out to restore control over Magna Graecia and allied tribal territories. These had come under attack during his absence, with the Samnites, Lucanians, and Italiotes being driven to ground and barely able to defend their home communities. Marshaling his own forces and attaching picked Tarentine troops, Pyrrhus formed two columns that advanced in tandem on consular armies operating separately in Samnium and Lucania.

Pyrrhus must have intended that his Lucanian detachment avoid serious engagement with a likely understrength consular army of only two legions/alae (9,000 in infantry and 1,200 horsemen) as appropriate for operating in that lower priority theater. Its assignment instead was to prevent reinforcement of the consul in Samnium until Pyrrhus could drive him from the field. He could then unite his columns and engage in Lucania to complete a defeat of the Romans in detail. We can therefore reasonably expect his Lucanian force to have been no larger than what was needed to intimidate the opposition and pin it down on the defensive. That would have taken no more than 10,000 men. Looking at available manpower, Pyrrhus might have allotted something like 5,000 pikemen (more than half probably less capable Tarentines), 3,000 hoplites (there were plenty of mercenaries for this), and 1000 each in cavalry (maybe Tarentines plus an Epiriote guard for the column's commander) and foot-skirmishers.

Retaining the bulk (and best) of his troops, Pyrrhus moved into Samnium. It's likely that his command included some 9,000 pikemen,[76] 9,000 hoplites, 5,000 in light foot, 4,000 horsemen,[77] and up to 17 elephants. At around 27,000 combatants, this was comparable to the Grecian host deployed five years earlier at Heraclea. In addition, Pyrrhus had a small contingent of Samnites as well, despite those allies being both in bad shape from recent Roman attacks and no longer fully supportive due to his having abandoned them when he went to Sicily.[78] We might thus put his overall strength at as much as 29,000 combatants in all categories. That would have given him a slim edge in manpower over what was probably an army of 25,200 foot-soldiers and 3,000 in cavalry (nominal strength for four Roman and two allied legions).[79]

Unlike his first two engagements against Rome, which had taken place on relatively flat ground, Pyrrhus now had to operate in uplands; indeed, over the very terrain in Samnium whose ruggedness had led the Romans to adopt a manipular array. And his foes had clearly taken their past harsh lessons at his hands to heart. Refusing to descend from an elevated camp near the town of Maleventum (later Beneventum), the Romans were not only keeping to broken ground unfavorable for phalanx maneuvers but had also built field-works as a further defensive measure. Additionally, the width of line that Pyrrhus required to match the enemy front and prevent overlapping of his flanks took most of his men, even after filing the hoplites at minimum depth.[80] The latter had been required at Heraclea as well; but there, he'd been able to address the risk posed by dangerously thin sections within his phalanx through executing a mounted attack on relatively weak forces guarding one end of the Roman line. The terrain and/or field-works acting as anchors here made that sort of flanking action impossible.

As a purely tactical matter, reasonable caution should have dissuaded a seasoned phalanx commander like Pyrrhus from assaulting so strong a position. However, it seems that the need to address potential loss of the Samnites and other allies vital to any hope for long-term strategic success now compelled him to find a way to score a major victory on the spot. He was surely aware of Seleucus' end-run at Cyrrhestica nine years earlier that had snuck behind and defeated the similarly anchored army of Demetrius. And both commanders (the elderly Seleucus by personal observation and Pyrrhus in studying his cousin's campaigns) would have been familiar with comparable stratagems employed by Alexander the Great.[81] Assessing that such a risky maneuver presented the only viable route to victory in his current situation, the Epirote warlord kept his main force in place and set out on a stealthy night march with a select detachment. His intent was to circle through the hills and come down behind the opposition's extreme left in conjunction with a frontal assault along that same narrow sector. If he then broke through the enemy troops on that side of the field and proceeded to roll up the remainder of the Roman line, a general attack by the rest of his army could reasonably be expected to deliver a campaign-sustaining triumph.

The modest contingent that Pyrrhus led out for the skirting action consisted of "his best men and most serviceable elephants."[82] In parallel to the earlier team of Seleucus and the key elements of Alexander's deployments as well as using troops in excess of those needed to man his primary line of battle, it's likely that this detachment included 3,000 hoplites (the Chaosian agema plus other picked men), maybe half that in light infantry, and at least ten elephants along with a few local Samnites to lead the way. But no matter how familiar his guides might have been with the countryside, negotiating it in the dark proved extremely difficult, and it was therefore an exhausted pack of men who finally came into position above the Romans at dawn.[83] Looking to push through by main force, Pyrrhus filed his hoplites at depth (maybe sixteen shields) and anchored their left along broken ground and/or heavy vegetation. He then sounded a salpinx and descended on the enemy's far left rear. The elephants and skirmishers marched on his right to screen that otherwise vulnerable flank. Meanwhile, his loud signal for action had also triggered a charge from below at the same target. That task must have fallen to the Samnite maniples posted far right, which were best suited to negotiate the rough slope and presented a modest length of front matching Pyrrhus' own.

All appeared to be going well at last for Pyrrhus despite the trials of his night march. But the next few minutes would bring a most unpleasant surprise when, instead of taking a panicked mob from behind, he ran head-on into a well-disciplined formation poised to fight. It seems that the Romans had used the interval of their foe's Sicilian sojourn to develop new ploys for combating his elephants. They were not only prepared to avoid level ground to drop envelopment exposure, but ready to actively counter frontal assaults as well. With horsemen useless within this hardened position, a portion (200 per legion) could dismount and stand between each pair of front-rank legionaries. These repurposed equites might then ply their long spears (*paltae*) with both hands against any attacking beasts, dealing out wounds while protecting the swordsmen alongside. And should the legions then face human foes, they would simply slip into the interfile spaces behind and free up room needed on the leading edge for swinging a sword. Long aware of Pyrrhus' approach, it must have been just such a hybrid, spear-reinforced front that received his subsequent rush. Though intended to join the hastati heading an acies triplex, the improvised spearmen had apparently spun about to stand among the principes instead, with that middle segment of the Roman array having reversed direction to move through the triarii and make their formation double-fronted.[84]

The attacking hoplites closing downhill at a deliberate pace came to an abrupt halt, stalling against the principes' unyielding stance. At the same time, the hastati also managed with the aid of their field-works to stymy the Samnites rushing up from below. And that coupled resistance bought time for Rome's spear-armed front-fighters to function as designed against the elephants and accompanying teams of skirmishers. Two of the great beasts went down mortally wounded and eight more wheeled away from the fight to be isolated and captured. As the elephants fled, the principes closed against the right side of Pyrrhus' modest formation and tore it apart. The warlord's tactical gamble had failed utterly, but he managed an escape along with a good share of his men due to the need of his victorious foes to restrain their pursuit and deal with the main phalanx still threatening from below. Even so, the Roman swordsmen are said to have inflicted "great slaughter"[85] on the Greeks as they ran from the field.

Manius, the consul in command, now focused on the remainder of Pyrrhus' forces still arrayed out on the open plain.[86] Having his men abandon their ramparts save for a strong reserve of the triarii (3,600), improvised equites spearmen (1,200), and some light infantry, he led a charge downhill. Plutarch says the ensuing clash saw mixed results along the front. Past patterns suggest that there were stalemates with modest bloodshed where Rome's swordsmen met enemy pikes, while legionaries elsewhere made headway at great cost against spear-armed contingents. Perhaps sensing that his minimally filed hoplites were near to giving way, the commander on hand, probably Pyrrhus' son Helenus, brought up the remaining elephants. These passed through the Samnites to pierce the Roman line's far left, scattering the legionaries there and creating a gap that at least foot-skirmishers, if not horsemen, might exploit. But that never came to pass. Even as the elephants broke into the Roman rear, Manius' spear-armed reserve raced from its battlements to drive them back. Wounded and frightened, the great beasts fled, crowding to plug the breach they had cut as well as running among their own infantry. The Greek phalanx might well have already been on the verge of suffering a deadly penetration; but even if not, this elephant stampede shattered its right wing and the subsequent Roman envelopment from that end of the field was rapidly decisive.

With some contingents in full flight and others maybe falling back in better order, the ensuing Greek retreat must have benefited greatly from cover by its large and capable cavalry reserve. Our more reliable sources provide no casualty figures,[87] but a reasonable guess at rates might be 5–10 percent for the Romans (bloody for sure) and 15–20 percent for Pyrrhus (clearly a substantial defeat). The latter's Lucanian column also met with failure; though, lacking any report of a battle, its commander probably just withdrew without risking engagement once he learned what had happened at Maleventum. The longer-term consequence of these Roman successes was that Pyrrhus, having effectively lost his barbarian allies and with Magna Graecia now wavering in its enthusiasm for his leadership, elected to go home. He sailed for Greece with 8,000 foot-soldiers and 500 horsemen, leaving behind a garrison (no doubt largely mercenary) under a trusted officer (Milon) and his son Helenus to hold Tarentum. That city would fall to Rome three years later after being betrayed by some of its Greek defenders.

3. Gauls, Pyrrhus, Carthage and Rome

Gallic Invasions, Last of Pyrrhus and the First Punic/Mercenary War (279–237 BCE)

The middle decades of the 3rd century saw major military campaigns that affected the Mediterranean world from Asia Minor all the way to the western edge of Europe. This began with a massive invasion of the Successor kingdoms by multiple tribal armies of Gauls; an event that was highly traumatic for Greeks of the day despite the ultimate results yielding strong evidence for the superiority of their own way of war. More important for the region's future was initiation at this time of the first of three wars between Carthage and Rome. Spawned out of the latter's desire to extend its dominance of the Italian mainland onto Sicily, this opening clash of empires would range across that much-prized island and onto the soil of Carthage's African homeland. And the war's conclusion would shift Carthaginian interest onto Spain (Iberia) and spark even wider conflict with Rome before century's end.

Gauls and Greeks

Gallic (Celtic) tribes migrating across Europe from the west had settled for a time in Illyria, down into the northern portion of Paeonia, and along the modern Danube (ancient Hister) river valley as far as the Thracian frontier. A party of these Gauls first threatened Greece in 298 but was met in the passes of the Haemus Mountains (today's Balkan range) by Cassander, king of Macedonia. The barbarians made one assault at minimum (and likely several) against blocking elements of that monarch's heavy infantry, which must have anchored within key chokepoints along narrow passages. Failing to gain entry at some cost, the tribesmen finally retreated. However, by 279, Gallic strength had grown and, seeking both plunder and resources to allow an expanded population to flourish, three separate bands descended upon the Greek world. One tribal grouping under Cerethrios headed eastward through Thrace toward Byzantium and the Hellespont, while another led by the chieftains Brennus and Acichorios came down through lower Paeonia above central Macedon. But it was the third tribal coalition farther west that was first to see action. Led by Bolgios, this nation on the move, unlike the expedition of 298, managed to invade Grecian territory unopposed, skirting northern Epirus to enter Upper (western) Macedonia. Refused a fortune to withdraw, the Gauls then awaited a military response on ground of their own choosing.

Gallic Warfare and Orestis Plain (279)

Gauls/Celts were shock fighters who relied upon long (up to 90cm) slashing swords as their primary weapon, though often using longche-type spears and heavy javelins as well in opening volleys. They were effectively theurophoroi, having large, flat shields made of wood covered in leather with an oval shape and central grip—much like the Greek theuros and Roman scutum in all critical aspects. These were the only form of protection utilized by most Gallic warriors, many of whom are said to have gone into battle naked to the waist or even nude. This was partly a cultural phenomenon, being a display of bravery cultivated from primitive instinct,[1] but was also a function of simple economics, as only the wealthiest chieftains and other aristocrats had the means to purchase expensive helmets and body armor. Certainly, the near-universal shortage of protective gear didn't reflect ignorance about such things, since it was Gauls who had significantly advanced armor technology by inventing chain mail near the beginning of the 3rd century.

The most commonly cited form of attack for Gauls was a frantic frontal charge behind a rain of spears that took them within sword-reach. Once engaged, length of the Gallic sword and the flamboyant way in which it was plied must then have called for wide lateral spacing along the battle-front, perhaps as much as 2–3m per man. But some of this should be taken with caution, since colorful contemporary descriptions of such assaults probably caused later writers to underestimate use of more tightly aligned formations as well as to overestimate both the frequency and impact of those first, wild rushes. We have several accounts of close-ordered arrays being used by Gallic armies, though primarily when standing on the defensive or operating in mountainous terrain unsuited to rapid movement.[2] It's quite possible, however, that Gauls also initially charged into battle in reasonably tight formation, only to then have a portion of their front-fighters spread out as needed to bring their long blades into play. As for Gallic warriors overwhelming foes with the opening fury of their attacks, this shouldn't be discounted when dealing with lesser quality opponents, but is dubious where seasoned troops are concerned, especially those standing in tight formation with longer-reaching polearms. Indeed, it's likely that horsemen and accompanying infantry played a greater role in the subject era's victories by Gauls than their more frequently mentioned opening charges.

Gallic cavalry consisted of rich men able to pay for a string of horses for themselves and a few companions. They carried thrusting spears (much like the Macedonian xyston or Roman palta) and small shields of several different designs. As members of the wealthiest class, these horsemen could afford helmets and armor, including the aforementioned chainmail. Since Gallic cavalry lacked thrown weapons, it was entirely dependent upon infantry to protect both riders and precious mounts from enemy missiles. There were usually a few javelin-armed skirmishers available for that task, but it seems that the much more numerous theurophoroi also provided support for their horsemen. Contingents of these better shielded fighters apparently lent their spears and javelins to screening barrages whenever they could be spared from the main line of battle. With this assistance, mounted Gauls were quite effective and received high praise for their courage and prowess.[3]

Degradation and even complete loss of known accounts along with a tendency for exaggeration in those still extant introduce an unavoidably strong element of speculation into any attempt to assess the manpower that Bolgios brought into Macedonia. Sorting this out begins with Justin's claim that the earlier Gallic exodus out of west-central Europe involved some 300,000 souls.[4] And while a portion of that migration had branched off into Italy before its arrival above Macedon in the early 4th century, his number may well mark the scale of population needed to pressure a similar mass relocation in 279. This was not a matter of strictly military deployments, but rather involved transfers of entire communities with women, children, servants, and the elderly in addition to fighting-aged males. Applying a standard ratio of three non-combatants for each warrior suggests that a comparable early 3rd century population might have produced some 75,000 combatants. Splitting these between the four named chieftains would give them 15,000–20,000 apiece. Though quite hypothetical, that order of manpower is a good match with a report that the eastward-moving band of Gauls might have had 20,000 warriors.[5] Likewise, the bands of Brennus and Acichorios may well have fielded 20,000 each for a combined force of around 40,000 fighters.[6] These tallies suggest that Bolgios perhaps had only about 15,000 men under his command. If so, they probably broke down into 12,000–12,500 theurophoros swordsmen, 500–1,000 foot-skirmishers equipped with javelins and small shields, and 2,000 or so cavalrymen.[7]

It was the young Macedonian king Ptolemy Keraunos who had rejected Bolgios' demands for payment in return for a withdrawal, doing so in a high-handed manner that included killing at least some of the Gaul's envoys. Though the invasion had caught him by surprise, Ptolemy refused to pause and fully gather his resources before taking the field. He even spurned an offer of 20,000 men from the Dardanian Illyrians, who were long-time enemies of the Gauls settled along their western borderlands.[8] As a result, we are told that "he went out to meet them [the Gauls] with a small number of poorly organized troops."[9] Evaluating this claim, it seems most unlikely that the well-drilled professionals in Macedonia's military were truly disorganized despite a hurried muster; however, they would surely have been short of a complete mobilization under such rushed circumstances. Ptolemy must have drawn upon royal guards and contingents from nearby in coring his force and then bulked it out with levies gathered along his route of march from the several recruiting districts of Upper Macedonia. At best, this would have let him approach the site of battle with only about half of his kingdom's available manpower. He might therefore have had something like 18,000 men in all, perhaps consisting of 9,000 pikemen, 3,000 hoplite hypaspists, 4,000 foot-skirmishers, and 2,000 horsemen that included xyston-lancers as well as javelineers.[10]

Bolgios had likely traveled down the Haliacmon river valley to emerge onto Macedon's central plain in its western district of Orestis. Having transited potential chokepoints in the canyons behind him, he could now deploy on open ground and avoid the grave tactical disadvantages that facing a terrain-anchored phalanx would have presented. And this imposed a countervailing challenge upon Ptolemy when he finally came to array against the barbarians spread across the plain in front of him. While his numbers probably at least modestly exceeded those of the opposition, the need for Grecian heavy infantry to maintain close order meant that he must file very shallow to keep the enemy from overlapping his line of battle. With the Gallic swordsmen perhaps stretching across a nearly 2.5km front, Ptolemy had no choice but to match it at an absolute minimum of four men deep.

Yet even with the Macedonians so widely spread, Bolgios could have equaled their frontage at a depth of ten and still spared a good many theurophoroi to reinforce the cavalry and skirmishers off both his wings.[11] And it appears that potential for these enhanced flanking contingents to play a key role in the looming battle was something the Macedonian king found easy to ignore. After all, his own screens not only boasted some of the world's finest horsemen, but also expert javelineers at nearly twice the enemy's strength in supporting infantry. That would presumably set up Macedon's famed phalanx to frontally stall its unarmored foes while his superior flankers enveloped them to win the day. Having grown up hearing his father's stirring tales of gaining glorious victories in just this way at the side of the great Alexander, young Ptolemy must have advanced full of confidence, riding much like that famed conqueror of old among the royal mounted guard off his right wing.

The Gauls would have rushed to meet Ptolemy's well-ordered phalanx as it slowly came on across the flat. Sadly, our surviving sources provide no details on the following combat; however, though it has often been proposed that an initial barbarian charge might have swiftly broken the Macedonian line, this seems improbable in view of our better documented examples elsewhere of similar Gallic assaults being stopped dead by such spear and pike-fronted arrays. What seems more likely to have happened is rapid failure of Ptolemy's flanking skirmishers against the theurophoroi of Bolgios. Using much superior shields to ward incoming missiles, those ferocious swordsmen rapidly closed into shock contact, where pelte and repurposed javelin proved inadequate against them. They and their following horsemen then got in among the Macedonian cavalry, cutting down vulnerable mounts and otherwise unhorsing shocked foes unaccustomed to this sort of assault. Ptolemy himself fell wounded and was captured as the Gauls, both mounted and afoot, swept around either end of his phalanx to inflict tremendous slaughter. We are told that the Macedonians were "cut to pieces" and, having been doubly enveloped, "flight proved the salvation of a small number … the rest were either taken prisoners or killed."[12] Ptolemy was subsequently beheaded as fitting payback for the atrocity of his own earlier murder of Bolgios' envoys.

With Ptolemy's heavy infantry sealed off from escape, the handful of Macedonians that got away would mostly have been horsemen fled from the rear of his collapsed wing-screens. It must have been a time of great dismay and fear the day those riders reached the capital at Pella to report the king's defeat and death. Fortunately for Macedon, there was salvation in the short term from two sources. The first was that Bolgios and his men chose to thoroughly plunder the upper provinces instead of moving immediately against Lower Macedonia. The other saving grace was that someone quickly came forward to devise an effective defense. This was Sosthenes, a general that Ptolemy Keraunos had inherited from the fallen Lysimachus after assassinating that Successor's conqueror, Seleucus I, to seize the Macedonian throne. Leaving others to dispute the once more vacant kingship, this patriot rallied the considerable military assets that Ptolemy had left behind in his rush to doom.

Sosthenes drew upon untapped district levies that possibly included seasoned veterans just returned from serving Pyrrhus in Italy. These professional regulars gave him a ready force roughly equal to the one lost in Orestis. And he could boost that manpower with the youths under twenty and old sweats over fifty that made up the emergency reserve in most Greek states. With the latter garrisoning lowland cities, Sosthenes led the rest of his army against the Gauls. Though it's often said that he then waged a "guerrilla war," that is probably only a partial truth. Being strongly biased in favor of heavy infantry for its phalanx, the composition of Macedonia's military was poorly designed for a campaign of swiftly moving insurgent attacks from concealment. Sosthenes had no doubt served in Cassander's victory over Gallic invaders back in 298 and would surely have now called upon that valuable experience in designing a strategy aimed at similar success. It's therefore probable that he established heavy-armed blocking forces within all the passes leading onto the still untouched Macedonian coastal plain followed by a series of quick strikes from those strongholds using his cavalry and light foot. The strategy was to discomfit rather than defeat the invaders and demonstrate that they occupied a land destined to be ever hostile to their presence. And Bolgios seems to have taken that message to heart, withdrawing his booty-rich horde as winter approached.

Thermopylae, Northern Aetolia and Delphi (279/78)

Greece's respite from Gallic threats would prove brief as the bands of Brennus[13] and Acichorios that had been ravaging Paeonia regrouped and dropped down into Lower Macedon that fall. Seeking to exploit the damage that Bolgios had dealt the region's defenders, this new wave of Gauls swept through the eastern plain. Sosthenes must have made some minor counterstrikes with his light-armed auxiliaries in an obligatory effort against this invasion. But the reality of his situation was that such resistance provided little more than symbolic comfort for the populace. He clearly knew it would be utter folly to throw away his nation's remaining forces against a significantly more numerous foe across relatively open country bereft of terrain features that might allow him to multiply the impact of his modest resources. Sosthenes therefore kept to fortified sites that the barbarians were loath to assault in light of their having no aptitude for (nor interest in) siege work. Husbanding his strength, he hunkered down to await a better future opportunity for reclaiming the land. His patience was rewarded when the Gauls moved on of their own accord. Inspired by tales of even greater wealth to be had, they began to march south toward the fabled Greek shrine at Delphi.

The path to those supposed riches[14] led through Thessaly and the narrow coastal pass of Thermopylae at its base. A coalition army gathered there to bar the way, much as one had done two centuries earlier to oppose the Persian king Xerxes and his vast host of conquest. Forces gathered in the pass came largely from the central Greek states most at hazard from a Gallic advance; these included: Boeotia (10,000 hoplites and 500 horsemen), Phocis (3,000 infantry, perhaps mostly skirmishers, and 500 cavalry), Opuntian Locris (700 hoplites), and Aetolia (7,000 hoplites, nearly 800 light footmen, and perhaps 700 horsemen at a tenth the hoplite count[15]). But there were men from the nearest southern poleis as well, with Megara sending 400 spearmen and Athens another 1,000 hoplites, 500 cavalrymen, and all the city's serviceable warships.[16] Even the Asian Successor kingdom of Antiochus chipped in with 500 mercenaries, no doubt expert missilemen, as did Macedonia with a like contribution; this last being of particular value in that it came with critical intelligence on the strengths and weaknesses of the Gauls' way of war. The combined Grecian armament gathered at Thermopylae thus came to roughly 20,000 heavy spearmen, 4,000 foot-skirmishers, and 2,000 horsemen.[17]

Ranged against the Greeks standing in the pass was the largest of the Gallic hosts that had taken the field that summer. Judging its combat strength in context of the conflicting data that has filtered down to us over the intervening millennia poses a challenge, but compositing all available information suggests more than half again the opposing Greek manpower at something like 40,000 fighting men.[18] Brennus, who apparently held overall command, first came up against resistance along the Spercheius River above Thermopylae's western entry or "gate" in the form of a Greek cavalry detachment supported by 1,000 light infantrymen protecting the far bank. He dispatched a contingent to ford the river upstream at night and forced this small team to give way, allowing him to move down, enter the pass, and launch a daybreak attack on the coalition army anchored within that narrows.[19]

Said to have been contemptuous of the enemy's lesser numbers, Brennus signaled for one of the Gauls' patented wild charges at the unbroken front of spears and rim-to-rim aspides standing between him and the road to his much-coveted prize at Delphi. The hoplites met this clamorous assault "silently and in good order"; and as "they came to close quarters, the infantry did not rush out of their line far enough to disturb their proper formation." It was a pure infantry battle, with the cavalry on both sides proving "useless, as the ground at the pass is not only narrow, but also smooth because of the natural rocks." The opening flight of barbarian spears and javelins had had little impact upon the well-armored and shielded Greek spearmen, contrasting with the support that their own light foot provided in return. Those missilemen fired arrows and hurled sling bullets and javelins over the heads of their deeply filed hoplite comrades to much greater effect. These barrages came blindly from far behind a battle front that also hid enemy front-fighters in the lee of its own spearmen,[20] yet they nevertheless took a bloody toll in plummeting down among the poorly protected men being held static within the Gallic rear ranks. Nor was the Gauls' lethal exposure to ranged weaponry only from ahead, as Greek marksmen tormented them as well from the cliffs on one side (manned by Aetolian javelineers at this point) and from offshore on the other flank, where "the Athenians on the triremes … brought their ships as close to the barbarians as possible and raked them with arrows and every other kind of missile."

Brennus and his men "were in unspeakable distress" from the long-range death raining thus from the heavens on three sides. Moreover, "in the confined space [of the pass], they inflicted few losses [along the front] but suffered twice or four times as many."[21] The stark battlefield reality being forced upon the Gauls trumped any false sense of confidence they had brought to the fight, making it clear that they "were worse armed than the Greeks, having no other defensive armor than their national shields." Bloodied and thoroughly defeated before mid-morning, Brennus finally gave the order to retreat, only to have his troops suffer further as pursuit struck at the backs of those trailing the withdrawal. We have no surviving count of Gallic losses on the day, but they must have run well into the scores if not hundreds. Opposing phalanx fighters, on the other hand, reportedly lost only forty men.

The Gauls now found themselves stalemated above Thermopylae, and they licked their wounds in frustration for a full week while seeking some means of overcoming the Greek blockade without risking further fruitless punishment in another unequal shock fight. The first ploy attempted was to send a detachment around Thermopylae via a narrow track over Mount Oeta to the south. But this ended in failure when Aetolian peltasts guarding the cliffs above mercilessly pelted the unarmored Gauls and sent them packing. Brennus next decided to send a powerful force westward above the mountains so it could drop into Aetolia from the north.[22] His plan was to convince that nation's large contingent to abandon the pass and march against this threat to its homeland. And, indeed, the Aetolians reacted just as desired, rushing back to defend their own territory.

Having accomplished its diversionary objective, the Gallic detachment in Aetolia broke off plundering and began retracing its course back to Thermopylae. A modest force of Achaean hoplites from Patra (probably no more than a lochos/battalion 500-strong), allies from across the Corinthian Gulf, made a frontal attack on the van of the barbarian column only to be met by vastly superior numbers and dispersed with severe losses (perhaps 20–30 percent slain). These overmatched spearmen undoubtedly dodged complete annihilation only with the aid of intense covering fire from Aetolian peltasts on the enclosing cliffs. And javelin bombardments didn't stop there but continued to inflict pain and death throughout the remainder of the Gallic retreat. When the tribesmen tried to go after those showering missiles upon them, the nimbler Aetolians easily skipped to higher ground; they then turned about and resumed the long-range assault as soon as their foes ceased chasing. Much as in the Gauls' failed attempt on the Mount Oeta pass, this expert Aetolian sniping wrought a great deal of unanswerable damage "among enemies protected by nothing but their national shields."[23]

Despite loss of Aetolia's contribution, the defenders at Thermopylae retained more than enough troops to prolong their blockade, forcing Brennus to essay yet another indirect maneuver toward bypassing the Greek position. That involved a second attempt to cross Mount Oeta, this time using the same path that the Persians had exploited in their past passage of Thermopylae. Ironically, with the Aetolians gone, defense of this track had fallen to the Phocians, the same people who had failed to hold it two centuries earlier. Led by locals eager to get the invaders out of their country, the Gauls took advantage of a misty day to surprise the Phocians and send them into retreat. As for those holding the pass below, they learned of this critical reverse from Phocian messengers and were able to rapidly evacuate aboard Athens' fleet, thus avoiding the necessity of sacrificing a rearguard to delay overland pursuit as Sparta's Leonidas had done with his heroic last stand in 480.

Brennus immediately set off for Delphi once Thermopylae was cleared, leaving behind half or so of his men with Acichorios to defend the families and plunder within his camp still situated above the pass. At the head of perhaps 16,000–26,000 fighters,[24] including 13,000–21,000 of his best theurophoros swordsmen (80 percent of the total) and 1,600–2,600 in cavalry (a 10 percent share), the Gallic chieftain marched in rapidly worsening winter weather conditions toward his target, moving eventually through the frosty canyons below Mount Parnassus in winding his way up to that lofty sacred site. He was confronted there by a small Greek defense force. This consisted of 4,000 men per Justin, who offers no details on origins or troop types, but must have been referencing only the heavy infantry present. Pausanius mentions 400 hoplites from the Phocian polis of Amphissa, which lay nearby within Delphic territory, and adds that others came "from all their cities." He also cites the Aetolians, of whom "a few came at once" and 1,200 later, noting that the flower of that nation's strength was at the time deployed against Acichorios back in Thessaly. However, descriptions of the ensuing battle make it clear that an even greater concentration of lighter javelineers and bowmen was also on hand, coming from both Aetolia and Phocis.[25]

Taking stance upslope across a slim passage below the shrine, the Greeks received Brennus' charge aligned in phalanx formation. And per other actions that had recently unfolded within this sort of anchored setting, those tightly ranked spearmen with their close-set aspides (possibly aided by low works as a further barrier) stopped the fierce Gallic rush cold in its tracks. While their hoplites held the barbarians all along that short, terrain-framed front, missilemen went to work from the heights off either flank, sending a stream of projectiles of all types into the crowded and poorly armored Gauls. Nor was that all with which the embattled tribesmen had to contend, as previously positioned Phocian skirmishers issued from defiles at the rear of the stalled Gallic array to launch a ranged attack from that direction as well. With flat shields warding but a single direction at a time, the Gauls suffered under a savage rain of javelins, arrows, and stones coming from every quarter. Brennus went down mortally wounded and his men soon had to fall back from a manifestly hopeless fight.

Leaving behind some 6,000 of their dead and dying on the field of battle,[26] the Gauls retreated under nightmarish conditions, beset by both constant Aetolian sniping from all sides during the day and freezing temperatures at night. Thousands more died before the remnants of Brennus' expedition rejoined Acichorios back above Thermopylae. By then, Athenian and Boeotian armies were also nipping at the barbarians' heels, "killing those who happened to be the last."[27] The surviving Gallic combatants, numbering perhaps as few as 10,000,[28] retraced their steps up the length of Thessaly amid frequent ambushes by light-armed locals. Despite claims in our sources of their destruction to the last man, many of these fleeing Gauls and their accompanying dependents must ultimately have found safety beyond the broad and unguarded frontiers of northern Macedonia.[29]

Lysimacheia (277) and the Elephant Victory (c. 273)

Cerethrios and his followers were joined in Thrace by a portion of the tribal coalition of Bolgios and, in 277, a force drawn from this base descended upon the Hellespont in search of more land to plunder. Antigonus Gonatus, warlord son of Demetrius the Besieger, was at the time operating with an army of mercenaries in that region preliminary to making a bid for Macedonia.[30] The barbarians descended upon his position at Lysimacheia. That former capital of Thrace sat on the western shore of the Propontis Sea just east of the Chersonese (modern Gallipoli) Peninsula, and Antigonus' fleet of triremes and transports was pulled sterns-first upon the beach there a short distance below his fortified camp.

The Gallic force moving on Antigonus came to 15,000 foot-soldiers and 3,000 horsemen per Justin, though this might not include a couple of thousand javelineer skirmishers attached to the cavalry as auxiliaries.[31] Much as Bolgios had tried with Ptolemy two years earlier, the Gauls offered to depart in return for a substantial fee. Antigonus, having no mind to be so extorted, nevertheless hosted the barbarians' envoys opulently, taking care to show off both his fleet and elephants toward intimidating them against attempting any future aggression.

The size of Antigonus' army seems unlikely to have been much greater than what the Gauls had fielded in light of his eventual decision to conserve his strength for use elsewhere by avoiding a straight-forward, pitched battle. Judging by the theoretical capacity of the armada he had inherited from his father, the largest force he might have deployed for the sort of amphibious operation at hand would have been about 24,000 men not counting sailors and oarsmen.[32] Such an armament would logically have included something like 18,000 hoplites, 4,000 in light foot, and 2,000 horsemen plus a small number of elephants, with the latter two elements having come aboard transports within an overall fleet of 300 ships. Suspecting that the tribesmen still meant to attack him after his refusal to meet their demands for payment, Antigonus set a trap for them. He abandoned camp and divided his troops into two contingents, one to take cover in a nearby forest and the other to protect his ships along the beach.

The Gauls decided to make a nighttime assault on the Greek encampment; but finding it deserted, they then descended toward the grounded fleet at daybreak. That brought them up against a stout defensive front stretching across perhaps as much as 3km in front of the sterns of the vessels beached some 10m apart along the shore. Likely reinforced by a low field-work of ditch and following mound dug from the sand, a third of Antigonus' hoplites must have ranked two-deep along the strand with maybe 1,000–1,500 expert missilemen and thousands of rowers and sailors at their backs.[33] The Gallic swordsmen fanned out at 2m spacing against this rampart only to then come under attack from the rear as Antigonus and the rest of his army took advantage of their occupation along the front to advance out of hiding. The warlord's hoplites could have matched widths with the anchorage beyond at a depth of four shields, having their skirmishers, elephants, and horsemen close down around both ends of the barbarians' deployment to cut them off from any sort of lateral escape. Completely enveloped, the tribesmen were subjected to a "slaughter" so devastating that its later report "secured peace for Antigonus, not only with the Gauls, but also with his barbarous neighbors."[34] The Greek warlord would go on to exploit this victory in securing Macedonia before year's end.

With their defeat at Lysimacheia having blunted expansion opportunities in the eastern Greek borderlands, the Gauls of Thrace pushed into Asia Minor instead. This came in two waves, with one group led by the chieftain Luturios crossing over on its own during the winter of 278/77, and the other under Leonorios being transported across the following spring or summer to serve as mercenaries in a dispute over control of the province of Bithynia. We are told that the combined tribes in Europe boasted 20,000 fighters, but when reunited in Asia, fielded only 10,000 combatants from a community of 20,000.[35] However, since a population of at least twice the latter size would be needed to produce so many warriors, it's much more likely that this was a confused reference to the same 20,000 fighters, which represented contributions averaging 10,000 men apiece from each of the two chieftains. These tribesmen settled in northern Asia Minor to form a new homeland known as Galatia and soon began raiding throughout the region. That finally provoked a response from the Seleucid ruler, Antiochus I, this happening sometime around 275.[36] The resulting battle took place somewhere on the open Anatolian plains and is not widely documented, with most of what is known coming courtesy of a fictional dialogue written by the 2nd century CE satirist Lucian.[37]

Antiochus' preparations are said to have been "hurried on no great scale," resulting in him taking the field with "quite a small force." His army was built around modest contingents of guards that were resident at the capitol and thus at the king's immediate disposal plus a system of military colonies that provided the bulk of the nation's troops. Not feeling that he had time to gather his extended host from its several widely spread base communities, Antiochus marched out with a force cored by only his smaller, elite units. These included a 10,000-man heavy infantry guard known as the *Argyraspides* (Silver Shields), which boasted 8,000 pikemen and 2,000 hypaspists, the latter cross-trained to use either hoplite dory/aspis or phalangite sarissa/pelte as best suited for any given engagement. Also, there were mounted guards with xyston and shield contained in two 1,000-man units. And in addition to these various select troops, there were sixteen elephants, with each having a fifty-man team of supporters on foot.[38] Lucian claimed that Antigonus' army was "mostly skirmishers and light-armed troops" and thus "more than half of his men were without defensive armor." However, this is unlikely, though there must have been some light footmen backing up his phalanx's heavy line-infantry (*stratiotai*) and horsemen.[39] More reasonably numbered per historical deployments, we might propose no more than 3,000–4,000 foot-skirmishers including those with the elephants, therefore bringing the Seleucids up to 16,000 men at most.

Lucian cited the Gauls as having 20,000 cavalrymen plus 320 chariots, with at least the first of those numbers not being at all realistic. Reducing this by a factor of four as seen likely to apply elsewhere to Gallic deployments would suggest a still rather high count of 5,000 riders even ignoring the chariot contingent. Should we assume an overall tribal manpower of just over 20,000, that would indicate about 15,000 foot-soldiers. These would normally break down into 11,500–12,000 theurophoros swordsmen and 3,000–3,500 javelineers (two for each three horsemen). The swordsmen closed on the opposing phalanx at twenty-four deep per our lone account, thus covering a 1,000m front at 2m per man with their chariots ahead and cavalry off both wings. If so, Antigonus, who was restricted to a frontage of only 2/3m per pikeman, had no choice but to file dangerously thin if he was to avoid an overlap of his flanks. This would have forced him to stack his regular phalangites at eight (half the optimum, but a common depth all the same) while casting the die that his select hypaspists could stand their ground adequately in files no more than the practical minimum of four-deep.

Lucian informs us that this clash featured the Gauls' chariots opening action by crossing the field ahead of their infantry and engaging half of Antiochus' pachyderms doing the same. The latter is highly improbable for an experienced operator of elephants to have done, especially when in possession of so very few of them.[40] The described split of these beasts onto both flanks much more likely involved their entire complement rather than merely a portion as the satirist assumed. And flankward is thus where their confrontation with the chariots must have taken place; all the chariots probably facing half the elephants on a single flank.[41] Meanwhile, along the main line of engagement, the Gauls' theurophoroi soon proved incapable of gaining quick success against an opposing, multi-layered front of pikes, though apparently suffering only modestly from those lengthy weapons due to their entire front-rank sporting chainmail. That failure then turned decisive when the barbarian chariots and cavalry, having only poor light-infantry support, fled before a deadly onslaught of charging elephants and thick missile fire. Sweeping in from both sides, Antiochus' flankers were now free to envelop the Gallic footmen to such deadly effect that "the carnage was great, and all the Galatians were either killed or captured, save for a quite small band which got off to the mountains."

This victory by Antiochus I would earn him the title of "Sotor" (Savior) as it put an end to the ongoing round of Gallic raids. And though he would later make cash payments to prevent the Galatians from resuming predation upon his territory, they would in future form a valuable mercenary asset for his and other Seleucid armies. In approving a commemorative for the battle, Antiochus insisted that it solely celebrate his elephants, which certainly had played an important role in this "Elephant Victory" as it came to be known. However, the larger lesson taught here and by the other early 3rd century confrontations with Gallic foes was that Grecian heavy infantry with either spear or pike was far superior to theurophoroi in pitched battle. Yet at the same time, though effective at long range, peltast javelineers were no match for those same barbarians hand-to-hand. This would lead Greek skirmishers to replace their pelte with a theuros. These upgraded light infantrymen would then go on to prove more efficient in both detached operations and the provision of phalanx support.

Pyrrhus and Greece

Even as Antiochus suppressed Gallic raiding in Asia Minor, the Greek mainland was experiencing internal turmoil from one corner to the other. In the northeast, Antigonus Gonatus had taken charge of Macedon following his victory at Lysimacheia; but he now faced a challenge from Pyrrhus, who had reinvigorated Epirus after returning from his failed Italian/Sicilian ventures. Meanwhile, trouble was brewing in the southwest of Greece as well, where Sparta's disputed succession was only one of several sources of regional disquiet.

Haliacmon Pass (273)

Following his return to Greece at year's end 275, Pyrrhus set about restoring his military strength, replacing losses sustained in Italy in addition to incorporating troops left behind to defend Epirus. The latter had failed to prevent some of the Gallic raids of the early 270s from reaching into Epirote territory but were able to join with the repatriated Italian veterans in training a flood of new recruits needed to refill the nation's ranks. Pyrrhus would even use some of the very Gauls who had proven so troublesome in his absence, hiring them as skirmisher support for his phalanx. Ready at last, the warlord set out to revive his imperial ambitions in the summer of 273,[42] marching east into the Macedonian province of Elimeia in opening a campaign against Antigonus Gonatus.

Antigonus took the field in response, but apparently felt overmatched; thus, he refused battle on open ground. Instead, the king saw 2,000 of his Upper Macedonian troops defect in disgust when he abandoned their homelands in falling back upon a pass through the mountains that led onto his more highly prized eastern coastal plain. His route must have been through the canyon cut by the Haliacmon River in its passage out of the Elimeian heights and down to the sea. Pyrrhus caught up with Antigonus there, and "meeting him at a narrow passage," he "put the whole army [of Macedonia] in disorder."[43] The exact nature of that action is unreported; however, Pausanius cites the Epiriotes as "overpowering the native [Macedonian] troops of Antigonus and his Gallic mercenaries,"[44] which suggests a sizeable pitched fight. This likely saw a pike-armed blockade across the pass give way before the frontal attack of like-equipped, but more battle-savvy veterans of Pyrrhus' western campaigns, with the Macedonian phalangites then tossing their heavy weapons for speedier flight.

Antigonus, like Pyrrhus, had contracted Gallic warriors, and these along with his elephants, which the barbarians were screening, ended up guarding the rear to let their army escape annihilation. Trying to stand against what must have been slowly pursuing Epirote heavy infantry (Pyrrhus' skirmishers and cavalry being mired at the rear in this confined setting), the Gauls, despite being "numerous," suffered defeat in a "sharp encounter," their lack of armor and shorter-reaching weapons no doubt once again letting them down. Most of the tribesmen were "cut off," and those "who had charge of the elephants, being surrounded every way, delivered up both themselves and the beasts." Beset with further desertions, Antigonus and those still loyal to him retreated into fortified cities across the Macedonian lowlands, thereby ceding control over Upper Macedonia and Thessaly. Dedications of Gallic and Macedonian shields at a shrine in Thessaly demonstrate both "the extent and decisive nature of the victory of Pyrrhus" with their inscribed boast that "he had destroyed all the host of Antigonus."[45]

Sparta II/III, Charadrus Pass and the Streets of Argos (272)

Pyrrhus might at this point have seemed on the verge of completely reducing Macedon, but the long series of sieges that would require must have been a daunting prospect. This sent him casting about for another means of increasing his authority; something less demanding or, perhaps, simply better suited to his available resources and personal set of skills. And just such an opportunity now arose when Cleonymus, a failed claimant to Sparta's recently vacated crown, invited Epirote intervention on his behalf. Pyrrhus agreed and marched into the Peloponnese that spring with a powerful force. In fact, at the head of

25,000 foot-soldiers, 200 horsemen, and 24 elephants,[46] it seems clear that his intention was to begin subduing that entire region rather than simply help a potential ally gain the Spartan throne.[47]

The Spartans were caught short-handed by this unexpected aggression, their new king, Areus, being off to Crete earning coin as a mercenary commander in the company of at least a portion of the polis' dwindling pool of crack, full-citizen spearmen (spartiates). And had Pyrrhus immediately attacked their capital, he might well have beaten them at little cost on that account. However, he instead chose to open with a campaign of plundering the countryside, which gave his foes critical time to improve their defenses.[48] That included digging a trench in front of the city's main entryway that must have had a low wall behind it composed of the excavated dirt and any other useful debris near to hand. This ran across a front some 250m in length and was nearly 3m wide and 2m deep. Packed tightly to more than its material's original density, the backing wall might have exceeded a meter in height to protect a defender's lower body as he speared above over top of his aspis. The Spartans anchored this hardened front against envelopment by burying wagons up to the axle as artificial topography on its flanks. These field-works allowed for as few as 500 prime-aged hoplites (likely all the spartiates available at about half the polis' complement) to hold the line two-deep, supported by an equal number of old-age/youth reservists and other spearmen (perioeci) plus some Cretan archers and a host of other missile-bearing folk in back and among the wagon-hillocks either side.

Pyrrhus launched an attack on the Spartans at daybreak, personally leading an advance by his heavy infantry, which probably consisted of 2,000 hoplites aligned across the fixed enemy front in files eight-deep.[49] He meant "to force through the shields of the Spartans ranged against him," but found the trench "scarce passable, because the looseness of the fresh earth afforded no firm footing."[50] As Pyrrhus' frontal assault was thus foundering against Sparta's works-strengthened phalanx, his son, Ptolemy, was going after one of the flank barriers of sunken wagons with a contingent (likely a 500-man lochos) of Chaosian elite hoplites supported by 2,000 Gallic mercenaries. The spearmen stood at the fore and shielded the Gauls as they disinterred the wagons and began hauling them out of the way. But this exercise came to naught when some Spartans circled around to strike from behind. A chaotic melee then ensued that ultimately saw Ptolemy and his men withdraw, perhaps largely due to a dense rain of lethal projectiles that began coming at their backs once they had turned to face the rearward attack (the unarmored Gauls being particularly vulnerable to such fire). That same sort of bombardment must have been pelting Pyrrhus' hoplites along the main line of battle as well, but it would have had only a rather modest effect from the front on men so heavily equipped.[51] Yet even if the warlord's casualties were relatively light, he simply could not crack the hardened Spartan formation and eventually had to retreat in frustration.

The next morning, Pyrrhus initiated a second battle, sending his spearmen once more at Sparta's field-work and the phalanx holding it. This time, he planned to have his after-rankers undo in short order the ditch that had taken the Spartans substantial time to dig, doing so behind cover from his front-fighters if only they could somehow cope with both bad footing and skilled enemy hoplites lancing down across the earthen wall above. Carrying up material from the rear, the Epirotes threw it in with whatever already lay in the excavation, including their own dead. Pyrrhus urged them on, riding close behind his infantry. The danger of thus exposing himself soon made itself known when a Cretan arrow took down his horse and threw the warlord to the ground. He managed to survive this incident, but his men were unable to fill the trench under such trying conditions. Seriously disadvantaged against Spartan spearmen along the battlefront and harassed farther back by foes "making good use of their missiles," Pyrrhus finally "put an end to the combat"[52] and once again withdrew to his camp.

Powerless to take the city by main force, Pyrrhus was reduced to the hope that whatever damage he had inflicted so far on the Spartans had lowered their morale to the point where they might be willing to surrender without further fighting. However, that proved to be wishful thinking and, worse yet for his chances, Sparta began to receive reinforcements. These included not only hired troops sent by Antigonus, but also the Spartan king Areus, who arrived from Crete with 2,000 soldiers (mercenaries plus the spartiates making up his bodyguard). The situation was fast becoming hopeless and, after briefly contemplating siege operations, Pyrrhus pulled his army back into the countryside.

Pyrrhus now headed toward Argos, where he sought to intervene on behalf of a friendly party being opposed by a pro–Antigonus faction. Areus trailed him beyond Sparta, harrying the Gallic skirmishers and Molossian heavy infantry that were bringing up the rear wherever the topography favored it. Moving east from Mantinea through the mountains along the canyon cut by the Charadrus River, Pyrrhus had his son, Ptolemy, ride back to lead a counter against one such ambush in company with his personal team of mounted companions; meanwhile, the father took his army's main body out onto the Argive plain. Ptolemy led an advance against the spartiate and mercenary hoplites and auxiliaries engaging the column's rearguard, but when he then lost his life to one of the hired spearmen that had accompanied Areus from Crete, his close comrades turned and galloped away. Some of the Spartan horsemen present gave chase, cutting off a few of the fleeing Epirotes and closely following the rest onto open ground beyond the canyon mouth. Exposed there without light infantry support, the Spartan riders were hit by Pyrrhus at the head of his Molossian cavalry guard. The warlord was aware by now of his son's death and "satisfied himself with the blood and slaughter of the Lacedemonians."[53] He pursued the beaten horsemen back into the pass to engage their foot soldiers as well. Those were no longer in good order and, scattered under the Molossians' charge, many of them also died that day, including their spartiate commander.

The Epirote warlord had no time to grieve as he was soon confronted by Antigonus, who had likewise marched into the vicinity of Argos, making camp on high ground. That king declined a challenge from Pyrrhus to resolve their dispute over Macedonia's crown in a pitched battle out in the open. Instead, he kept to his safely elevated position and sent some of his best officers into town with a significant force to aid its defense. And Argos then got further help as Areus also arrived to add a contingent of his spartiates (500 or more) plus 1,000 mercenaries from Crete to the garrison. Faced with such growing opposition, Pyrrhus set out to capture the city as quickly as possible by means of betrayal from within. His Argive allies opened a gate and let him and some select contingents get inside the walls during the dark of night; his surviving son, Helenus, was to wait outside town with most of the army.

Pyrrhus' Gauls were first inside, racing to Argos' marketplace; however, a delay then ensued as the Epirote elephants' towers had to be removed to allow them through the gateway along with the warlord himself at the head of some chosen cavalry units. As little time as this probably cost, it was enough for the alarm to get out and arouse the city's defenders. The foreign troops in the garrison immediately descended upon the Gauls and threw them into disorder. Meanwhile, the Argives, soldiers and other residents alike, swarmed to impede Pyrrhus and his horsemen in any way they could. Plutarch remarks that "in this night engagement there was infinite uncertainty as to what was being done … there was much mistaking and struggling in the narrow streets … all generalship was useless in that darkness and noise and pressure."[54] Pyrrhus eventually realized that his ploy had failed and, retreating, he sent word for Helenus to break a passage for escape through the city wall. But that didn't come to fruition when the Epirotes' flight slowed to a crawl as its van jammed into the slender road leading out of town. This saw men "wedged into one mass" and at least one frenzied elephant raging about to trample all around it. Pyrrhus was wounded amid this chaos by one of the many objects being hurled from surrounding rooftops. Struck on the neck, he fell in a daze onto the street, where one of Antigonus' men found and killed him. This triggered defeat for the army of Epirus, which surrendered along with Helenus to the Macedonian king.

The Isthmus of Corinth (265), Megalopolis (263) and Sardis (262)

Pyrrhus' death reduced the scope of intermural conflicts among mainland Greeks for a while, but by 268 fighting broke out again. This featured Athens, under the influence of Egypt's Ptolemy II, leading a campaign of resistance to Antigonus' dominance in southern Greece. Sparta joined this cause and, when the Athenians came under siege in 265, its king, Areus, marched out to their relief.[55] His overland route into Attica passed through the Isthmus of Corinth, which featured a chokepoint only 6km wide. Antigonus had manned field-works there toward preventing just such a unification of his foes. This barrier was probably much like that in front of Sparta seven years earlier: a trench backed by a waist-high mound that would impose poor footing on an attacker while allowing defenders above to strike down from stable stances and with lower bodies warded by a barrier of well-packed earth. Unlike those older works, however, this construction must have been double-sided, since it sat between enemy centers to both west and east and might have to defend either direction. A satisfactory garrison for these works could have been some 7,000 men stationed at set intervals that would allow a prompt rally by sufficient numbers to any point under threat.[56]

Areus would have been leading his own Spartan hoplites (perhaps 2,000 strong with half citizens of higher classes and the rest perioeci), mercenary spearmen (maybe 1,000 as at Argos earlier), and some coalition allies. If the last equaled Sparta's own total contribution, then he might have had some 6,000 heavy infantrymen in all to which we can add 2,000 or so skirmishers and horsemen in support. Though Areus had not taken part in fighting along Sparta's trench-line, there were many with him who had, and he would also have been familiar with the effects of such barriers from other past combats.[57] That should have made him wary of emulating recently twice-beaten Pyrrhus by similarly assaulting so hardened a position,[58] yet he chose to attack anyway. Perhaps driving a phalanx filed eight-deep into a 750m stretch of enemy works easily defended by even half the garrison on hand, this act of bravado resulted in a defeat that cost Areus his life.

With the campaign of resistance to Antigonus fading in the wake of their failure at the Isthmus of Corinth, the Spartans made a last attempt to reenergize it by marching against the nearby polis of Megalopolis. That city owed its very existence to enmity against the Spartans, having been founded by Thebes as a refuge from which the Messenians, former downtrodden subjects of Sparta, could act as a regional counterweight. Fully in keeping with that history, Megalopolis was allied to the Macedonian king now trying to force his will upon Sparta's struggling coalition. Acroatus, uncrowned son of Areus, invaded Messenia in summer 263 only to be bested and killed by Aristodemus, tyrant of Megalopolis.

The undocumented scope of this action must have been modest. No allies are mentioned for Sparta, suggesting that it had only a couple thousand of its own spearmen, while Megalopolis' army probably wasn't significantly larger. Such reasonable parity of strength is indicated not only by what appears to be a mutual agreement to engage, but also by Pausanius' claim that this was a "fierce battle" concluded only "after many had fallen on both sides,"[59] suggesting (if more than simply literary flourishes) a long and closely matched slug-fest. Deployed across flat terrain, the Spartan left/defensive wing probably gave way before the right could best its own opposition, both those failures perhaps due in part to slightly deeper opposing files. If so, Acroatus must have gone down near his right flank, fighting close to the front at the traditional post held by Spartan commanders. As the Messenians had enveloped and rolled up his formation from the far end, those ranked behind him would have given way before that developing lateral attack, leaving their general and other lead-fighters (*promachoi*) still faced forward to be overwhelmed by the sudden surge of a victorious enemy front. This was the last major offensive undertaken by forces of the anti–Macedonian coalition, and their cause unraveled completely two years later when Athens finally capitulated.

With Antigonus cementing his position on the Greek mainland and Ptolemy II secure in Egypt, only Antiochus I's domain among the three great Successor kingdoms was now facing a rising challenge. This came from Pergamum, a new state spun off from the former holdings of Lysimachus that incorporated the old Persian satrapy of Mysia. Pergamum's tyrant, Eumenes, revolted against Seleucid rule in 262, and we are told that he scored a victory over Antiochus near the latter's capital of Sardis in Lydia.[60] If historical, such an action must have been quite small in that Pergamum lacked heavy infantry at the time and its light-armed forces were much inferior to what the Seleucid king could throw into the field even on short notice.[61] Any military success by Pergamum against Antiochus in 262 is thus likely to have involved no more than relatively minor skirmishing in front of or behind an otherwise uncontested Seleucid punitive expedition responding to Eumenes' rebellion.

The First Punic/Mercenary War

Carthage's involvement with affairs of Greek poleis in eastern Sicily was of long standing and reasonably justified in service of looking after the wider interests of its own holdings in the island's west end. However, that policy ultimately pulled the Carthaginians into matters in the Sicilian far northeast that would send them down the path to war with an ascending Rome. The flashpoint for the initial significant conflict between Carthage and Rome that would become known as the First Punic War was Messana, which sat southeast of Rhegium below the narrow strait separating Sicily from the Italian mainland.

Cyamosorus R. (c. 274), Longanus R. (c. 265) and Messana III/IV (264)

Campanian mercenaries occupied Messana after the death of their tyrant paymaster Agathocles of Syracuse in 289, adopting the name "Mamertines" from the war-god Mamers (Mars of the Romans). Equipped as Greek hoplites, they are said to have been capable in the mid–260s of fielding 8,000 foot-soldiers and might have had at least 5,000 a decade earlier, including maybe a thousand locals recruited as skirmishers.[62] These men took up piratical raiding to support themselves in what would normally have been an agricultural community. They had resisted Pyrrhus and even crossed over to Italy at one point to fight him in support of Rome. It was shortly after that foray when these freebooters found themselves facing the Epirote's ex-allies from Syracuse, who came against them under the pretext of putting an end to spoiling of their territory. However, the real purpose of Hiero, Syracuse's commander, was to deal with his city's current batch of hired fighters. He thought those men presented a risk of revolt and sought to get rid of them.[63] Hiero therefore marched on Messana with the Syracusan army but refused to come to the mercenaries' aid after sending them against Mamertine forces across the Cyamosorus River. Maybe only 2,500 strong[64] and handicapped by attacking through flowing water, the betrayed hirelings endured heavy slaughter even as Hiero and his citizen militia stole away without a fight.[65]

Hiero established a dictatorship and marched c. 265 to again confront the Mamertines, truly intending to stop their predation on his polis this time. He engaged them along the Longanus River on the plain of Mylae near Messana. Messanian strength had by this time risen to 8,000 infantrymen (probably 6,000 hoplites and 2,000 skirmishers) plus perhaps 400 in cavalry; however, Hiero's host was larger still at 10,000 foot-soldiers (likely 8,000 spearmen and 2,000 light-armed) and 1,500 horsemen.[66] And upon close approach, his cavalry drove its weaker counterpart back across the Longanus to seize high ground above its near bank. Said to have been encouraged by a favorable prophesy, the Mamertines launched a disadvantaged charge not unlike the one they themselves had defeated along the Cyamosorus. Possibly filed six-deep to the opposition's eight and having its foes further aided by elevated terrain, this ill-considered attack stalled against a stout front of shields and spears lined above the river's far bank. Pausanius reports that "for a while, the battle was evenly balanced," but then Hiero turned the tide with a well-prepared stratagem. Back when the engagement was commencing, he had sent 600 picked men, including 200 Messanian exiles familiar with the area, to secretly cross the Longanus at a distance and circumvent a hill standing off one side of the enemy rear. That detachment now hit the Mamertine phalanx from behind, shattering it as "the Syracusans, attacking in force, cut the whole army to pieces."[67]

This culmination of what has been called the "Mamertine War" proved to be the spark that ignited the First Punic War, as those defeated now sought help from both Carthage and Rome. It was the Romans who won that competition and came to the Mamertines' rescue. This saw Rome slip an army across from Rhegium at night on borrowed ships to enter Messana in 264. The city was by then under joint siege from Syracuse and Carthage, the latter having sent a fleet to open hostilities after its aid was rejected. The Roman force was under the consul Appius Claudius and thus presumably a typical consular army with a pair each of Roman and allied legions (alae sociorum). That would have given the consul some 9,600 heavy swordsmen, 2,400 triarius spearmen, and 4,800 foot-skirmishers. There normally would have been 1,800 horsemen as well, but it's unlikely that this first-ever amphibious deployment by Rome included so much cavalry. That would have required either constructing transport-conversions or employing an impossibly high number of unaltered ships.[68] It's therefore probable that Claudius brought only a few cavalrymen at the most.

The Carthaginians were camped on the north side of Messana with their fleet grounded behind on Cape Pelorias at the island's northeastern tip. Hiero and the army of Syracuse were in place south of the city. There is quite a bit of confusion among our sources as to what the consul did once on the ground in Messana. Polybius says that he defeated the Syracusans and then the Carthaginians in separate battles but cites Philinos as claiming that it was Hiero and the Punic army that were victorious. Philinos should be taken seriously in that he was a Greek historian from Sicily's Agrigentum (Acragas) and contemporary to these events. And then there is Diodorus, whose version has the Syracusan dictator retreating without a fight and only the Carthaginians being beaten in the field.[69] Dio, Zonaras, and Orosius are all in Polybius' camp in reporting the defeat of both forces opposed to Claudius. The soundest approach to this conflicting material seems to be that suggested by Lazenby, who recommends assuming that "both sides exaggerated what were at best minor successes."[70]

A reasonable reconstruction of the action around Messana in 264 thus begins with Claudius moving against Hiero from the nearest portal. He would have used his own troops for this but adding all the local cavalry with its small contingent of attached foot-skirmishers as well. As for the Mamertine phalanx, being tactically incompatible with Rome's manipular system, it must have briefly demonstrated toward occupying the Africans on the other side of town.[71] Philinos' Punic victory is therefore likely to be a surviving trace of the Messanians taking a minor reverse in that feint before pulling back under cover from their missile-men both on and outside Messana's barrier wall. Claudius had meanwhile exited the south gate, arrayed in acies triplex across 1,600m, and advanced on the Greek phalanx. Given manpower like that at Longanus River, Hiero could have matched the Roman front he saw gathering across the way by filing his men at a minimum four-deep along 1,200m of his line. That provided potential to deploy an eight-deep strike element across 400m far right. Syracuse's cavalry and skirmishers would then have taken post off both wings.

Claudius' swordsmen may well have broken through some part of the thin Syracusan phalanx, driving it at least back, if not entirely from the field. However, the cavalry that had bested the Mamertines' horsemen above the Longanus must have repeated that feat. Possibly having an overwhelming 3-to-1 advantage in numbers, the Greek mounted force and its much superior attached foot-support chased Rome's light screens and turned against the now exposed legionaries.[72] Harassed from front, side, and possibly even rear, the Romans couldn't exploit their gains and had to abandon the fight and fall back into town. Hiero could thus claim a tactical triumph of sorts per Philinos' version, with his men holding the contested ground at day's end; however, badly battered, he subsequently retreated (somewhat in line with Diodorus) to yield Claudius a much more important strategic victory.

A second action took place in the next few days[73] as Claudius turned his undivided attention on the Carthaginians still encamped north of Messana. The size of the Punic army is highly speculative but must have been rather more modest than the sort of 30,000-man hosts landed by 300-ship fleets that carried out major Sicilian campaigns in the past. Assuming the money-wise Carthaginians dug minimally into their treasury for no more than what was needed to deal with Messana in conjunction with an allied Syracuse, we might expect something like 10,000 men arriving aboard 100 ships. If so, this force likely had 6,000 African heavy spearmen, 3,000 mercenary missilemen, and 1,000 horsemen (10 percent of the total consistent with mounted content of past sea-borne operations). Zonaras describes the Punic position as a strong one, with the shoreline anchoring its left flank, marshes flanking on the right, and field-works stiffening everything in between. Width of the frontage is unknown, but it could have been manned along up to 1,500m at four-deep using hoplites alone, equaling what the Romans were able to span with their now slightly battle-depleted acies triplex.

Dio claims that Claudius threw his legionaries at the Punic works in vain, but that setback was immediately offset by an unwise Carthaginian counterattack sallying out onto open ground only to be driven back with heavy losses.[74] This would seem to effectively have been a drawn engagement, though the Romans might have claimed a technical victory based on maintaining control over the last ground contested. Of greater import, this action ultimately delivered a win at the strategic level when the Carthaginians refused to make any further advances and abandoned their ramparts in favor of widely dispersing the troops on hand in better defending several allied towns in the vicinity.

Heraclea Minoa and Agrigentum (262)

The Carthaginians' approach to the conflict with Rome mirrored their earlier strategy against Pyrrhus. This called for standing on the defensive within fortified sites and forcing all attacking responsibilities onto a tactically disadvantaged foe. And they were content to play that plan out over an extended timeframe, seeking to trade an endurable level of economic pain for a price in blood that might eventually become unacceptable to the enemy. For eight years after the battles at Messana, this policy limited the fighting to a series of Roman investments punctuated by rare episodes of open fighting when the Carthaginians either saw a favorable opening or were forced onto the offensive by desperate logistical demands.

The first prize opportunity for the Carthaginians came a full two years after Messana. They had established their main base at Agrigentum (Acragas) on the south-central coast of Sicily and a double consular army had skirmished into the area to put the city under siege. This involved building a camp on either side and connecting them with field-works. The besiegers then suffered from an outbreak of disease and the Punic general Hanno decided to exploit this from his post up the coast at Heraclea Minoa, where most of Carthage's mobile forces had been concentrated. He marched with what was probably over half of the Punic manpower on Sicily, including large numbers of mercenary infantry, perhaps 30 of the elephants added to Carthage's arsenal post–Pyrrhus, and a sizeable cavalry arm—possibly some 33,500 men in all.[75] Hanno's horsemen were allied Numidians for the most part, and these closed on the Roman encampments to entice their counterparts from at least one of them into giving chase. Riding toward Heraclea, the Romans soon found themselves blocked by a line of Punic infantry acting bastion for the Numidians, who then turned about and dealt their pursuers a heavy defeat. With his foe's mounted strength thus reduced, Hanno seized a hilltop near Agrigentum from which he proceeded to menace the Roman position.

After two months, Agrigentum's defenders fell into such distress from the still active investment that Hanno was forced into more aggressive action. Though perhaps well-matched in overall numbers,[76] the horse-poor Romans couldn't be lured into disadvantage across open terrain. Hanno therefore advanced reluctantly into confined space between the two enemy encampments. With his cavalry, elephants, and light foot kept to the rear in this restricted setting, he engaged a narrow width of legionaries. This employed what little African heavy infantry he might have had,[77] but mostly Iberian hirelings, who must have posted on either wing to form a compound phalanx with hoplites only at center. These Iberians were sturdily equipped with swords, theuros shields,[78] and most having some armor, and their contest against similarly armed opponents went on for quite a while per Polybius. Any Carthaginian hoplites present no doubt continued to hold their part of the line in close order, but the professionals from Spain were more vulnerable in such an extended engagement. The Romans, though comparative amateurs,[79] were more efficient as a group in the ability to bring up fresh front-fighters via their manipular system to slowly wear down the mercenaries' van-ranks. Legionary pressure finally drove the Iberians back into their auxiliaries and the entire Punic array fractured into disorderly flight. Most of those defeated got away under cover from their still intact force of cavalry and further aided by the victors' fleetest troops being stuck at the rear. Even so, some 3,000 foot-soldiers, 200 horsemen, and eight elephants were left dead on the field, while another 4,000 men plus the rest of the pachyderms fell captive.[80]

Segesta and Paropus/Thermae (260), Camarina (258)

Despite their defeat in front of Agrigentum, those under siege there managed to execute a stealthy withdrawal in the exhausting battle's aftermath. And before year's end, Carthage was able to strike a couple of counter-blows on the other side of the island.[81] The first came near the city of Segesta (Egesta) in the northwestern interior; a superior Punic force ambushed a tribune-led Roman contingent (possibly a lone legion) there and dealt it a sharp reverse. The other took place shortly thereafter and farther east, where the Sicilian allies of Rome were encamped between Paropus on the coast and Himeraen Thermae a little way inland. Hanno's able replacement, Hamilcar Barca, launched an assault on these troops while they were distracted in the act of relocating their camp. Perhaps catching a little over 6,000 of these Siciliot Greeks by surprise and out of order with a force that easily could have been twice as large, the newly arrived general made his first significant impact and put them to rout, killing a perhaps overstated 4,000 in what must have been a brief battle plus prolonged chase.[82]

With Carthage persisting in its defensive strategy across Sicily, the action on land continued to stalemate and it was two years before another rare opportunity for an advantaged attack presented itself. This time, a consular army was marching inland of Camarina (on the coast of southeastern Sicily) when stopped short by field-works thrown across its path within a narrow pass.[83] Assaulting the barrier on one end, a 300-man contingent was able to gain control over a low hill anchoring that part of the Carthaginian line, which caused nearly all of what must have been quite a modest defending force of mercenaries to wheel against the threat of lateral attack from that direction. Though the Roman contingent atop the hillock would be wiped out, its sacrificial diversion let the consul in command escape over and/or through the other flank's now undermanned works with the rest of his men.

Adys (256), Tunes and Aspis (255) and Panormus (250)

As the conflict between Carthage and Rome dragged on into the 250s, it increasingly evolved into a naval war with the Romans constructing fleets capable of competing with those of Carthage and interdicting its flow of men and material onto Sicily. Success at sea combined with continued deadlock ashore in prompting Rome's decision to row an army to North Africa toward bringing the war to a swifter end on enemy soil. Clearing the way with a major naval victory at Ecnomus, a double consular army landed on the African coast in 256. After spoiling the countryside without significant resistance, most of the Roman fleet sailed back to Europe with half the army, leaving the consul Regulus behind with 40 ships, 15,000 foot-soldiers, and 500 horsemen.[84] Meanwhile, the Carthaginians had collected their troops immediately at hand and brought Hamilcar Barca back from Sicily with an additional 5,000 infantrymen and 500 in cavalry. Total Punic strength might have run to some 23,000 men, including 4,000 horsemen and 19,000 foot-soldiers; the latter likely being 9,000 African hoplites (one division of Carthaginians and two of Liby-Phoenicians), 5,000 Iberian mercenaries (who had come with Hamilcar), and 5,000 skirmishers with some of them screening 100 elephants.[85]

The Punic host advanced to confront Regulus, who was preparing to besiege the city of Adys. Lodged upon a nearby ridge, the Carthaginians once more sought to passively provoke their enemy into a disadvantaged offensive, even though such positioning meant that their clearly superior cavalry and elephants were forced to stand down within the mesa-top's interior. Regulus readily took this bait and launched twin daybreak advances. These came at the elevated and entrenched enemy from either side of the ridge's long axis; each offensive featuring a brigaded native legion and ala sociorum, with what little Roman cavalry was present plus the light foot standing in reserve behind the triarii. Deployed in acies triplex, the attackers were set to swarm up a roughly kilometer-long front on either rise. This ignored those foemen sitting at each end of the mesa, which might have consumed up to half the Punic hoplites if that feature's length was twice its width.

The Carthaginians had no doubt anticipated an assault up the slope located nearest to the Roman encampment; thus, their best troops, the African heavy foot, would have defended that incline plus the mesa's flanking terminations to prevent an envelopment at those points. Such a strategy assigned a lower priority to the back-side slope, leaving it to be held by Hamilcar's Iberians. Though veterans likely standing ten-deep along that stretch of hilltop, those hirelings presented a less stout defense than the heavier-equipped Carthaginian infantry elsewhere. And it seems that Regulus' two-pronged approach was specifically designed to exploit that weakness, sending his "first legion" against the Iberians rather than their better equipped employers. Polybius says that the mercenary contingent fought well and drove its foes back down the hill despite their probably being more deeply filed. Always geared to charge, the Iberians gave chase, but then found themselves sandwiched between enemy forces when another legion appeared without warning and crashed into their rear.

Circumstances surrounding the surprise attack that took the mercenaries from behind are obscure, Polybius simply saying that the legion involved "was advancing from the other direction." Perhaps it was seeking another target after having been repulsed on the opposite slope; however, there is a distinct possibility that this was part of a deliberate scheme. Attacking uphill at an entrenched phalanx seems foolish on its face; thus, it's reasonable that Regulus' effort there was never meant to be anything more than a feint. If so, he occupied the Carthaginians on the fore-slope by keeping a legion in place while sending the other around one end of the mesa. That suggests that he had always planned to lure the barbarians down the reverse slope and the seeming failure of his legionaries against lesser opposition there was a ruse. Regardless of whether the maneuver was cleverly plotted or simply a matter of coincidence, Punic spearmen holding the circumvented mesa-tip had to watch helplessly as the Romans swept around to rout their mercenary comrades. With its backdoor now undefended, the Carthaginian army fled, horsemen and elephants getting away easily and its infantry, though suffering some damage from behind, largely escaping as well due to a shortage of Roman horsemen and skirmishers to mount an effective pursuit.

The reaction at Carthage to this defeat was to husband its surviving forces while replacing losses with mercenary recruits mostly from the Greek mainland. Among the latter was a Spartan soldier-of-fortune named Xanthippus. A product of Sparta's highly esteemed training system (*agoge*) that had for centuries groomed youths into Greece's most renowned warriors,[86] Xanthippus headed a small band of mercenaries and was perhaps in his late thirties or early forties. He might have taken part in his polis' victories over Pyrrhus and/or the defeats suffered thereafter by Areus and his son. More certainly, he had seen significant service for pay in the last decade, possibly including a hitch with the Hellenistic host of Ptolemaic Egypt.[87] Xanthippus was thus likely well-versed in the sort of classical phalanx warfare for which Carthage's native forces were designed as well as being knowledgeable on practical aspects of Macedonian warfare from both the opposing and participating points of view. Observing preparations to re-engage the Romans, he drew on this experience in boldly proposing some changes in tactics to his paymasters. Wisely choosing to adopt these, the Carthaginians went so far as to put Xanthippus himself in effective field-command of their army.

The key recommendation of Xanthippus was to abandon fighting on the defensive. Keeping to favorable ground had discomfited the Romans, but not sufficiently to deliver a victory. And that approach had not only ceded all operational initiative to the enemy but had also utterly squandered Carthage's overwhelming superiority in mounted forces. The Punic army thus spent the ensuing fall and winter under the Spartan hireling's close supervision in drilling hard to fight across open, level ground best suited for cavalry and elephants.[88] That let him take the field in spring 255 with a well-trained and confident host that numbered 12,000 footmen, 4,000 in cavalry, and nearly 100 elephants.[89] In assessing the possible details of this deployment, past Punic practice and what likely remained from the previous year's combat suggest an even mix for the infantry of native spearmen (6,000 Carthaginians and Liby-Phoenicians) and mercenaries of various types (maybe 3,000 Greek hoplites plus a like count of retained Iberians and newly acquired Grecian skirmishers). In support of these, we can add the same mounted contingents that had escaped from Adys.

Regulus was under pressure to finish the African campaign before expiration of his one-year term as consul. And this perhaps explains his considering an advance onto open ground upon the plain of the river Bagradas southwest of the city of Tunes against a foe so much stronger in its mounted elements. Whatever his calculation, the consul accepted that challenge and formed his men up for battle. The exact nature of both Roman and Carthaginian positioning is speculative, being dependent upon the Punic depth of file one choses to apply. Assuming thin filing to avoid overlaps by a more numerous opponent, the description of Xanthippus' formation by Polybius suggests that what he called the "heavy phalanx of the Carthaginians" formed the left and center at six shields deep having its best men far left, while the Greek mercenary hoplites made up the right wing at the same depth. Some of the hireling skirmishers (those "most active" according to Polybius) were then split off either side of the phalanx along with their cavalry. As for Xanthippus' elephants, they lined up with the remaining light infantry to span some 1,500m across the entire formation-front.

Regulus must have matched this frontage with his acies triplex, the hastati leading in the van at their standard 2m spacing and depth of six and his horsemen off each side much like their enemy counterparts across the way.[90] But as a counter to the elephants, he then made unusual placement of his light foot, spreading it out before the legions instead of off their wings as usual. Moving around 3,000 men from his outboard screens thus to stand at the fore made the Romans' array "less extended than usual, but deeper" per Polybius, yet so weakened its flanks that "their provision in that part of the field was altogether inadequate."

What happened next is said to have been a contest between the leading ranks of the acies triplex and Carthage's van of elephants. This, however, presents some difficulties;

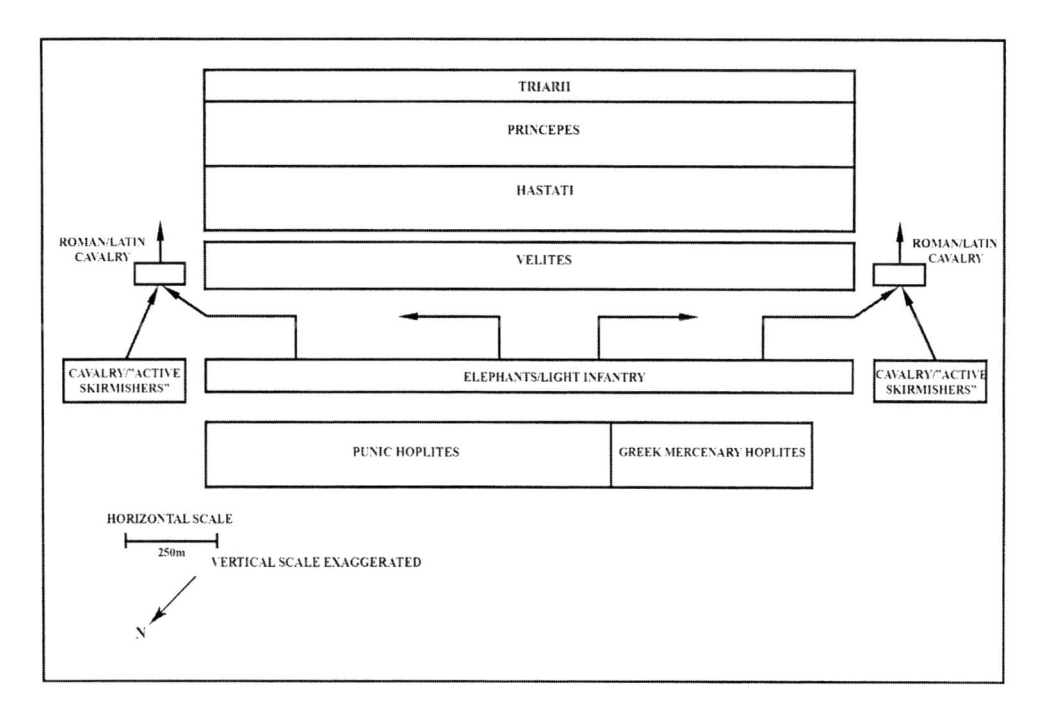

[Diagram: Battle of Tunes troop dispositions, showing Roman formation (Triarii, Princepes, Hastati, Velites with Roman/Latin Cavalry on flanks and Cavalry/"Active Skirmishers" forward) facing Carthaginian formation (Elephants/Light Infantry forward line, with Punic Hoplites and Greek Mercenary Hoplites behind). Horizontal scale: 250m; vertical scale exaggerated; north arrow shown.]

Battle of Tunes, 255 BCE.

somewhat as to the relatively modest size of the African forest elephants involved,[91] but mainly that the heavy infantry then engaged in that same space. It is more likely that the recent tactics of Pyrrhus would have informed Xanthippus, with that approach employing even its larger elephants against the Romans solely in flanking actions and almost exclusively to counter cavalry.[92] Pyrrhus, of course, hadn't fielded as many of the beasts, but Xanthippus would have been aware of two celebrated analogs involving larger numbers. At Hydaspes River in 326, India's Porus, who had never before fought Greek heavy infantry, threw 80–90 elephants in a leading line against Alexander and ended up getting many of his own men trampled in a costly defeat.[93] There was also Ipsus in 301, where 400 pachyderms led a phalanx; yet, that was a mere deception as discussed regarding the Elephant Victory of Antiochus. Xanthippus' use of elephants probably ran closest to this last model, initially spreading them 15m apart[94] as a forward screen, and then shifting them flankward before having his heavy foot close into combat. Zonaras is relevant on this unavoidably controversial point, claiming that it was the Spartan's elephants that routed Rome's flank-placed cavalry.[95] And critically, this scenario seems by far the best reconciliation for the subsequent engagement of legionaries with all segments of Carthage's phalanx; something only practical if the animals had already evacuated the interval between so that those opponents could physically get at each other.

What then are we to make of Polybius' description of the havoc wrought by Carthage's pachyderms upon Regulus' infantry? This is perhaps best seen as a misplaced echo that has filtered down to us about what happened to the skirmishers standing before the acies triplex, who otherwise completely disappear in a mysterious manner from the historian's further account. If so, the battle must have opened upon a charge from Rome's light footmen up front only for the elephants to swiftly rout them. Having disposed of that threat, the beasts and their supporting light infantry teams were then clear to move out onto both flanks and join attacks against the small contingents of opposing horsemen there. This in turn left the heavy-armed formations free to close into shock combat against each other as described.

During the brief but fierce fight that followed, the Punic spearmen were apparently able to hold firm against their legionary foes while Carthage's mercenary hoplites didn't fare nearly as well.[96] Perhaps suffering a turned flank,[97] Polybius says they were chased from the field. That pursuit was apparently carried out by some 2,000 of the hastati and principes committed against them even as the remaining Romans on that wing (presumably all principes) folded in upon the now exposed right side of what would have been Carthage's least capable militiamen holding its formation center. But before their pending envelopment could prove decisive, overriding disasters struck the Romans off either flank.

A potent mixture of elephants, horsemen in large numbers, and supporting foot-skirmishers of superior quality swept away the woefully inadequate outer screens on both ends of the acies triplex and closed about in a doubly enveloping encirclement. Suddenly under attack from front, left, right, and rear, the Roman formation quickly broke apart with heavy slaughter. Polybius says that every Roman was slain save for 500 taken prisoner along with Regulus plus the 2,000 that had gone after the Greek hirelings, but such an 85 percent fatality rate is probably overstated.[98] As for his claim that 800 Carthaginian mercenaries were killed, that produces more acceptable rates of 27 percent among those intensely pursued men and 5 percent overall. Nevertheless, one cannot reasonably credit that no others went down in so large an engagement, making it likely that at least another 200–300 died to run losses up to around 6.5 percent. Still, regardless of actual casualty ratios, this was a crushing defeat for Rome.

The Romans were able to respond to this setback ashore with a naval victory off Cape Hermaeum (modern Cape Bon), and landed more troops that then bested a Carthaginian army on the cape near Aspis. This engagement is mentioned in passing by Zonaras, who says that the victors took many prisoners, while Orosius claims that the two Carthaginian generals in command there lost 9,000 men.[99] If that number actually reflects the entire Punic army engaged (maybe the same 6,000 militiamen seen earlier plus 3,000 in light infantry and cavalry), its relative strength perhaps encouraged the Carthaginians to risk an open fight against what might have been a couple of legions, doing so despite having much more modest screening forces than at Tunes. Reinforced by that battle's survivors holed-up at Aspis, the Roman deployment could have come to some 8,000 in heavy foot plus whatever horsemen and foot-skirmishers had been embarked (presumably sub-nominal based upon Regulus' precedent). As to what happened in the battle, the report of a bevy of prisoners being taken suggests that the Romans might have exploited their greater numbers and less compact spacing to pay back the victors at Tunes with a double envelopment of their own. Yet, no matter the true scope of their tactical success at Aspis, all Roman forces still withdrew from North Africa in its aftermath, turning the focus back onto Sicily and the war at sea.

Fighting on land was minimal in the wake of Rome's failed African initiative, with what little there was consisting of a few successful investments by the Latins plus some amphibious spoiling of Carthage's remaining Sicilian territory. As before, Punic commanders kept to a cautious game plan that had them standing down unless some highly advantageous situation should arise; and it wasn't until 250 that such an occasion presented itself. The Romans had stationed one of two consular armies at Panormus on the northwest coast while the other returned to Italy for the winter. Seeing an opening in this,

Carthage's Hasdrubal took to the field at last. Orosius puts 30,000 men in the Punic force (though the 20,000 he and Eutropius claim as casualties is probably a better estimate of total strength), among which Diodorus notes the presence of both Gallic mercenaries and 60 elephants.[100]

Hasdrubal ravaged the countryside right up to Panormus, where the consul Metellus stood on the defensive. Having dug a trench with backing mound in front of the city's barrier wall, his skirmishers charged out to harass the Punic van, retreating behind the field-works whenever pursued. Hasdrubal closed to draw up his army before the Roman ramparts in a compounded phalanx with Gallic swordsmen holding its left wing. Metellus had arranged his works such that the Gauls would sit within striking distance of a city gate that hid his heavy infantry (some 12,000 legionaries) poised to sally. Meanwhile, Hasdrubal's elephants went after the Roman skirmishers as at Tunes, chasing them all the way to their ditches; but then, a storm of missiles hit the beasts, wounding many and reversing all back to trample and disorder their own troops. That was the signal for Metellus and his men to charge from their portal and take the unready barbarian swordsmen in flank. A devastating rout followed that saw much of the Punic host put to the sword and its entire complement of elephants captured. Panormus would prove to be the last significant land action of the First Punic War. The conflict dragged on with Hamilcar Barca waging a brilliant guerrilla campaign on Sicily, but Carthage would surrender at last in 241 after its navy had been decisively beaten. Chief among the Carthaginian concessions were to abandon Sicily completely and pay hefty cash reparations to Rome.

The Mercenary War, Bagradas Bridge and "Naravas' Victory" (240) and Leptis Minor (238)

Despite Carthage's surrender, fighting related to its conflict with Rome would not come to an end for another four years due to withdrawal from Sicily requiring return of Hamilcar's army to Africa before it could be disbanded. Composed over half of Libyan draftees with the rest foreign mercenaries, these more than 20,000 men[101] had not been paid for years, something even harder for Carthage to do now under the heavy burdens of reparations and its need to rebuild vital naval assets. And in November of 241, these soldiers rose up in what is generally known as "The Mercenary War" and were joined by much of Libya, which had borne a great deal of the Roman war's cost through onerous taxation and conscription. The rebel veterans set up a mere 18km southwest of Carthage at Tunes as volunteers streamed in from the Libyan countryside[102]; meanwhile, the Carthaginians scrambled to gather a response.

The insurgents put two loyal Liby-Phoenician cities under siege. These were Utica and Hippo (Hippacra), located in that respective order northwest up the coast from Carthage. As the Carthaginians continued to rearm in early 240, a modest advance force under Hanno[103] attacked the rebels at Utica with some success but suffered significant reverses as well and failed to drive them away. Hanno shifted operations to Hippo that spring and Hamilcar Barca took over as supreme commander at the capital. After intensely drilling his new army for several months, Hamilcar marched to Utica's relief. The insurrectionists led by a Campanian named Spendius had bridged the Bagradas south of the city and perhaps 10,000 from their 25,000-man local strength guarded that approach. Hamilcar avoided this chokepoint by fording at night well to the east at the river's mouth, taking advantage of seasonal conditions that lowered the depth of water over its sand bars. He then advanced toward the bridge, his elephants, horsemen, and light foot in that order leading their phalanx with the Bagradas flanking on the left.

Hamilcar's army numbered around 10,000, likely including 7,000 in heavy infantry (perhaps one full 3,000-man division of Liby-Phoenicians and two under-strength totaling 4,000 Carthaginians) plus 1,000 citizen horsemen and 70 elephants, each of those latter contingents having support from 1,000-man teams of mercenary skirmishers (most newly hired but some loyalists as well from Hamilcar's old Sicilian cadre).[104] Spendius, having left a large detachment at Utica to continue its blockade, probably had some 20,000 men on hand. Most were recent Libyan volunteers armed similarly to Hamilcar's own heavy foot and thus much like traditional hoplites save for wielding shorter spears than their Greek counterparts. A mixture of green troops and a few grizzled veterans of past Punic campaigns, these maybe composed four divisions of 3,000 men each and were accompanied by around 6,000 veterans of the war with Rome. The latter were 3,000 or so "Mixed Greeks" (*Mixellenes*, mostly theurophoros spearmen directly associated with Spendius, some from his native Italy) and a like count of other foreign soldiers more lightly armed with various types of missiles. These last would have been allotted between providing support for the rebel phalanx and screening a contingent of mercenary horsemen that was perhaps 600–800 strong.

Hamilcar got within distant sight of Spendius and his men before ordering a halt. Polybius indicates that the rebels formed two bodies (one having come from Utica and the other from the bridge), but Spendius had surely by this time composited his troops and the ensuing battle narrative seems to bear this out.[105] The Campanian commander would have been able to see that his opponent's formation was a little over a kilometer wide with a van of widely spaced elephants and its cavalry standing four-deep behind them. The phalanx, however, must have been barely visible at the far rear and its dimensions difficult to make out. Nevertheless, Spendius probably had at least a rough idea of Hamilcar's strength in heavy foot from scouting and arrayed his own troops accordingly, no doubt confident of enjoying significant numerical superiority in all but his mounted elements. Likely deploying his 15,000-man phalanx ten shields deep across a 1.5km frontage, the rebel leader eliminated any risk of rightward drift by anchoring the Libyans along the river on that side, thus ensuring that the veteran mercenary spearmen on his left as well as cavalry outboard of them could easily overlap and envelop the Punic right flank. Deployed as such, the insurgents started forward on signal only to then fall prey to a cleverly designed maneuver.

Hamilcar had used his few months in charge back at Carthage wisely, drilling his freshly formed army over and over in the execution of a false retreat. Putting that hard work now to use, he directed his phalanx to come about and march rearward, with its withdrawal shortly thereafter to be emulated in turn by the light infantry, horsemen, and elephants. What the rebels across the way saw were foes apparently so cowed by pending opposition that they chose to run rather than fight. Cheering an easy victory, Spendius' forward ranks broke into a hasty pursuit that left them jumbled pell-mell across the intervening plain. That's when Hamilcar struck as carefully planned, giving a command that had his phalanx spin about and stand fast in close array with a precision reflecting long hours of grueling practice. His equally hard-drilled light foot, cavalry, and elephant corps then stopped and reversed as well to mount a counter-charge, their heavy infantry comrades rearward slowly joining that surge in disciplined ranks with spears lowered at the fore. The chasing insurgents "were so much surprised that they at once turned and fled panic-stricken in the same loose order and confusion in which they had advanced."[106] Crashing into those still coming up from behind, the fleeing men threw their entire host into disarray as Hamilcar's elephants crushed some and his horsemen and skirmishers took down many more, with the measured advance of his hoplites then finishing off any stouter pockets of resistance still standing. Spendius got away but 6,000 of his followers were among the dead and another 2,000 fell prisoner.[107]

Hamilcar proceeded to liberate areas that had come under rebel control, but found his progress delayed by the escaped Spendius, who was shadowing across high ground at a safe distance and then descending to inflict small attacks whenever chance provided an opportunity. The Campanian initially had 8,000 men including 2,000 Gauls led by one of their own named Antaritus, suggesting that most if not all of the remaining European veterans from Sicily were aboard to make this as elite a force as the rebellion could probably field. Some Libyan infantry and Numidian cavalrymen (whose nation had lately decided to join the uprising against former ally Carthage) then arrived to pump rebel numbers in excess of 16,000, well past the size of the Punic army under pursuit if it was basically the same one Hamilcar had fielded just a month or two earlier along the Bagradas with the citizen divisions there having since been brought to nominal strength.[108] The insurgents advanced to trap the Punic general when he errored in camping upon a plain enclosed on three sides by high ground.[109] Spendius and his main force suddenly appeared to threaten from the heights on one flank even as the Libyans did likewise on the other and the Numidians took post uphill at the rear.

It wasn't personal tactical brilliance that allowed Hamilcar to fight free of this predicament, but rather vital aid from Naravas, who commanded the Numidian cavalry. This young noble was inclined toward Carthage and chose to bring his men over to Hamilcar. The insurgents still had the larger infantry force and they elected to descend and challenge in open combat. That proved an exceedingly poor decision that resulted in a devastating defeat said to have cost them 10,000 dead and 4,000 more captured. We have no description of the action, but Hamilcar's superior horsemen (now at least 3,000 strong including Naravas' men versus no more than a few hundred mounted mercenaries) and elephants no doubt led a double envelopment in producing so vast a slaughter and mass surrender. Those giving up the fight must have constituted the bulk of the recently arrived Libyans, who had been forced to watch as Spendius, Antaritus, and a select band of hireling companions fled to safety at some point in a long and arduous struggle that was going badly for their side. Most of these prisoners (perhaps a complete division of 3,000) agreed to enlist with Hamilcar while the rest were allowed to go free as a gesture of good will.

This rebel defeat, often identified as "Naravas' Victory" for the critical role he played, served to put the insurrection on a downward path over the next couple of years despite it having some scattered successes. Then a truly mortal blow was inflicted on the insurgents in the summer of 238 when they (somewhat like Hamilcar earlier) found themselves trapped in a box canyon at a location known as "The Saw" due to jagged peaks nearby resembling that carpenter's tool. With all escape routes barricaded by a much more powerful foe, the rebels refused combat for so long that hunger drove them to eat their prisoners and slaves. And when Spendius, Antaritus, and other key commanders were then taken hostage during negotiations, their now leaderless men (numbering a reported 40,000) were attacked in camp and utterly wiped out.[110] The captured chiefs were later tortured and crucified in retaliation not only for heading the uprising, but also for carrying out similar atrocities of their own.

Mathos was now the last major insurgent commander still standing. A Libyan national who had fought with Hamilcar against the Romans, he led his countrymen's faction of the uprising, which had been its largest from the beginning. But the disaster at The Saw had put an end to the rebellion's prospects for ultimate victory no matter how many short-term triumphs it might claim, and Mathos soon came under blockade in his base at Tunes. He was able to break out, however, when Hamilcar foolishly split his forces either side of the town and the camp of his subordinate Hannibal fell to the Libyan's sneak attack. Hamilcar withdrew until reinforced by a fresh draft of troops from Carthage under his political rival Hanno. The Punic generals closed in that winter on Mathos, who was operating south of Carthage on the eastern coast below Cape Bon near the Phoenician colony at Leptis Minor. Running out of options, the Libyan rebel committed to a final pitched battle in December 238.

Sadly, we have no details about this engagement at Leptis Minor save for Polybius' claim that it was an all-out effort by both sides, which means that Mathos would have been badly outnumbered. Hoyos has suggested that he might have had as many as 20,000 men if able to draw upon modest reinforcements from a few friendly garrisons in the region.[111] Even so, Hamilcar and Hanno likely fielded half again more and were strong in mounted troops of which the Libyan was almost entirely bereft.[112] Thus, though the rebel leader might have been able to throw a smaller yet still reasonably competitive phalanx at his foes, he must have been quickly and completely crushed outboard by irresistible waves of light foot and cavalry sweeping forward behind a thunderous elephant charge. Probably enclosed around either flank, most of Mathos' troops died on the spot and he was captured alive, while those few who did manage to escape the killing ground surrendered in a body shortly thereafter. The victors hideously disfigured and then crucified Mathos; and within a couple of months, all of Libya was securely back under Carthaginian control.

Not only having lost Sicily, Carthage's even more valuable province of Sardinia (including Corsica) off northern Italy had also slipped away when its hired garrison went rogue early in the Mercenary War. The locals eventually expelled these bandits, but then declared independence on their own behalf. And when the internal conflicts in Africa had finally been settled and preparation begun to recover Sardinia, Rome unjustly declared that to be an act of war. Too weak to contest this, Carthage agreed to abandon Sardinia and pay an additional reparation, those terms simply being appended to the existing treaty regarding Sicily. The Carthaginians were now confined to their North African homeland and a meager toehold in the southwestern corner of Iberia; yet, they would rebound over the next quarter century, going on to elevate their empire to greater heights than ever before.

4. Sundered Realms

Achaean, Illyrian, Anatolian, Cleomenean and Syrian Wars (245–217 BCE)

As Rome was challenging Carthage and beginning to cast its ambitions more broadly in the Mediterranean, conflicts in the Grecian world to the east continued to have an internal focus within the shattered remnants of Alexander the Great's empire. New aspirants sought the several crowns now scattered across that vast and disunited land, while those who already wore them strove to either defend or expand their kingdoms. These dynamics would spawn battles that roiled both mainland Greece and Anatolia (Asia Minor).

Achaean League and Illyrian Actions

The Greek mainland was embroiled in internal conflicts over dominance entering the second half of the 3rd century. This saw a multi-faceted dance of diplomacy and increasing violence as Macedonia imposed upon resurgent states and rising coalitions to the south that battled each other as well. Achaea in the northwestern Peloponnese had formed a federal union of its ten small agricultural communities prior to the mid–5th century, but that had fallen away for some time before its revival in winter 281/80 amid a period of lessened outside influence upon the decline of Demetrius Poliorcetes. Initially frail, this reborn Achaean League grew in the mid–3rd century through addition of cities outside of its original territory. First and significant among these was Sicyon, a Dorian center to the north on the Corinthian Gulf. That polis had ousted its tyrant in 251 under the leadership of Aratus, a native son returned from exile at Argos. Seeing that his polis was at great risk of interference from Macedon, he sought to bolster its security by joining the Achaeans' federation.

Chaeronea III (245), Pellene (241), Chares R. and Cleonae (235) and Phylacia (233)

Gaining fame and respect within the Achaean League through outstanding cavalry service, Aratus was elected in 245 to the office of general for all its forces, a feat he would repeat across many alternating years as term-limited by League policy. Details for the army he now commanded are somewhat controversial in that Plutarch's claims about the light-armed nature of Achaea's military in the late 3rd century (see Chapter 7) contrast strongly with what we know or can reasonably infer on its marked propensity for heavy arms through the end of the 4th century and into at least the middle 3rd.[1] Tactical events in Aratus' subsequent campaigns seem most compatible with his leading a conventional hoplite force whose core-region ranks of spearmen had been reinforced by troops from Sicyon. Nonetheless, it's possible that the native Achaeans in his service included a larger percentage of skirmishers than common elsewhere in the otherwise hoplite-dominated Peloponnese. This could reflect general poverty that created a smaller than usual population able to afford heavy panoplies as well as significant limitations on the ability to financially compete for the services of those lesser numbers that did have expensive hoplite gear, with the last leading many to emigrate in pursuit of more lucrative foreign opportunities. Based on documentation for later Achaean standing units and past Sicyonian potential, it's likely that the 10,000 troops that Aratus led out in the autumn of his first year as general was a nearly full League muster of 6,000 hoplites (evenly split between Achaeans and Sicyonians/mercenaries) plus 4,000 skirmishers and cavalry (perhaps 3,000 javelineers and 300 horsemen from Achaea with the rest being Sicyonian and/or hired men).[2] He moved north with this army to assist Boeotia against Aetolian opposition aligned with Macedon's Antigonus Gonatus as well as hostile to Sicyon and thence the League.[3]

Aratus' march proved futile when he arrived too to take part in a decisive battle in the Boeotian west. The Aetolians had launched a surprise incursion there timed to catch their foes ill prepared to fight as they celebrated an important local festival that was to have been protected under a traditionally recognized truce. Despite this gross violation of Grecian martial protocol, Boeotia's Aboeocritos managed to gather an army and meet the Aetolian column about 20km north of the festival site on the broad plain east of Chaeronea.[4] Plutarch provides no numbers, but Polybius indicates that the Boeotians fielded their "full available force."[5] In the past that was generally some 10,000 men, breaking down into 7,000 spearmen plus 2,000–2,500 foot-skirmishers and 500–700 horsemen, and subsequent Boeotian casualties reported by Plutarch appear consistent with that sort of strength. Aboeocritos seems at any rate to have felt confident enough that he had sufficient manpower versus his prospective opposition to risk engagement prior to the arrival of Achaean reinforcements.

As for the Aetolians, we have manpower data from a generation earlier at Thermopylae where they fielded some 7,000 hoplites plus 790 foot-skirmishers and a mounted contingent that might have been 700 strong at a tenth the number of spearmen present.[6] But that does not include a detachment of additional peltasts posted in the adjacent mountains at the same time.[7] A roughly similar effort at Chaeronea would have set near identical quantities of spearmen and cavalry against each other, but would have given the Aetolians a hefty two or even nearly three-to-one advantage in light foot—something their hoplite-centric foes apparently chose to discount. This perhaps best explains the battle's results; those undervalued light infantrymen enveloping a Boeotian flank to win the day and take the life of Aboeocritos on that wing along with a thousand of his countrymen overall.

Artatus got another opportunity to oppose the Aetolians in his third term as League general in 241. Word had leaked that they were launching an overland raid into the Peloponnese, and both the Achaean League and Spartans marched armies toward Corinth to block their entry.[8] This seems to have happened late in the campaigning season and, finding only a modest force that apparently was not aimed at either Achaean or Spartan territory (the true target is unknown), Aratus and Sparta's king Agis IV refused to endanger their soldiers needlessly and led them home.[9] However, whatever the original objective of the Aetolians might have been, they ended up capturing Pellene, an addition to the Achaean

League close upon Sicyon. Aratus responded with a hastily gathered scratch force and took the raiders by surprise while sacking the place. An initial engagement was fought at the city gate and among the suburbs in which the unprepared Aetolians were quickly put to flight. The beaten men raced toward the city-center, where they spread panic throughout the main body of their army, which had formed up for action and was advancing to meet the attack. Aratus and his troops engaged these Aetolians in the streets and routed them as well. We are told by Plutarch (per Aratus' own commentaries) that 700 of the raiders were killed.[10] If accurate, this suggests that the invading force was rather small, perhaps no more than 1,000–1,500 men given that it must have lost half or more of its count in so confined a combat space with limited opportunity for escape. And Aratus probably was not much stronger, having compiled his own force so hurriedly; however, he possessed a decisive edge in having caught his foes disorganized and unready for a battle.

In his first decade of alternating command, Aratus' campaigns added more poleis to the Achaean League roster, including Corinth, Megara, Troezen, and Epidaurus. Then, in 235, he moved against Argos and its tyrant, Aristippus, marching into the Argolid and spoiling the countryside until confronted by the Argives near the Chares River.[11] This likely involved some 6.000 hoplites on either side based upon past Argive and Achaean League deployments. The battle seems to have been quite out of the norm in that, rather than the right wing being dominant, it was the Achaean left that prevailed. But as that wing pursued its fleeing foes, Aratus was either misinformed about or unaware of this within his position at the other end of the field; and fearful that his left was failing, he had the right wing withdraw despite not being overly pressed by what should have been less capable opposition. Besides illustrating how little combatants knew about what was happening at even a modest distance away amid the clamorous chaos of phalanx battle, this highlights a lack of confidence where actual fighting was involved that would dog Aratus throughout his long career. His timorous retreat here on the verge of total victory ceded the contested ground to his enemies, who erected a trophy to mark their surprising triumph. The men of Aratus' otherwise successful left wing were "extremely vexed" at this turn of events, and their harsh criticism led him to deploy for a second engagement the next day. However, the Argives had received significant reinforcements overnight and, rather than accept combat when outnumbered, Artatus confirmed his defeat by asking for a truce that he might recover his dead.

Aratus was humiliated by this self-inflicted failure but salvaged his reputation in short order. He learned that Aristippus was planning to attack Cleonae, a former client of Argos on the northern fringe of its territory that had joined the Achaean League. Secretly marching his army, Aratus entered Cleonae at night and, when Aristippus drew up his troops before the city next morning, the Achaeans sallied out with vastly more strength than the tyrant was expecting to face. With perhaps 7,000 hoplites closing in upon their own no more than 5,000 in heavy infantry,[12] the Argives were so shocked and unprepared to fight that they immediately bolted. A running slaughter ensued as fleet Achaean theurophoroi chased the escapees southward along the track through the hills for 14km until reaching Mycenae at the edge of the Argive Plain. Aristippus himself fell to the pursuit there, adding to a reported body count for Argos of 1,500 on the day, which at perhaps 30 percent of those engaged fits well with so extended a chase. Aratus, on the other hand, is said to have lost not a single man.[13]

Achaean League ascendance after Cleonae proved short lived. Demetrius II of Macedon had succeeded to the throne upon the death of his father Antigonus Gonatus in 239.

70   4. Sundered Realms

Concerned thereafter about loss of influence to the League in the Peloponnese, he sent his general Bithys down in 233 to restore Macedonian authority there. Bithys marched into Arcadia and engaged Aratus near Tegea at Phylacia. Based on past deployments, we might propose that the Achaeans arrayed 7,000–8,000 hoplites in phalanx with a depth of eight shields, pitting them against a mixed-arms formation of as many as 9,000 pikemen standing eight-deep and 3,000 hoplites filed at up to twelve shields, with both sides having roughly equivalent light foot and horsemen outboard. Such an arrangement could have let Macedonian spearmen and shock cavalry envelop Artatus' left wing to carry the day.[14] Regardless of any such unconfirmable details, Macedon's invading army thoroughly defeated the Achaeans, triggering a retreat so chaotic and costly as to give rise to false but credible reports of Aratus' own demise.

Illyrian Warfare, Medion (231) and Phoenice (230)

Demetrius had reasserted Macedonia's influence in southern Greece at Phylacia, but within a couple of years he faced a new challenge from Aetolia. Detached from Macedon since Chares River, the Aetolians invaded Acarnania in the Greek northwest to send its leaders pleading for help from their long-time Macedonian allies. Demetrius bribed the Illyrian king Agron to intervene in this affair, and that ruler sent 5,000 fighters in pentekonters to land and march on the Aetolians where they were investing the city of Medion. Taken unaware, the besiegers nevertheless rose resolutely to the challenge. They aligned most of their hoplites below the city and posted the light foot with a cavalry contingent on a gentle anchoring hill that extended forward off one flank. That allowed the bulk of their horsemen to screen the flat on the opposite end of the heavy infantry line.[15] Said to be a full deployment, the Aetolian phalanx would have had 7,000 hoplites filed eight shields deep across a front nearly 900m in width with several thousand skirmishers and at least 500 horsemen in flanking support.

Though the Illyrians never fielded much in the way of cavalry, the warriors transported solely by sea in this case were entirely infantry mostly armed with a long, heavy-headed, thrusting spear (*sibina*) plus javelins for initial bombardments as well as a kopis-like sword or axe as sidearm. They wore helmets and carried shields either oval-shaped per Italian variants on the scutum or a smaller, highly convex type likewise fitted with a central grip.[16] Skirmishers using javelins or slings were likely present only in very small numbers, perhaps making up no more than a tenth of the landing party. Polybius applies the Macedonian term *speira* to the Illyrians' internal organization, suggesting that "the order customary to their country" included division into contingents of perhaps 200–300 men. This would have provided a degree of tactical flexibility not unlike the manipular system gave some of the Oscans of Italy with whom the Illyrians seem to have been distantly related.

The Illyrians must have demonstrated along the entire Aetolian front but concentrated a massive charge in close order against the light-armed men on the low, flanking rise.[17] Employing "irresistible weight," this attack dispersed the foot-skirmishers and drove the attached horsemen down among their hoplites on the plain. With that sector now entirely bared of its screen, the barbarian spearmen were free to move swiftly downhill and take the opposing phalanx in flank, routing its already confused ranks "without difficulty" with the aid of Medionians sallying from the city against the Aetolian rear. This twin assault killed "a great number" of the Aetolians with "a still greater number" falling prisoner.

Agron died of natural causes shortly after Medion, and his wife, Teuta, came to power.

She set out over the next year on an unrestrained campaign of piracy along the western Greek seaboard. This led to a descent upon the major Epirote city of Phoenice, which the raiders captured in league with a band of Gauls 800-strong. The latter had been hired to guard that place, but instead betrayed it from within. Epirus raised a general levy, which marched to Phoenice, taking position across a river that separated it from the enemy and removing planks from the floor of an intervening bridge to further secure their camp.

The Epiriote army must have been much like past deployments in character even if somewhat less stout in numbers during a period of decline from Pyrrhus' time, while the Illyrians were perhaps similar in strength to those at Medion. This was seen by the Epirotes as sufficiently favorable to risk detaching maybe a third of the troops on hand to march against a second Illyrian force 5,000-strong that was simultaneously approaching overland. This suggests that the undivided levy was stout, maybe no more than a third below what Pyrrhus had last deployed. At around 16,000 men, that would likely have tallied 9,000 pikemen, 3,000 hoplites, and better than 3,500 in light foot plus a few hundred horsemen. And the contingent remaining before Phoenice would still have retained 8,000 heavy infantrymen with 2,000–3,000 in attached skirmishers and cavalry—a force presumably adequate to hold less than 6,000 enemy troops in check given a seemingly safe position behind the river. Yet if that was indeed the Epiriote calculation, it was destined to prove disastrously wrong.

The Illyrians occupying Phoenice had observed the enemy's foolhardy division of its manpower as well as that the Epiriotes were not bothering to post a nighttime watch. They therefore set out in the dark, replaced the planks taken from the bridge, and crossed undetected in full force to lay low until morning. Realizing their peril when the enemy advanced from hiding at dawn, the Greeks formed up for battle only to be beaten in an open engagement. Being taken unprepared must have put the Epiriotes at a severe psychological disadvantage as one factor in their losing despite likely having significantly superior numbers. Another could be that the necessarily thinner-filed barbarians managed to hold firm along the main line of battle long enough for their greater tactical flexibility to prove decisive in turning a flank. Whatever its keys, the Illyrians' triumph at Phoenice was devastating to the Epiriotes as "a large number of them fell, still more were taken prisoners, and the rest fled."[18]

The Illyrians at Phoenice now joined their fellows moving cross-country to form an army approaching 10,000-strong. Meanwhile, the Aetolians and Achaeans, likely seeing themselves and/or their allies as potential future targets of these barbarians, joined with what remained of the Epiriotes to offer a defense. In the end, however, it was decided to avoid further loss of Grecian lives by simply having Epirus pay the invaders to leave. Releasing all freemen prisoners and control of Phoenice, the Illyrians withdrew with that ransom in addition to a great deal of already gathered plunder.

Anatolia in Turmoil

A civil war broke out within the Seleucid Empire after the death of Antiochus II in 246 and the ascension of his oldest son as Seleucus II. Seleucus had a power-sharing arrangement that placed his younger brother Antiochus Hierax (Hawk) in a subordinate role, but they soon came to blows in bids for sole control. Hierax took position in the northern portion of the realm, where the brothers met on the field of battle.

Lydia I/II and Ancyra (c. 237)

Seleucus, who had been campaigning against Egypt's Ptolemy III in Syria, led up the army he already had in tow to confront his rebellious sibling. With the lower portions alone of the nation to draw upon, his force must have been smaller than the one his grandfather had deployed from a nearly intact recruiting base in the late 280s, but larger than what his father fielded less than a decade before in a very limited mobilization. This is consistent with the report of Seleucus later losing 20,000 men if that is a surviving indication of contemporary estimates on his total strength.[19] As such, his command might have included some 15,000 in heavy infantry, 3,000 foot-skirmishers, and 2,000 horsemen. As for elephants, Seleucus had recently lost his stable in Syria to Ptolemy and probably had few, if any, of those on hand.

Hierax had hired large numbers of Galatians for his own army, which must have had little Seleucid content. If he had gained about two-thirds of available Galatian manpower, that would have provided some 10,000 foot-soldiers and 2,500 in cavalry based on the likely tribal muster at the Elephant Victory. Adding perhaps 6,000 ethnic Macedonian adherents (a 5,000-man division of heavy infantry plus 1,000 in cavalry and light foot) would have given him a significant force, yet one still somewhat inferior to his brother's in both magnitude as well as recent combat experience. And those twin weaknesses probably played important roles in the younger man then taking two defeats in the field. We know nothing more about these actions; however, that Hierax remained in active rebellion and that his brother was unable to take the capital city of Sardis from him suggest they were either effective draws or (more likely) relatively minor engagements involving only modest detachments.

Operating outside of Sardis with his forces having been exposed as inadequate, Hierax pulled up into the homeland of his Galatian mercenaries. He managed to boost his strength there through an alliance with neighboring Pontus. The exact content of the ensuing Pontic contribution to Hierax' army is uncertain. Pontus was a modest state at this point and surely not able to supply the sort of massive manpower sometimes claimed at its height in later centuries. Perhaps the 6,000 Greek hoplites that initially cored that future build-up might provide a clue. A similar heavy-armed contingent at this time with support from light infantry and cavalry in equal parts might have yielded 10,000 men,[20] letting the young pretender field a formation of Grecian heavy infantry not much inferior in size to that of his brother. And even should his troops have been of lesser quality, the mass of Gauls available in surplus of those needed to equal-out his phalanx would give him a huge advantage against Seleucus' auxiliary counterparts at the edges of any open battlefield.

Hierax was thus able to challenge Seleucus' advance on the Galatian capital of Ancyra and deal his fraternal rival a sound defeat.[21] We have no direct tactical details on this engagement, but ancillary data are informative. Both Seleucus and the commander of his royal cavalry fled the defeat in haste and remained separated for some time from others that had escaped within sizeable mounted and infantry contingents.[22] This implies that: (1) Seleucus took a thorough beating that precluded orderly withdrawal; (2) survival of "a large number"[23] of his infantry makes a double envelopment doubtful; and (3) Seleucus' successful retreat from off what was probably his right wing points to his phalanx collapsing either along the front or due to turning of a left flank held by somewhat less shock-capable theurophoros swordsmen. Should the foregoing speculation on Hierax's manpower apply, a reasonable interpretation might then be that Galatians screening his far right dispersed their less robust opposition and rolled up the Seleucid heavy array from that side, sending it into disorderly flight. Such a scenario would certainly make an optimum fit with Justin's claim that Hierax had gained his victory here "thanks to the valor of the Gauls."[24]

Aphrodision, Caicus Sp., H. Phyrgia, Harpassos R., Coloe and the Royal Road (c. 237–228)

Hierax controlled all Seleucid territory above the Taurus Mountains, which marked the boundary between Anatolia and Syria, but his Galatian hirelings now turned on him and were only dissuaded by the paying of a ransom. Both he and they then met defeat shortly thereafter at the Aphrodision just outside the walls of Pergamum, the two Gallic tribes that had stood with Hierax earlier failing because "they were still weak from [the Ancyra] campaign."[25] This was the first of six actions won by Attalus I of Pergamum in this period.[26] Those that followed were: (1) against a single Galatian tribe near the springs of the Caicus River some 60km east of Pergamum[27]; (2) against Hierax in Hellespontine Phyrgia to the north of Pergamum; (3) against Hierax at the Harpassos River in Caria to the south; (4) against Hierax at Coloe in Lydia; and (5) against the forces of Seleucus, perhaps in Lydia as well per participation by Seleucid allies from along Persia's old Royal Road that ran through the Lydian expanse.

The scope of these actions is quite speculative without further input from our meager sources. Given what we know about the limitations of Pergamum's manpower in the 3rd century,[28] Aphrodision, should it have seen the defeat of Hierax's troops from Ancyra sans his Pontic allies, is best explained by a surprise sally from the immediately adjoining city. That would have let Pergamum's light-armed but highly mobile forces catch a larger and heavier foe out of formation and mentally unready to fight. That last would have had a major effect on Hierax's excitable hirelings and lightly experienced Grecians. The Gauls were understandably upset at this setback against outmanned opposition and broke with Hierax, going on to launch a raid of their own on Pergamum. Apparently forewarned, Attalus met this new threat out toward his border and inflicted a defeat on the Galatian raiding party at the spring source for the Caicus River. With perhaps no more than half their manpower at Ancyra, the tribesmen might well have fallen here to an enemy not only similar in strength of numbers, but one taking advantage of chosen terrain and/or circumstances favorable for its own way of war.

While Attalus' battles against the Galatians were defensive, the three against Hierax seem to represent offensive operations meant to expand his territory at the expense of that now much weakened ruler. Bereft of Gallic mercenaries, Hierax appears to have struggled with his small remaining Seleucid force against highly mobile strikes targeting his territory both to the north (near the Hellespont) and south (Caria) and, finally, in Lydia at its very heart. Based upon what Hierax had probably been able to deploy from his own population at Ancyra and his having taken losses there and at the Aphrodision, he was most likely undone by a less formidable, but more numerous opponent in these actions, either ambushed or his modest phalanx overwhelmed on a flank. Coloe was clearly the most substantial of these reverses and was particularly costly, leading Hierax to abandon his kingdom.[29]

Seleucus now engaged Attalus in attempting to reclaim his lost holdings but suffered defeat along with a contingent of his Anatolian allies. The scope of this action is not recorded; still, it could not have been overly large and perhaps involved less than 10,000 troops on either side in light of the apparent limitations on Attalus' potential manpower and the reduced condition of Seleucus. Possibly enticed into a trap of some sort or compelled to withdraw by either the reality or threat of an envelopment, Seleucus nonetheless seems to have suffered something well short of overwhelming defeat, living to fight another day. Attalus was now a self-proclaimed king in control of an expanded realm that incorporated all Hierax's former territory; however, this was more a reflection of his foes' passing disarray than of any lasting strength at Pergamum. And by 222, Attalus was back within his old borders, driven there by the army of a new Seleucid ruler, Antiochus III.[30]

Cleomenean War

Sparta had been in decline for over a century when Cleomenes III came to the throne in 235 full of ambition to restore his polis to some of its old customs and prominence.[31] He was influenced in this by the unfulfilled reform concepts of Agis IV; something on which he was educated by his wife, who was Agis' widow. There was, however, bound to be great resistance to any such changes from the upper echelons of Spartan society, whose citizens were comfortably privileged within the current system. Cleomenes seems to have eventually concluded that the best way to get widespread backing for his plans was to court a conflict that might then unite the entire nation behind him against a common enemy. The seeds for this strategy were perhaps inadvertently sown by Aratus, whose ambition to gather all the Peloponnese within his Achaean League saw campaigns against still independent city-states toward compelling them into that union. Cleomenes took advantage by attaching several Arcadian poleis eager to gain protection from this aggression, a move which also gave his Spartans access to a sizeable reservoir of hoplites to boost their own long-shrinking ranks. The ensuing friction between Sparta and the League would lead to a formal state of war by 228.

Mount Lycaeum, Ladoceia and Arcadian Orchomenus (227)

Aratus was contemptuous of the inexperienced Cleomenes and celebrated his reelection to the generalship in 227 by spoiling Arcadia without concern for potential reprisals. Sparta would, however, answer in kind by sending its young king on an incursion into League-allied Argive territory. Cleomenes' invasion force of around 5,000 men (most likely a count of the heavy infantry alone) was confronted there by a host with 20,000 foot-soldiers and 1,000 horsemen.[32] Yet, despite having so huge an advantage in numbers, Aratus was uneasy about the situation and relayed orders for his commander on the spot to withdraw without risking an engagement. Our sources provide scant illumination on the motivation for this decision, and the only rationalization would seem to be fear of taking disproportionately steep losses even in what almost certainly should have been a tactical victory.

Whatever his reasoning for inaction in the Argolid, Aratus elected to strike instead in the opposite direction by personally leading a foray against Elis on the northwest coast, perhaps utilizing a smaller force drawn solely from Sicyon and Achaea proper against that presumably softer target.[33] However, this turned bad as well when Cleomenes surprised the expedition's return, apparently catching it strung out in line of march near Mount Lycaeum in Arcadian territory. The king's combat force is not described, but whatever the native content, mercenaries financed by Egypt's Ptolemy III were in the mix, that monarch having come to appreciate Sparta as an ally in his ongoing rivalry with Macedonia.

The engagement probably had Cleomenes' men charge downslope from forested cover to unexpectedly hit the Achaean column along one side while blocking both its forward and rearward avenues of escape with modest hoplite arrays. Any of the Achaeans not carrying all their gear on the march must have scrambled to grab something with which to defend themselves as their foes rapidly closed about. Dealing out heavy casualties and disaggregating Aratus' thin and disorderly formation, the Spartans and their allies isolated segments of the ambushed men and accepted their surrender. Aratus managed to escape the debacle but did so under such extreme circumstances of chaos that convincing rumors once more circulated widely that he had been killed. Back in Sparta, Cleomenes used the impetus of this success in combination with family resources and funds acquired from Egypt to overthrow the polis' traditional governing body of elders and seize sole authority for himself.

Despite his setback at Lyceum, Aratus was not neutralized, and he immediately rebounded by capturing Sparta's most important Arcadian partner at Mantinea. Cleomenes answered by invading Messenia, a long-standing foe of Sparta now joined to the Achaean League. His army must have grouped Sparta's small levy of some 1,000 crack spearmen of various ranks still able to afford heavy equipment along with a larger body of hoplites drawn from its perioeci. The latter had made up an increasingly greater majority share of Lacedaemonian musters since at least the late 5th century and it's likely that they currently supplied around three-fourths of the polis' heavy infantry. That apparent potential to field around 3,000 spearmen suggests the perioeci here probably provided 2,000 in accordance with the two-thirds standard contribution to foreign expeditions that Sparta normally required of allies dating back to the late 6th century under its old Peloponnesian League.[34] The rest of the heavy foot would have come courtesy of Arcadian poleis. Without Mantinea, these likely included 1,000 hoplites from Tegea (another "two-thirds" call-up)[35] as well as a similarly sized contingent composited from Orchomenus and other cities of lesser note. These additions brought Cleomenes' spearmen up to some 5,000 in total to rival what he had managed to deploy earlier at Argos. Light-armed support might have amounted to 1,000–2,000 both mounted and afoot, including not only local draftees but also some Cretan archers and javelineer horsemen with shields ("Tarentines") hired through the largess of Ptolemy.

Aratus learned of this menace and rushed to his allies' defense; however, with but short notice to gather and not having recovered from Mount Lycaeum, Plutarch says that he "was much inferior in numbers" to the enemy. And though that probably applied only to hoplites (perhaps no more than 4,000-strong), it would profoundly affect his thinking once he finally came to grips with Cleomenes.[36] That took place a short distance outside Messenia's capital of Megalopolis on the plain at Ladoceia. The action there opened with a clash of light infantry and, regardless of any edge their army might have held in heavy foot, Sparta's skirmishers proved rather the weaker. Taking a beating, they withdrew across a dry gulch toward their still well-separated main body. Aratus pursued with his host but, leery of openly engaging Cleomenes' larger phalanx, halted to take a defensive posture behind the ravine even as some of his light foot continued to chase as far as the enemy camp.

Lydiades, the former tyrant of Megalopolis, was a political opponent and fierce critic of Aratus who had often lambasted his timidity and past failures to exploit favorable combat opportunities. Fearing that the man was letting yet another promising chance slip away, this fellow led an insubordinate charge of mounted volunteers and other auxiliaries in a bid to sweep around the right side of a Spartan heavy array seemingly bereft of light-armed protection. But it soon became apparent that Cleomenes had anchored his right flank abutting ground full of trees and ditches difficult for cavalry to negotiate. Thus frustrated, Lydiades fell back and was killed when Sparta's Cretan and Tarentine-style hirelings attacked the retreat. The Megapolitan's surviving followers fled to throw the rest of their army into a panic as the Spartans advanced into shock contact. How their hoplites spanned the intervening gully is not described, possibly they just went over pell-mell against opposition in even worse disorder. Yet Plutarch's comment on the arroyo's depth so emphasizes the difficulty of such a crossing that a better solution might rest in Spartan exploitation of superior manpower to overlap the flank of a shorter enemy front that had been robbed by Lydiades' impetuous action of its outboard screens. The extension of at least one end of Cleomenes' array could then have transited the ravine unopposed to envelop an already distressed foe. Irrespective of how this played out, Artatus' phalanx was routed with heavy slaughter and numerous prisoners taken.[37]

Aratus at this point fell into disrepute around the League and seriously pondered giving up his generalship. But reconsidering, he led a late-season campaign against Orchomenus designed to quiet his most vocal critics at Megalopolis. Orchomenus was a long-running local foe of theirs and they were sure to applaud any damage he could impose upon it. While a direct assault on Orchomenus was sure to be perilous due to its easily defendable location on a mountainside, investment offered a much more viable threat. And it was probably a bid to preempt the prospect of such a siege that led the city's defenders to challenge in the open what must have been a much stronger enemy force.[38] Megistonus, step-father of Cleomenes, led this foolhardy sortie and it failed miserably, losing 300 killed (probably a tally of only hoplite casualties) with many more falling captive, including Megistonus himself.[39]

Cleomenes' Reforms, Hecatombaeum (225) and Sellasia (222)

Cleomenes used his newfound control of the Spartan state to institute sweeping reforms. These included canceling debts and elevating the most capable among his poorer or otherwise less privileged residents to full citizenship as spartiates.[40] Many of these men had previously served as skirmishers but were now obligated for phalanx duty, which raised the issue of how to arm them given that the traditional method requiring self-provision of costly hoplite gear was out of the question for the vast majority having very limited financial means. Cleomenes would solve this problem much as Macedon's Phillip II had 132 years earlier, equipping the new troops with cheaper pikes and shields at state expense. This had the further benefit of giving these mostly neophyte stratiotai a less demanding role in combat, the Macedonian phalanx being better designed than its classical counterpart to facilitate the largely defensive duties required of them in pitched battle. Addition of these phalangites to the 1,000 or so spearmen already on hand expanded Sparta's native heavy infantry to 4,000-strong.[41] Further manpower then came from Lacedaemonia's remaining non-citizen perioeci plus whatever troops could be attached from allied poleis. As for light-armed fighters, Cleomenes could still draw from Sparta's less promising poor; however, mercenary missilemen financed by Egypt continued to serve as key components in his otherwise retooled military.

Having significantly boosted his polis' homegrown strength, Cleomenes became even more aggressive, opening the campaign season in 225 with a fresh incursion into Messenia followed by helping Mantinea expel its occupying garrison. He then marched through

Arcadia to threaten the Achaean League polis of Pherae. A League army responded to this last move by taking position near its westernmost city of Dyme. This was at a site for religious sacrifices known as the Hecatombaeum and Cleomenes rapidly descended there to compel an engagement. Plutarch says the Achaeans' host represented their "whole strength"[42]; however, it's unlikely distant contingents such as that from Argos had time to join in. That suggests a more modest complement of around 10,000 soldiers with maybe 8,000 spearmen supported by some 1,500 foot-skirmishers and 500 horsemen. Cleomenes probably had an army built upon the one employed at Ladoceia, now having reinforced it with the pikemen and a levy from newly freed Mantinea. The last probably included 1,000–2,000 hoplites, giving him at least 6,000 spearmen plus 3,000 phalangites with light infantry and horsemen outboard in numbers roughly equivalent to their counterparts abutting the Achaeans' flanks.

The deployments at Hecatombaeum are not known but, should the foregoing speculation on troop strengths be reasonably correct, the heavy-armed on both sides would perhaps have faced off eight-deep across an 800m front (spaced at 1m per hoplite and 2/3m per pikeman). Cleomenes must have placed his phalangites far left while standing among Sparta's crack spearmen on the other wing of the phalanx. This suggests that the ensuing action featured his newly minted citizens using their long sarissai to keep hoplites across the enemy's right in check long enough for Sparta's savvy spearmen to carry the day at the opposite end of the battle-line, throwing the Achaeans into flight and inflicting significant casualties even as enveloping foot-skirmishers and cavalry cut off escape and drove many more to surrender.

Cleomenes was at his height after the resounding victory at Hecatombaeum and he took advantage to press the Achaeans across the whole of the Peloponnese. Many Achaean League cities came over or were taken, including Argos and Corinth, though the latter's all-important fortress on the heights of Acrocorinth remained defiant. The Spartan king even put Sicyon under siege. Aratus was desperate and brokered a deal that chiefly ceded Corinth to Macedonia's Antigonus III (Doson, who had succeeded Demetrius in 229) in return for assistance. This news reached Cleomenes and he withdrew from Sicyon to position behind field-works across the Isthmus of Corinth that he might block Macedonian access to the Peloponnese. But that strategy came to naught when Argos rebelled to besiege its Spartan garrison and Aratus landed with 1,500 of Antigonus' men at Epidauros just east of the Argolid. Cleomenes' father-in-law Megistonus, who had vouched for Argos' loyalty, marched with 2,000 men to re-take the city, but was slain trying to gain entry. Cleomenes became fearful of being caught from behind and abandoned the isthmus to fall back on Argos and protect his rear. However, this simply left the way open for Antigonus to enter and he promptly descended onto the Argive plain, forcing Cleomenes to retire into Arcadia lest he be cut off from Sparta itself.

Over the course of the ensuing months, Antigonus and Aratus captured or otherwise attached all of Cleomenes' allies to isolate him in Laconia with only its modest resources at his disposal. And those limited means were then further stressed as outside funding from Ptolemy dried up as well. Cleomenes sought a bold solution to his pressing problems of inadequate manpower and finances through a program that let Spartan serfs buy their freedom. He raised a reported 500 talents in this way with which he armed 2,000 of the former helots as pikemen and hired a significant number of mercenaries as well.[43] Meanwhile, he avoided battle toward exhausting the time that Antigonus could afford to keep his huge and costly invasion force in the field. This delaying strategy finally paid dividends near year's end 223 when the Macedonian king sent his men to winter at home after a year and a half away.

Cleomenes exploited this by feinting due north toward occupied Tegea as a distraction for the Achaeans that were still a threat before diverting westward and seizing Megalopolis by surprise. Plundering the place when the Messenians refused to cooperate under the influence of a young cavalry officer named Philopoemen, Cleomenes left the city in deserted shambles as he carried its spoils back to Sparta. He then spent the rest of the winter improving the polis' defenses by fortifying all potential accessways, following up in the spring with an incursion into the Argolid. Though in residence at Argos with some hirelings, Antigonus refused this bid to lure him into battle on unfavorable terms and instead marshaled above Laconia after his Macedonians returned that summer to complete a host of some 30,000 combatants.[44]

Cleomenes elected to meet this menace by blocking all practical routes from the north into his homeland and funneling the enemy advance through a slender pass leading to the Spartan hamlet of Sellasia as a chokepoint where his smaller army might be able to make a successful stand. The Oinous River cut a north-south path there, creating a flat valley about 200m wide between flanking hills (*lophoi*). Olympos on the east was the loftiest portion of Mount Provatares and separated by a gorge (*rhevma*) from a high, east-west ridge that marked the mountain's northern boundary. Evas to the west sloped down northward from its peak onto a terminating low ridge (the Dagla) that sat above a tributary stream (the Gorgylos) feeding into the Oinous from the northwest.[45] The Spartan king set up camp atop the crest of Olympos and built north-facing field-works from there to the pass below. Troop deployments under his personal command here consisted of 6,000 Lacedaemonian heavy foot (1,000 elite spearmen, the 3,000 recently enfranchised phalangites, and those 2,000 newly liberated helots armed with pikes) plus some 5,000 in supporting light infantry.

Over on Evas, Cleomenes' younger brother Eukleidas led a heavy division of similar size that boasted around 6,000 hoplites consisting of 3,000 or so perioeci and up to an equal number of allies (possibly including some mercenaries).[46] These were positioned behind field-works that ran down the Dagla Ridge from steeply rising terrain on the west toward the edge of the valley some 600m beyond. A contingent of maybe 1,000 light foot held post within fortifications on the very peak of the hill as a guard against any enemy attempt to make an end-run around Evas' western extreme. As for Sparta's cavalry, it arrayed a probable 1,000-strong down in the pass, stretching across the road toward Sellasia that ran along the western bank of the river. The flat on that side was perhaps 100m wide and the horsemen would have spanned about half this in standard order (four-deep and about 2m across per mount). The remaining space between the cavalry and the valley wall hosted a contingent of 1,000 skirmishers forming a flank screen. All of these Spartan deployments at Sellasia appear to have added up to a total of 20,000 combatants in agreement with a claim by Plutarch.

Antigonus spent several days observing Cleomenes' strong positions and attempting to entice him out of them. But once it became clear that his foe was not about to give up such advantageous terrain, the Macedonian monarch arranged his own troops as best he could to engage. This saw him lead the bulk of his countrymen as well as 5,000 skirmishers (including both Gauls with sword and theuros and Thracian javelineers that might also have by now adopted theuroi) up Provatares' northern ridge, deploying them across from the enemy works on Olympos to the south. The only element of Antigonus' native forces

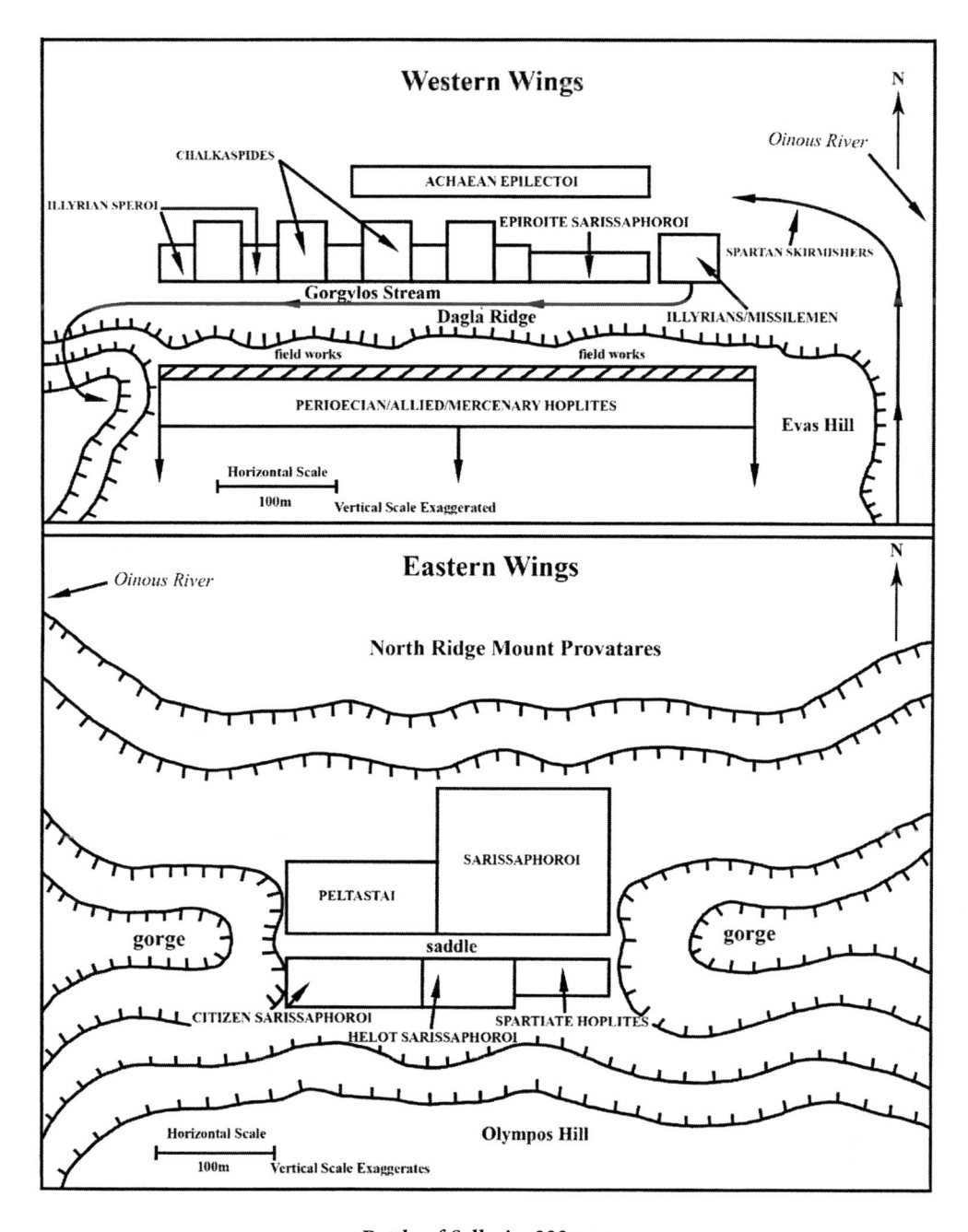

Battle of Sellasia, 222 BCE.

not to take station with him there was the crack division of pikemen known as Chalkaspides (Bronze Shields), whose number is not recorded in our sources but might have been 3,000.[47] The indication is therefore that about 10,000 heavy footmen stood alongside the Macedonian ruler on the eastern ridgeline in the form of 7,000 phalangites and 3,000 hoplite peltastai.[48]

The Chalkaspides arrayed on the far side of the Gorgylos streamed below the Spartan position on Dagla Ridge, their phalanx extending from the west and abutted on its left by a combined force of 1,000 similarly armed Epirotes plus maybe 800 hoplites and 200 expert slingers from Acarnania[49] as well as a contingent of mercenary archers from Crete. Sans skirmishers, this formation stretched across a front of perhaps a little over 400m due to the interspersing of five speirai of 300 Illyrian spearmen apiece on either flank of each 1,000-man pike contingent. The phalangites likely stood in files of 16 and 2/3m apart, the hoplites eight-deep with 1m/man frontage, and the Illyrians in 10-man files spaced at 1m. That arrangement made the resulting composite phalanx more flexible (very much like those Pyrrhus had utilized in Italy). Behind this lead formation was a second phalanx composed of 2,000 Achaean epilektoi. Possibly eight shields deep, these spearmen were apparently meant to stand bastion, but their positioning is surely more reflective of the restricted ground at Sellasia than of any real tactical considerations on the part of Antigonus.[50]

Antigonus' other pre-battle arrangements saw him place his cavalry opposed to its counterpart in the pass. Amounting to some 900 horsemen from Macedonia (300), Achaea (300), Boeotia (200), Epirus (50), and Acarnania (50) plus 300 mercenaries, these were backed by a formation of 1,000 Megapolitan pikemen probably aligned 16-deep beyond their rear. The latter were inexperienced, having just recently been supplied with sarissai and other gear by Macedon, but would not be required to maneuver. They had only to act as a refuge behind which the cavalry could retire if needed, their lengthy weapons being well designed to fend off any mounted pursuit that might follow. Also present in the pass were some 1,000 Achaean theurophoroi additional to their nation's hoplites in place rearward to the west.[51] These skirmishers would have been vital to screening Antigonus' horsemen from the missiles of opposing light foot and, based on their subsequent failure to block enemy movement along the west side of the pass, they were most likely mixed in between the cavalry ranks, possibly one man either at or near the rear of each mount.[52]

Having his troops thus in place, Antigonus opened action at dawn with a surprise maneuver. The Acarnanian slingers and Cretan bowmen attached on the west plus a speira of spearmen and 100 or so skirmishers (making up that last portion of the Illyrians not incorporated into the phalanx there) had hidden along the Gorgylos during the night. These troops included their army's longest ranging missilemen and struggled up onto the high ground anchoring Eukleidas' line on that side of the pass.[53] While this elevated terrain formed an effective barrier to a heavy-armed phalanx, the potential danger from lightly equipped fighters determined to negotiate such a slope no matter how intimidating had been badly underestimated. And it was just such agile marksmen that now began a deadly bombardment, sending thousands of sling-bullets, arrows, and javelins into the Spartan position from behind a barricade of Illyrian shields as they threatened an envelopment. Realizing the extreme difficulty of trying to hold off a frontal assault from below while being simultaneously struck from the side in this manner, Eukleidas pulled his men back onto the top of the hill where he would be less exposed to the enemy's rain of projectiles and his own skirmishers could screen his now endangered left flank from their crestal redoubt.

The Macedonian phalanx had joined the assault by climbing up the northern incline of Evas with relative ease thanks in part to its interspersed-arms design and must now have encountered some difficulty in crossing over the abandoned Spartan field-works.[54] Polybius levels a great deal of criticism toward Eukleidas at this juncture for not attacking downslope to break his foe's advance.[55] Yet getting his own men reorganized after so hurried an uphill retreat would have been a major chore, and by the time his formation was again somewhat coherent, the Macedonians surely had already reformed above the Dagla works. All Eukleidas could really do then was try and hold higher ground in hope that it just might provide a winning edge. But that hope would soon prove false, as the Chalkaspides and their allies closed in good (perhaps tellingly superior) order and drove the Spartan's stratiotai over the crest of Evas, sending them into stumbling flight under hot pursuit down the hill's treacherously dipping reverse slope where many, including Eukleidas, would lose their lives.

As all of this was playing out on the western heights, there was considerable drama in the adjacent flats as well. Some sparring between the opposed mounted contingents in the pass had begun when Eukleidas, who had now repaired to the crestal position on Evas that he would ultimately fail to hold, sent an attack-directive down to his light infantry to exploit what he could see from his lofty vantage point was an opening that movement of Antigonus' right-wing phalanx upslope had exposed off its left flank. Leaving their cavalry and racing along the western valley wall to skirt the right side of the forward-focused enemy horsemen and their backing pike array, the Spartan light foot looped around to hit the Achaean reserve phalanx at side and rear. Those much less mobile hoplites lacked light-armed support and had no way to effectively counter, their plight threatening to leave the main allied formation above vulnerable to an attack from behind. The situation was rescued by Philopoemen, the same young officer who had counseled against meeting Spartan demands after the capture of Megalopolis. Defying a command to stand fast, he charged with his own cavalry and others to drive off Sparta's attackers. Those skirmishes returned to their previous post alongside Cleomenes' mounted men as fighting in the pass began to rage more intensely.

Action on Provatares until this time had been limited to dueling between the large auxiliary contingents there as both heavy arrays stood back. But Cleomenes, having a good view of the contested ground from atop Olympos, saw both the devastating collapse of his brother's effort on Evas and that Sparta's mounted formation in the pass was also at hazard of failure. The only possible way for him to avoid defeat now was to seek an invasion-ending stalemate by leaving his field-works and somehow forging a victory in pitched battle against Macedon's larger phalanx. And due to unique configuration of the terrain on his eastern side of the field, this was not so long a shot as to be a forlorn hope. Antigonus' position on Provatares' northern ridge was separated for most of that feature's length by a gorge that his phalanx could never fight its way across.[56] The only practical access onto Olympos was therefore via a modest saddle that split that channel in two. This level stretch was about 275m long west-to-east and 75m wide,[57] creating a restricted fighting-ground that would prevent Antigonus from taking full advantage of his greater manpower.

The Macedonian king watched as Cleomenes scuttled some of his defenses to descend onto the saddle on Olympos' north side and set his own men in motion toward there as well. In order to accommodate the limited area available, he had to stack his troops at double optimum depth, the 7,000 pikemen in files of 32 at 2/3m spacing and the 3,000 peltasts/hoplites 24-deep at 1m frontage each to span 270m in all. Cleomenes was able to fit his approximately 1,000 spartiate spearmen and 5,000 phalangites across that same expanse using like spacing and best-practice files of 12 and 16 respectively. Once so arrayed, both monarchs recalled all skirmishers and advanced, their phalanxes filling the central 50m or so of width along the saddle's entire length as leading ranks closed into violent contact.

Our sources describe a stubborn contest between the two formations, with Plutarch indicating that Antigonus was pressed back for a length of around 800m and Polybius less precisely stating that his men gave way under duress "for a long distance."[58] Yet, the idea that the Macedonian retreat was forced seems unlikely. Beyond the high improbability of a phalanx of such immense depth being shoved back against its will under any circumstance, let alone by files half those of its own, there are the battleground's physical constraints to consider. As Morgan notes: "the presence of a hill behind either line would make it difficult for one side to push back the other farther than the depth of the plain."[59] And after accounting for volume occupied by the phalanxes themselves, the measure of flat at their rears would probably have averaged less than 15m. What are we to make then of these reports of a lengthy Macedonian withdrawal? The best answer appears to be that it was a deliberate maneuver.

A hint of conscious design in Antigonus' retreat up the back-slope of Provatares' north ridge can be seen in Polybius saying that his formation "gradually fell back facing the enemy." That is consistent with the sort of well-practiced evolution that Antigonus' famed predecessor on the Macedonian throne, Philip II, is said to have executed to turn the tide in his favor at the battle of Chaeronea. Deliberately withdrawing his right wing there to lure its untried opponents from Athens into disorderly pursuit, he reversed on rising ground for a decisive counter-attack.[60] And use of a similar ploy here would have exploited Cleomenes' neophyte helots in direct parallel to what Philip did to those "green" Athenians back in 338. We are thus told that "upon Antigonus ordering the Macedonians to close up [presumably at some set point on the slope] ... they delivered a charge,"[61] which broke the Spartans (or at least their helots and possibly some of the new citizens as well), who were now "disordered and unable to maintain the fight."[62] Antigonus' light foot then came forward to give lethal chase even as the victors from Evas and the cavalry action (now also resolved in Macedon's favor) cut off escape to ensure a heavy slaughter. Cleomenes fled to Egypt as the lone Spartan king to survive a lost battle but would commit suicide in the end. As for his defeated polis, it was compelled to ally with Macedonia and accept imposition of a foreign garrison.[63]

Aratus' Last Battle, Molon's Revolt and the Fourth Syrian War

Antigonus retired on Macedon after Sellasia to address an ongoing incursion by Illyrians not among his current hirelings. According to Polybius,[64] he repelled those barbarians in a pitched action about which we have no further information, but the more than 12,000 well-drilled and battle-tested Macedonians he commanded would alone have been more than needed to overwhelm a probably smaller tribal deployment bent much more on plunder than decisive confrontation. Antigonus passed away the next year to be replaced by Philip V, the son of his predecessor Demetrius. Not long thereafter, serious conflict resumed in the Peloponnese despite Sparta having been humbled. This came when the Aetolians justified a campaign of plunder there as reprisal against the Achaean League's embrace of Macedonia.

Caphyae and Babylonian Apollonia (220)

The Aetolians had invaded the Peloponnese from the sea with what must have been a fairly modest embarkment of perhaps less than 5,000 foot-soldiers and a few hundred horsemen. Theirs was at any rate a small enough force as to be intimidated by the threat of facing a full levy of the Achaeans and their allies. They therefore offered to retreat to Elis and ship home with the loot gathered to date. Aratus agreed and demobilized save for the picked Achaean brigade that had fought at Sellasia with its 2,000 epilektos hoplites, 1,000 theurophoroi, and 300 cavalrymen. He also had a Macedonian mercenary division maybe about 1,000-strong under Philip's representative Tauron. The Aetolians, seeing Aratus' strength thus reduced, treacherously turned about and marched on his position near Caphyae in Arcadia.

The Achaean general was well placed to defend, having a river and broken terrain protecting his front, which caused the invaders to defer and fall back toward high ground as their horsemen rode behind. Aratus responded by sortieing a few hundred of his cavalry and light foot. But by the time those pursuers drew near, the Aetolian van had already moved upslope and its mounted rear-guard was following in good order. Observing his foes climbing away in the distance and wrongly thinking them in distress, Artatus dispatched his epilektoi to join the fight as he led the remaining Achaeans and Tauron's men in a wide flanking maneuver that dangerously divided his command in the close presence of the enemy.

The Aetolians had by now regrouped and, taking advantage of both elevation and local superiority in numbers, they rushed down to utterly rout the small force of horsemen and light infantry opposed below. Those beaten troops fled back across the plain to panic and scatter their heavy-armed countrymen, who were not approaching in battle order, but rather strung out in their separate units. The calamitous result was that "whereas the actual number of those defeated on the field was less than 500, the number that fled was more than 2,000."[65] The Aetolians sailed away with their booty, while Aratus, having handed them an easy victory in detail, saw his long career go into final decline.

Even as Aratus' star faded in Greece, turmoil was once more wracking the Greek world in Asia. Shortly after succeeding to the Seleucid throne in late 223 or earliest 222, Antiochus III had to deal with his governor Molon, who led an uprising from his own satrapy of Media along with that of his brother in neighboring Persia. Taking advantage of ongoing diversions of Antigonus' forces in suppressing Attalus of Pergamon in the northwest and an expansionist Syrian campaign to the southwest that occupied the young monarch himself, this rebellious satrap seized a vast area spanning much of the kingdom's eastern portion. Antiochus dispatched two generals to suppress the revolt using garrisons on hand near the troubled region. But when that plus all subsequent remotely directed efforts failed and the insurrection persisted, the king left Syria in 220 to lead his royal host against Molon.

Most of Antiochus' heavy infantry had either been in Syria or holding post in western provinces removed from Molon's influence. Save for mention of ten elephants, we have no numbers, but can project from what is deducible about Seleucid military potential during this period in general and specifically from the force fielded three years later at Raphia. Given some desertions to the rebellion, these suggest that the king's phalanx might have contained 30,000 pikemen plus 5,000 mercenary Greek hoplites with support from around 9,000 in lighter infantry of various types plus 2,000 horsemen and those ten elephants. Molon's heavy array would have been much smaller at perhaps no more than 10,000 Greco-Macedonian phalangites plus 5,000–10,000 Galatian hirelings. However, the rebel leader must have had a solid edge in both Asian skirmishers and cavalry, maybe being able to field 20,000 of the former and 4,000 of the latter along with a modest contingent of scythed chariots.[66]

Molon chose to pull back into his home province. He would have optimum logistical support there and be better able to bring about engagement on an open plain where his numerical edge in cavalry and light infantry might prove decisive. But Antigonus' pursuit seems to have moved faster than anticipated and cut off the rebel's planned escape route, bringing him to bay near Apollonia along the mountainous border between Babylonia and

Media. When a nighttime ambush had to be called off due to deserters possibly having given warning, Molon prepared for a daylight battle. Opinions differ over whether he made this stand on high ground or within a broad pass, though the former seems to better fit the ensuing turn of events.[67] Either way, there was room to deploy his heavy foot and mounted troops upon level terrain behind the chariots, which were spaced out at center-front. This formation stretched across up to 3.5km if the Galatian contingent was of maximum size.[68] Molon placed all his skirmishers farthest outside as opposed to their normal station between the cavalry and phalanx, apparently addressing both a lack of secure footing for horses off either flank and that the line of sight and trajectories of slingers and other missilemen would suffer should they have to retire behind their own heavy infantry. Antiochus responded by matching width of this array using equivalent depths for his own horsemen and phalangites with the Greek spearmen at 12-deep far right. Standing next to the hoplites were some Cretan archers and what was probably an attached screen of Gallic mercenaries, while most of the cavalry was divided outboard. The latter saw the king's elite guardsmen at a likely 1,000-strong posted alongside his pikemen on the left with perhaps 500 lesser lancers taking up position to the right of the Cretans and Gauls. The remaining royal light infantry and cavalry were tucked in hiding behind the flanking horsemen with orders to attempt envelopments at first action. As for the elephants, they took forward station at center to confront the enemy's chariots.

With Molon holding fast on the defensive, Antiochus advanced into shock combat with at least his right/strike wing, which decisively bested the rebel left. It's not clear how this came about, there being serious doubt about Polybius' claim that the Median horsemen on that side of the field, who should have been among Molon's most loyal followers, surrendered upon seeing Antiochus to trigger a wholesale capitulation. Bar-Kochva has proposed instead that the king's light foot and cavalry concealed at the rear actually did swing out to envelop per design.[69] Yet one might question this as well given a probable better than 2-to-1 edge in rebel mounted strength along that flank supported by thousands more missilemen farther outboard. Another possibility is that Antiochus' Greek mercenaries were critical in carrying the day. Those hoplites might well have turned the left flank of the Galatians immediately opposed, taking advantage of greater file-depth, favorable spacing (Gallic swords being less effective in close order), and longer reaching weapons. And they had an edge in morale as well against foes badly shaken by the previous night's aborted attack.[70] Whatever its true cause, the subsequent collapse of Molon's entire host put an end to the uprising and he took his own life.

Raphia (217)

Ever since the battle of Ipsus in 301 brought about a final fragmentation of Alexander the Great's empire, there had been a growing competition among his Seleucid successors in Asia and their Ptolemaic counterparts in Egypt for control of Coele (southern) Syria. An unofficial "gentlemen's agreement" for Seleucus I to cede nominal sway there to Ptolemy I had initially kept the peace, but subsequent rulers had actively engaged over the area in three so-called "Syrian Wars" between 274 and 241. Largely conflicts of maneuver, skirmish, and city seizures along with a pair of major actions at sea,[71] these did little to alter the basic balance of dominion. The Ptolemies were generally more successful militarily and were able to hold onto Cole Syria in the end.[72] Things had remained relatively calm for a couple of decades before Antiochus III renewed conflict in the region, looking to restore his dynasty's reach to the farthest limits claimed at its foundation. Dealing with Molon had stalled that effort for a few months; however, the ambitious young monarch was back in Syria before year's end 220.[73] The next two campaign seasons saw Egypt on the defensive as it both built up its long dormant forces and dealt with matters lingering from the ascension of Ptolemy IV upon the death of his father (Ptolemy III) in 221. It wasn't then until 217 that the new Egyptian ruler led his revitalized military against Antiochus, who was marching along the Mediterranean strand near Gaza in a bold advance on the Ptolemaic homelands.

The Seleucid host boasted some 62,000 foot soldiers, 6,000 horsemen, and 102 Indian elephants against Ptolemy's more than 70,000 infantrymen plus 5,000 in cavalry and 73 pachyderms of the smaller North African variety. Similarly large, these armaments were quite different in detail with the Egyptians having much more numerous line-infantry (over 60,000 heavy foot versus 35,000 heavies and a few thousand other shield-bearing spearmen for their foes).[74] That left Antiochus facing a challenge not unlike the one before Molon three years prior: how to exploit his superior mounted force (in quality if not so much in size) plus a larger number of light foot against a foe stronger in heavy infantry. His chosen approach was to post upon a battleground wide enough to favorably accommodate his entire army, yet sufficiently restricted so as to force Ptolemy into deeper and less efficient files. This saw him set up his phalanx below the city of Raphia within a shoreline parallel pass running between a trend of coastal dunes and a series of slow-drifting sandhills inland to the southeast. At some 5.6km wide, this provided just the sort of modest chokepoint desired.[75]

In reconciling Antiochus' reported manpower with the apparent dimensions of the battlefield in 217 and what we are told by Polybius of his dispositions,[76] the following arrangement appears most probable: (1) His heavy array occupied the center of the field with its troops deployed toward prioritizing the right wing as its primary strike element in traditional manner. This placed his Greek mercenary hoplites far right at 5,000 strong in 12-man files,[77] followed leftward by the various pike contingents (the Argyraspides all using sarissai) totaling 30,000 at 2/3m lateral spacing in files of 16 and then the Iranian mixed-arms contingent of 5,000 at ten-deep and a meter across for each of the shield-bearing spearmen in its forward ranks. This heavy formation covered some 2,150m of the available front. (2) The larger share of Antiochus' cavalry (4,000 riders) reinforced his right-wing strikers by taking post off that flank, including the king with his royal guard at 1,000-strong. Ranking 2m apart, the horsemen had to file eight-deep at twice the norm that they might accommodate the field's restricted dimensions, thus covering 1,000m of frontage. Between this mounted formation and the Greek hoplites capping the phalanx's right extreme were 2,500 Cretan bowmen, who probably ranked a meter each at a depth of five, their short files allowing for optimum sighting and trajectories along a 500m front.[78] (3) Standing next to the Iranians on the heavy array's far left were 14,500 light-armed troops including (right to left) 10,000 Arabs and other tribesmen,[79] 3,000 unidentified skirmishers,[80] and 1,500 Anatolian javelineers, all fronting over 1,450m at ten-deep. Antiochus' remaining horsemen (2,000) completed the 5.6km span of his formation, holding station far left in ranks and files like those of their mounted comrades on the other end of the field. The elephants were divided and spread out in front of the cavalry screens on either flank, 42 on the left with 12m separations and 60 on the right spaced 15m apart.[81]

Ptolemy scouted the opposing army for several days and distributed his own troops accordingly for a late afternoon assault.[82] Though crowded within the pass, he was still able to file his spearmen in their accustomed depth of 12-shields on either side of the pike array but had to set up the latter an unusual 24-deep with contingents of 20,000 native Egyptians newly equipped with sarissai on the right, 25,000 experienced pikemen of Graeco-Macedonian descent at center, and 3,000 hired Libyans also recently retrained as phalangites on the left.[83] Ptolemy then placed light infantry either side of his heavy-armed troops and split the cavalry off the flanks to fill the entire breadth of field. This arrangement was exceptional in that its "strike" element was on the left where picked hoplites of the royal guard (3,000 strong) stood with 2,000 similarly outfitted peltastai to their right.[84] On the other side of the guardsmen were Cretan and neo-Cretan archers (3,000 at five-deep) while the king rode far left with 3,000 horsemen filed at six to fit the terrain. By thus switching his offensive wing from its traditional position on the right, Ptolemy seems to have been targeting Antiochus' strength much akin to what the Thebans had done at Leuctra in their famous victory over Sparta.[85]

The right side of the Ptolemaic heavy formation was occupied by 8,000 hired Greeks. Though these troops had "exercised together in one body" with some of the army's phalangites, care is taken to differentiate them from those pikemen in describing them as posting on the "right wing" and thus (like their guard/peltast counterparts on the left) being distinct from phalangites standing alongside who were part of the phalanx proper as Polybius narrowly defined it.[86] Combining this with actions in the ensuing battle,[87] we can reasonably conclude that they were probably exactly what you'd expect to have come from Greece's mercenary recruiting hotbeds in the southern Peloponnese: classical hoplite spearmen just like those serving Antiochus on the other side of the field. Completing Ptolemy's formation on the right were 6,000 light foot next in line and 2,000 horsemen at six-deep on the far flank, while the African elephants fronted his cavalry with 40 on the left and 33 on the right.

The armies initiated combat using the elephants that led the directly opposed strike wings on the northwest side of the field. Most of Ptolemy's smaller African beasts refused to fight and ended up being driven back into him and his riders. Antiochus led his own cavalry around that flank to put the now disrupted Egyptian horse to flight. It seems, however, that he then chose pursuit over envelopment, perhaps being dissuaded by still effective arrow fire coming from the Cretans covering that side of the enemy line. This decision let Ptolemy and some of his horsemen escape the general rout and shelter behind their infantry. Yet that soon proved a less than secure haven when the Seleucids' Greek mercenaries began to spear into the peltastai and presumably the royal guardsmen as well, shoving them back such that "the whole of Ptolemy's left wing was hard pressed and in retreat."[88] At this crucial juncture, it was the right side of the Egyptian ruler's formation that saved him from defeat. It had stood refused to allow the crack troops on the other end of the field to carry the day, but now went into action when this pre-battle scheme came to naught.[89] And as Ptolemy's elephants and cavalry carried that flank, his spear-brigade of Greek hirelings closed into the Median shield-bearers directly ahead, punching through to send their light-armed after-ranks as well as the tribesmen alongside running for the rear. Thus, though the Egyptians' left had been perilously wavering on the verge of defeat, it was their foes' own left wing that ultimately ended up driven from the fight.

The sarissa-bearers on both sides in the center of the field had been stalemated in a shifting contest of well separated fencing with those long weapons at the heads of their deep files. That phase now came to a sudden halt as Antiochus' left fell prey to envelopment by the enemy's locally victorious Greek hoplites and horsemen. And though the Argyraspides posted farther rightward held firm for a while, their fellow pikemen closer to this lateral assault quickly gave way. That led to the entire Seleucid heavy formation collapsing from left to right like a line of falling dominoes, with even its previously successful mercenary spearmen at the far end eventually taking to their heels as Ptolemy's troops seized full control of the battleground. By the time Antiochus realized what was happening and broke off pursuit to address this looming disaster, all he could do was join in the escape. His losses are said to have included nearly 10,000 foot soldiers and over 300 horsemen killed plus another 4,000 men captured. Ptolemy paid a lesser price as victor; still, the early reverses on his left had helped run up a hefty toll of 1,500 foot soldiers and 700 cavalrymen slain.[90]

The truce that emerged after Raphia rendered results of the Fourth Syrian War little different from the first three in that Egypt remained in possession of Cole Syria. Antiochus pulled back and dealt with Achaeus' fading resistance in Ionia. However, ambitions to expand his empire remained alive despite the setback against Ptolemy, and if they couldn't be achieved to the south and west, then he would look toward the east instead.

5. Phalanx Triumphant

The Second Punic War, Phase 1
(c. 236–211 BCE)

Hamilcar Barca had emerged from the trials of the First Punic and Mercenary conflicts as the leading power in Carthage. And with ink hardly dry on the agreement to abandon Sardinia and pay additional reparations in avoiding another conflict with Rome, he marched an army to the Pillars of Hercules (Gibraltar) in the summer of 237 and crossed into Iberia (Spain) to set up camp near the Phoenician foundation at Agadir/Gades (Cadiz today) just above the Pillars on the west coast of modern Andalucía. He was intent on expanding Carthage's modest holdings in the Iberian southwest and thereby access rich silver and tin mines, verdant farmland, and ample export markets farther inland to restore his people's prosperity and prestige.

Carthaginian Operations, 237–219

We know little about Hamilcar's military actions on the Iberian Peninsula save for some passing references in Polybius and a few surviving fragments of Diodorus' history. It appears that he largely fought local tribes and tribal unions. The force he led to begin was not huge,[1] its core heavy infantry perhaps being half that fielded at the end of the Mercenary War with some 9,000 hoplites (citizens and Liby-Phoenicians looking to colonize as well as Libyan conscripts). His cavalry might have been limited to a couple thousand Numidians per their numbers against the mercenaries. Once at Agadir, he must have contracted native tribesmen to boost his mounted contingent while tacking on a division of colonial heavy foot. Additional hires from tribes that had supplied such to Carthage in the past would have then completed support for his elephants (requiring about 5,000 men) as well as the phalanx and cavalry (another 2,000), all serving to push Hamilcar's manpower above 20,000.

Agadir and Numidia (c. 236)

The sole pitched action of record waged by Hamilcar in Iberia came against a coalition led by the chieftain Istolatius. This probably took place near Agadir, suggesting a date early in the campaign amid an initial uprising by many of the locals in concert. We are told that Hamilcar "cut to pieces" the entire enemy force of Iberian tribesmen (probably the largest component), Celts, and "Tartessians" (inhabitants of the region derived from

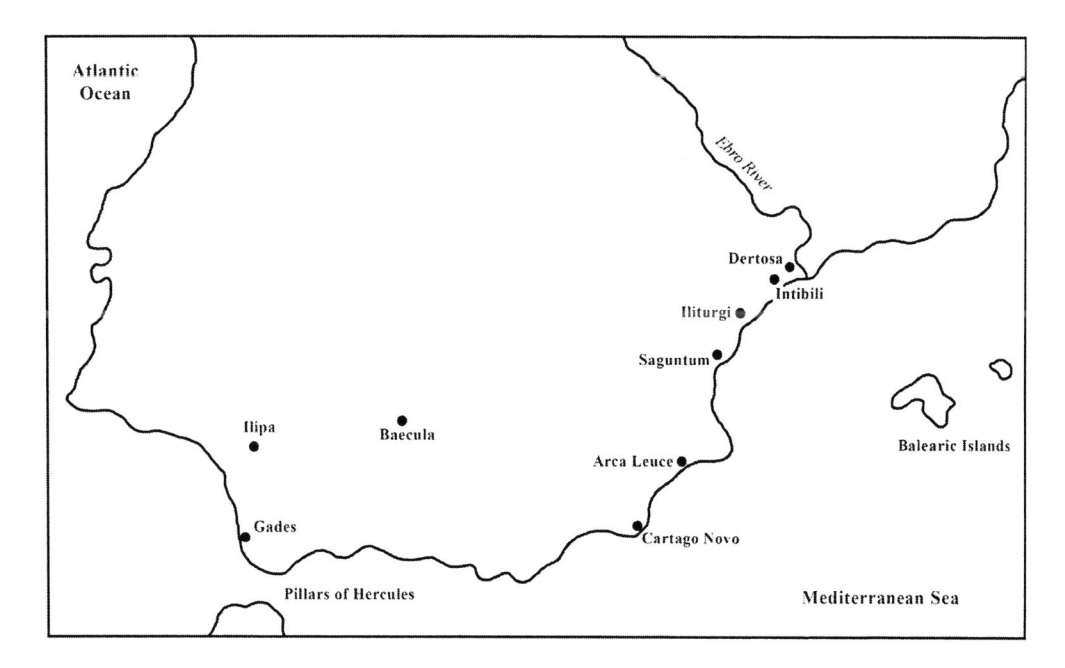

Iberia, 3rd–2nd centuries BCE.

the former urban center of Tartessia).[2] These peoples likely all fought in similar fashion, even the Celts having adopted local culture to effectively become "Celtiberian." The coalition army would have included upper class horsemen (some being javelineers using small shields and others called *jinetes* operating as heavier lancers) at 12–15 percent the infantry count with two-thirds of the foot soldiers being theurophoros swordsmen (scutarii that also plied heavy javelins) and the rest light javelineers (caetrati) carrying round bucklers (some of these provided missile support for the cavalry much like the Greek skirmishers known as *hamippoi* in some classical Greek armies). Body armor was far from common and more costly types like chain-mail of Gallic design must have been rare among the less affluent infantry masses. Some 3,000 surviving tribesmen went into Punic service. Had that been around 10 percent of their full deployment, the resulting projection of 30,000 fighters seems reasonable, being on the same order of magnitude as an Iberian tribal gathering soon thereafter and later ones of 34,000 and 35,000.[3]

It's likely that Hamilcar won this engagement by using his elephants to panic opposition horses unfamiliar with those alien creatures, doing so in coordination with an attack by his superior shock infantry. That tactical pattern would have applied to any further actions of this type as well, though Hamilcar's only other such confrontation on record (with the chieftain Indortes, who reputedly led 50,000 men) saw the tribesmen so intimidated that they fled without a fight as 10,000 meekly surrendered. In fact, the lone additional battle actually described in this period took place back in Africa, where Hamilcar dispatched his son-in-law (and second in command) Hasdrubal to deal with a Numidian uprising.

Hasdrubal must have brought contingents of hired light foot and cavalry from Europe, but most of his army would have been African, including citizen and Liby-Phoenician hoplites (perhaps equal to the 9,000 heavy foot sent to Iberia) as well as like-equipped Libyan draftees (another 3,000 or so). Hasdrubal probably had 2,000 citizen horsemen added to a comparable count of mercenary and other riders plus at least a few elephants to contend with lighter Numidian cavalry perhaps some 5,000-strong. That seems to have been adequate to hold his own off the wings and buy time for his much more shock-capable phalanx to break the theurophoros javelineers and even lighter skirmishers that made up the rebel formation of foot. This keyed a decisive Punic victory that took the lives of 8,000 Numidians and sent 2,000 more into captivity, with the fatalities at around 25 percent being plausible for a badly beaten force of 30,000 suffering heavy pursuit.[4]

Tagus River (220) and Saguntum (219)

Hamilcar Barca was killed in 229 while trying to escape a betrayed siege operation. Hasdrubal then took over with tremendous success until assassinated in 221. The leadership in Iberia now passed to Hamilcar's oldest son, Hannibal. Though relatively young at 26, he was a keen student of Alexander the Great and Pyrrhus as well as superbly schooled in the many practical aspects of making war through 16 years in the company of his father and brother-in-law. Hannibal inherited a powerful military of 60,000 foot soldiers, 8,000 cavalry, and 200 elephants,[5] immediately putting it to work reducing the few remaining pockets of resistance to Punic rule in the Iberian south. He went on to extend that campaign northward the next year, capturing the cities of Salmantica (modern Salamanca) and Arbucale. However, Hannibal's return march from the latter came under threat from a large coalition force led by the Carpetani, a tribe from the vicinity of modern Toledo in central Iberia. Perhaps facing some 25,000 warriors with not much more than a fifth of his own military,[6] he elected to retreat.

Hannibal retired behind the Tagus River so that he could use it as a force multiplier for his smaller host. The Carpetani et al launched assaults over that flow but failed to gain a foothold due to counterattacks from Hannibal's cavalry and elephants with supporting teams of skirmishers. These melees included Punic horsemen using their height advantage to wade out and slaughter floundering foot-soldiers. With his opponents confused and distressed in the wake of this disastrously failed crossing attempt, Hannibal charged through the river and swiftly put them to rout.[7]

Having shown his ability along the Tagus to tellingly exploit both favorable terrain and a well-timed offensive, Hannibal's next (and last) battle on Iberian soil presented a much lesser tactical challenge; yet, it was to have profound strategic implications. This came a year later at Saguntum (Zacantha), which he had put under siege in the final stage of his suppression program. The militiamen of that sole remaining outpost of unbowed resistance sallied in desperation and were annihilated, though only after "having themselves inflicted many casualties."[8] This must have been a relatively small affair involving just a few thousand defenders bested by more than twice their number. The rub was that Saguntum had recently allied with the Romans despite being below the Ebro River, which Rome had agreed by treaty would mark the northeast boundary of Punic Iberia. Demanding Hannibal's surrender for attacking its ally (despite any possible justification under the Ebro terms), Rome went to war upon refusal of the leadership at Carthage to comply.

Northern Italy, 218–216

Hannibal moved quickly upon learning of Rome's declaration of hostilities, first arranging protection for Carthage's European assets and home territories. This included assigning a substantial part of strength on hand to his brother Hasdrubal for use in lower Iberia, amounting to some 2,500 horsemen (a mix of Liby-Phoenicians, Libyans, Iberians, and Numidians), 12,000 African heavy foot, and 800 slingers plus 21 elephants[9] and all available warships. He also contracted fresh Iberian contingents, sending 19,000 foot-soldiers and 1,200 horsemen to Africa.[10] Hannibal then marched beyond the Ebro and, leaving 10,000 foot-soldiers and a thousand horse with the general Hanno to hold the trans-Ebro frontier,[11] crossed the Rhodanus (Rhone) as well. From there, he headed into the Alps toward Italy, having calculated that the key to overcoming Rome lay in disaffection of its many allies and called for besting the Romans in spectacular fashion on their own soil.

Ticinus R., Trebia R. and Cissus (218)

The Romans had mobilized both their consular armies to prosecute the conflict with Carthage, shipping one under Publius Cornelius Scipio to assault Iberia while the other under Tiberius Sempronius Longus crossed to Sicily and staged at Lilybaeum in preparation for an attack on the Africans' homeland. Scipio came ashore at the allied Grecian city of Massilia (modern Marseilles) at the mouth of the Rhone to confront Hannibal only to find him already gone by a couple of days. Realizing the potential threat this posed, the consul left his brother in command at Massilia and hastened back to Italy with just a handful of companions to lead the resistance to Hannibal once he emerged from the Alps. And as news of these events reached Sempronius, he and his troops turned back as well in a rush to reach Rome.

Hannibal's passage through the mountains was difficult and costly, his army being greatly reduced due to attacks from local tribes, bitter cold, misadventure on icy precipices, and mass desertions by dispirited auxiliaries. Reaching the Po Valley in late September of 218, he had only some 26,000 combatants left: 12,000 in African heavy foot, 8,000 Iberians (maybe 4,000 scutarii, 2,000 caetrati, and 2,000 others including slingers), and 6,000 in cavalry (likely 2,000 Numidian light horse with the rest heavier Iberian and African riders).[12] Of his 37 elephants perhaps 20–25 had survived, among them a sole Indian beast (known as "The Syrian" for its place of origin) that Hannibal used for personal transport. Camping on the Po River, the Carthaginians began replacing lost cavalry mounts and pack animals, trading with local (Cisalpine) Gauls whom they also solicited to join the fight.

Rome had recently put down a revolt among those tribesmen, which was a boon for Hannibal's recruiting; however, it worked to his detriment as well in that a substantial Roman peace-keeping force was still stationed in the Po Valley. This was under the praetor Lucius Manlius Vulso and consisted of a pair of Roman legions (8,400 infantry and 600 horse) plus 10,000 foot and 1,000 in cavalry provided by alliance partners.[13] The allied footmen were equivalent to (if not in actuality) the infantry contingents from two alae sociorum plus another 1,600 in javelineers, the latter adequate to support the cavalry on hand at one per horseman. The riders were less than the 2,400 typical for a true consular army, the allies being deficient by at least half the normal count (1,800 for a pair of alae sociorum) with only partial compensation from some 200 mounted Gauls. But regardless of that shortage, it was this ready force that let Scipio march against Hannibal soon after his arrival.

Hannibal and Scipio approached each other from the west and east respectively along the northern bank of the Po, the Roman crossing its south-flowing Ticinus tributary to establish camp. Lead elements for the armies then came into contact and both generals sortied their cavalry. Hannibal had much the larger mounted force and his decision to attack was sound; however, Scipio's choice to do the same is certainly questionable. Based upon having bested some Numidian scouts back along the Rhone,[14] he might have been misled about the possible superiority of his own riders. Hannibal's approach to the ensuing engagement mimicked the tactics of hoplite battle in that he set his heavier troopers in the middle much like a phalanx while spreading the Numidian horse outboard. Scipio countered by putting auxiliary javelineers in front of his cavalry, which stood perhaps five-deep along a 720m-wide expanse at 2m per mount. That spread would let him match up "front to front" with the opposition's lancers comprising a likely 2,000 Africans and 600–800 jinetes (30–40 percent of the mounted Iberians) deployed in files of six and eight respectively.[15]

Hannibal opened with a charge that drove Scipio's skirmishers back through their mounted files before they could have any significant impact. The cavalrymen then closed into a melee with some either dismounting or being unhorsed to fight on foot. Meanwhile, the Numidians swept forward on either wing and, aided by intermixed caetrati, chased infantry contingents guarding Scipio's flanks (most likely 300–600 Roman and/or ala sociorum velites on either side with possibly some auxiliaries relocated from the front). The Numidian riders ignored those scattering foes and (perhaps joined now by Iberian mounted javelineers and more caetrati from reserve) struck at the enemy rear, dispersing any light foot still huddled there to then break up the Roman horse. A wounded Scipio escaped to his camp, collected what he could of the battle's other survivors, and withdrew to Placentia on the far bank of the Po. He thus preserved the army's unblooded heavy foot from mounted threats that couldn't be countered with its cavalry and light infantry so badly damaged. The local tribes now hastened to join Hannibal with even some of the consul's own Gallic auxiliaries switching sides.

Scipio continued to withdraw until eventually taking position to the south on the eastern side of the Trebia, a north-flowing tributary of the Po. Sempronius joined him there, having marched from Rome upon hearing of the Ticinus action that he might throw another army into the fight. That consular force comprised the usual two Roman legions and pair of alae sociorum. Unlike their counterparts taken over by Scipio from Manlius, these contingents carried not only the normal count of foot-soldiers (16,800) but full complements of horsemen as well (1,800 attached to the alae sociorum plus 600 Romans)—something badly needed in light of Hannibal's mounted strength and Scipio's losses. Sempronius also brought more than 7,000 additional infantry, probably all light missilemen of whom at least a third would have been dedicated to providing support for the cavalry.[16] Finally, some still loyal Gauls were on hand with modest contingents that included light footmen.

Scipio was still recovering from his wound at Ticinus, which effectively left his fellow consul in sole command. And a combination of Sempronius' pride in having so large a force plus his desire to gain glory apart from Scipio and before his consulship's end of term is said to have led him into engaging Hannibal under unfavorable conditions. Somewhat like Scipio's small victory on the Rhone, Roman horsemen chased off some of Hannibal's riders who were scavenging on the Trebia's far side. Thus encouraged, Sempronius went on the offensive the next day when a portion of the Numidian horse forded for a pre-dawn attack on his camp. But his savvy foe was, in fact, goading him into just such a foolhardy act, possibly even having stage-managed a weak response in the previous day's action for that same purpose. And once he had drawn the unwary Roman into an ill-advised engagement, not only would Hannibal have the edge with his larger and more capable mounted force taking on opponents with a river at their backs to hinder retreat, but he could spring a lethal surprise as well. His brother Mago with 1,000 picked foot and the same in horsemen had hidden under cover of darkness behind a heavily vegetated area on the near side of the Trebia wherefrom he could launch a surprise assault on the left flank/rear of any Roman formation crossing to do battle.[17]

Sempronius sent his cavalry after the Numidians, who quickly rode back across the Trebia to resume opposition there. Seeing this, he fatefully took the bait and dispatched most (6,000) of his javelineer auxiliaries to join the horsemen in securing a foothold on the far bank so that he could cross safely with the rest of the army. The latter required his legionaries to wade in the dark chest-deep through a swampy network of flood-swollen channels on an exceedingly cold day (around the winter solstice) under falls of freezing rain, sleet, and snow. They emerged chilled to the bone yet still willing and ready to fight. Being some 36,000-strong, the infantry formed its usual acies triplex with 24,000 heavy foot in the center at 15-deep and over 12,000 skirmishers split off the flanks to be joined by their cavalry.[18] Hannibal for his part deployed 8,000 light footmen as a van (4,000 caetrati and specialists with missiles plus an equal number of recently recruited Gauls) behind which he set up a phalanx. That consisted of 6,000 African heavy foot forming each wing with 3,000 scutarii and 5,000 Gallic swordsmen intermingled by unit at center. His cavalry (sans Mago's Numidians) moved to divide evenly off either side at better than 10,000 riders including 6,000 Gauls.

Hannibal knew how the acies triplex would deploy and arrayed his compound phalanx to counter along a 3,200m expanse with the Iberian and Gallic theurophoroi in close order at 1m spacing and ten-deep while the hoplites on either side stood equally tight, but at a depth of only five. The defensive set of Hannibal's Europeans (such swordsmen requiring twice their current width to attack in optimum fashion) as well as the high risk of disorderly advance by his Africans in such short files signaled weakness, seeming to justify their standing to receive (rather than charging to meet) the slow and steady Roman advance now closing on them. But this was in reality all part of a calculated trap, drawing Sempronius' legions far enough beyond the Trebia to make room for Mago's moving behind them. Hannibal set up more aggressively outboard. Facing some 2,000 horsemen stretching 800m or so beyond either Roman flank, he opposed around 5,000 riders on each of his outer screens. Iberian, Gallic, and heavier African horse were intermixed by units in some fashion at the fore, with the Numidians that had attacked the Roman camp now having regrouped in the rear. The few elephants on hand took broadly separated posts in order to front for the flanking cavalry.[19]

After some dispersed skirmishing by missilemen in the no-man's-land between heavy arrays, both sides' light foot withdrew to join the mounted contingents outboard as armored infantry lines closed into an extended shock action. This saw the Punic troops hold their ground to keep more deeply filed Romans from breaking through, thus allowing for the action to turn in favor of Carthage flankward. Hannibal's elephants there, though set upon and wounded by skirmishers assigned specifically to oppose them, managed to badly frighten their foes' mounts. The leading Punic horse took advantage of that disorder plus much greater numbers to then charge between the widely spaced pachyderms and rout the enemy screens from both ends of the battlefield. As most of these victorious riders gave chase, the rest folded in on the now naked flanks of the Roman heavy formation, being joined by their foot-skirmishers along with those Numidians that had been in rearward reserve. And at this key moment, Mago and his men joined the fight from behind, adding to a vicious multidirectional assault that rapidly collapsed Sempronius' army. Many Romans were cut down either on the spot or in flight, but 10,000 slashed in desperation through some Gauls in the middle of Hannibal's line to make a truly miraculous escape in that most unlikely direction.

Hannibal now held effective control over Cisalpine Gaul. He had taken little damage to his core African and Iberian troops at Trebia, casualties having largely been among the Gallic allies, especially those penetrated in the middle of his line. However, this battle was to mark the last appearance of his elephant corps. Suffering from wounds and subjected to a harsh winter, all the beasts would die by spring save for the Syrian, Hannibal's sturdier Indian mount. Scipio and Sempronius (the latter having fled back over the Trebia under cover of foul weather) were forced to retreat within the protective walls of Placentia and await arrival of a new consul (Gaius Flaminius) to take command. The situation was grim, but all had not gone against Rome in 218. Publius Scipio's brother, Gnaeus, had taken several enemy coastal sites and gained local allies. He then marched beyond the Ebro, where he defeated Hanno near Cissus in a "pitched battle" that saw the Carthaginian and his companion Iberian general lose 6,000 killed with themselves and 2,000 others falling prisoner.[20]

The Romans should have had a significant numerical advantage in this engagement. Gnaeus had his "whole army" in tow per Polybius, including two legions, two alae sociorum, and some 5,600 allied light foot in addition to 1,600 horsemen. That gave him 12,000 in heavy infantry plus over 10,000 skirmishers not counting whatever his new Iberian partners provided. Hannibal had left Hanno with 10,000 infantrymen (perhaps 3,000 Africans plus 4,000 scutarii, 2,000 caetrati, and 1,000 other missilemen) and 1,000 in cavalry. His Iberian compatriot could have brought in some more tribesmen; but even if so, they might have no more than offset the locals Gnaeus had added. Frontinus is our sole source on how these troops were utilized, saying that Hanno deployed the African heavy foot on his left wing with Iberians (presumably scutarii) on the right.[21] Frontinus then claims Gnaeus defeated this compound arrangement much as the Thebans had Sparta at Leuctra, refusing his own left while attacking and routing the Africans as their Iberian allies "stood apart after the manner of spectators."

There is much here that departs from previous Punic practices in neutral terrain. Those usually placed their best spearmen on the right when deploying a fairly uniform phalanx; however, they set up less homogeneous arrays by either splitting the heavy foot onto both flanks (should it constitute a strong plurality or majority of the line as at Trebia) or (when much in the minority as at Cissus) placing it in the center with other arms on the wings. We can't discount Frontinus entirely, yet it's quite plausible that he had misconstrued some of his source material. A major red flag in this regard is that a few of the dead must by simple calculation have come from Iberians he paints as non-combatants. It's notable that had the Africans been in the middle here as under similar circumstances past, it would not have kept Gnaeus from withholding a wing, targeting half the Iberians while leaving those on the opposite end to join the Africans at center in being turned with steep losses. And that might well have been due to developments elsewhere on the field. It's possible that Gnaeus' huge complement of foot-skirmishers had bested the considerably smaller flank screens opposed to accomplish a double envelopment irrespective of any refusal tactic also in play, with such a scenario perhaps offering the best explanation for the high death and surrender rates observed here.[22]

L. Trasimenus and L. Umber (217)

The spring of 217 witnessed Hannibal passing from Cisalpine Gaul toward Rome via Etruria, which sat immediately above Latium along the southwestern Italian coast. He took an unlikely route in doing this, transiting pestilent marshlands associated with the Arno River in an effort to avoid observation that could lead to an attack in route. This trek was punishing and took a toll in particular on his allied Gauls struggling along at the rear of the column of foot. Hannibal himself, though riding high above the mire upon the Syrian's back, contracted an infection that could not be treated on the move and cost him the sight in one eye. He emerged into Etruria and set about confronting Flaminius, who was camped upstream on the Arno at Arretium. Seeking to lure that new foe into disadvantaged battle as he had with his predecessors, Hannibal laid waste to the Etrurian countryside as an open provocation; he then marched past the enemy camp and turned south in the direction of Rome with the consul close behind.

Flaminius' army was apparently a reconstituted version of that originally assigned to Sempronius for the invasion of Africa. Casualties at the Trebia had been replaced by fresh recruits and allied drafts in bringing its components (two legions and a matching number of alae sociorum plus nearly 6,000 additional light-armed auxiliaries) back up to some 25,000 strong.[23] Hannibal had if anything a mightier host than before. He now fielded the larger contingent of heavy foot, retaining most of his 12,000 African hoplites and 4,000 scutarii (these upgraded with captured equipment)[24] versus 12,000 heavies of all types for Flaminius. And his past small edge in medium and light infantry had likely grown with new Gallic allies added in the former category and a majority of the Iberian light foot previously employed still on hand.[25] Finally, even without added Gauls, his cavalry at over 10,000-strong would have dwarfed Rome's 2,400 riders. And there was more still going for Hannibal than these numbers imply. Many of the Romans were raw recruits serving in an army wracked with doubt after a recent defeat of disastrous proportions, while all of his men save for the latest Gallic arrivals were assured veterans that had just routed an even larger enemy host than the one now on their heels. Yet in the end, Carthage's greatest plus on the coming battlefield would stem neither from superior manpower nor higher levels of experience and confidence among its soldiers, but rather from the unique tactical genius of its commanding general.

Hannibal had gathered intelligence about the local terrain and now occupied a strip of flat ground that stretched along the north shore of Lake Trasimenus. This had slopping uplands bordering its landward side with slim entrances at either end that made it the ideal setting for a deadly ambuscade. Timing his movement here for late in the day, the wily Carthaginian concealed lighter-equipped troops across the high ground above the lake and set up camp at the east end of the shoreside pass from whence his phalanx could deploy at great depth as a forward barrier. Meanwhile, he hid cavalry and foot-skirmishers above the pass' western gateway in position to move rapidly on signal and block that direction. All would work to near perfection the next morning as Flaminius broke camp and resumed ardent pursuit by leading his entire column into this carefully prepared killing ground.[26]

Regular order for a Roman army on the march would have had Flaminius and company moving behind a contingent of picked men from the alae sociorum. Known as *extraordinarii*, these were a third of allied horsemen (600 for a normal consular force as here) and a fifth of their foot soldiers (1,680). The extraordinarii were followed by an ala sociorum and then both Roman legions with the other ala sociorum bringing up the rear. Flaminius' baggage train would have been nestled between the legions from Rome, having all his remaining cavalry riding alongside and/or in separate units trailing the infantry divisions to which they were attached.[27] Marching in a thick mist on this early morning in mid–June, the consul's long array came to a premature halt when its lead elements encountered the heavy phalanx of Africans and scutarii blocking the way ahead. Masses of enemy soldiers charged down out of the hills on signal at that moment to smash into the stalled column's northern/left flank even as cavalry and more skirmishers closed off any path for escape to the rear. Nic Fields has aptly characterized what followed over the next three hours as "the murder at Lake Trasimene, for battle it was not." Polybius says that most of Flaminius' men "were cut to pieces in marching order" while Livy reports them (metaphorically?) to have been in a state of confusion and panic so profound that an earthquake went unnoticed amid the slaughter.[28]

Somewhat akin to events at Trebia, most of the extraordinarii and the ala sociorum immediately behind (around 6,000 men in all) managed to flee across high ground by barging ahead through lighter-armed troops stationed off one flank of the Punic phalanx. They left behind some 15,000 comrades dead or dying as well as the body of their slain commander. This rather amazing escape was, however, no more than temporary as Hannibal's horsemen forced their surrender the next day to join some 4,000 others captured previously. According to Livy, Hannibal suffered 2,500 killed on the field as well as others later from wounds (though but 1,500 total per Polybius), which was only a fraction of Rome's losses with most of it being highly replaceable Gauls. He would release a majority of the prisoners, those being Latins and Italians whose nations he sought to attach, while holding onto the Roman citizens.

Word of Flaminius' pursuit of Hannibal had reached Gnaeus Sempronius where he and his consular army were encamped near the mouth of the River Po. Knowing his infantry could never reach Etruria in time to help, he dispatched 4,000 horsemen under the praetor Gaius Centenius. Hannibal learned of this and sent out his subordinate Maharbal with a portion of his own cavalry plus some light infantrymen (longchophorai with throwing spears). The two forces met southeast of the Trasimenus battleground close to the Umber, a small lake near modern Assisi. We lack details on Maharbal's command; however, Hannibal could have held back as many horsemen as Centenius had in total and still opposed him with a force half again larger. It's likely that Maharbal emulated his general's tactics at Ticinus, matching the Romans along their entire front using heavy African and Iberian horse flanking a mass of Gallic riders while sending fleet Numidians galloping into flank attacks round either wing. Nearly encircled, about half of the Roman cavalry was slain on the spot as the rest fled under hard pursuit only to be surrounded on high ground and compelled to surrender the next day.[29]

We are told that Hannibal rested his men and "re-armed the Africans in the Roman fashion with select arms," though later clarification makes it likely that this was restricted to adoption of superior chainmail that had been captured.[30] Lazenby notes that "Hannibal would not have tried to turn spearmen into swordsmen in the midst of such a campaign" and "unless the Roman equipment they used was purely protective" his men would have to have been sword fighters all along.[31] Yet there is abundant pictorial evidence for Carthage's heavy African infantry always having been hoplites using a thrusting spear as their primary weapon. This along with Polybius' statement on Libyan heavy foot sporting Roman armor a year later at Cannae and his oblique reference to its use of spears in executing a classic hoplite envelopment there makes Lazenby's "protective" proviso near certain; thus, any re-arming of the Africans must have been confined solely to defensive gear. This would not have included shields as use of scuti would have put an end to the aspis-based fighting style that had twice now devastated Rome's legions. It is simply not credible that Hannibal traded his men's deeply ingrained and successful combat method for one it had so badly beaten in recent days.[32]

Gerunium (217), Cannae and Nola I (216)

Panic was widespread in the wake of so many heavy defeats close to home, which led the Romans to unify their military command for a six-month term under Quintus Fabius Verrucosis, appointing him to the formal office of Dictator. Twice a consul and having gained some past fame fighting the Ligurians, Fabius was a pious 63-year-old naturally inclined toward caution and he set out to contain rather than confront Hannibal. Shadowing opposition movements, Fabius frustrated his tactically brilliant foe by waging a successful war of attrition; still, Hannibal managed to retaliate at least modestly that summer, escaping a potential ambush and killing around a thousand Romans in the process.[33] Neither this relatively small yet painful setback nor his slow and deliberate operational approach did anything for the Dictator's popularity among a citizenry desperate to see the enemy quickly driven from Italy, and he was soon tagged with a derisive nickname, Fabius the Delayer (*Cunctator*).

A major problem for Fabius was his Master of Horse, Marcus Minucius Rufus. A fierce critic appointed by political foes, Minucius declared his commander a coward for avoiding battle and accrued increasing authority from backers at Rome. Hannibal would set sight on this fellow as just the sort of "useful idiot" he might exploit, and the chance to do so came that fall after the Romans took post near where he planned to winter at Gerunium in Apulia. Fabius had traveled home to fulfill duties required by his office and left Minucius in charge. He took advantage by sending his light foot to drive some of Hannibal's skirmishers off a small hill on the far side of the Fortore River. Occupying the rise, Minucius followed up the next day with a wider assault on Carthaginian foraging parties that carried all the way to the walls of their fortified encampment. Hannibal retreated but lingered in the vicinity. News of these actions was so overhyped at Rome that when the Dictator returned to the army, he found himself compelled to share it with his now greatly admired subordinate. Each took some 20,000 men: two legions, two alae sociorum, and around 1,600 irregular skirmishers.[34] Fabius remained in his original camp on high ground behind the Fortore, while Minucius aggressively settled beyond the river atop the hill he had recently captured.

Hannibal immediately set about ensnaring Minucius. Moving at night, he concealed several large contingents of light foot and horsemen within ambushing distance of the plain between the Roman's position and a ridge farther inland toward his own campsite.[35] He then secretly deployed his phalanx behind the ridge's crest as a small body of skirmishers made a show of demonstrating at dawn on the fore-slope.[36] Knowing that Minucius was likely to see this as a chance to duplicate his much-lauded earlier feats, Hannibal must have smiled when the overconfident Romans came out to fight and duly marched into his trap with their heavy infantry in close order behind a van of cavalry and light foot.

Seeing so few of the enemy, Minucius likely counted on an easy victory that would give him the high ground should a larger engagement develop. The shock must therefore have been considerable when his velites found the going difficult and were ultimately repulsed as Hannibal's heavy array crested the ridge and his cavalry descended to drive the Roman skirmishers back among their own horsemen. With their comrades streaming past in flight, Minucius' legionaries maintained orderly lines in admirable fashion, stoically awaiting an advance by the enemy's phalanx that seemed sure to be coming. But it was Hannibal's ambushers who struck instead, smashing into both flanks as well as at the rear. This assault came as a complete surprise and "worked such havoc and alarm" among Minucius' men "that not one of them had any courage left for fighting or any hope of flight."[37]

Yet another Roman defeat at hideous cost seemed imminent when Fabius unexpectedly appeared, marching his own hastily gathered army onto the field to cut his countrymen's losses. Minucius and his beleaguered soldiers, "though they had entirely broken their ranks … retreated and took refuge under cover of Fabius' force after losing many of their light-armed troops, but still more of the legionaries."[38] Hannibal broke off pursuit, allowing the Roman survivors and rescuers alike to withdraw without further damage. He then retired to fortify his camp where he would spend the winter. Having absorbed a painful lesson on the value of unity, Minucius pledged loyalty to Fabius as they returned to having a single encampment. The Dictator's term expired shortly thereafter and his badly battered army once more came under consular authority as two freshly elected consuls, Lucius Aemilius Paulus and Gaius Terentius Varo, took charge in the spring.

While Gerunium had for the moment resolved the divisive conflict over who was in effective charge of Rome's military, the status of Paulus and Varo as equals brought that troublesome issue back into play. Our sources portray Paulus as assuming a version of Fabius' role in advocating a careful operational approach while Varo channeled early Minucius in being more daring and pugnacious. And while Fabius and Minucius had rejected alternating in authority and split the army evenly instead, these new consuls began to rotate in command on a daily basis. Historically a questionable practice,[39] this has been seen as opening the way for yet another incautious Roman leader to be lured into a major tactical test on terms heavily weighted in Hannibal's favor. However, there is evidence to indicate that no matter which of the consuls might have held authority at any given time, he would have been operating under a mandate to decisively engage the enemy with all reasonable dispatch.

This aggressive intent for Roman strategy can be seen in the massive resources deployed to carry it out. Regardless of how many citizen legions might have been in service on various missions at any one time, the largest single army fielded by Rome to this date had included no more than six of them. Now, however, the consuls were set to confront Hannibal with an eight-legion host. That kind of force would theoretically have included eight alae sociorum as well plus perhaps some 400 irregular auxiliaries per legion to bring its troop count up to 80,000. Yet Polybius reports even that colossal total was exceeded with more than 86,000 combatants being put into the field.[40] This extraordinary call-up was so immense that it apparently overtopped the allies' capacity to provide cavalry at the usual 3-to-1 ratio with Roman horse. They thus supplied just over 3,600 riders (about normal for a double-consular army of four legions) against 2,400 horsemen from Rome (300/legion as customary). This shortage was addressed (inadequately as it would prove) by overstocking the legions with infantrymen to the tune of some 1,200 extra apiece. Standard practice when that was done called for keeping the triarii at their nominal 600 per legion while boosting the accompanying velites, hastati, and princepes by equal amounts, putting each at 1,600-strong in this case.[41]

The consuls marched to Apulia where Hannibal held position near Cannae along the Aufidus River just below where its northeasterly flow entered the sea. They set up two camps downstream with a third of their troops on the southeast and the rest across on the far bank. Hannibal approached the larger of these sites and challenged Paulus; but he refused, judging the ground there too favorable for the enemy's cavalry. Hannibal tried again the next day, arraying along the opposite riverbank to tempt Varo. And even though this location was hardly less advantageous for horsemen, the Roman elected to engage anyway. While that might have reflected military naiveté and/or undue aggression on Varo's part as has often been suggested, it's quite possible that Paulus was actually in step, with neither man seeing a better prospect on the horizon for swiftly besting Hannibal as directed.

Hannibal was deployed in what appeared to be the same type of compounded formation used at Trebia, having cavalry either side of a line featuring African heavy infantry on both wings with alternating units of Gauls and Iberian scutarii in the center. His total manpower came to just over 40,000 foot-soldiers and 10,000 horsemen.[42] There were some 11,000 Africans and maybe 5,000 scutarii forming the backbone of his phalanx with perhaps an equal number of Gauls then filling it out utilizing scavenged Roman gear.[43] The remaining 8,000 or so footmen would have been divided in some fashion between cavalry support and guarding the army's camp and baggage. The heavy array ranked 1m per man across its front, standard for the African spearmen and for the Iberians and Gauls as well when in defensive posture; however, while the hoplites were at their regular depth of ten on the wings, it seems that the swordsmen forming the phalanx's mid-section might have been filed at twice that, ostensively in compensation for the weakness against legionaries they had shown at Trebia. The resulting formation stretched across something like 2,150m. Hannibal had his cavalry divided off either wing with the Numidian light horse extending onto the plain to the right and Iberians abutting the Aufidus on the left. Notably, Polybius says that all of the Gallic horsemen now making up the majority of his mounted force were grouped leftward as well, which rendered his right cavalry-poor in that there had never been all that many Numidians even before any losses of the last two years. Hannibal must therefore have posted most of his foot-skirmishers to that flank (though this is not specified in our sources), standing them inboard of the African riders.

The Roman command staff had observed Hannibal's deployment the day before on the other side of the river, which must have been a mirror-image of what he was doing now. They would also have been well aware of the results when legions faced a very similar arrangement on the Trebia. Confident their current more open setting would preclude an ambush such as had contributed to that defeat, they were prepared to employ tactics formulated to counter the very sort of formation now standing across the way. This called for massing their heavy infantry at exceptional depth to punch through the weaker, sword-armed middle of the enemy array by brute force much as some of their troops had done in escaping the killing field at Trebia. If performed with sufficient speed, this would allow the Roman horse to the right and allied on the left to hold their mounted counterparts long enough for the legions to roll up both ends of the Punic line from the center. Apparently assessing that any possible increased depth in the targeted heart of the Punic line would not invalidate this equation, Varro moved out to engage with his heavy foot filed 50-deep at 2m spacing across a frontage approximating that of the phalanx opposite.[44] Yet the calculations incorporated

100   5. Phalanx Triumphant

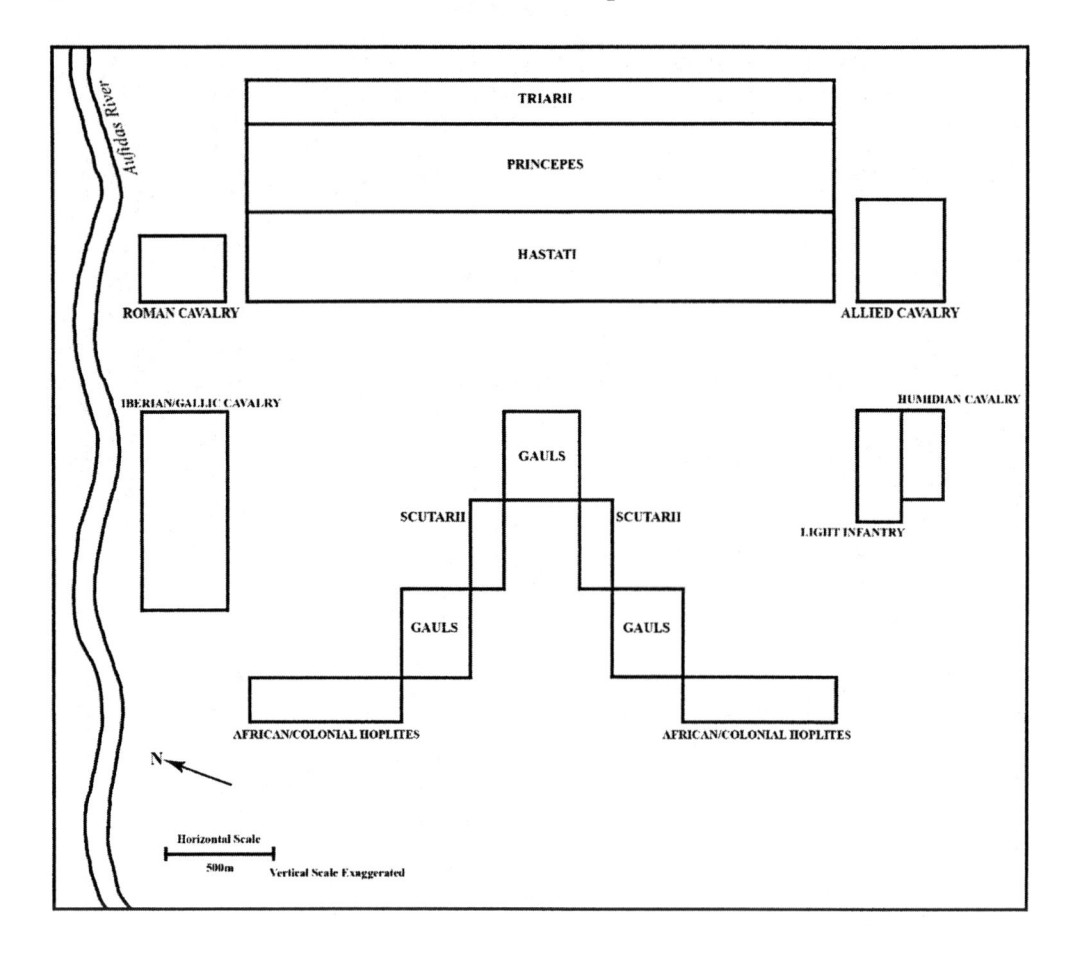

Battle of Cannae, 216 BCE.

into his plan of attack had been foreseen by Hannibal and all would soon go horribly wrong for the consul and his huge army.

    Hannibal had no intention of letting the opposition's infantry break through before his superior cavalry could succeed, and he put an ingenious counter-measure into motion even as the Romans closed distance. This saw him throw forward his Gallic and Iberian contingents in echelon to form what Polybius describes as "a crescent-shaped formation" at mid-field.[45] This presumably was based around a rectangle of Gallic swordsmen farthest in front that then had smaller sets of scutarii alternating with other Gauls stepping back off either side until those last segments contacted the inner flanks of the African heavy foot. The approaching Roman front-fighters would thus first encounter and be forced to drive back the Gallic block at the apex of this bluntly protruding wedge before being able to do the same with the next-forward set of flanking units, repeating that process if they wanted to push the entire enemy center back to its original position between the wing contingents on either end. Only then could they break through to begin outward-turning envelopments. The configuration of Hannibal's formation guaranteed this would be a difficult, time-consuming slog that would tend to draw the leading attackers inward against resistance in the middle of the battleground.

    It was therefore by design that Rome's swordsmen were able to collapse Hannibal's formation extension by main force, battering the Celts and Iberians back despite increased depth until almost flush with their wings. The Africans had held post as these allies gave ground; but when the fighting came near enough, they surged forward on signal, spearing into the fringes of Varo's battle array. The opposing troops there were probably slightly contracted and disrupted along their first couple of ranks as a result of some having edged closer inboard where all the action had been taking place. They thus quickly gave way when the well-ordered and more tightly spaced hoplites hit at either side, instinctively crowding toward the center of the field and taking those behind with them. And as interior line-mates pinned those Romans directly in front, the Africans' best men in the outermost sub-units on each wing began to execute a traditional phalanx maneuver to deadly effect. This saw them wheel by section to their "spear-side" on the left and "shield-side" on the right in a classic double envelopment.[46] The legionaries, suddenly at hazard not only from the front but also now on both flanks, were then entirely surrounded as cavalry and light foot crashed into their rear.

Hannibal's horsemen had driven away their counterparts on both ends of the battlefront as his cleverly overloaded riders beside the river exploited a numerical edge of probably better than 3-to-1 to quickly chase opposition there and then cross behind the legions to join their Numidian comrades in rapidly routing Rome's allied horse as well. The Numidians essayed a pursuit as the rest of the Punic cavalry turned against the rear ranks of Varo's infantry according to plan. Pushed hard from all quarters and forcefully compressed into a tight and helpless mass, those legionaries unable to escape fell to spear, sword, and lance in unprecedented numbers. As that terrible slaughter progressed from the outside inward, the increasingly desperate mob of Romans steadily dwindled, ranks shrinking until the last man went down. Among the dead was Paulus as well as Marcus Minucius, who had survived Gerunium only to die in command of the centrally deployed legions at Cannae; Varo, however, somehow managed to get away.

Rome's losses at Cannae were staggering with nearly 48,000 reported dead plus over 19,000 more falling captive and less than 15,000 escaping.[47] The Romans remained resolute and set about not only regrouping the survivors, but also organizing a large body of slaves for temporary defense as recruiting of fresh citizen and allied troops got underway. They also appointed another Dictator, the elderly Marcus Iunius Pera. Meantime, in the wake of so enormous a disaster for his foes, Hannibal made some headway in detaching a few of their allies as he marched down into Campania in southwestern Italy. But there, he fought an action in front of the town of Nola in which his assault party was rebuffed upon approach.

The praetor Marcus Claudius Marcellus held Nola with some of those who had escaped from Cannae and he made a surprise sally with a picked team of them from a city gate. With support from cavalry emerging from other portals on each side, he drove off Hannibal's men, inflicting what were claimed to be either 2,800 or 5,000 casualties at a cost of but 500 of his own. However, even Livy, never one to undervalue his countrymen's achievements, doubted those reports.[48] Probably little more than a melee between modest contingents, the reputed low-side Punic losses are better seen as perhaps the entire force defeated. And Marcellus' squad could have been even smaller considering both its select nature and the physical limitations that the gate would have imposed on any rapid attack. Indeed, the noisy fanfare that reportedly accompanied the Roman charge might have done as much to carry the field as any actual bodily harm imposed. Nevertheless, Hannibal's subsequent withdrawal surely came as a rare and much needed bit of good news during a very dark time for Rome.

5. Phalanx Triumphant

Italy, Sardinia and Iberia, 215–211

Grumentum, Nola II, Cornus and Carales (215)

Nola illustrates the sort of uncertainty that dominates our information on the period immediately after Cannae, for which most of Polybius' work has been lost to leave us dependent on even more strongly biased pro–Roman sources. This certainly applies to the first battle fought the following year at Grumentum in Lucania. Livy tells us that the losing commander at Trebia, Tiberius Sempronius Longus, scored a victory there over Carthage's Hanno in which he slew over 2,000 at a cost of only 280 men.[49] As a reality check using ancient averages of 15 percent loss for those defeated and 5 percent for victors, such casualties indicate that a Punic army more than 13,000-strong was bested by a force less than half its size. Though certainly possible, Sempronius would have needed an ambush or some similar force-multiplying advantage to pull this off; thus, the lack of any such in Livy's barebones account casts his reported result into reasonable doubt. At very least, the figure for Hanno's casualties is suspicious, since he likely had a mounted contingent that was easily an order of magnitude larger than that of the praetor. The Carthaginians should therefore have been able to severely limit the sort of pursuit required to claim so high a body-count during their retreat.

Hanno shortly thereafter collected reinforcements from Carthage to the tune of 4,000 foot-soldiers and 40 elephants and united with Hannibal, who had returned to investing Marcellus' base at Nola.[50] The Roman refused to come out for a pitched engagement but eventually sallied upon scattered Carthaginian provisioning activities.[51] Again, it's likely that a lone report of 5,000 of Hannibal's men being killed is much overblown; though his losses perhaps did include four of the recently arrived elephants as related by Plutarch. These fell to "long lances" issued to Marcellus' foot soldiers to deal with the beasts, repeating a tactic with repurposed cavalry weapons used to good effect against Pyrrhus 60 years earlier (see Chapter 2 re: *Maleventum*). And whatever the truth was regarding his damage, Hannibal once more backed off Nola, ending the year in control of much of the Italian south, yet frustrated by resistance from a Rome in no way inclined toward surrender.

No matter what might actually have taken place at Grumentum and Nola II, Rome did have real success during 215 in Iberia (see below) and on Sardinia. The latter's Punic coastal cities had risen up against Roman control. They were led by Hampsicora, chief magistrate of Cornus, which was centrally located along the island's western shore. Hoping to exploit serious crippling by disease of Sardinia's garrisoning legions, Hampsicora raised troops from nearby cities and sent to Carthage for assistance. While the latter gathered, he left the men on hand under his son Hiostus and set out to recruit from the rest of the Punic population as well as from native tribesmen in the mountainous eastern interior. Hiostus had about 4,000 combatants per reports of his subsequent losses,[52] these likely being about 75 percent line infantry and 25 percent auxiliaries (including wealthy horsemen at 10 percent of the total army). Meanwhile, the praetor Titus Manlius Torquatus arrived in the far south at Carales (Decimomannu) with a second legion/ala pair to reinforce the debilitated existing garrison. He immediately advanced upon Cornus hoping to catch his foes by surprise. Manlius had brought his ships' crews ashore to boost available manpower to a nominal 22,000 foot and 1,200 horse; however, the resident legion and ala sociorum had been cut down to maybe as little as half strength. If so, he took the field with closer to 12,600 foot (9,000 heavy-armed) and 600 horsemen plus perhaps some 2,500 of the landed crewmen (the rest serving as camp guards).[53] Yet even if thus limited, Manlius would still have been able to outnumber his pending opposition by nearly 4-to-1.

Hiostus sallied against the Romans upon their arrival before Cornus, which strongly implies that he was unaware of their true strength, likely thinking them no more than a portion of the disease-thinned garrison of long-standing with a count of heavy foot about equal to his own. Advancing in what was probably a 3,000-man classical phalanx filed at a maneuverable minimum of six-deep and with some 300 light infantrymen plus 200 horse off each wing, the Sardinian rebels quickly found themselves enveloped and overwhelmed by a much deeper acies triplex not only arrayed at twice their width but with outboard support from half-again more mounted troops as well as better than six times as many foot-skirmishers. The 200 or so of Hiostus' men that managed to flee the ensuing debacle must have been almost exclusively horsemen and light infantry while nearly all of the hoplites either surrendered or met death along with their young commander.

Aid for the rebellion came from Carthage shortly thereafter in the form of Hasdrubal "The Bald" with what likely was 6,000 African heavy and 2,000 light infantry.[54] These joined with Hampsicora and his men from outside the Cornus region for a march on the Roman camp near Carales. The combined Carthaginian force of perhaps 20,000 combatants would have deployed a Doric phalanx of 12,000 hoplite-style spearmen comprised of 6,000 Africans under Hasdrubal on the right wing and the same number of Sardinian colonials with Hampsicora on the left, all probably filed at a depth of ten across a 1,200m front. Split on the flanks of that line were some 6,800 tribesmen and light foot with 1,200 or so Punic and tribal horsemen farthest outboard off each side. Advancing to meet this threat at a distance, Manlius perhaps had much the same army as at Cornus, which let him not only deploy around 9,000 heavy infantry at 2m spacing in acies triplex over the same frontage as that of the Carthaginian phalanx, but also throw 6,000–8,000 velites and armed crewmen onto his wings to offset Hasdrubal's tribal spearmen and other skirmishers as well as provide critical support to his riders in their efforts to keep the larger enemy cavalry contingent at bay.

Should the foregoing projections on forces engaged at Carales be reasonably accurate, the tactical details that Livy offers provide useful insights on the practicalities of legion versus phalanx warfare.[55] More lightly equipped troops flanking the heavy arrays were well-matched and came to no conclusion throughout the engagement; thus, the decision fell entirely to their better-armed comrades along the main line of battle. But the dynamics there were those of stalemate. The Carthaginian phalanx lacked adequate flexibility to force itself onto more agile foes, while Rome's swordsmen had ample freedom of movement within wider spacing to dance away from spear thrusts, making the choice of accepting close engagement entirely theirs. But whenever they did take that risk, the opposition made them pay dearly. Carthage's hoplites not only had stout individual defensive gear and stood behind a cooperative front of overlapping shields, but they also wielded longer-reaching weapons at half the lateral separation from two ranks deep with the resulting 4-to-1 edge in strike frequency letting them deal out much the greater share of damage inflicted in the ensuing shock-fights.

With neither side able to promptly impose its will on the other, Carales became a drawn-out affair that lasted an astounding four hours if we are to believe Livy. The habitually cavalry-poor legions with their relatively weaker species of light foot could normally expect to fall victim under such conditions to an envelopment by superior enemy mobile troops. The best past examples of this come from Pyrrhus' first two Roman battles. At Heraclea in 280, though the Epirote's phalanx also endured a lengthy impasse, his mounted forces still finally turned a Roman flank. However, despite winning a year later at Asculum in similar fashion, things almost went against him there when the decisive envelopment took so long that legionaries had time to break through a vulnerable phalanx contingent and very nearly carry the field. And what came close to bringing down Pyrrhus at Asculum seems to have been Hasdrubal's undoing here. This saw the Romans, after hours of costly sacrifice, close at last into his less capable Sardinians and put their wing to rout. With those colonials fleeing in terror, Manlius' swordsmen swarmed against the still resisting Africans' now exposed left flank and swiftly broke them as well. Some 2,000 of Carthage's troops were killed, maybe three-quarters of them on an enclosed right wing that likely also yielded most of the reported 3,700 prisoners, including Hasdrubal himself. Rome's losses are not recorded but must have been fairly high with those slain perhaps topping 1,000. As for Hampsicora, while he survived Carales, the loss of both the rebellion and his son was too much to endure and he took his own life.

Dertosa/Ibera, Iliturgi and Intibili (215)

The other area where Rome managed to somewhat offset Hannibal's triumphs on the home front was in Iberia. Hasdrubal Barca had been waiting there for a fresh army from Africa to take over his current duties safeguarding Punic interests in the west so that he and his men could join his brother's campaign in Italy. But when those replacements finally arrived in spring 215, Publius and Gnaeus Scipio set out to keep him occupied on the far side of the Alps by crossing over the Ebro to menace the town of Ibera. Preparing for his departure nearby, Hasdrubal responded as the Romans had hoped by mounting a threat of his own against Dertosa on the Roman (north) side of the river.

Drawing upon Polybius' report of troops left with Hasdrubal in 218 and Livy's claims on the double consular army of the Scipios along with his description on events here, we can make some reasonable projections of the forces present on either side. Hasdrubal's army was around 22,300-strong with some 19,800 foot-soldiers (5,000 Punic colonial and 5,000 Libyan heavy spearmen, 6,000 Iberian scutarii, 3,000 Iberian caetrati, and 800 slingers) plus 2,500 horsemen (Iberian, Punic, Libyan, and Numidian contingents) and 20 or so elephants. And there were about the same number of men with the Scipios having 12,000 heavy infantry (4,800 hastati, 4,800 princepes, and 2,400 triarii), 10,400 light foot (4,800 velites and 5,600 other allies), and 2,200 horsemen (600 Roman and 1,600 allied) for a total of some 22,400.[56]

After observing each other for several days, both armies arrayed for battle. Hasdrubal's phalanx resembled a smaller scale version of the compound one deployed by his sibling at Cannae with the scutarii standing in close/defensive order in the middle and having wings of heavy spearmen on each flank, Carthaginian colonials to the right and Libyans on the left. His elephants, cavalry, and light infantry took post outboard of the hoplites with the Numidians and their screen of skirmishers alongside the colonial foot and the other horsemen and auxiliaries next to the Libyans. This varied most significantly from what Hannibal did at Cannae in the lack of any attempt by Hasdrubal to strengthen his centrally placed swordsmen by arraying them in the sort of projecting wedge that had worked so well in that previous engagement. Across on the other side of the field, the Scipios set up their heavy foot in acies triplex ("in triple line" per Livy) with cavalry and supporting light foot on either flank; however, they gave this otherwise standard Roman arrangement an unusual twist in standing half of their velites at three-deep in the 1m gaps between hastati files at the head of their formation. Both heavy arrays would thus have covered fronts around 1,200m wide when they closed into action.

There are a number of issues with our lone account of the ensuing battle from Livy, who appears to have incorporated a number of highly improbable elements from pro-Roman sources into his narrative. What seems fairly certain is that the competing approaches that Hannibal and Varo had employed at Cannae remained operational among their countrymen at this later date. Hasdrubal clearly meant to carry out another double envelopment with his spear-armed wings while the Romans were again looking to cut the opposing formation in two by breaking through its more vulnerable center—and both tactics had some success. Despite Livy's claim of Roman mounted superiority, Hasdrubal's uncountered elephants, well-regarded cavalry, and better-equipped light foot must have cleared the way on either side of the front if Hasdrubal's spearmen rolled around both ends of the Scipios' infantry as attested. Yet at the same time, the hastati, not being delayed by the kind of "crescent-shaped" formation extension encountered at Cannae, were able to rapidly penetrate and chase Carthage's swordsmen in the middle of the field. This must have been further accelerated by a preceding barrage of javelins of exceptional proportions due to contributions from the velites intermingled along the Roman front, with those same light footmen then setting out in pursuit of the fleeing Iberians while their heavier-armed comrades attempted to wheel outward and envelop the enemy's newly created and completely exposed inner flanks.

Livy's version of what happened at this point is extremely improbable, saying that the two armies reordered on the fly to fight a double-sided engagement with the Romans transforming their flanks into fronts and literally wiping out twin heavy infantry arrays likewise spontaneously rotated through 90-degrees against them. The logistics required to do this seem impractical at a level approaching impossibility and, even had they somehow been engineered, any realistic prospect of Roman success under such daunting conditions looks no more plausible. What then might actually have happened? A rather more likely scenario would have both armies reeling from their exchange of victories on different parts of the field and scrambling to reform for another go at each other. This resembles a number of well-documented actions in which opposing phalanxes gained simultaneous successes on opposite flanks.[57] And here, as often in those cases, one of the participants decided to withdraw. Hasdrubal had already suffered the rout of his Iberians as well as serious losses to his spearmen in separating from legionaries better suited for that chaotic melee's individual combats; he therefore elected to take advantage of cover from his dominant mobile forces and retreat to friendlier territory on the other side of the Ebro. The Scipios would surely have been content with that, not only claiming a politically valuable tactical triumph, but also having significantly postponed any attempt by Hasdrubal to merge his army with that of his brother in Italy.

This less impressive take on Dertosa/Ibera finds support in the following engagement nearby at Iliturgi. Hasdrubal had laid siege to that town with what Livy claims was 60,000 men[58] forming three separate armies: (1) the one bested by the Scipios under Hasdrubal; (2) the reinforcements that had arrived that spring now led by Hamilcar son of Bomilcar; and (3) a force of recent Iberian hires and troops brought from Africa by Mago Barca. The last included 12,000 foot diverted from intended Italian duty (perhaps as many as 9,000 with heavy arms), 1,500 cavalry, and 20 elephants. Mago must also have contracted some 6,000 Iberians (maybe 4,000 scutarii and 2,000 caetrati) in boosting his strength to nearly 20,000. And Hamilcar's Iberian defense force would have been of a similar size, being equivalent to the army previously assigned to that same task under Hasdrubal. This all indicates that Hasdrubal still personally led 20,000 or so troops should the 60,000 total be anywhere near correct, serving as a strong rebuttal to the claim of his earlier near-annihilation.[59]

Livy's summary of the battle at Iliturgi is even less creditable than his tale about Dertosa/Ibera, asserting that a Roman army of only 16,000 defeated four times that number while inflicting more than 27 percent casualties and taking another 5 percent prisoner. Evaluating this action and one cited thereafter in the same general area at Intibili in which Livy says his countrymen killed 13,000 Carthaginians and captured 2,000 more,[60] Lazenby has come to the judgement that "we can, surely, not accept the details of Carthaginian losses."[61] While perhaps not entirely fictional events, these actions (and others of their ilk reported for 213—see below) abound in gross exaggerations regarding the magnitude of Roman success. All the same, the Scipios must have achieved some at least minor positive results to inspire such stories, likely breaking up a series of modest Carthaginian investments rather than actually winning major set-piece battles. More importantly, their aggressive activities (along with a continual state of unrest among many Iberian tribal factions) served Rome well at the strategic level in keeping much needed Iberian resources from flowing across the Alps.

Calor R. and Nola III (214)

The next year saw the war in Italy continue at no more than moderate pace with only one really significant battle being fought. This was a rather unusual action that played out along the Calor River near Beneventum (Maleventum) between the Carthaginian Hanno with an 18,200-man army and a force from Rome that included some 8,000 slaves (two legions of foot) that had been inducted immediately after Cannae plus what was probably the same number of legionary regulars and/or like-equipped allies. The latter host, perhaps some 20,000-strong per its apparent four-legion/ala composition and subsequent casualties, advanced eagerly to engage under Tiberius Sempronius Gracchus, who had promised freedom to any of his slave contingent able to deliver the head of an enemy soldier.

Hanno's 17,000 infantrymen were mostly allied Bruttians and Lucanians (including maybe 10,000 heavier theurophoros spearmen) with only a small contingent of Carthaginians (perhaps a single division of 3,000 hoplites), though the majority of his 1,200 horsemen were African (Numidians and Moors). The Italian allies were likely divided between the wings in close order at ten-deep with the Carthaginians thinned to half that depth at center in order to extend their entire line along a 1,600m front matching that of the enemy's acies triplex. The cavalry and light foot for both armies must have been spread off either wing with those of the Romans having a quantitative edge but being inferior in quality.

Much as at Carales a year earlier, this engagement is said to have featured well matched light-armed forces off the flanks that were unable to deliver a decision for either army. This led to another lengthy slugging match inboard between the competing heavy-armed arrays. Though longer/denser weaponed with superior protection from more closely aligned shields, the hoplites in the middle of Carthage's line finally had to give way out of sheer exhaustion against deeper-filed foes able to rotate fresh princepes into the front when their hastati tired and then put those men back into the fight once their replacements in turn grew weary. And as soon as the Carthaginians broke, the tribesmen on either flank took to their heels as well, sending Hanno's whole army into frantic rearward flight. This immediately transformed the hoplites' restrictive panoply from a combat advantage into a deadly burden as agile legionaries having rather less specialized gear pursued, caught, and cut them down from behind. Livy records that only about 2,000 of the defeated men managed to escape death or capture with many of those more fortunate individuals, like Hanno himself, being horsemen. That costly tally probably only applies to the Carthaginians present, since quite a few of the tribesmen must have been able to get away as well; yet, even if so limited, around half of Hanno's hard-to-replace Punic troops were lost including over 60 percent of his heavy infantry. Gracchus' losses are put at a quite realistic 2,000 (10 percent) to mark a hard-fought Roman victory.

The only other engagement of any note during 215 was yet another rerun of past events at Nola, where a Carthaginian siege attempt was again foiled by a Roman sally. Marcellus was there with a contingent of 6,000 foot and 300 cavalry (apparently a single legion with some 1,800 or so additional skirmishers attached) which he had reinforced with more troops from his base camp nearby in the hills on the edge of the Campanian plain.[62] (These additions might represent an ala sociorum that doubled his strength, but more likely fell short of that.) Marcellus' plan was to send out most of his horsemen via a backside exit so that they could come around and strike the investment from behind while he made a frontal attack with infantry from the main gate; however, his riders missed the fight due either to becoming lost or (most probably) having been dispatched too late to complete their assignment in time. Nonetheless, Marcellus still managed to take the besiegers by surprise and chase them away, though his lack of mounted support precluded pursuit. Roman claims of having killed more than 2,000 of those in flight at a cost of only 400 are therefore very questionable (Livy himself attaching the qualification "are said" to those assertions) and we are probably looking at no more than a limited tactical success against rather modest enemy assets.

Hannibal had made no progress by year's end toward forcing Rome to capitulate, having neither inflicted further combat damage of consequence toward discouraging its citizens from further resistance nor adequately cut outside resources through detachment of their allies. The war in Italy thus began to devolve into a series of contests for control of key cities with both sides leery of engaging each other without having some strong advantage in hand (Hannibal husbanding imported manpower and the Romans seeking to avoid his tactical wizardry while battling rebellious native populations). Iberia had been relatively calm after Dertosa/Ibera, but the Scipios were still able as a force-in-being to keep Hasdrubal from transferring resources to his brother's all-important Italian campaign. This general strategic stasis would extend into the next year with no battles of import between the principles in Italy and those few accounts we have of combats in Iberia looking very much like pro–Roman inventions.[63] Still, 213 did see one significant train of events set into motion on Sicily, where Syracuse elected to ally with Carthage against Rome and came under what would prove to be a truly epic siege.

Lucania and Herdonea I (212)

Back-and-forth dueling around targeted Italian cities either allied to or against Rome continued in the new year, with most of the action involving Hannibal's troops being minor melees between ancillary forces. Yet even such peripheral skirmishing could turn serious, doing so several times in 212. These included Roman forces taking a camp in Samnium near Beneventum while its commander (Hanno) and most of his men were absent. The Carthaginians profited in turn against a Roman garrison caught in the open near Thurium (that town and others in Italy's far south having joined Hannibal) and in a couple of clashes just south of Rome at Capua in Campania.[64] The latter city had come under siege by the Romans and sallied both Punic horsemen and its own riders to kill some 2,000 of the enemy. Hannibal came to Capua's support shortly thereafter; however, he failed to force a battle when the Romans timidly withdrew, first to their camps and then altogether. Still, they did not get away unbloodied as the Carthaginian cavalry had punished their initial flight from the field.

The Romans retreated from Capua in two columns, Hannibal following one of them toward the front-instep of the Italian boot into Lucania intent on bringing it to action. He was confronted there by the former centurion Marcus Centenius. Centenius had gained an appointment as general and led an 8,000-man force composed half of Roman troops and half of allies (essentially equivalent to a legion/ala pair), which he had strengthened on the march by adding volunteers.[65] Livy claims that this make-shift host was "for the most part tumultuary and half-armed" (perhaps all having shields with sword or spear but most lacking armor) and might have had just a few hundred horsemen at best. That would have ceded overwhelming numerical superiority to Hannibal, whose army likely numbered some 27,000 combatants with 15,000 heavy infantry (maybe 11,000 African-style spearmen plus 4,000 scutarius swordsmen), 2,000 Gallic medium infantry, 6,000 light foot (2,000 Iberian caetrati and the rest hired missilemen including 750 or so attached to at least 15 elephants), and 4,000 horsemen (squarely divided between Iberians and riders from Africa).[66] It was therefore an act of suicidal bravado when Centenius lined his men up and engaged the Carthaginian phalanx in pitched battle. Despite Livy's claim that Centenius' troops put up a long and spirited resistance before he fell fighting, the actual combat must have been brief. Hannibal's horsemen encircled the rapidly disintegrating Roman line and barely 1,000 of those enclosed survived the ensuing slaughter.

Straight away after this walkover victory, Hannibal marched north and east to take on a more substantial Roman army in Apulia. The praetor Gneius Fulvius Flaccus was there at Herdonea (Ordona) with two legions and a pair of alae sociorum coming to 18,000 overall though apparently understrength in cavalry.[67] Seeing opportunity in this, Hannibal challenged him with the still almost completely intact host of veterans used to overrun Centenius' little command. Fulvius' troops, having enjoyed success in their operations, seem to have been unduly confident about being able to handle anything their foes might throw at them. Given what had just happened to the similarly incautious Centenius, this was a dangerous attitude; but whether sharing it or not, Fulvius let his men's enthusiasm influence his decision to march out the next day and engage the approaching Carthaginians on open ground. Also anticipating a fight in the morning, Hannibal had camped not too far away. Livy indicates that he was aware of a state of poor discipline within the opposing camp,[68] and that plus the observed shortage of opposition horse would inspire him to plan a more aggressive approach than in the past, when he had for the most part counterpunched attacking Roman arrays from a defensive posture. He looked to surprise as well as a way to gain an edge, hiding 3,000 foot-skirmishers under cover of darkness for a possible ambush. Hannibal was so confident of victory in all of this that he then withheld half of his cavalry from the coming action, distributing it before dawn along all routes leading out of the vicinity to keep the Romans from escaping once beaten.

When the armies emerged and took position at daybreak, Livy tells us the Romans lacked good order with units that "came up as chance directed and took their positions just as they pleased" rather than in a proper lateral scheme. Still, there seems to have been an effort to match fronts with the phalanx across the way. Hannibal must have deployed at ten-deep as usual with heavy spearmen on the wings; however, his compound formation was geared toward offense this time, having the Gauls and Iberian scutarii at center in attack mode requiring 2m spacing. His front thus would have spanned some 2,300m and extended beyond either end of Fulvius' acies triplex if at standard depth. The praetor was therefore forced to set up shallower in order to avoid that dangerous overlap, the result being that his "line was extended to great length" but "there was no strength in it."[69] Added to general indiscipline, this proved fatal when the formations then closed and "the Romans did not so much as sustain their shout and first attack." Not only did Fulvius' overly thin line break almost at once under intense frontal pressure from Punic spears and blades, but his anemic mounted screens outboard did no better as the enemy's elephants, horsemen, and light foot swept them aside to loop onto the Roman rear even as their heavy foot folded in to envelop both flanks.

His victory at Herdonea was so rapid and complete that Hannibal never got a chance to employ the ambush he had taken the trouble to prepare. Livy says that the Roman troops, "beaten in front and surrounded on the flank and rear, were slaughtered to such a degree that out of eighteen thousand men, not more than two thousand escaped." It seems that Fulvius and 200 horsemen had run at the first sign of trouble to count among the latter. Rome once more went into a panic when news arrived of this brutal defeat on top of the disaster in Lucania just a few days earlier; thus, Hannibal ended the year with a pair of triumphs that very much echoed Cannae in their negative impact on enemy morale.

Himera R. II[70] and Castulo (211)

Hannibal's latest tactical successes had put nearly all of southern Italy under his control; still, there was no sign of a Roman capitulation. Indeed, Capua once more came under attack and Marcus Claudius Marcellus was able to capture Syracuse in late 212 and thereby seriously damage prospects to funnel supplies from Africa for the Italian front via Sicily. But all was not yet lost on the island as a Punic host remained in place at Agrigentum along the southern coast. This boasted some 25,000 foot, 3,000 cavalry, and 12 elephants plus perhaps 800 Syracusan horseman stranded by their city's fall.[71] It was yet another Carthaginian named Hanno that led that force assisted by a Syracusan, Epicydes, and Mutines, a capable veteran sent by Hannibal to take charge of the army's Numidian horse and provide tactical guidance. Serving in the latter capacity, Mutines persuaded Hanno in early 211 to take a position toward Syracuse just west of the Himera River; and when the Romans came out and set up on the far bank, his mounted attacks forced them to shelter inside their encampment. However, Mutines then had to go after a party of Numidians who had deserted and, despite his sound advice otherwise, Hanno and Epicydes elected to do battle in his absence.

Marcellus had employed at least three and likely four legions along with their associated allied contingents in the siege of Syracuse.[72] His attack force on the Himera therefore probably included a trio of legion/ala pairs with the remaining troops staying behind on garrison duty sans cavalry. That would have given him a nominal total of 25,200 foot and possibly up to 4,800 horse to match or exceed the Punic counts in those arms.[73] Vital to the willingness of both sides to openly engage was that the balance of heavy infantry must have been close with deployments around 18,000-strong of legionary swordsmen for Rome and African spearmen for Carthage. Hanno and Epicydes could well have been somewhat disadvantaged in cavalry strength had Marcellus been at full allotments for four legions; however, even if so, Mutines' recent mounted success would suggest that Carthage's riders were of such higher quality as to overcome any Roman edge in numbers. Yet it was those same horsemen whose superiority Hanno and Epicydes were banking upon that then betrayed them, the Numidians approaching Marcellus just prior to battle with a pledge not to fight. And stripped of the best of their cavalry, the Carthaginians' classical phalanx then quickly went down to defeat as "the first shout and onset determined the business" with thousands reported slain or captured during the subsequent flight along with eight elephants taken alive.[74]

But as well as things had gone for Rome on Sicily, the story was dramatically different in Iberia. The Scipio brothers there had spent a couple of years consolidating their gains above the Ebro following the victory at Dertosa/Ibera before crossing south of the river into Punic territory during the 212 campaign season and recapturing Saguntum where the war had first ignited. The following spring, they hired some 20,000 Celtiberians for an offensive against the three Punic armies of roughly 20,000 men each that were still active in the Iberian west.[75] Marching into south-central Iberia, the Scipios split up. Publius led two-thirds of the original Roman force against Mago Barca and Hasdrubal (son of Gisco), his manpower counting half the legionaries on hand (a legion and ala totaling over 8,000 men) with some 5,000–6,000 irregular skirmishers plus all the Italian allied and Roman cavalry at around 2,000 for 16,000 combatants.[76] Gnaeus remained camped near Hasdrubal Barca, having the other legion/ala pair plus the new Celtiberian hirelings (likely 12,000 scutarii, 6,000 caetrati, and 2,000 horsemen) to complete a force better than 28,000-strong.

Seeing that his immediate opposition mainly consisted of Iberians prone to pursuing their own interests above nearly all other concerns, Hasdrubal waited until Publius and his troops were well removed and then made a counter employment offer to the tribesmen that saw them accept and march home to leave their former employer in the lurch. Now being badly outnumbered as well as blocked from reuniting with his brother, Gnaeus chose to retreat with the Carthaginians in close pursuit. Publius was at the same time having troubles of his own near the town of Castulo along the Upper Baetis River. Perhaps initially intent on carrying out a diversionary action that would allow Gnaeus to confront Hasdrubal Barca without interference, he found himself bedeviled by Numidia's Masinissa with 3,000 of his nation's light horsemen, these being attached to that prince's prospective father-in-law, Hasdrubal Gisco. Publius then learned that the Iberian chief Indibilis of the Ilergetes was bringing 7,500 men to support the Carthaginians.[77] Looking to avoid detection by Masinissa, he took the unusual tack of setting out at night to let his own vanguard (extraordinarii) skirmish against that of the Iberians in a bid to turn them back before they could join his foes.

Publius' stratagem turned against him when the fighting dragged on until Masinissa's riders joined the fray the next day, harassing the flanks of the Romans, who were still in order of march. And then disaster struck as H. Gisco and Mago came up at full strength from behind to force a pitched battle at dreadful odds. The combined Punic host likely numbered about 40,000 with maybe 21,000 heavy spearmen, 8,000 scutarii, and 7,000 light foot (including 4,000 caetrati) plus 1,500 horsemen as well as Masinissa's men and 35–40 elephants. Adding in Indibilis' contingent gave the Carthaginians at least a 3-to-1 edge in manpower overall and nearly 5-to-1 in compounded heavy foot. This would have let them engage a normally deployed acies triplex using a phalanx that was significantly wider with twice the spacing density and depth of file while enjoying support off each flank from vastly superior cavalry and light infantry led by 15–20 elephants. And those advantages plus contributions from the Numidians and Iberians still lurking on all other sides turned the engagement into a massacre. Publius Scipio died on the spot along with many of his men while those Romans forming a modest majority that did manage to flee were cut down in equal number by pursuit.

As terrible as was its defeat at Castulo, the bad news out of Iberia for Rome did not end there as the army of Gnaeus Scipio was shortly thereafter run down and destroyed as well. Hasdrubal Barca had been chasing close behind Gnaeus and his men with a much stronger force that was then joined by the victorious troops of his brother Mago and H. Gisco. With around 60,000 combatants against less than 10,000 Romans, the latter would have had no chance in a stand-up fight. Yet, Gnaeus couldn't get clear and Masinissa's Numidians brought his retreat to a halt near Ilorcum (Illorci) in the countryside above Cartago Novo. The Romans occupied a nearby hilltop under cover of darkness and piled packs and saddles around the perimeter for a last stand. But that make-shift barrier showed woefully inadequate next day when massive Punic forces quickly overran it to kill Gnaeus and most of his command as but a few legionaries escaped by slipping into the surrounding forest.[78]

Hannibal had proven tactically brilliant, being responsible in half a dozen victories for 90 percent of the 40 legions/alae defeated by Carthage's phalanxes and their auxiliaries. Still, all those heavy blows and unprecedented casualties had not driven the Romans to their knees. It must have been growing ever clearer to Carthaginian leadership that there was a vast difference between merely winning battles versus winning a lengthy war against so vibrant and populous a foe. Indeed, the most recent round of Punic triumphs had taken a full five legions and an even larger number of attached allies out of the fight yet failed to incapacitate a nation that could simultaneously field as many as 25 legions without exhausting its manpower.[79] And those immense resources were slowly but surely wrecking Hannibal's strategic plan as Rome captured one after another of his hard-won local allies, Capua falling by year's end 211 to reduce him to only a handful of remaining bases in Italy. Without resupply from Iberia or Africa and increasingly bereft of Italian manpower, he was being forced onto the defensive in preserving an irreplaceable pool of imported troops. Hannibal's ambitious campaign of conquest had now turned into a more modest one of delay and survival.

6. The Road to Zama
The Second Punic War, Phase 2 (210–202 BCE)

The Second Punic War was at a crossroads going into 210 with the Carthaginians facing a difficult choice. One option was to withdraw from Italy, abandoning an operation clearly failing in its strategic aim despite great combat success. Advantageous peace terms might then be negotiated from a position of relative strength based upon both recent victories in the field and concentration of all resources on defense under the guidance of Hannibal's tactical genius. The alternative was to keep fighting on enemy soil in hope that that very same genius could somehow overcome stubborn Roman resistance and deliver a more complete victory. Whether either of those favorable outcomes was realistic for Carthage in light of manifest Roman determination and belligerence is highly debatable; nevertheless, defeat of the Scipios had improved prospects for reinforcing Hannibal from Iberia and that was probably what ultimately inspired a decision to continue the Italian campaign.

Italy and Iberia, 210–205

Herdonia II and Numistro (210)

Hannibal made a forced march from Bruttia to relieve one of his few remaining bases in central Italy at Herdonea, which was on the verge of surrendering to the proconsul Gnaeus Fulvius Flaccus. Taken unaware but reluctant to pass up a chance to bleed the Carthaginians of hard-to-replace strength, Fulvius deployed his four legions/alae in what must have been standard 15-man files and 2m spacing. He could thus equal the width of the enemy front, which would have had heavy spearmen on either wing of a 15,000-man compound phalanx standing at 1m apart and ten-deep.[1] These well-matched arrays then fought to a stand-still; however, though having "preserved their ranks and stood their ground ... after many ... had fallen in the close contest,"[2] the legionaries suffered failures of the mounted forces screening both ends of their line. Hannibal held the edge there, where his 4,000 or so riders and a few elephants faced only 2,400 Romans at best. The latter now gave way on either flank, freeing the Punic cavalry contingent on one side to ride toward Fulvius' camp even as its counterpart on the other curled in upon his after-ranks.[3] Destruction rippled down the legionary line with those distant from the envelopment fleeing even as their commander and comrades on the near wing were enclosed and cut down. Livy's sources gave

Roman losses running from 7,000 up to 13,000, and Appian cites 8,000 killed (42 percent) consistent with the sort of heavy defeat described.[4]

Shortly after this second victory at Herdonia, Hannibal faced yet another Roman army in Lucania willing to fight, this time at Numistro. The consul Marcus Claudius Marcellus challenged him there with four legions/alae arrayed for battle despite the Carthaginians holding a strong hilltop position. Accounts of the ensuing engagement suggest that only a portion of either army actually came to action as one of Marcellus' legions and its attached ala tackled Hannibal's Iberians, who were backed by slingers and had help of some unspecified sort from elephants. Rather than a pitched battle, this seems to have been a light-armed skirmish with Marcellus' velites charging upslope in front of a bastion of legionaries, hurling their javelins, and then running back down, possibly covering beneath small shields (parma) recently introduced yet otherwise suffering a deadly rain of missiles coming over the enemy's barricade of scutarius shields above. Marcellus rotated in fresh troops as the strength and/or ammunition of his attackers gave out, but darkness fell after three hours to bring the effort to a close.[5]

Hannibal was clearly reluctant to descend onto the plain and expose his valuable heavy infantry to anything like an equal match, while Marcellus had no intention of fighting upslope at great disadvantage. The next day thus saw both refuse battle on the other's terms. Hannibal slipped away that night and made good his escape, thereby preserving strength for a future opportunity more to his liking. Still, the sort of victories he might now deliver (like Herdonea II) would not win the war even as the demands of self-preservation made obvious at Numistro severely limited his ability to save local allies from succumbing to Rome one by one.

Canusium and Novo Cartago (209)

The following spring, the new consul Quintus Fabius Maximus instituted a siege of one of Carthage's Italian allies at Tarentum, detailing Marcellus to keep Hannibal from coming to the city's rescue. Marcellus made contact in Apulia near Canusium with the Carthaginian, who again sought to avoid a battle that might endanger troops he would need in the future. But Marcellus kept up pressure and finally forced an engagement late in the day when Hannibal was setting up camp for the night. Having taken little harm at Herdonia II and since, the Punic army was probably around 25,000-strong with some 14,000 heavy infantry (10,000–11,000 hoplites and 3,000–4,000 scutarii), 7,000–8,000 light foot, 3,000–4,000 horsemen, and maybe a dozen or so elephants. It seems that the terrain leading to Hannibal's campsite must have constrained Marcellus' deployment in some fashion as he had to post his two legion/ala pairs with one behind the other. This created a roughly 800m-wide front that Hannibal could match with a Doric phalanx having its spearmen fronting at the usual 1m apart but in deep files of twelve or more. That let him hold all of his scutarii in reserve. However, the engagement began at so late an hour that darkness put an end to fighting with nothing resolved.

Action resumed the next morning as the same troop dispositions ground on with neither legion nor phalanx able to frontally penetrate its opposite number. Since this combat unfolded in a laterally confined setting, Hannibal's elephants and horsemen couldn't execute his favored tactic of envelopment; yet, his spearmen were still able to inflict much the greater share of damage on wider-spaced foes whose weapons had lesser reach. Adding to this offensive shortcoming for Marcellus' legionaries was that the tight battlespace with crowding from a mass of men in the rear made it nearly impossible for those at the front to dance back from spear-thrusts as in past shock fights with hoplites. In consequence, Marcellus eventually saw that the ala on his right was so hard-pressed as to be in danger of giving way and he tried to relieve those men by moving up the unengaged legion standing idle to their rear.

Marcellus perhaps believed what he was doing ran akin to how he had rotated fresh troops into the front a year before at Numistro. But that long-distance missile skirmish was profoundly different from the present face-to-face shock fight. As a result, this maneuver only served to throw his own troops into confusion, which Hannibal's spearmen rapidly exploited to break the affected wing and then run the rest of the Roman army off the field. The Romans suffered a reported 2,700 killed (14 percent) and that kind of significant damage seems unlikely to have come from pursuit due to the Punic mobile forces being stuck behind their intact phalanx and the covering capability of similarly rear-located velites that were now better equipped with shields (*parmae*). This suggests Marcellus' casualties more likely reflect losses among his legionaries during the initial front-fighting, when perhaps as many as 20 percent went down before the rout had even begun.[6] All the same, their sacrifice would serve its purpose, as Hannibal was now unable to relieve Tarentum before it fell to Fabius.

There was a fateful development outside Italy at this time with assignment of Publius Cornelius Scipio (later titled Africanus) to replace his slain father and uncle. Rome supplied this talented 24-year-old with fresh troops counting some 20,000 foot and 2,000 horse, which he added to around 8,000 infantry and 1,000 cavalry still present in Iberia.[7] Avoiding the Carthaginian armies active in the region that had more than twice his strength, Scipio descended suddenly on Novo Cartago. He bested a sortie by some 2,000 defenders[8] and an assault from both land and sea let him take the city within four days. Scipio then spent the next year adding allies and rigorously drilling in preparation for going on the offensive.

Petelia H., Epizephyrian Locri and Baecula (208)

Though Hannibal had lost Tarentum, he still retained a base nearby at Epizephyrian Locri. That city on the underside of the Italian toe soon became the target of both a Roman landing force from Sicily and what was probably a legion/ala pair out of Tarentum representing half of the garrison there. Informed of this, Hannibal sent out 2,000 foot (presumably Iberians) and 3,000 horsemen to ambush the overland party. These hid on the small hill of Petelia along that column's route and charged down to take it completely unprepared. Caught strung out in line of march, nearly 50 percent of the quickly routed Romans fell victim as 2,500 died either on the spot or in flight and almost as many were taken prisoner.[9] Bad as this was for Rome, its luck soon took an even worse turn when both current consuls, Marcellus and Quinctius Crispinus, were killed in another hillside ambuscade while making a mounted reconnaissance of Hannibal's position outside Venusia in Apulia.[10]

Nonetheless, the seaborne assault on Locri continued despite these setbacks ashore as one of the praetors in charge on Sicily, Lucius Cincius, landed troops and siege-engines to envelop the place. Based upon an apparent strength of 100 ships in his fleet (presumably the quinquereme count),[11] Cincius could have transported two legions-worth of infantry along with better than thirty loads of equipment in a single passage, which was more than enough resources to keep the garrison penned up behind its walls. Hannibal marched to the city's relief and sent a contingent of Numidian cavalry ahead to speed the effort. Alerted that these horsemen were drawing near, Mago, the local Punic commander, charged out with what must have been several thousand men.[12] Cincius' troops put up a brief fight, but then abandoned the siege and escaped on their ships when the Numidians arrived, no doubt doing so less due to the mounted threat than in mistaken belief that Hannibal was following close behind with a large force of foot.

Nothing more of note transpired in Italy that year as the war remained in stalemate; however, things were moving in Rome's favor elsewhere. This included damaging raids by Roman ships upon the African coast as well as a major tactical success on the ground in Iberia. The last saw young Scipio take advantage of several opposition armies being spread out to engage one of them in isolation.[13] This involved him marching to Baecula in south-central Iberia to challenge Hasdrubal Barca's host of perhaps 25,000 men built upon the 9,000 hoplites, 7,500 Iberians (5,000 scutarii and 2,500 caetrati), 1,000 other foot-skirmishers, 2,500 cavalry, and at least 15 elephants that he had led against Gnaeus Scipio three years prior with the likely addition of another division of 3,000 colonial spearmen and 2,000 others (maybe 1,500 foot and 500 horse) that might have been Iberian for the most part if not entirely.[14] Scipio could deploy four legions/alae that had been reinforced by drafting men from the fleet and also had a good many new local allies to give him more than 35,000 combatants and possibly as many as 40,000.[15] He thus enjoyed a significant edge in manpower; however, the terrain threatened to render that moot since his foe had taken a highly favorable position on top of a broad plateau.

Scipio pondered this tactical challenge for two days, hoping in vain that Hasdrubal might agree to fight on the flat. Concerned that any further delay risked additional enemy forces descending upon him, he appears to have drawn from past Roman success over a Punic army atop a mesa for a way to tackle this somewhat similar situation. That action in 255 (see Chapter 3 re: *Adys*) had involved Regulus diverting the enemy's attention with a frontal demonstration that let him swing a legion around one end of the ridge to introduce a surprise element into a decisive attack on its less well-defended rear slope. Scipio's variant here had him open battle much as Marcellus had done at Numistro by establishing a thin bastion of picked heavy foot at the base of the plateau and sending a portion of his velites up to duel with Numidians and slingers on its fore-rise. Committing the rest of his skirmishers to further hold the focus of Hasdrubal's phalanx ranked across the highland's crest, Scipio than divided his legionary contingents to climb what are said to have been unguarded inclines at either end of the upland. Hasdrubal was suddenly under simultaneous attack from three directions and he wisely broke off action, somehow managing to successfully withdraw both baggage train and the bulk of his army down the plateau's still open backside.

Our sources report that Hasdrubal took steep losses in getting away, Polybius claiming that 8,000 of his men died and Livy that more than 12,000 fell captive. Yet it seems clear that most of his command not only survived, but continued to be dangerous as well; certainly, Scipio's refusal to give chase implies as much, reflecting fear that those in flight remained sufficiently potent to turn about and pin him against one or both of the other Carthaginian armies present in the region. This plus the astonishing nature of Hasdrubal's escape from near-encirclement has led to skepticism concerning Polybius' and Livy's numbers.[16] Yet these figures could actually have some bases in reality.

Walbank has noted that Livy's claim for captives is "probably exaggerated" and that Polybius' count is "plausible only as a combined figure for dead and prisoners," while Bagnall opines that "a large number of [those captured] were Spaniards wishing to desert rather than escape" and notes that "all of them were later released without ransom after the tribal chiefs had assembled to offer their submission."[17] As such, Livy's prisoners are a good match for the probable number of Iberians with Hasdrubal and 8,000 of them might well have been captured/killed to influence Polybius' death toll. Rather than ignoring flank security, Hasdrubal more likely posted the Iberians to that task, selecting them for the same reason their ilk got a similar assignment at Adys: it was thought an easier chore suitable for less capable soldiers. And dimensions of the battleground are compatible with just such dispositions in that Hasdrubal had to protect a front only some 1,200m wide.[18] That is something he could (and would) have done with his hoplites alone filed in a classical phalanx at their standard depth of ten shields, thereby freeing all his scutarii for duty on either lateral.

It was the resistance of these Iberians and the light-armed men below-forward that then allowed Hasdrubal to make a relatively uncontested withdrawal. His troops had no doubt drilled hard over the last few otherwise inactive years, rendering their phalanx expert in executing a classic about-face maneuver to march out of harm's way with mounted men and camp auxiliaries fleeing before it carrying all the valuables they could snatch on the fly.[19] The sacrifice of his Iberian contingents would have dealt Hasdrubal a harsh blow, but hardly a crippling one as they could be replaced easier than his precious African horse and heavy foot. Indeed, support for that idea can be found in it being just such Iberians that composed the entirety of troops shortly thereafter transferred from the armies of H. Gisco and Mago in order to bring Hasdrubal's depleted host once more up to strength so that he could finally make his long delayed march into Italy (see below).

Metaurus R. (207)

It was decided after Baecula that Hasdrubal Barca would lead his army over the Alps to support his brother's Italian campaign. Mago Barca and Hasdrubal Gisco ceded Iberian contingents from their armies to him with the latter assuming command of all the remaining African and colonial troops to be reinforced by recruiting more locals and Mago adding Balearic slingers and other auxiliaries. Gisco was to retire toward secure territory in the southwest and avoid battle with Scipio while the Numidian prince Masinissa harassed the Roman using some 3,000 horsemen from his native land.[20] Waiting for the passes to clear, Hasdrubal crossed into Italy that spring. Appian claimed that the combined host left in Iberia numbered 70,000 foot-soldiers, 5,000 horse, and 36 elephants and, after a preliminary cavalry engagement, Scipio led less than 25,000 men against it.[21] It's generally considered that this is an error-filled version of the battle of Ilipia, which was not to take place for another year. Similarly, our Roman sources cite victories over Hannibal in this period that are questionable at least as to damage inflicted upon him.[22] Nevertheless, the Romans were successful enough to keep the Carthaginian from joining his younger sibling straightaway.

Hasdrubal had emerged from the mountains to move along the Adriatic coastal plain with an army much exaggerated in our surviving accounts.[23] Considering what he'd salvaged from Baecula plus subsequent restoration of his Iberian losses there, he probably started out with nearly 30,000 combatants. These would have included approximately 12,000 "African" spearmen and 8,000 scutarii for a total of 20,000 in heavy foot; 4,000 caetrati plus 1,500 slingers and other expert missilemen as well as 500 additional skirmishers assigned to support ten elephants for 6,000 light infantrymen in all; and, finally, some 3,000–4,000 horsemen. Unlike Hannibal's much contested passage, there is no hint in our sources that Hasdrubal took significant losses in getting over the Alps. Once down in Cisalpine Gaul, he added 5,000 or so Celts to his host, bringing it up to some 35,000-strong,[24] and we are told that 8,000 Ligurians had also been gathered for his use. Livy reports the latter as engaging at Metaurus River; however, they garner no mention whatsoever from Polybius and it is most probable that Hasdrubal's choice to advance down the opposite side of the peninsula from Liguria had prevented them from joining him in time for that battle.

The Carthaginian advance out of the Alps was being followed by the praetor L. Porcius Licinus with two legions and it shortly found its progress blocked by M. Livius Salinator and his consular army of four legions/alae. The other consul, C. Claudius Nero, then joined the effort. Leaving most of his troops behind to continue opposing Hannibal in the south, he had stolen away in the night with the 6,000 heavy infantry from one of his legion/ala pairs and 1,000 horsemen (probably half of what he had on hand) to rapidly reach the northern campaign area in a series of forced marches. But all that work at deception came to naught when horn signaling in the newly combined Roman camp revealed his presence.

Hasdrubal might have been willing to fight Salinator and Licinus, pitting his 20,000 or so heavy foot against some 18,000 legionary counterparts; however, not knowing that Nero had brought only a portion of his army, he must have thought the opposition had perhaps now swollen to ten legions/alae with up to 30,000 in line-infantry. Those were unacceptable odds and the Carthaginian withdrew under cover of darkness to move inland along the south side of the Metaurus.[25] This route proved to be full of difficult topography that slowed progress and Nero's horsemen eventually caught up. Fending off what Zonaras says was believed to be mere harassment well in advance of any more serious pursuit, Hasdrubal set about making camp on a riverside hill. However, the Roman infantry soon arrived in force.

Realizing that engagement was unavoidable, Hasdrubal deployed as best he could. The recently added Gauls were not as yet integrated into his system; moreover, many of them had assumed their day was over as an excuse to drink heavily. All he could do as a practical matter was assign defense of the camp to these mostly intoxicated men in hope that they could get by with the aid of its elevated position. He then arrayed the rest of his troops to exploit the terrain, abandoning the normal compounding that divided hoplites onto each wing when they formed a majority or strong plurality; instead, he aligned them in a single body at left and center while manning the rest of the phalanx with scutarii. This had the benefit of allowing Carthage's spearmen to anchor their left flank against the campsite hill, which freed the entirety of his skirmisher and mounted contingents to secure the open right flank.

The Romans closed on Hasdrubal's formation with Licinus and his legions on the right, Salinator and his men positioned center through left, and all of the skirmishers and horsemen outboard far left. Meanwhile, Nero led his picked soldiers beyond the right flank against the Celts atop their hill. We are told by Livy that Licinus' command was "weak," presumably consisting of only two citizen legions sans support from alae sociorum. That would have put his heavy foot at around 6,000-strong to line up beside the 12,000 legionaries of Salinator. If in a standard acies triplex arrangement, these troops extended along a front 2,400m wide. To match that, Hasdrubal most likely filed his hoplites at eight while keeping most of the scutarii ten-deep in defensive order with a tight spacing of 1m per man.

Once these arrays met in combat, the now well-established dynamic of phalanx versus legion seems to have asserted itself. This once more saw Roman swordsmen forced to take disproportionate damage in order to reach more densely aligned foes wielding longer weapons, while the phalanx's inherent lack of flexibility severely limited its ability to initiate harm on looser packed men able to dodge spear-reach. Thus, with none capable of seizing a decisive advantage, the action dragged on viciously in a manner Polybius describes as "doubtful."[26] The best path to victory for Hasdrubal was an envelopment of the Roman left by his mobile forces; however, his mounted troops and light foot were held at bay by cavalry and velites opposed off that flank. The numerical odds very slightly favored Rome in this ancillary struggle with some 11,000 men (just over 7,000 infantry plus 4,000 horse) facing no more than 10,000 for Carthage (6,000 foot-skirmishers and 3,000–4,000 riders) and all now having comparable gear. There is uncertainty as to the position of Hasdrubal's elephants, but Polybius' location on the far right makes the most sense. This would have pitted them against cavalry as per their most common role in pitched actions. It also best explains the harm they are said to have taken from javelin cross-fire, which would have dominated the skirmishing between their own light infantry and the velites screening on Salinator's left. These barrages not only wounded the beasts themselves, six of whom ultimately died, but also slew their mahouts to send unguided animals dashing about haphazardly to the detriment of friend and foe alike.

Improving on past performances, the Roman skirmishers and cavalry managed to stalemate their highly regarded opposition outboard even as Celts defending the hill on the other end of the field were surprisingly able to do the same, repulsing every attempt by Nero and his select legionaries to force that slope. Deciding that he couldn't take the high ground in a timely fashion, if at all, the consul then made a brilliant spontaneous decision. He withdrew his rear ranks and marched them all the way behind the acies triplex to throw their weight into the stalled light-armed fight. This proved decisive as Hasdrubal's mobile troops there, who might have finally begun to gain sway, quickly collapsed to expose the scutarii holding that wing. Hitting those already frontally engaged Iberians now from side and rear as well, a combination of Roman skirmishers and Nero's contingent broke them to fold in upon that part of the phalanx still in place. Hasdrubal and thousands of his troops were trapped against the flanking hill and compressed into a defenseless mass before being completely overrun. Polybius says that by the end of the action, the Carthaginian commander and more than 10,000 of his men were dead, and it has been estimated that a further 10,000 fell prisoner.[27]

Fatalities on the winning side were also stunningly high, with Livy citing 8,000 in total. That represents nearly 23 percent of all Roman troops present and more than 30 percent of the heavy foot engaged if, as seems likely, it took most of the harm; indeed, had triarii seen little or no action in their bulwarking task at the rear, then Rome's line-infantry losses might have approached an astonishing 40 percent. Given that there would have been no rational motivation for Livy to inflate his side's damage in touting a celebrated victory, Polybius' alternative of only 2,000 slain must be rejected as being far too few even should it be confined to losses solely among ethnic Romans.[28] And in that case, the legions' cost in this battle actually better fits the concept of a "Pyrrhic Victory" than anything Pyrrhus himself experienced.[29]

The foregoing speaks not only to casualties taken by swordsmen against denser arrays of similarly armored troops with spears in which the Romans might have lost roughly two of their own for every foeman they killed,[30] but also to the heroic intensity with which Rome's legionaries threw themselves at the enemy, putting their lives at unequal risk to turn the fight into what Livy calls "a furious contest [in which] the slaughter on both sides was dreadful." And great credit must go to the upgraded velites, who fought their better-respected opposite numbers at least close to even and thereby prevented a fatal turning of the Roman left before Nero's masterful (even if unplanned and fortuitously opportune) maneuver could win the day. Metaurus River was a smashing strategic success and a major turning point in the Second Punic War. For while the continuing presence of strong forces in Iberia under Gisco might still allow for reinforcement of Hannibal, that would be a very difficult proposition. The destruction of Hasdrubal Barca and his army thus went a long way toward sealing the doom of Carthage's long-running effort to win the war on Roman soil.

Ilipia (206)

His brother's defeat along the Metaurus sent Hannibal protectively retiring into Bruttium in the south. He continued to sting the Romans here and there but could not risk a major engagement that would put his now more surely irreplaceable manpower at hazard. Nor were the Romans eager to take him on, being more than happy to bask in their current ascendency without needlessly testing their luck against Hannibal's still much-feared tactical skills. If there was to be any hope of improving this unfavorable situation for Carthage, Hasdrubal Gisco, who had been preserving his strength in the Iberian far southwest at Gades, would have to somehow deal with the Roman presence on his side of the Alps and then march across with the fresh troops needed to let Hannibal go on the attack again. Gisco therefore took the field in early 206 to engage and clear Scipio's army out of the way.

Appian's earlier claims on size of the forces left behind with Gisco in Iberia likely derive from Polybius' over-estimate of his host at Ilipia.[31] Livy's alternative of 50,000 infantry and 4,500 cavalry appears more accurate in better fitting with the 40,000 or so men previously reported by our sources for the combined armies of Gisco and Mago. That host had by now replaced the Iberian hirelings ceded to Hasdrubal Barca over a year earlier and added new allies (Celtiberians supplied by the locally dominant Turdetani tribe) plus colonial and mercenary troops freshly recruited by Mago. A best-guess at how this manpower broke down suggests 24,000 Punic hoplites, 15,000 Iberian foot of unspecified origin (10,000 scutarii and 5,000 caetrati), perhaps 9,000 Celtiberian infantry (5,000 swordsmen and 4,000 javelineers),[32] 2,000 slingers and other missile specialists, 4,500 horsemen, and at least 30 elephants. As for the force that Scipio had in opposition, it consisted of four legions/alae (12,000 heavy foot, 6,000 velites with other light foot, and 2,000 horse) plus a large component of Iberian allies attracted since the taking of Novo Cartago that added perhaps another 28,000 men (18,000 scutarii, 9,000 caetrati, and 1,000 horsemen) if Livy's claim of 45,000 foot and 3,000 horse is correct.

Gisco took position near the southwest Iberian town of Ilipia on a ridge along which the Romans shortly thereafter also established themselves at some distance to the northeast. The Carthaginian's plan was to provoke a fight on the plain bordering on the east, which was relatively flat and well-suited for mounted contingents in which he deemed himself superior. And, after a failed cavalry raid on their encampment, the enemy did indeed deploy at mid-day well out on the plain in front of Gisco's campsite. Scipio seems to have arrayed his troops in fairly typical fashion with his velites in front of a battle-line that had legionary heavy foot in 15-deep acies triplex at center and Iberian swordsmen in files of ten on the wings, all spaced 2m apart for offensive action and supported off both flanks by cavalry and Iberian javelineers. Gisco countered by throwing out a matching van of skirmishers while setting all his heavy spearmen at center to engage Scipio's legionaries and dividing the Iberians/Celtiberians onto the wings opposite Rome's own locals. His elephants, cavalry, and remaining light foot took post on either end of this compound battle-line. With hoplites at 1m spacing, swordsmen offensively arrayed 2m apart, and all filed ten-deep, Gisco's phalanx equaled the width of the opposed heavy front at something over 5km across. The Carthaginians held position thus and waited for Scipio to advance, but he simply remained in place until dusk before retiring.

This same sequence of mid-day Roman deployment and Punic counter-placement followed by mutual retirement without combat went on for a couple more days. Scipio then took the field unexpectedly at dawn, using an opening cavalry charge to catch Gisco unprepared and goad him into rushing his army into action. Expecting Scipio to be set up in much the same way as over the last three days, the Carthaginian also deployed as before only to find the formation opposite much different than those seen previously. Scipio again had the Iberians ten-deep and 2m apart, but they were now in the middle of his heavy array. As for the legionaries, they suddenly reordered into columns to march outboard of either flank, moving faster than ever they could when in line and closing too swiftly for Gisco to have any chance of rearranging his own men. All he could do was watch helplessly as the Romans once more spread out in acies triplex and smashed into his sword-bearing wings even as the opposing Iberians at center, having been badly outpaced by their legionary comrades, were still short of (and effectively refused from) the deadly, spear-armed heart of his phalanx.[33]

The ensuing heavy infantry clash was accompanied off either flank by equally fierce skirmishing between like-armed mobile elements. As at Metaurus River, our sources disagree on placement of the elephants, but Polybius must again have it right that they led Gisco's light-armed attacks outboard. And their fate seems to have been much like their counterparts in that earlier battle, suffering under a rain of javelins that brought some of the beasts down and sent others rampaging through the men on both sides. The action here on the periphery of the battle was close-run, but Scipio's velites put both intense recent drilling and their new parmae to good use as they and the light-armed Iberians alongside gradually began to take control. Meanwhile, the legionaries with files half again deeper were pressing Gisco's scutarii hard on either wing. Rome's tribal swordsmen, in contrast, were staying outside spear-reach, Polybius noting that "the center occupied by the Libyans [Liby-Phoenician heavy infantry] … was never engaged at all … because the enemy in front of it did not come to close quarters." This might reflect the inherent inability of rank-bound hoplites to carry a fight into loosely ordered foes; however, a bigger factor was probably hesitation to push too far forward and risk lethal encirclement should their heavily embattled flank contingents collapse.

And as it turned out, with Gisco's outboard screens being driven away and his Iberians coming under assault from flank as well as front, just such a horrific double-envelopment scenario soon began to emerge. Descriptions of what happened next detail how the African spearmen in the middle of the phalanx began to edge back, their cautious withdrawal being enabled by failure of the facing tribesmen to maintain contact. Polybius says this began "step by step" and, though possibly spontaneous, it looks very much like a concerted maneuver that was not the product of direct enemy pressure. David Campbell has aptly noted in his recent analysis of Ilipia that the Carthaginians were moving "slow and steady, as if under the orders of Hasdrubal himself";[34] and given Carthage's roots in Spartan drill as instituted by Xanthippus during the First Punic War, it is by no means unreasonable that Gisco had issued a horn-blown command for his men to execute a practiced evolution bequeathed to them by that skilled spartiate mercenary. This called for exploiting a lull during a failing engagement to have your lattermost ranks turn around and deliberately walk away as their comrades farther forward follow in a backward shuffle while still facing a hopefully confused and static enemy; once beyond reach of a quick rush by such startled opponents, these last troops would then turn their backs as well and join in a rapid march from the battlefield.[35]

But if Gisco's plan was to escape through a controlled withdrawal, that soon came crashing down in ruin as either the enemy's fronting Iberians finally charged into close combat or (more likely) the already wavering contingents of allied swordsmen at either end of his phalanx suddenly gave way completely to expose both of his flanks. In either case, any attempt at orderly retreat immediately dissolved into a chaotic rush toward hoped for safety within the Carthaginian camp on the upland behind. Gisco's men briefly regrouped upon reaching the backing slope but ended up giving way as pursuit caught up and began once again to tear at them. Taking shelter within their barricaded campsite, the defeated men gained temporary respite due to a tremendous rainstorm that put an end to further assault.

During the course of that night, Carthage's Iberian hirelings and allies took to their heels, fleeing into what for them was a friendly countryside. Their loss made holding the camp impractical and Gisco elected to make a run for it as well; however, the Romans overtook him and Livy describes what happened next as being much less like a battle than "the butchering of cattle" as only Gisco and 6,000 of his men got away. With the extermination of its last field army in Iberia, the battle of Ilipia put an end to Carthage's overseas empire.[36]

Northern Italy and Africa, 204–202

With Iberia under Roman control, Scipio moved across to Sicily in 205 with a 7,000-man contingent of volunteers to join four legions/alae already on the island and train for an invasion of the Carthaginian homeland designed to force the Punic forces in Italy back to defend Africa. However, though Hannibal was being kept in check in Bruttia to the south, his brother Mago arrived to complicate this calculation, landing far to the north in Liguria with 12,000 foot-soldiers and 2,000 horsemen. After adding the 8,000 Ligurian mercenaries hired in vane earlier for his now lost sibling Hasdrubal, he then received reinforcements direct from Carthage to the tune of 6,000 foot, 800 horse, and seven elephants along with funds to pay the Ligurians.[37] This development might have caused some reevaluation of Scipio's plans, but did not derail them, since Rome managed to find adequate additional manpower with which to confine and reduce Mago's activities and keep him from joining Hannibal. Scipio was thus able by no later than early summer 204 to land on the African shore, from where he marched to encamp within 2km of Utica and a mere 35km from the walls of Carthage itself.

Salaeca (204), Great Plains and Mediolanum (203)

Scipio's first action on Carthaginian soil was successful as he repulsed a scouting party of 500 horsemen and killed its commander named Hanno. Undeterred, yet another Hanno (this one the son of one Hamilcar) emerged from Utica with 4,000 cavalry and light infantry to offer more serious opposition. Scipio dispatched Masinissa (who had defected to Rome after the fall of Iberia) with 200 or so of his fleet Numidian horsemen to draw that larger detachment into a trap. He succeeded in doing this as a well-supported force of Roman cavalry charged from hiding behind a hill near the town of Salaeca, surprising and slaying Hanno along with 1,000 of his men on the spot and another thousand in flight.[38] Scipio then began receiving supplies by ship in preparation for going on the offensive in the spring.

6. The Road to Zama

The Carthaginians' responded to this threat by moving up an army of their own men under Hasdrubal Gisco and a separate contingent of allied Numidian Masaesylii led by their chieftain Syphax. But, having camped about 3km apart and been lulled into a false sense of security by a pretense of peace negotiations, both these contingents fell victim in the night to sneak attacks. The Romans and their Numidian allies set tents and huts on fire and then slaughtered thousands as they tried to either fight back or flee the flames. This was no doubt a serious blow to Carthage; still, the strengths and casualty counts for these forces appear to be much exaggerated in our sources as evidenced by Gisco and Syphax not only getting away but being back in in action mere weeks later at Great Plains with another large army that must have included numerous other escapees from the holocausts.[39]

The battle at Great Plains probably took place about 110km southwest of Utica near a point where several tributaries enter the Bagradas River.[40] Syphax joined Gisco and a freshly gathered Carthaginian army there, having regrouped his own tribesmen and taken in a large body of Celtiberian mercenaries. The resulting host is said to have numbered 30,000–35,000 combatants[41]; however, details on its composition are limited to a count of more than 4,000 for the Celtiberians and comments on the presence of both Carthaginian and Numidian horsemen. We might reasonably assume that cavalry accounted for roughly 20 percent of the total at about 6,000-strong with perhaps 2,000 Numidians (Syphax's surviving troopers being about equal to those under his rival Masinissa—see below) and 4,000 heavier riders of various stripes representing Carthage. At a 75 percent share within the bounds of past Numidian musters, Syphax's light footmen would have come to 6,000; and, had the 4,000 figure cited for the Celtiberians been only their scutarius count, another 2,000 caetrati per common Iberian arms mixes could have boosted the skirmisher total. This implies that line-capable infantry for Gisco's phalanx in addition to the scutarii probably included at least 12,000 African hoplites.

Leaving behind some of his volunteers to keep up appearances of continuing operations around Utica, Scipio marched on Gisco's position with all his Numidian cavalry as well as the four legions/alae previously stationed on Sicily, the latter having likely been restored to nominal strength by drawing from the volunteer contingent. If so, he had around 12,000 heavy foot and 4,400 horsemen backed by nearly 5,000 velites plus perhaps a few tribal javelineers attached to the riders of Masinissa. This deployment at around 20,000-strong was significantly smaller than its pending opposition; however, Scipio's decision to fight well distant from a safe base shows he had great confidence in the superior quality of his own men.

After a couple days of skirmishing, the opposing heavy formations set up to engage in earnest. Scipio arrayed in standard fashion, spreading his acies triplex's ranks along an expanse of some 1,600m with cavalry and light infantry posted outside each flank. The heavier Roman and allied horse at maybe 2,400-strong held post far right while Masinissa and 2,000 of his Numidians rode off to the left[42] and the velites divided to station in front of both mounted contingents. Meanwhile, Gisco set up by having the Celtiberians take post in the center of his phalanx while the African spearmen formed the wings as was their practice when in the majority. Both the tribesmen and the hoplites stood in close order at a likely 1m per man and depth of ten. Gisco mimicked the opposition in splitting his mobile forces outboard, placing half his light foot before the cavalry from Carthage on the right to oppose Masinissa and the rest ahead of Carthage's own Numidians to face the velites and Latin horse far left.

The tactical setting at Great Plains offers some resemblance to the one at Cannae in having a solid formation of Roman and allied legionaries closing into a compounded Carthaginian phalanx that featured tribal swordsmen in the middle and tight-spaced heavy spearmen on either wing. However, these seeming parallels were no more than superficial as there were profound and ultimately pivotal differences between the situation here and what had attained more than a decade past on that otherwise similar Italian plain. Hasdrubal Gisco's troops on this occasion had drilled together, but though a few were veterans, the majority were nowhere near as experienced in actual combat as the seasoned winners of seven previous battles that Hannibal led to an eighth straight victory at Cannae. Nor were Scipio's legionaries the sort of untried draftees that had been crowded into an impotent mob and cut to pieces on that sad day for Rome; indeed, some of his men were among the longest serving soldiers that city had ever put into the field.[43] Most important of all, however, was vast improvement in the performance level of Scipio's velites in comparison to those at Cannae. Having gained the protection of shields since that time, these javelineers were not only products of improved training under their current commander but benefited greatly from his being much more adept at the art of light-arms tactics than any previous Roman general.

Once the formations entered into combat, these vital factors all came into play. First, Scipio's battle-savvy legionaries kept the Punic phalanx pinned along its entire front without overly pressing matters and exposing themselves to excessive casualties. That allowed for the velites to penetrate leading screens largely composed of inferior Numidian skirmishers before joining their horsemen charging up from behind to rout the opposing cavalry from both ends of the field. While their riders gave chase, Scipios' victorious velites turned against the now exposed flanks of Carthage's phalanx even as legionaries finally began surging into its front. The effect of this sudden tandem assault upon raw recruits among the hoplites holding Gisco's wings proved decisive. Panicking, these tyro soldiers tossed their shields and broke for the rear in a terrified stampede that became general as even the stouter veterans in their ranks were compelled to follow suit. This flight by the Carthaginians from either wing abandoned the Celtiberians to a grisly fate. Unlike the spearmen alongside, who had been largely unchallenged in the early going, these sword-fighters had hotly engaged with the legionaries to their front and could not so easily break free; as a result, they were quickly surrounded and forced into a hopeless fight to the death. Concentration of Scipio's men on these mercenaries' futile last acts of resistance plus the fall of night then served to limit pursuit, enabling Gisco, Syphax, and sizeable portions of their commands to escape the killing ground.

The defeat at Great Plains pressured Carthage to prepare a defense of the homeland by recalling all available forces from abroad even as another lost battle underscored the forlorn nature of its overseas operations. Livy records that proconsul Marcus Cornelius and praetor Publius Quinctius Varus met Mago Barca in pitched combat near Mediolanum (modern Milan) in the Italian far north.[44] Some aspects of his account have been discounted, but it appears that the action took place within restrictive terrain allowing only two of the legions/alae present to actively engage while the other two had to stand behind. At the same time, one end of the contested ground was open and saw Roman velites and horsemen dual a mixture of Numidian skirmishers and cavalry who were supported in later stages by elephants originally kept in reserve. Analysis of the sort of setting these various elements would have required indicates level ground about 1km wide with topographic barriers of some sort on the boundaries. Mago's phalanx must have fixed its more vulnerable right flank against the terrain impediment on that end of the field in facing a legion (identified as the 12th) similarly anchored on its left. The opposing formations then would have extended across some 800m with the 12th's paired ala sociorum confronting the Carthaginian left wing and the 200m or so of flat ground beyond hosting the described light-armed fighting.

Mago's force contained not only most of the men that he had first led from Africa and later received direct from there as reinforcements, but also locals acquired in Italy since and identified by Livy as Gauls, presumably of the Insubrian tribe that occupied the surrounding region. The troops from Carthage likely consisted of 12,000 heavy Liby-Phoenician spearmen, 6,000 light infantry mostly (if not entirely) from Numidia, and 2,800 cavalrymen of whom perhaps 2,000 were Numidians and the rest heavier African lancers. Mago had apparently left behind his Ligurian mercenaries to defend their own territory and his base. We have no details on the Gallic contingent, but it's unlikely to have exceeded a couple of thousand foot-soldiers plus a few hundred horsemen. Mago therefore had some 21,000–24,000 combatants to oppose 19,000–20,000 on the other side. Both armies would have fielded around 12,000 heavy footmen should Carthage's Gauls be considered skirmishers rather than line-infantry as their reported role in this battle would seem to indicate.

The ground to be contested must have been chosen by Mago; as such, it allowed him to cover most of its open expanse with hoplites at a probable depth of 15 shields and thereby present the kind of deep Doric phalanx that had proven effectively impenetrable to past legionary foes. At the same time, he kept his Gauls in the rear, leaving room by design off to the left for deployment of his mobile forces in anticipation that they could best inferior counterparts and envelop the otherwise stalled enemy heavy array. Given recent Carthaginian defeats in which improved Roman light arms had carried the day, that sort of thinking seems obsolete; however, due to the well-demonstrated inability of the Punic phalanx to penetrate more agile acies triplex formations, Mago probably had no other option if he wanted to avoid an indecisive engagement that might prove his undoing in the long run.

But if Mago was more or less compelled to employ recently outdated tactics, Marcus Cornelius, who led the Roman army, appears to have deliberately focused on methodologies long known as ineffective and potentially disastrous. This called for deeply massing his legionaries for a narrow, head-on assault that specifically echoed key aspects of the failed approaches taken at Cannae and Canusium. Meaning to carry the action with heavy foot alone, the proconsul held back his 2,400 or so cavalrymen and relegated the almost 5,000 velites on hand to merely neutralizing Mago's mobile troops. The results of this once the battle began was to produce stalemates across the entire field. Cornelius' javelineers stalled the Carthaginian light infantry, but his heavy foot could not crack the deeply filed phalanx. And while his allied legionaries cautiously engaged the hoplites they faced only lightly, the men of the 12th Legion drove hard into the enemy spear-front such that "a great number were slain" per Livy and they came close to not being able to hold their ground.

Seeing that his heavy infantry's costly efforts "produced no impression on the enemy," Varus approached Cornelius and got him to bring up their cavalry to join in the fighting outboard. Mago responded by advancing his half dozen or so elephants and they terrified the Romans' horses, sending them reeling about ineffectively. That allowed the opposing Numidian javelineers both mounted and afoot to rain destruction from a distance at no cost to themselves. It was at this crucial point that the Roman commanders dispatched the 13th Legion that had so far stood idle at the rear to aid their horsemen. These fresh troops came around and hit the elephants at the enemy's fore with an opening salvo of javelin fire that drove the animals back among their own men into whom the Romans then charged. Mago sought to counter by committing his Gauls, but the legionaries soon put those less capable foes to rout as well. Just like Nero's analogous move at Metaurus River, it was thus an improvised redeployment that exposed one flank of the Carthaginian phalanx to decide the battle.

Much as Hasdrubal Gisco had done at Ilipia three years prior, Mago recognized this deadly development in progress and signaled for his troops to break off and withdraw. Executing what must have been a well-practiced maneuver, the hoplites took advantage of their facing opponents being either too badly battered (the Roman 12th) or only weakly engaged (its ala) and "stepped back slowly, preserving their ranks and not relaxing their ardor in fighting." It was during this process that a javelin pierced Mago's thigh and Livy claims the Punic retreat fell into disorder to become a general rout. But that description is somewhat misleading in that Mago and most of his men escaped the field with their lives. Livy, who is very unlikely to have understated Punic losses, puts them at 5,000 (20–24 percent). That is for sure a heavy defeat indicative of serious damage taken from hard pursuit; still, it was well short of total disaster.

As for the Romans, their casualties are given as 2,300 (12 percent). Not only is that steep for a victorious army overall but Livy reports that "by far the greater part of [the dead] belonged to the 12th Legion." If two-thirds of the slain came from that unit's hastati, princepes, velites, and cavalry (the triarii not engaging), then about 30 percent of its men at hazard were lost. And had the horseman and light foot suffered at a 5 percent rate consistent with the sort of combat they seem to have endured, then some 60 percent of the legionaries that the 12th threw at Mago's phalanx died in action. Applying other assumptions could certainly moderate this staggering number; all the same, the unfavorable dynamics previously noted as afflicting Roman swordsmen when aggressively attacking close-ordered spearmen appear to have been operating at Mediolanum in spades. And the heavy casualties taken in such "old school" efforts at bashing headlong into intact phalanxes stand in stark contrast to the much more modest losses incurred by Scipio's sophisticated use of restrained frontal engagement in tandem with flanking assaults carried out by properly equipped/trained light armaments.

Zama (202)

Desperate to counter Scipio's invasion, the Carthaginians recalled Hannibal in the fall of 203, putting him in command of protecting their home soil. In this role, he had the troops that had sailed back with him from Italy, the similarly repatriated men from Mago's army, and all the survivors from Great Plains for a grand total according to Appian of around 50,000 combatants.[45] This host likely consisted of 32,000 line-infantry (20,000 heavy spearmen and 4,000 Iberian scutarii plus 6,000 Ligurian and 2,000 Gallic theuros-bearing swordsmen), 13,000 light foot (Celtiberian caetrati, Balearic slingers, and Moorish archers plus javelineers from Numidia and elsewhere across North Africa), and 5,000 cavalrymen (probably around 3,000 Numidian lights and 2,000 heavier Iberian and Carthaginian horse).[46] Hannibal also was able to field a force of more than 80 elephants.

After months of non-decisive operations and fruitless peace negotiations, Hannibal marched out in spring 202 to confront Scipio where he was encamped above a broad plain approximately 120km southwest of Carthage near the village of Zama. He set up his own camp across the flats about 5.5km from the Romans.[47] A personal meeting is said to have taken place between the opposing generals at this time; however, if true, it seems to have produced nothing more than agreement to settle matters on the field of battle. The two armies deployed to that end out on the plain and closed to engage. Scipio had some 40,000 men based around four legions/alae whose infantry had not only replaced losses to date by drawing from the pool of volunteers he had brought from Italy but had attached the rest to number 23,000-strong. Likely 15,600 hastati and princepes and 2,400 triarii plus 5,000 velites, these troops cored Scipio's formation with cavalry on either flank. Up to 2,400 Latin lancers rode on the left along with 1,600 Numidians, each of the latter with a foot-skirmisher, and Masinissa was on the right with 4,000–6,000 of his horsemen likewise accompanied by javelineers.

Scipio marched toward Hannibal's position in typical Roman fashion, doing so in a preliminary array that has come to be called a quincunx. Designed to avoid formation disruption during lengthy and/or difficult pre-battle movements, there are varying theories on exactly how this poorly described and somewhat mysterious technique worked. Developments at Zama suggest that in this instance it involved a division by maniples in which every other one was recessed along the line at a distance behind those on either side. At the same time, the block-like heavy arms-segments of each maniple (those of the hastati, princepes, and triarii) were separated and positioned far enough behind any segment ahead so that the entire deployment formed a checkerboard pattern six rows deep. The velites were spread out loosely in front of this arrangement to skirmish as appropriate for any given situation, normally then withdrawing into the gaps between the fronting maniples and moving around the blocks rearward to redeploy where needed, usually in support of cavalry on the flanks. Once those skirmishers were out of the way, the hastati in the recessed maniples could advance to form a single battlefront and all the following blocks of princepes and triarii would close up behind the hastati and thereby complete a standard acies triplex for close combat.

Hannibal must have seen this common opening procedure many times during his Italian campaigns and assumed Scipio intended to fight him very much in traditional Roman style as far as the legionaries were concerned. His problem seemed to lay elsewhere in that he had never had to face an army from Rome that was so strong in cavalry. He was now looking at a foe not only boasting a numerical advantage in horse possibly as great as 2-to-1, but also fielding riders as skilled (if not rather more adept in the case of Masinissa's men) than his own. Even the edge his elephants might provide by spooking enemy mounts was partially negated here in that the opposing Numidians were well used to operating around those beasts.[48] Among his solutions to this challenge appears to have been calling upon a defensive tactic that his hero Alexander the Great had used in all of the major battles in Persia against opponents whose cavalry was more numerous. This called for deploying a second phalanx rearward that could counter a mounted turning of his first/leading formation or reverse facing to present a united front against any encircling horsemen.[49] Adapting that tactic to conditions at Zama, however, required Hannibal to make some significant modifications.

Unlike Alexander's host, Hannibal's in 202 was neither armed entirely in Grecian fashion nor as uniformly seasoned; and those were major issues he had to address not only in employing the famed Macedonian's double-phalanx ploy, but in formulating an offensive plan as well. The troops inherited from Gisco and Mago comprised more than half of his spearmen but lacked positive combat experience. What little exposure most of them had to pitched battle involved running from the field at either Great Plains or Mediolanum. Hannibal could not trust these now likely battle-shy troops to stand their ground without support from more reliable soldiers.[50] But being intimately mixed in among such questionable fellows must have been unacceptable to his veterans, who knew that tact had failed miserably when green troops in those past defeats bolted to tear their entire formation apart and abandon steadier men like themselves for slaughter. Maintaining vital morale therefore dictated assigning Mago's and Gisco's 12,000 surviving heavy footmen to a leading classical phalanx in hope that those among them with more experience could exert a steadying influence in the first and last ranks.

This let Hannibal place the old sweats from Italy, also around 12,000-strong,[51] at the rear in a second phalanx. Their leveled spears there could stiffen the resolve of potential faint hearts up ahead that might entertain thoughts of flight, but the primary reasons for posting his best men at the very back were purely tactical. Should things go badly and

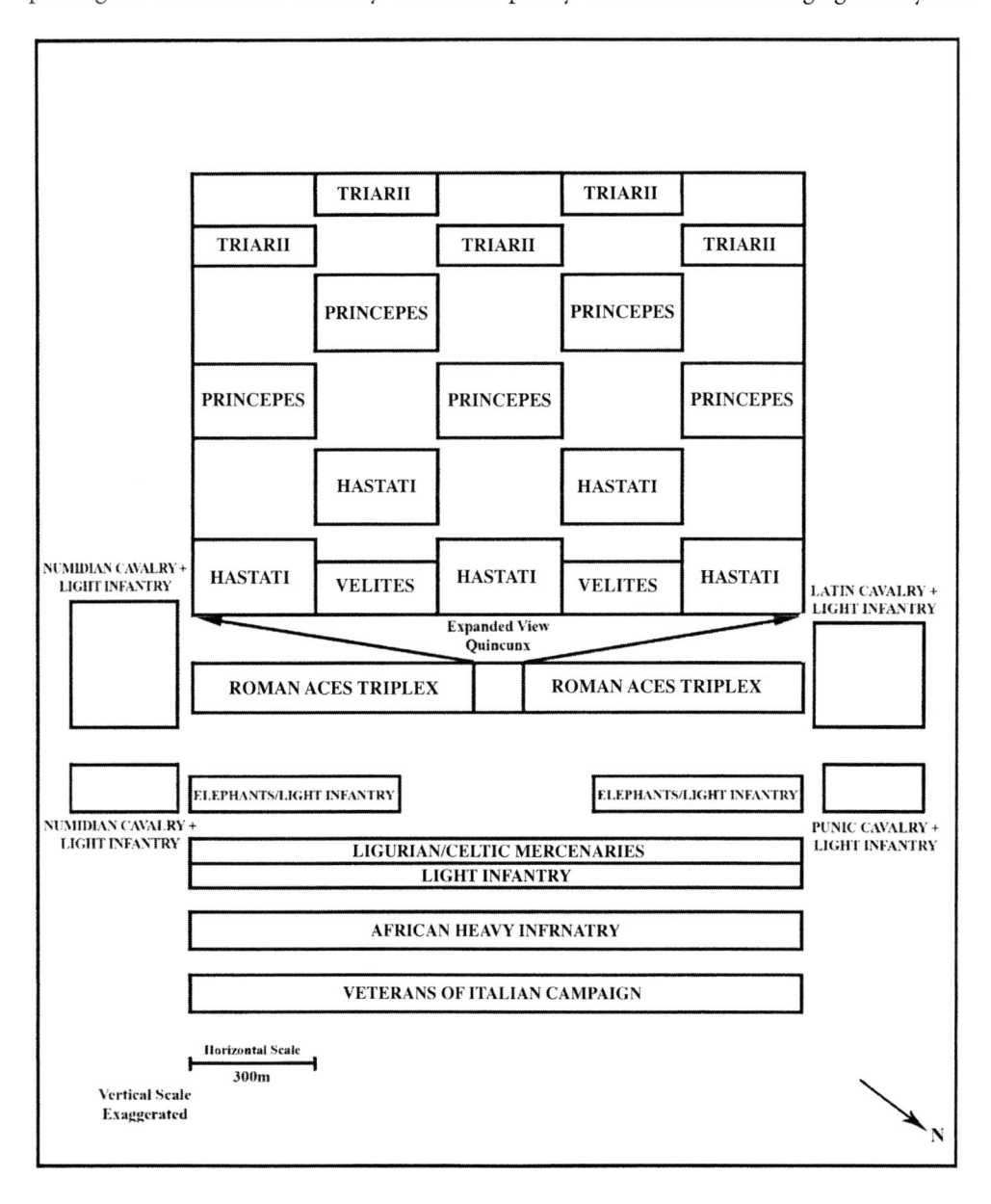

Battle of Zama, 202 BCE.

Scipio's legionaries frontally penetrate the forward lines, these highly capable troops could advance from reserve and repulse that threat. On the other hand, if all went as planned, they would be preserved at full strength and positioned for the same sort of late-stage envelopments that some of these same men had executed so successfully at Cannae. Emulating that battle, Hannibal's veteran scutarii would have occupied the middle of this rear phalanx with his crack spearmen divided into similar-sized contingents of 4,000 on either wing.

The forwardmost element of Hannibal's infantry array was composed of a mixed formation of heavier Ligurian and Celtic mercenaries in its leading ranks with expert light missilemen sheltered barricade-style behind them.[52] More widely spaced at 2m than the close-ordered spearmen rearward to optimize their swordplay but at greater depth (ten versus five-man files) and covering the same frontage, these 12,000 men were meant along with the first phalanx to function much as had the crescent-shaped extension in the center of the Carthaginian line at Cannae. Absorbing and slowing the Roman attack, they would try to channel it toward the center of the field while buying time for their mobile forces to prevail outboard, all toward enabling ultimate envelopments by Hannibal's veteran spearmen at the rear.

With the foregoing tripartite infantry arrangement in place, Hannibal then had to devise a way to sweep the enemy flanks as that too was critical to any realistic chance for success. As the cavalry standing outside either end of his line was relatively weak, he had to rely for this upon his elephant corps, the one mounted arm in which he was superior. Hannibal drew once more from a past master of phalanx warfare by channeling Xanthippus' triumph over the Romans at Tunes in 255. This saw him copy the Spartan by placing the elephants in front of his infantry; however, the setting at Zama argues against their being distributed across the entire front as at Tunes. Hannibal had only around 80 elephants versus the nearly 100 of Xanthippus to cover a much wider expanse at 2,400m versus 1,500m. The normal spacing of 12–15m for each animal and its 50-man light infantry support squad would therefore have limited them to fronting 600m or so at most before each wing; and that is consistent with Polybius' and Livy's descriptions of their subsequent fate, which can be viewed as unfolding solely on or partially spread beyond those posts. But regardless of any such debatable details of initial positioning, Hannibal must have intended for his elephants to duplicate Tunes by smashing Scipio's light-armed van prior to moving onto the flanks and leading his horsemen and skirmishers there to victory just as their kind had done for Xanthippus.

Hannibal's battle plan was clearly not without major risk for failure, but it ran along lines proven successful in past actions and must have looked sound for countering the velites-led quincunx that was approaching in a manner very much resembling that of his previous Roman victims. What happened next, however, would signal that he was up against an opponent like no other he had seen. Just as Scipio had surprised Gisco at Ilipia by transforming his formation in the final stages of its approach, he had his fronting javelineers here fall back to shelter within the still open gaps in the quincunx behind. It's also possible that either dismounted horsemen or velites using long cavalry lances came up from the rear to provide a stronger front against the elephants as Romans had done in the past.[53] Instead of Hannibal's pachyderm teams being able to rampage through a highly vulnerable crowd of loosely spread skirmishers, they thus suddenly found themselves facing an unbroken front of alternating Roman units against which they had no real chance to make headway. Savaged by javelins raining into them from not only the velites but the hastati as well, the beasts recoiled with some plunging about driverless and a few of them rushing fatally into the Roman line.⁵⁴ Denied their intended initial targets, the surviving mahouts guided their animals and out-runners flankward, not in flight as our pro-Roman sources suggest but merely carrying out the second phase of their role in Hannibal's plan of attack that called for them to add their weight to his horsemen and skirmishers outboard. And Scipio's velites duly followed suit, withdrawing rearward themselves to relocate in support of their own mobile forces now entering into battle.

With both elephants and velites out of the way, Scipio's heavy foot filled the gaps in his front and closed up from the rear to form a solid acies triplex that then engaged the mercenary swordsmen in Hannibal's first line. Fighting in a cohesive manner against foes darting up and back like skirmishers, the legionaries forced the Ligurians and Celts backward as the Punic phalanx behind gave ground to stay unengaged. Finally, the mercenaries routed and ran, taking rear-ranks missilemen with them. Most fled toward the wings, but some rushed directly at the first phalanx only to be slain by its hoplites, who stood in close order and lacked room to let the fugitives pass without becoming dangerously disrupted themselves. The hastati advanced aggressively upon that still unbroken front of Carthaginian spears and shields but suffered such heavy losses that Livy claims they were "driven from their ground" and Scipio had to rotate in his princepes.⁵⁵ Our accounts of what followed next are confusing and appear to conflate subsequent action, but the lead phalanx rife with poorly experienced African spearmen that had fought surprisingly well up to this point seems to have exhausted all endurance and/or courage to finally break and flee laterally from the field. Essaying no more than token pursuit, the victorious princepes then closed into the remaining formation of Italian veterans. This initiated a vicious melee whose contenders Polybius claimed were so "nearly equal in numbers, spirit, courage, and arms" that "the battle was for a long time undecided, the men in their obstinate valor falling dead without giving way a step."⁵⁶

As it turned out, this brutal shock action would not resolve the engagement; rather, it was the mounted contests outboard that proved decisive. Hannibal had positioned his Numidian horsemen and skirmishers off his left flank to face their countrymen under Masinissa, placing the Carthaginian and other heavier cavalry units on the right against Scipio's Italian horse. Outnumbered either side, any hope for success rested upon pivotal contributions from his elephants. But the velites, having repositioned in the van off both flanks, were able to absorb significant casualties and still inflict serious damage on the beasts. All the elephants were ultimately wounded and/or shorn of the mahout/javelineer pairs aboard to be driven back into their own soldiers.⁵⁷ Hannibal's cavalry and light foot fled from either end with pursuit by Scipio's mobile forces carrying them far from the still ongoing infantry fight; however, they eventually turned about and descended upon Hannibal's trailing ranks.

Carthage's rear phalanx of veterans had held up well against Scipio's princepes, whom Livy says were fighting men "equal to them in the nature of their arms, experience in war, [and] fame of their achievements." But being so engaged, they couldn't reverse facing as designed against the cavalry suddenly striking from behind and these last-standing Punic troops quickly routed. Carthage is said to have suffered 20,000–25,000 (40–50 percent) killed at Zama with Polybius claiming those captured were nearly as numerous (though Appian cites only 8,500 prisoners). Roman losses are put at 1,500–2,500 plus 2,500 Numidian allies. At 10–12.5 percent overall, Scipio's casualties exceeded those in his previous victories as fitting for so aggressively fought an action against mostly spear-armed heavy foot.⁵⁸ All the same, he had scored a crushing triumph over Carthage from which it would not recover. Hannibal escaped to assemble another army from the battle's survivors and fresh levies,⁵⁹ but there was no desire to continue a clearly lost war. The Carthaginians sued for peace, and in 201 they accepted exceedingly harsh terms in order to avoid outright occupation. The Romans would not tolerate even the distant possibility of Carthage rising again, and when its military took to the field against a threat from Numidia in the late 150s, they developed pretexts to declare a Third Punic War. And despite some initial tactical ineptitude on Rome's part that extended this conflict, Carthage was ultimately stormed and burnt to the ground in 146, the site remaining barren for a century thereafter.

7. Twilight of the Phalanx
Antiochus III, Philopoemen and the First/Second Macedonian Wars (214–196 BCE)

As the later phases of the Second Punic War played out to the west, other conflicts were raging not only on the always contentious Greek mainland but in Asia as well, where Antiochus III was seeking to extend the Seleucid kingdom's borders to their greatest extents. Though this project had been stalled on the southwest, where his defeat at Raphia in 217 had forced an agreement not to further contest Coele Syria with Egypt's Ptolemy IV, a vast region stretching all the way to India remained ripe for reclamation. Antiochus set out in the spring of 210 with a powerful expeditionary force on an ambitious crusade of showing the flag and reconquest through those wavering and splintered territories that would not see him return to his core realm in Babylonia and Syria for a full six years.

Seleucia's Frontiers

Antiochus' long march (*anabasis*) through Asia is not well documented at the tactical level but seems to have involved at least two pitched battles early in the campaign. The first of these took place as he was moving thorough elevated terrain south and east of the Caspian Sea in pursuit of Arsaces, king of the breakaway state of Parthia. Components of Antiochus' expeditionary force probably encompassed some 6,000 horsemen (including a guard unit of 2,000), heavy infantry consisting of 13,000 phalangites and 2,000 hoplite "peltastai" (picked men within the two elite Argyraspide divisions that were trained to use either spear or pike), and maybe 14,000 light infantrymen (many being mercenaries and including slingers, javelineers, and 2,000 Cretan bowmen with small shields) for about 35,000 combatants in all.[1] The strength of this armament dissuaded the Parthian leader from a direct confrontation and he fled eastward from his homeland into Hyrkania.

Mount Labos Pass (210) and Arios R. (209)

The Seleucid column marched toward Hyrkania through canyons in the Elburz Mountains where local tribesmen aligned with Parthia set up barricades and hurled missiles from the enclosing heights. Antiochus countered by reforming his van, putting skirmishers familiar with mountain-fighting in front followed by the Cretan bowmen and then heavy foot "armed with breastplate and shield" as a rear bastion.[2] With archers and spearmen forming a reserve below, the Seleucid skirmishers were able to climb above the ambushing tribesmen and shoot down to drive them off. This approach allowed Antiochus to move slowly but without significant loss through the mountains for eight days until reaching the pass atop Mount Labus, where the barbarians flushed ahead of him chose to make a stand.

Antiochus advanced his phalangites in phalanx upon the tribesmen's position, which occupied the modest crestal passage at considerable depth. Heavier armed men along the barbarian front "kept well together and fought desperately," holding their ground "as long as they were engaged with the phalanx face to face."[3] But Antiochus' pikemen had not been tasked with dislodging these opponents; rather, they were carrying out an operation for which they were much better equipped, that of pinning the enemy in place so as to render them vulnerable to action from more mobile forces. This classic Macedonian "hammer and anvil" tactic usually relied upon envelopment by elite hoplites and cavalry on the phalanx's right wing; however, the ruggedly narrow topography here forced that critical role onto contingents of Antiochus' light infantry instead.[4] Circling through the hills at daybreak, these now appeared in command of high ground at the enemy's rear. The startled tribesmen "fled in a panic" and Antiochus resumed his march without wasting time giving chase.

Antiochus descended to campaign against Parthian strongholds in the lowlands and successfully brought the region back under Seleucid control by forcing a negotiated settlement upon Parthia's king, Arsaces II. Antiochus next pushed on toward Bactria (modern Afghanistan) and the only other battle recorded in the course of his campaign to the east. It appears that the Bactrians were defending their border at a key fording point along the Arias River with what Polybius says were 10,000 soldiers,[5] though his claim that these were all mounted is surely incorrect. Should the total be accurate, it's much more likely that there were no more than 5,000 riders along with an equal number of foot-skirmishers. The opposing Seleucid armament was but modestly larger, being a fast-moving advance party that had failed to secure the crossing before the enemy could do so. Details of this "flying column" are uncertain; however, it apparently contained horsemen, light infantry, and heavy foot with a best guess suggesting perhaps 4,000 cavalrymen (including the 2,000 mounted guards) supported by the same in javelineers and accompanied by the 2,000 elite spearmen attached to the Argyraspides along with another 4,000 skirmishers.[6]

Disappointed upon arrival to find the enemy already in place across the Arius and blocking the ford, Antigonus quickly recovered the situation due to his foes' failure to hold continuous station. It seems that the Bactrians kept post only until sundown and then retired to more comfortable quarters some distance away. Antigonus thus simply made a nighttime crossing, getting most of his men over the river before being discovered. The Bactrian response to this unexpected development seems to have been hopelessly bungled, consisting of attacks in several small waves rather than via a single, massive effort. With the heavy infantry standing in bastion, Antigonus and his mounted guards turned back the first three of these piecemeal assaults before being relieved by the rest of their horsemen, who then routed one last, poorly organized enemy charge. Euthydemus of Bactria retreated and a siege of his capital and other fighting played out over the next two years before a settlement was reached for him to recognize Seleucid authority. That freed Antiochus to cross the Hindu Kush into modern day Pakistan. Penetrating as far as the Indus River region, he awed the locals there into yielding riches, food, and a herd of elephants (bringing his total to some 150) to get him to go away. Antiochus left a representative behind to collect the promised payment and began a return march that brought him back to his home provinces early in 204.

Mount Panium (200)

The same year that Antiochus returned from his eastern anabasis saw the death of longtime rival Ptolemy IV of Egypt. This suddenly opened up the possibility of capturing much-coveted Cole-Syria from newly installed Ptolemy V, a mere child whose succession had thrown his kingdom into a state of disarray including local uprisings. Having now fully reunited his military, the Seleucid monarch marched south in 202, capturing Damascus and putting Gaza under siege over the course of a couple of campaign seasons. Antiochus then retired for the winter in late 201 only to have the garrisons he had left behind come under attack from forces under the mercenary general Scopus. That Aetolian was serving the Egyptian monarch and had brought 6,000 foot-soldiers and 500 horsemen with him from Greece. Adding these to what African troops were available after dealing with desertions and meeting internal demands arising from ongoing revolts in Egypt, he had been able to field perhaps 40,000 combatants for an effort to reclaim his client's lost territory.[7]

A best guess at the composition of Scopus' host suggests 31,000 heavy infantrymen (6,000 Greek hoplites and 25,000 pikemen, the latter consisting of 10,000 ethnic Macedonians [half the strength of those at Raphia], 10,000 Egyptians [all those still loyal at half their Raphia count, having been deployed abroad here as a precaution against further insurrection], and perhaps 5,000 Lydians [increased since Raphia to full division strength]), 6,000 light foot, and 3,000 horsemen (half the Raphia number plus 500 Aetolians). Antigonus countered in the spring of 200 with resources on a par with those employed at Raphia. And despite garrisoning requirements, his field force likely held a significant advantage of 40 percent or more in overall manpower with at least 30,000 in heavy infantry[8] as well as 6,000 cavalrymen and as many as 150 elephants that boasted perhaps another 450–600 riders at a mahout and javelineer pair or trio each. All of these would then have been supported by nearly 20,000 skirmishers at one per horseman and per five heavy footmen plus another 50 per elephant.

Being weaker in mounted troops and skirmishers, Scopus sought to compensate by positioning across favorable terrain near what our sole source calls Mount Panium, which lay somewhere along or near the northern end of the Golan Heights.[9] Bar-Kochva's interpretation of the ensuing battle places this site between the Heights and Mount Hermon to the north, positing that our surviving, second-hand account of the engagement conflates two simultaneous actions that were physically separated.[10] This is an elegant solution to the many difficulties presented in a fragmentary report whose author casts great doubt upon the accuracy of his source material, and it may well be correct. However, an alternative reconstruction more consistent with the action's course as anciently described is possible should we recognize what seems a clear point of confusion on the placement of just one of Antiochus' contingents (see note below on the Seleucid lancers). This favors location of the battle farther south where a ridge west of the Golan Heights bounds a flat some 4.5km wide and well able to accommodate Scopus' entire army. His phalanx's right could anchor here upon the Heights while light forces screened its left, with the only less than ideal factor being a narrow stretch on the far right where the ground was too rugged for heavy foot to maintain adequately tight order yet remained at least marginally passable for horsemen. As our source details, this latter complication required Scopus to post a few riders and attached light foot outside his right flank.

Scopus' strategy must have been for cavalry and skirmishers on the left to stall their more numerous counterparts and give his phalanx a decent chance in this partially anchored position to repulse an enemy heavy array perhaps little if any larger than itself and maybe having fewer of the sort of well-shielded spearmen best-suited to an offensive press. Those last for Scopus were the Aetolian hoplites he had brought along from Greece, who, standing inside the small mobile screen far right, spanned a probable 500m at an optimum depth of twelve shields. The pike-armed African comrades on their left then formed eight-man files in spreading the phalanx westward across another 2.5km of the plain. With his skirmisher-supported horsemen off either flank aligned four-deep at 2m-wide per mount, Scopus was therefore able to cover the entire distance between the Golan Heights and the ridge to the west.

Antiochus had camped beyond the Jordan River and moved out in the morning to engage. Having observed the benefits of his opponents' position, he had dispatched a contingent of what was probably light infantry just before dawn to scale the Heights and get above their anchored flank; however, no more is said of this unit and it must have been unable to get into position in time to influence the battle. Once crossed over the river, the Seleucid phalanx formed up along an expanse similar to that of the opposition with its peltastai and any mercenary spearmen present taking up their left wing across from the like-armed Aetolians. A modest contingent of cavalry deployed to cover the noted tricky ground on that end of the field while a much larger body of riders including the heavier lancers (cataphracts) posted outside the right flank.[11] During this alignment process, the king and his 2,000 guardian cavalry stood out in front along with the elephants and a contingent of Tarentine horsemen (shielded javelineers), warding against any early enemy charge that might catch their army before it was ready.

Once arrayed for action, Antiochus led his mounted van aside to join the cavalry and light foot outboard to the west, clearing the way for the heavy infantry to engage. A "stubborn fight" then ensued in which Antiochus' peltastai on his left wing, finding themselves "outmatched in agility and forced backward by the Aetolians, retired step by step." As their spearmen pushed ahead, the flanking Ptolemaic horse "remained unbroken" to put Scopus on the verge of accomplishing a classic envelopment of the enemy left.[12] Just then, however, his terrain-enhanced tactical scheme came to ruin on the other end of the field.

Fighting beyond Scopus' left wing had been dominated up to this point by foot-skirmishers exchanging missiles at some remove. But as their ammunition began to dwindle, the mounted contingents shielding behind were free at last to brave what light fire remained and move up into action. This saw the Aetolian mercenary horsemen of Scopus "thrown into a panic because they were unaccustomed to the look of the elephants" that now came against them, and this was quickly exploited by a charge from Antiochus' cataphracts. Battered by pachyderm and lance, the Ptolemaic forces outboard on that side of the field fled under hard pursuit. Some of those giving chase then circled back against Scopus to launch an attack "on the rear of his phalanx." Finding much of his line suddenly "surrounded by elephants and cavalry," the Aetolian wisely accepted defeat and broke away with that portion of his command still intact on the far right, including most of the Greek hoplites. Yet this provided only a temporary respite as he and 10,000 of his men were then besieged at Sidon and forced to surrender.[13] With the capture of Gaza in 198, Antiochus put

The First Macedonian War and Philopoemen's Reforms

Cole Syria under Seleucid control, reuniting Alexander the Great's Asian holdings for the first time in more than a century.

The First Macedonian War and Philopoemen's Reforms

Even as Antiochus worked to expand his domain, the Greek mainland was serving as a sideshow to the Second Punic War. This began in 214, when Antigonus III's successor, Philip V, allied with Carthage after the crushing Roman defeat at Cannae. Recognized today in a Roman context as the First Macedonian War, this saw direct confrontation between the forces of Macedon and its Latin foe limited to no more than minor campaigning by the latter around Illyria at the westernmost fringe of Macedonia's reach. In Greece itself, the Romans committed very few men on the ground, settling instead to advance their interests via a proxy war that mostly relied upon the operations of local allies to weaken Philip and his supporters. Chief among those last was the Achaean League, which had recovered some of its old authority in the Peloponnese after joining the Macedonians to defeat Sparta at Sellasia in 222.

Larissa R. (210) and Lamia I/II (208)

Having risen to prominence in the war with Sparta, Achaea's Philopoemen had gone on to expand his martial resume by serving for a decade as a mercenary for Macedonian interests on the island of Crete. Upon his return to the mainland, the Achaean League selected him to head its cavalry, which he is credited with significantly upgrading and leading in heroic fashion against Elis in 210. Long-standing rivals of the League, the Eleans had received mounted reinforcements from Roman-allied Aetolia and the resulting combined cavalry force was either out in front of an infantry advance or preparing to make an independent raid into Achaean territory when Philopoemen and his horsemen met them at the frontier along the Larissa River.[14] Probably striking while their foes were disadvantaged in crossing the river, the Achaeans scored a victory during which Philopoemen is said to have personally speared down the Elean cavalry commander. The fame gained from this action helped to assure his election to the League generalship in the coming year.

Philopoemen took charge of the Achaean army with an aim to reform its capabilities beyond what he had already done with the cavalry. Having served beside and on behalf of the Macedonians, he had great respect for their way of war; moreover, he had seen how Cleomenes III of Sparta nearly subdued the Peloponnese after adopting elements of that system. He thus set out to emulate the Spartan revival by remaking Achaea's military in a like manner. Long prone to favor skirmishing, the Achaeans had over the course of more than a decade's association with Macedon adopted a narrow theuros for use by their javelin-armed conscripts in support of that ally's phalanxes. Philopoemen now equipped those light infantrymen with helmets, body armor, and shock weapons, though arraying them in Macedonian style rather than in their Doric battle formation of old. This saw not only the outfitting of a majority of his troops with sarissai and matching shields of modest size, but also either the retention or reintroduction of something akin to classical hoplites plying a heavier Argive aspis and thrusting spear.[15] These last formed small, elite contingents as per Macedonia's hypaspists/peltasts, though as a body of partially state-supported epilektoi rather than true professionals.

7. Twilight of the Phalanx

Being able at best to hold the generalship during alternating years due to limitations imposed by the League's constitution, Philopoemen was out of office in 208 as fresh threats arose from the Spartans making trouble to the south and Aetolian raids coming across the Corinthian Gulf. With their reinvented phalanx still only lightly drilled and not really fit to fight on its own, the Achaeans called upon Philip V for assistance. He responded by leading an army against the Aetolians, who marched to preempt him near the city of Lamia in southernmost Thessaly. The intercepting force under Pyrrhias included not only his countrymen but also some auxiliaries sent from Asia by Pergamum as well as troops drawn from a Roman fleet operating in the region under the former consul Sulpicius Galba.

There are no recorded strengths for either army beyond Pyrrhias' Romans amounting to 1,000 men and that the Aetolians lost that same number in each of two recorded engagements.[16] It seems that these battles were fought close to a refuge at Lamia, suggesting Aetolia's losses probably fell within the 5–10 percent range typical for soundly beaten phalanxes spared from excessive pursuit. Combined with data on past deployments, this indicates that the Aetolians likely went into these actions with roughly 15,000 combatants. Those might have broken down into 10,000 hoplites backed by 10 percent that count in light infantry and a like number of horsemen along with another 1,000 foot-skirmishers. The Roman and the Pergamum contingents at 1,000 apiece would then have completed a 15,000-man roster. Given Pyrrhias' willingness to engage, it's likely that Philip had an army smaller than the 24,000 thousand he would later deploy at Ithacus or the 26,000 or so at Cynoscephalae (see both below), perhaps being under 20,000 per his nation's muster at Sellasia sans significant mercenary input. This might have included 12,000 in heavy foot (9,000 phalangites and 3,000 peltastai),[17] 2,000 cavalrymen, and around 4,500 foot-skirmishers (20 percent of the heavy infantry count plus one per rider).

If the foregoing speculations on manpower at Lamia are at least in the ballpark, then it's likely that the phalanxes came to blows for the first time somewhere on the wide plains in that vicinity with both having their cavalry and light foot split off either end of a heavy-armed front 1,350–1,500m wide. Maybe placing the Roman swordsmen far left, the Aetolian spearmen could have stood across the rest of their phalanx filed at eight while the opposing phalangites formed eight-man files with the hypaspists to their right at a minimum depth of four that only the most elite troops might realistically hope to maintain for long against foes twice as deep. And that's probably just what transpired, with Philip's pikemen pinning Aetolian hoplites and Romans alike leftward even as the peltastai heroically held their own on the other wing. All that effort bought time for a superior Macedonian mounted force off at least one flank to chase its opposition and threaten an envelopment in quickly sending Pyrrhias and his men running for the safety of Lamia's fortunately nearby walls.

With a rapid escape having preserved most of Pyrrhias' manpower, he at some point sallied to engage the Macedonians for a second time. But though it's likely that the Aetolian made some attempt to adjust his approach toward gaining a better result, the Macedonians must have once more exploited their mounted advantage to deal him another defeat every bit as damaging as the first. Falling back again into Lamia, the Aetolians made no further effort to openly engage Philip's army as it then closed about to initiate a siege. This passive response most likely stemmed from Pyrrhias' recognition of his inferiority in mounted capability critical to any hope for tactical success upon the surrounding plain—a capability further reduced by his disproportionate loss of horsemen in the defeats taken to date. In the end, a negotiated settlement was reached that let the Aetolians withdraw safely from Lamia, freeing Philip to concentrate on other affairs of greater concern.

Mantinea V (207) and Scotitas (201)

Among Philip's problems at this time were the activities of Machanidas, a former mercenary leader of Tarentine-style horseman who had seized an effective dictatorship at Sparta by becoming regent for its child king, Pelops. Though courted by Rome, this tyrant was not only plaguing Macedon's Achaean allies, but even posed a threat to Roman-friendly Elis, though he abandoned the latter activity after Philip marched briefly into the Peloponnese and left behind some of his troops to help preserve the peace. Philip's men apparently returned home at the end of the 208 campaign season; however, Philopoemen decided to launch an attack upon the troublesome dictator the next year using Achaean resources alone. After spending eight months gathering an army from all the League members, he finally marched on Sparta and engaged Machanidas just outside the Arcadian city of Mantinea.

The contending forces at Mantinea in 207 were likely about the same size at roughly 20,000-strong.[18] The earlier League muster at Hecatombaeum (see Chapter 4) that likewise lacked outlying manpower provides a good low-side analog with 8,000 in heavy foot, 1,500 skirmishers, and 500 horsemen. Philopoemen might have improved on this to the tune of 10,000 for his reformed phalanx (maybe 8,000 draftee pikemen and 2,000 epilektoi with spears) and 1,000 riders with perhaps 1,000 light infantry attached to the horsemen and up to 2,000 elite theurophoros javelineers. Elevated from the skirmisher majority previously on hand, these last had gained body armor, most likely as epilektoi supported by the state, becoming medium infantry called *thorakitai* (cuirass-wearers).[19] There were probably around 6,000 mercenaries present as well, possibly including 1,000 Tarentine-style horsemen with a matching number of foot-skirmishers plus 1,000 additional light missilemen and 3,000 Illyrians.[20]

Machanidas learned of the Achaean presence at Mantinea and marched north to meet it. His local troops would have been much like those previously deployed at Sellasia of around 9,000 heavy foot (1,000 spartiate hoplites, 3,000 perioeci/allied hoplites, and 5,000 citizen/helot pikemen), 3,000 skirmishers, and 1,000 horsemen. Mercenaries then filled out his roster at some 7,000-strong, providing maybe another 1,000 horsemen of the Tarentine type (Machanidas' old command) and 5,000 light foot (possibly including Gauls, Thracians, and other foreign fighters in addition to 1,000 specialist javelineers that had been operating with the Tarentines).[21] The tyrant had also brought along dozens of artillery pieces in anticipation of putting Mantinea under siege once he had disposed of Philopoemen.

Philopoemen elected to take up a defensive position rather than move out and meet the Spartans in open battle. This involved expanding upon an existing drainage channel running south of Mantinea's walls to create a field-work. We are told without further explanation that he formed up his phalanx behind this barrier with gaps between its sub-units (speirai of around 250 men each). Walbank has suggested that this could have been an attempt to copy Pyrrhus' tactical innovations in Italy toward creating a more flexible combat array[22]; however, Pyrrhus did not insert spaces within his ranks but rather alternated spear-armed with pike-armed contingents while keeping all in close contact. There is no sign that Philopoemen similarly intermixed weaponry here, apparently deploying his spear-armed epilektoi all together on the left wing instead (where they presumably would face the enemy's best troops).[23] While having room between speirai might have been useful advancing over broken ground (as per Rome's quincunx), leaving those kind of gaps in a battle line seems nearly suicidal.

What then was the object of Philopoemen's uniquely segmented combat formation? One possible answer might lie in the length of the ditch/field-work that he had chosen to defend. Estimates for the trench's span range from 1,400m for the natural channel still in existence today to a more likely 2,000m with extending excavations, and Philopoemen could have covered less than 1,200m even using slender files of four for the spearmen and eight for his phalangites.[24] The gaps could have let him span the entire trench and then close ranks either to the left or right to defend a given portion most at hazard with a unified front. This might have been especially appealing in that the enemy's heavy foot, if it was composed as proposed here, would have been able to outflank him by something over 200m (if both sides were closely arrayed at similar depths) due to its greater proportion of hoplites (44 percent versus 20 percent) having shields half-again broader than those of pikemen.

Regardless of the true reasoning behind Philopoemen's curious formation design, he posted the crack Achaean horsemen with their supporting light foot behind the ditch outboard of the right wing of his phalanx,[25] placing the mercenary Tarentines and other cavalry plus attached skirmishers across the open ground beyond a temple (of Poseidon) and the field-work's leftward terminus. He then aligned the Illyrians and thorakitai in bastion behind his mercenary horse across the lowermost slope of Mount Alesion rising above Mantinea's eastern perimeter. Machanidas confronted these dispositions with his own heavy array matched against the opposing entrenched Achaean right wing and stretching out eastward to where his elite spartiates faced their epilektos counterparts. He personally led his own Tarentines and their associated light foot to threaten the mounted force opposed on his extreme right and, though not described in our sources, must have deployed some Peloponnesian horsemen beyond the termination of his phalanx at the other end of the field.

The Spartan tyrant came up with an innovative ploy in an attempt to overcome the advantage imparted to his foes by their field-work, moving his artillery pieces forward with the intention of providing cover for his heavy foot to cross over that impediment without undue loss.[26] Seeing this in progress, Philopoemen immediately attacked with the openly deployed mobile forces off his left flank in a bid to preempt the pending barrage. Machanidas then countercharged with his Tarentine riders and skirmishers to quickly prevail in a sharp melee that not only broke the Achaeans' mercenary cavalry and light foot but carried on to likewise scatter and chase the contingents of Illyrians and thorakitai standing on the slope behind. It was at this crucial juncture that the dictator made a serious mistake in choosing to pursue the beaten foes directly ahead rather than turn laterally against their phalanx's exposed flank.

Those leading Machanidas' own heavy array had seen their commander's outboard victory and, distaining now seemingly unnecessary artillery fire, launched an immediate assault into the trench under the badly mistaken belief that their opponents were being enveloped and on the verge of collapse. But actually unmolested, the Achaeans closed ranks and heavily punished the Spartans as they became badly disrupted in futilely attempting to cross over the depression. Philopoemen then took full advantage of this failed attack, maneuvering the well-drilled epilektoi holding his far left wing, who made a quarter turn and marched across the sector abandoned by Machanidas to again face forward and swing around the enemy's unshielded right in a cyclosis-like envelopment of their own. Suddenly taken in flank, the Spartan phalanx fell apart and its terrified members were pursued by horsemen and skirmishers that now came racing across the bridged western end of the trench.

Meanwhile, Machanidas had finally turned back from his ill-advised chase only to be met by the stunning sight of his beaten army in full flight. Seeking to escape this debacle, he made for the bridge only to find it still under guard. He then tried to cross directly through the ditch but was ridden down and killed, reportedly by Philopoemen himself. At day's end, the Achaeans' victory was complete, claiming the lives of their tyrannical tormentor plus more than 4,000 of his men with as many more falling prisoner.[27]

The First Macedonian War ended in 205 after the Aetolians withdrew from the conflict and the Romans, still needing to concentrate on battling Carthage, joined their remaining allies in signing the Treaty of Phoenice. This ceded control of Illyria to Philip in return for cutting his Punic ties. However, conflict between Achaea and Sparta continued to fester. A new regent named Nabis had taken charge upon the death of Machanidas and this bloodthirsty fellow quickly claimed royal descent for himself, usurped young Pelops, and went on to execute all other candidates for Sparta's kingships. He then set about recovering from the defeat at Mantinea V via a radical reapportioning of land and wealth. This elevated many slaves to citizenship, pulling them into a rebuilt army further expanded through the addition of mercenaries funded with riches impounded as part of the reapportionment program. An inherent foe of Philip's Achaean allies, Nabis had signed the Phoenice Treaty as a partner of Rome but continued to harass Achaea. He was initially unopposed in this by Philopoemen, who had resumed mercenary work on Crete; however, upon the latter's return to the Peloponnese in 201, he quickly put knowledge of that island's dominant irregular warfare to good use in engineering a successful ambush of some of Nabis' troops just above the Spartan border.

Philopoemen secretly gathered an army at Tegea and sent a picked force to raid into Laconia followed by a rapid retreat. This drew a pursuing Spartan contingent into thick woods near the village of Scotitas where it was ambushed. Our sources yield very little detail on this action beyond being successful for Philopoemen. The raiding party sent out as bait must have been a modestly sized combination of epilektos hoplites, javelineers (thorakitai), and horsemen per other such "flying columns" seen in this era. And the men that gave chase were probably not much if any more numerous, consisting perhaps of a small mercenary brigade better suited than conscripted citizens to garrison the frontier for an extended period. Philopoemen had collected a sizeable host from "all the cities of the Achaean League"[28] and no doubt had something grander in mind than merely snaring a few mercenaries, likely hoping to lure Nabis out in force so that he could be eliminated like Machanidas. But if so, he was frustrated and had to ultimately march home with nothing accomplished worthy of the effort.

The Second Macedonian War

Philip V and Antiochus III agreed to a non-aggression pact toward the end of the 3rd century with the aim of exploiting the disputed reign of young Ptolemy V in Egypt. This helped pave the way for Antiochus' attachment of Coele Syria (see *Panium* above) while at the same time encouraging Philip to expand his influence in and around the Aegean Sea. The Rhodians responded to the latter threat against their own interests by going to war with

Macedon in 202, and Pergamum joined them lest it be isolated as Philip's next target. With Egypt in turmoil and Seleucia cooperating with the Macedonians, Pergamum had no other source for help than Rome. And the Romans, having now ended their long conflict with Carthage, felt free to intervene on their former ally's behalf. Initially this saw them apply diplomatic pressure, but when Philip rejected their ultimatums, they again declared war.

Ithacus/Otolobum and the Dardanian Frontier (199)

Rome opened hostilities in 200 by landing an army in Illyria under the consul Sulpicius Galba.[29] He marched northeast into the Upper Macedonian district of Lyncestis the next summer, where he was met by Philip with 20,000 foot and 4,000 horse.[30] We have no breakdown of the king's troops but they might have included 12,000–14,000 heavy-armed men (including 9,000 phalangites) plus 6,000–8,000 medium (Illyrians and Grecian theurophoroi) and light-armed (slingers, bowmen, and Thracian javelineers) with a goodly portion of the latter types assigned to the cavalry at one per horseman. Sulpicius' host is not enumerated either; however, it must have been a typical consular army of four Roman/allied legions with some 9,600 hastati and principes plus 2,400 triarii, 4,800 light-armed velites, and 2,400 horsemen. In addition to that standard muster, we need to add some light infantry attached to a force of elephants captured from the Carthaginians and now accompanying a Roman army for the first time. The number of those beasts is unknown but no doubt rather modest, probably requiring no more than 1,000 skirmishers to serve as out-runners and perhaps well less.

Sulpicius camped near an otherwise unknown location identified as Ithacus (Athacus) and Philip occupied a hill nearby. With both camps fortified, neither leader wanted to make a disadvantaged attack on the other and they simply kept mutual watch for a couple of days. A skirmish developed between the camps on day three that saw Rome's horsemen and light foot rebuff a like-sized collection of Illyrians and riders sent out by Philip. Taking a day to prepare, the Macedonian king threw his cavalry and light foot in strength at the Romans, seeking to defeat their similarly composed contingents outright. However, should his men again meet failure, they were to lead the enemy into an ambush from a team of peltastai hidden along the intended path of retreat. But though Sulpicius' horsemen and velites did indeed once more prove successful, they managed to avoid that trap when the spearmen emerged prematurely and prompted the Romans to break off pursuit and retire safely.

Having somewhat weakened Philip's larger mobile contingents, Sulpicius deployed his entire army for battle the next day with the elephants positioned in front of its acies triplex. Philip refused to come out and fight and the consul then elected to pull back nearly 13km to Otolobum and set up a new encampment. He believed that his foragers would be free from attack at such a remove, but that idea was quickly proven erroneous when Philip personally led a speedy advance of his horsemen and Cretan archers to cut off the restocking detachments. Learning of this disaster in the making, Sulpicius dispatched cavalry to rescue his foragers and mustered the legions for action outside the camp. The Roman horsemen advanced in haphazard fashion and fared poorly, especially against the Cretans and javelineers accompanying Philip's cavalry that had set up in formation. However, the king and his riders would then suffer a similar fate when they gave chase and ran into a storm of javelins from legionaries likewise standing bastion at the Roman rear. Philip's own mount went down and he barely escaped with his life as the Macedonians fell back.[31]

Philip now decided not to risk an open combat with Sulpicius and retired eastward, moving through upland defiles toward home. The Romans followed for a time and engaged in some skirmishing, but ultimately swung through the Upper Macedonian district of Elimeia before returning to Illyria at the end of the campaign season. While Philip had failed to inflict an outright defeat on Sulpicius, he had sufficiently occupied the consul so as to keep him from invading Lower Macedonia. That preserved strength needed to confront threats to those more valuable eastern districts that were developing from the actions of others seeking to exploit his feud with Rome for their own benefit. The most pressing of these came from the Dardanians of Illyria, who had raided into the Macedonian northwest about the same time as the action at Otolobum. Philip's general Athenagoras chased the invaders back across the frontier, where they turned to fight when he caught them from behind.

We are told nothing of the forces that engaged here save that the Illyrians lacked cavalry and light foot such as opposed them and stood in a heavy line of battle against what was presumably a phalanx spread across a corresponding interval.[32] Reasonable speculation suggests that Athenagoras commanded the minimal operational force of a single strategia with 1,000 peltastai and 3,000 phalangites supported by 1,000–2,000 foot-skirmishers and 500–1,000 horsemen with the opposing Dardanians having some 5,000 spearmen. If so, the resulting heavy arrays would have been evenly matched across a front 500m wide that quickly fell into stalemate. It was Athenagoras' horsemen and skirmishers who then proved decisive by assaulting the Illyrians' unscreened or (perhaps more likely) poorly screened flanks. Though the barbarians' burdensome gear prevented an adequate response to this and many of them took wounds, we are told that few died and none fell prisoner "because they rarely quit their ranks, fighting and retreating instead in a close body."

Aous R. (198)

The following summer saw Titus Quinctius Flamininus take over command of the Roman effort against Philip and march a four-legion army rich in Punic War veterans to confront the king where he had aggressively set up southeast of the consul's base at Apolonia within a pass cut by the Aous River.[33] Philip occupied a strong position here that spanned the passage, having protection on either side provided by mountainous terrain which was reinforced with elements of light infantry. Our sources provide no figures on the Macedonian manpower deployed[34]; however, it was surely at least on a par with the 24,000 men thrown against Sulpicius the year before as well as similar in composition.

Flamininus hesitated before this impediment and engaged in fruitless negotiations until local men approached after 40 days with an offer to lead him around the Macedonian blockade. As the consul occupied his foes with harassing frontal sorties, a picked force set out on this mission with 4,000 foot and 300 horse, numbers suggesting that it was probably one of his citizen legions. The cavalry had to stop when the climb got too difficult, but the legionaries utilized night marches under a full moon to get above Philip on the northern side of the pass three days after their departure from camp. Signaled that this ambuscade was in place, Flaminius then advanced in three columns, each perhaps at legion-strength with the consul and his remaining citizen legion having an ala sociorum on either flank. Plutarch tells us that a phalanx of pikemen occupied the valley floor and had support from various types of works (Livy cites trenches, barricades, and even towers). In addition to the missilemen deployed above on each lateral, Philip sent out light infantry ahead of his phalanx. And though the heavier-armed legionaries soon drove these skirmishers from the field, that simply brought the king's remaining defenses into action and they proved highly effective.

Flamininus and his men could make no progress against the dense enemy pike-front[35] even as they took casualties from barrages of javelins and arrows cascading down from the enclosing heights. But the consul's ambushing detachment finally descended on the attack to save the day. Taken by surprise and seeing his position now badly compromised, Philip ordered a hasty retreat and managed to get away with most of his host. He suffered no more than 2,000 casualties in the end, with that relatively modest butcher's bill being ascribed to the terrain having hampered effective pursuit. However, while no doubt true for ambushers forced to negotiate rocky slopes, other factors must have been in play elsewhere such as needing to cross abandoned works, Rome's horsemen being stuck behind a crowd of foot soldiers, and effective cover by Philip's own cavalry.

Cynoscephalae (197)

Flamininus chose not to chase Philip and swung down instead into Greece, where he was able to establish control as far up as Thermopylae pass by year's end. The consul marched into Thessaly that spring, camping near Pherae even as Philip and his restored army came down into the same area. The country thereabout was "thickly wooded and full of walls and gardens"[36] and thus sure to disrupt any attempt at orderly mass maneuver. As this suited neither commander, both withdrew after a brief mounted skirmish and headed inland, losing contact in the process. A Roman patrol then blundered into some of Philip's troops moving south on the road from Larissa within a pass through the Cynoscephalae Hills above Pharsalus in a chance meeting that would lead to the war's decisive battle.

Plutarch informs us that the opposing forces were "about the same size" with Flaminius having over 26,000 men including 6,000 light foot and 400 cavalry from Aetolia.[37] This indicates a four legion/ala consular army of 12,000 heavy foot, 4,800 light-armed velites, and 2,400 horsemen in addition to the Aetolians plus a modest contingent of elephants with skirmisher support. Livy records Philip's phalanx at 16,000-strong, suggesting 1,000–2,000 regular peltastai and 14,000–15,000 pikemen with the latter being an unusually high count due to the inclusion of elderly and youth reservists.[38] Added to these were 2,000 elite agema peltastai, 2,000 Illyrians and Thracians, 1,000 other mercenary missile specialists, and 2,000 horsemen for a total of 23,000 combatants. It's possible, however, that Livy's figure for the Macedonian cavalry is an undercount in that he himself had said this was 4,000-strong just two years earlier at Ithacus and it would later number the same in a similar all-out effort at Pydna (see Chapter 8). It's thus conceivable that Philip rather than Flamininus had the larger mounted contingent as well as more attached light infantry than Livy claims, combining to boost his manpower above 26,000 in compliance with Plutarch's rough estimate.

Philip's men initially dominated the small Roman advance force; however, subsequent reinforcements sent by Flamininus forced them back onto a crestal position from which they sent for help from the king's camp to the north. He responded by dispatching contingents of Macedonian and Thessalian horsemen along with a strong force of mercenary skirmishers, and these drove the Romans down into a defensive stance. Seeing his lead elements thus in peril, the consul deployed the rest of his army at the foot of the slopes on either side of the contested roadway, strengthening the battered vanguard with heavy legionaries that allowed it to repulse the lighter-armed mercenary opposition.

Meanwhile, Philip organized into column and personally marched the right wing of his host upslope to take post atop the ridge on the west side of the pass. Behind this, his subordinate Nicanor was tasked with leading the army's left wing into a corresponding position on the hills to the east. Philip was certainly not compelled to accept battle in this rugged setting, which would clearly be disadvantageous for normal phalanx tactics designed for employment across flat ground. Why, then, did he accept combat here rather than withdraw onto the plains to the north and await the enemy on that seemingly more favorable terrain? Our sources suggest that the opening successes reported against the Roman vanguards had elevated his enthusiasm to the point that it overrode prudent caution and, once he was atop the ridge, the enemy moving up from below forced the issue. However, while Philip might indeed have been encouraged by the results of those early skirmishes and then quickly drawn into combat by his foes' close approach, it's quite likely that his original decision to

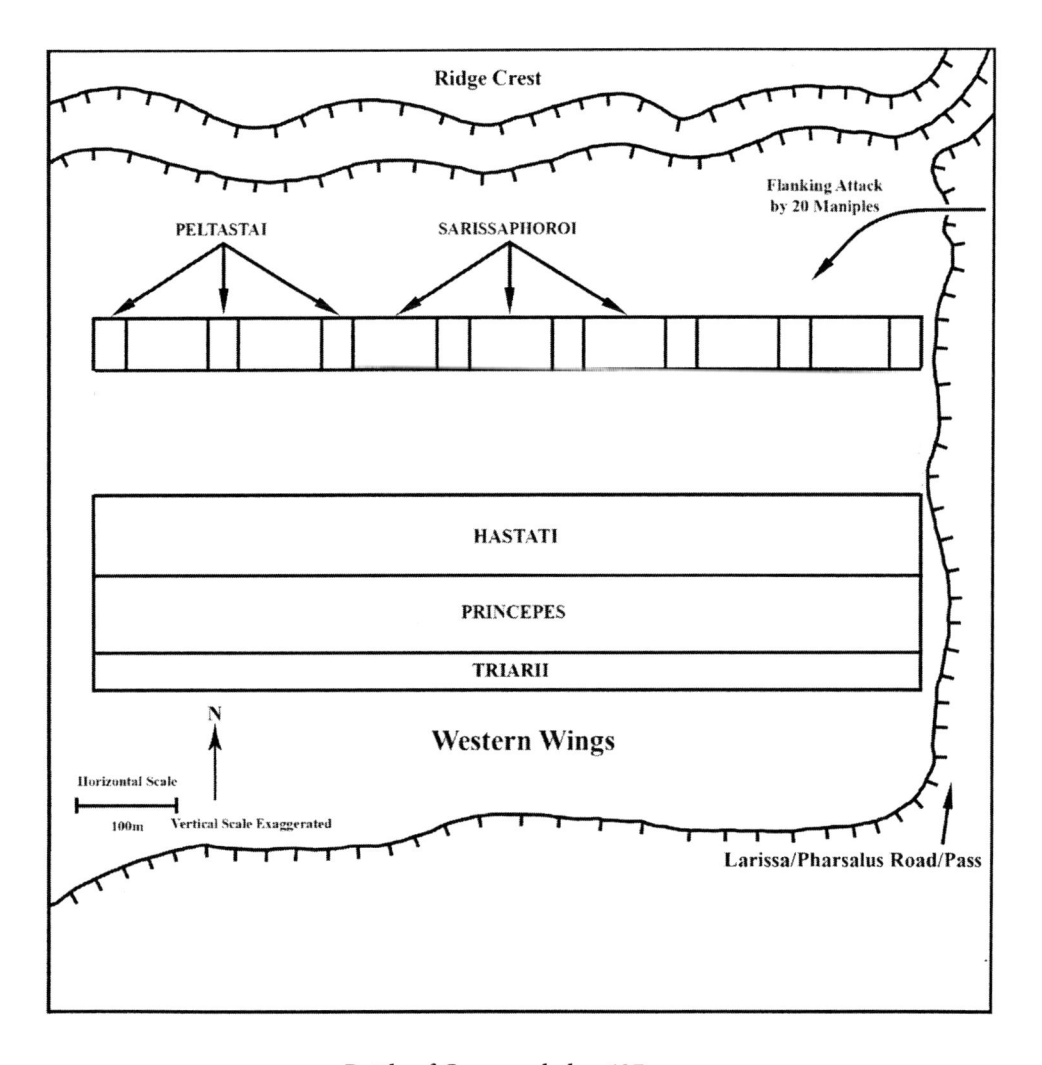

Battle of Cynoscephalae, 197 BCE.

engage was not rash, but rather soundly based on a notable past triumph by his stepfather Antigonus Doson.

The battle of Sellasia in 222 (see Chapter 4) had seen Antigonus' right wing (separated as was Philip's here from its left by a mountain pass) achieve victory after initiating an assault across a significant incline; indeed, doing so fighting uphill rather than with momentum from a downslope advance such as the present situation would provide. That had been engineered through emulating Pyrrhus' ploy against the Romans in Italy of interspersing units of heavy spearmen between phalangite contingents to create joints within his phalanx for greater flexibility. This enabled the Macedonian right wing at Sellasia to maintain order in an upslope charge that broke through and destroyed its crestal Spartan opposition. And with that favorable experience in mind, Philip probably tried much the same at Cynoscephalae. This would have called for forming a column four-men-wide that interspersed his eight speirai of crack agema peltastai among seven pike chiliarchies comprising the phalanx's right wing. He then led these troops up and reeled them leftward to double into a depth of eight and close toward the right into a mixed-arms line some 800m across, thus matching that half of Flamininus heavy array climbing up from below at two legions strong in acies triplex. In concert, the cavalry and mercenary skirmishers bested in the pass relocated to screen Philip's right, leaving his left flank to be covered by Nicanor's deployment still in progress.

The Macedonians descended against the Roman front and "came off brilliantly in the encounter, for they were charging downhill and were superior in weight, and their arms were far more suited for the actual conditions of the struggle."[39] The legionaries slowly gave ground under irresistible pressure enhanced by gravity, falling in multiple sectors to deadly spear thrusts even as sarissai elsewhere prodded them into awkward, rear-stepping retirement.[40] "Seeing that his men were unable to stand the charge of the phalanx," Flamininus left his rearward post on the west and rode over to the other side of the pass in "hopes of saving himself"[41] by conquering that so far uncontested part of the field.

The situation that the consul discovered on his right was that Nicanor had not yet managed to get the Macedonian left wing into position and was just now cresting the ridge with it still in column of march. Unable to properly form their phalanx, his men gave way and fled before even coming to close quarters with the well-formed acies triplex that Flamininus sent charging uphill with his elephants rampaging at the fore. While most of the Romans gave chase, one tribune on his own initiative led some twenty maniples (around 2,400 men) down and across the pass to come over the ridgeline on the other side and attack both the back and left flank of Philip's wing. Taken utterly by surprise, the Macedonians at rear and side tried to turn about in response and their resulting disarray allowed the previously retreating legionaries in front to recover and go on the offensive from that quarter as well. Simultaneously put to the sword from three directions, the Grecian formation disintegrated as panicked men tossed shields and weapons to run for their lives.

Philip was able to escape and gather a large number of survivors; nonetheless, he had absorbed a truly damaging defeat, which had cost half of his army at 8,000 killed and another 5,000 taken prisoner while claiming only 700 or so Romans in return.[42] Philip gained a truce to collect his dead and began negotiating a cessation to the war. There were incentives in play at this time for both sides to come to terms. The Romans were experiencing increasing friction with the Aetolians and growing ever more concerned that Seleucia might throw in against them; and for Philip, his combat losses plus the continuing menace from Rome were not his only threats as allies began to desert and local foes grew bolder.

Nemea R. and Alabanda (197)

Among Philip's most dangerous local enemies were the Achaeans. Their league had not contributed to Flamininus' campaign in Thessaly but elected instead to exploit that operation by independently attacking Macedonian interests closer to home. The key to reducing Philip's influence there was neutralizing his garrison at Corinth, which controlled the overland pathway into the Peloponnese. Led by Androsthenes, this force was ravaging League territory in the coastal region of the Peloponnesian northwest shortly after Cynoscephalae when suddenly confronted by the Achaean general Nicostratus.

Androsthenes' troops comprised a mixture of Philip's men, allies, and mercenaries.[43] An original 500-man contingent of Macedonians had recently been boosted by the arrival of a heavy reinforcement that included another 1,000 of their countrymen. Being too small a force to act as an independent phalanx, that first 500 must have been peltast spearmen well suited for executing a variety of other operations in concert with 800 mercenary skirmishers also initially on hand. The newly arrived Macedonians could have been a chiliarchy of either phalangites or more hoplites, with the latter maybe a better choice for garrisoning duties like manning ramparts on defense or carrying out detached offensives. The other reinforcements fit that more flexible mold as well, being 1,200 Illyrian spearmen, 800 Thessalian javelineers and Cretan bowmen plus 1,000 others consisting of Boeotians and Thessalians (probably mounted)[44] as well as Acarnanians (skirmishers including slingers). Some 700 young Corinthians (perhaps mostly hoplites) joined these foreign troops to total 6,000 combatants in all.

Confident that he was dealing with cowed foes after meeting no resistance while pillaging their coastal regions, Androsthenes had dismissed half his men and organized the rest into three detachments to more widely spread a campaign of ravaging across the inland territories of Pellene, Phlius, and Cleonai. Livy tells us that the troops retained for this operation included Macedonians and cavalry, with the latter moving in separate bodies ahead of each detachment. A fair guess at how Androsthenes could have used half his total manpower to form these independent raiding teams suggests that each might have been 1,000-strong and cored around a 250-man speira of Macedonian peltastai with support from 200 Illyrians, 500 javelineers and other skirmishers, and 50 horsemen.

The Achaean general Nicostratus was nearby at Sicyon and, initially too weak for retaliation, stealthily gathered an army of 5,000 foot and 300 horse. We are told that a portion of his infantry was light-armed and, while their exact number has been lost, these included Thracian javelineers and Cretan bowmen.[45] In assessing his manpower, it is related that Nicostratus split this force in two for advance on the enemy, with one division containing mercenaries and light infantry and the other all the heavy foot. Most likely done to further speed movement by reducing column lengths along narrow roads, this might well represent a nearly even split of the troop population. If so, a reasonable breakdown of the army's components might be 2,500 heavy-armed, 1,000 theurophoroi hirelings of medium weight, and 1,500 Thracians, Cretans, and other skirmishers in addition to the 300 cavalrymen. The detailed composition of Nicostratus' heavy infantry is particularly unclear due to it consisting not only of Achaeans for whom we have some past numbers, but those from "other states" as well. We do know, however, that these troops were a mixture of both pikemen and spear-armed hoplites,[46] with the last almost surely counting some League epilektoi.[47]

Androsthenes had set up a fortified camp along the Nemea River and Nicostratus descended upon it at a time when the Macedonian's horsemen and most of his lighter equipped foot were scattered about the countryside. Taken by surprise, Androsthenes quickly called in any auxiliaries close to hand so as to distribute them on one flank as he led out his modest force of spear-armed countrymen and formed a thin phalanx with its other end anchored on the riverbank. Having underestimated the opposition in abandoning ramparts for a fight in the open, Androsthenes and his peltastai found themselves hard pressed to withstand the attack that now struck. This came from a pike-hedge across most of the opposing line so deep as to be virtually impenetrable for their shorter Macedonian spears, while even the comparably equipped hoplites facing them on the wing farthest from the river had the benefit of longer files. Still, they valiantly "kept the victory a long time doubtful" before succumbing to a lateral assault. This saw their hastily gathered auxiliaries give way to let the enemy's light foot close around a now unscreened landward flank. Continuing to battle the heftier phalanx ahead, the Macedonians "at first gave ground," but "soon after, being vigorously pushed, they turned their backs" with most "throwing away their arms" in a desperate effort at speedier escape. It was during the subsequent pursuit and in clearing those of Androsthenes' men unaware of his defeat (and still despoiling the countryside) that the victors inflicted the greatest damage, allowing them to slay 1,500 and capture another 300 in total before the day was done.

The last pitched battle of the Second Macedonian War took place about the same time when the allies of Rome on Rhodes tried to exploit Philip's woes by recovering territory lost to him inboard on the southern mainland of Caria. This involved landing 800 Achaeans along with 1,900 other troops representing half a dozen nationalities and then reinforcing that beach-head with a further 1,000 foot and 100 horse also provided by Achaea. Learning of this threat, Macedon's local commander, Dinocrates, drew men from his garrisons and prepared to resist. Among his scratch force were 500 Macedonians (probably a bodyguard of peltastai), local hoplites (some Ionians but mostly Carians), Thracian javelineers (dominated by a crack team of Agrianians), Cretan bowmen, and Thessalian cavalry. Dinocrates confronted the invading army outside the city of Alabanda (Antiochia of the Chrysaorians) and, facing off across a small stream, both sides deployed for battle. The Macedonian general placed the peltast spearmen on the right extreme of his phalanx per custom, spread out the Carian and Ionian heavy foot along its center and left wing, and screened his far left with all the Agrianians. Dinocrates' archers and other javelineers posted on the opposite flank while the Thessalian horse divided outboard on either end of his infantry array. The Rhodians countered with Achaean hoplites on their right wing, a picked force of heavy-armed allies at center, mercenary spearmen standing farthest left, and skirmishers and cavalry off each flank.

Livy tells us that the armies were "an equality with respect to numbers and the kind of arms which they used" and provides strengths for a few of the units present.[48] He gives 1,000 heavy-armed men to the Achaeans serving Rhodes, suggesting that nation's 800 footmen with the initial landing party probably came from its state-supported contingent of armored javelineers (thorakitai), thus making it likely that the thousand infantrymen arriving later were similarly supplemented hoplites. Both those classes of epilektoi would have been more readily available and much better suited than a draft of amateurs for such an overseas adventure, whether serving in a truly allied capacity or as short-term hires. Mercenary and select-allied spearmen (probably mainland Greeks and Ionians respectively) would then have comprised the other 1,900 men originally brought ashore. The Rhodians' heavy infantry count was therefore 2,900, which added to the thorakitai and 100 horsemen to complete the 3,800-man strength cited by Livy.[49] For Dinocrates' part, the Carians and other locals in his service could easily have furnished 2,500 spearmen to go along with his 500 peltastai in forming a like-sized phalanx. This would have had equivalent auxiliary support as well in the form of 600 theurophoros javelineers (400 of them Agrianian), 100 archers from Crete, and 100 horsemen.

Neither army was eager to advance across the intervening rivulet and they mutually retired after doing no more than exchanging javelin fire. The same positions and deployments were resumed the next day; but this time, the Rhodians initiated battle, sending the thorakitai screening on the right against their Agrianian counterparts. This assault apparently opened in a sufficiently encouraging manner to then trigger an advance across the streambed by the entire Rhodian phalanx. The ensuing combat is said to have "continued doubtful a long time"; however, it finally turned in Rhodes' favor when its thorakitai broke the lighter equipped Agrianians. The local spearmen holding the left wing of the Macedonian heavy formation then collapsed in turn as they came under combined pressure from those elite javelineers attacking their flank and the epilektos hoplites pressing from in front.

As for the peltastai and allies on Dinocrates' other wing, Livy tells us that "no impression could be made against the Macedonians so long as their phalanx preserved its order, each man clinging as it were to each other; but in consequence of their flank being left exposed, they endeavored to turn their spears against the enemy, who were advancing on that side, and they immediately broke their ranks." Thrown into disorder and most tossing their arms, these men fled in a frenzy toward the rear. The victors gave pursuit until dark but many of those defeated, including Dinocrates himself, managed to escape and join a garrison in the nearby city of Stratonice. They would go on to withstand a siege there, largely negating the effects of their defeat to still firmly hold that bastion when negotiations finally brought the Second Macedonian War to an end in 196.

8. An End to the Greek Way of War
Seleucia in Decline and the Fall of Macedonia (195–167 BCE)

The peace agreement between Rome and Philip V ending the Second Macedonian War was destined to hold for a generation, but the conflict had set a precedent for large scale Roman military participation on the soil of mainland Greece. That opened the way for the Romans to usurp the role Macedon had played in affairs of the region's lesser states as a new reality with ominous implications for future Greek independence; something that would become apparent within a year as turmoil once more erupted in the Peloponnese.

The Wars Against Nabis and Antiochus

Argos split from the Achaean League in 195 and appealed to Macedonia for support. Though still reeling from his recent defeat, Philip was loathe to let so inviting an opportunity for reasserting influence slip away and asked Sparta's Nabis to undertake the task on his behalf. That tyrant jumped at the chance to advance his own interests; however, his subsequent harsh treatment of the Argives was so odious that they soon sought outside protection from their erstwhile savior. With Macedonia having proven both weak and duplicitous in inflicting this crisis upon them, the Argives approached Rome's local commander, Flamininus, for help. He duly convened a council of affected poleis to legitimatize his intervention and succeeded in convincing them to declare war on the Spartans.

Eurotas R. (195)

Flamininus marched a force of his own men and Grecian allies into Sparta and approached the Eurotas River immediately across from its capital city. What little we know of his army's is that its Latin component was multi-legion complete with light foot and horse and that the attached Greeks included troops from Achaea who might have formed those contingents' majority in quest of regaining authority over Argos.[1] A minimum assumption along those lines would be that Flamininus had a single legion/ala pair plus Achaea's epilektoi along with a squadron of its cavalry and a lesser body of light foot provided in concert by other northern Peloponnesian states. If so, we're looking at a Roman contribution of

6,000 heavy legionaries, 2,400 velites, and 900 horsemen accompanied by 2,000 elite hoplites, 2,000 javelineer thorakitai, and at least 100 mounted men from Achaea as well as some 2,000 other Greek skirmishers likely composed for the most part of theurophoroi.

Whatever the true size of Flamininus' army, Nabis refused to challenge it in heavy-armed combat. Well aware that his own long oppressed citizenry was of highly dubious loyalty, the tyrant chose to confine its most questionable members under close watch and employ what remained of Sparta's 10,000 or so native line troops and auxiliaries in defense of ditches and ramparts around the city as well as within other key fortified sites spread about the area. This forced him to rely exclusively on mercenary light foot and cavalry for any desired offensive operations. We are told in this regard that Nabis had 2,000 Cretans and 3,000 other hirelings in his employ, and all of those listed men might have been infantry in addition to a separate contingent of Tarentine-style horse.[2]

The Spartan tyrant sallied his mercenaries to where the newly arrived Flamininus with a vanguard had crossed the Eurotas and begun setting up camp. Caught by surprise, the Romans were at first thrown into disarray, but ended up being rescued when the lead elements of their heavy foot arrived to send the attackers into retreat. The next day, the Roman commander collected his entire force and set out along the riverbank with legions at the fore and the cavalry and allies marching behind. This presented Nabis with another opportunity for an ambush and, having kept his hired men ready next to the city's gates, he launched them against the rear of Flamininus' column. But to their surprise, the Roman's rearguard was prepared for this and spun about to present a unified front, turning what had been expected to be an open-ordered skirmish into a "a regular engagement ... as if two complete lines had encountered."[3] We are told that the ensuing action "lasted a considerable time; but at length Nabis' troops betook themselves to flight ... closely pressed by the Achaeans." Most of the Spartan hirelings threw away their weapons with the more fortunate managing to then get back inside their walls. They didn't dare emerge again and Flamininus proceeded to camp alongside the Eurotas, investing both the city and its port of Gytheum while his men spoiled the region. By year's end, Nabis found it prudent to negotiate terms that yielded not only Argos, but Sparta's coastal region as well in return for retaining control over what remained of the state.

The Camp of Pyrrhus (192)

Nabis had been greatly weakened by the loss of so much of his hinterland, which had ended access to the perioeci living there that had always been so valuable for Sparta's army. Seeking a remedy, he tried to reclaim Gytheum, whose harbor had been the main gateway for imports and thus the most treasured site within the now separated territories. And when a Roman fleet arrived with a garrison, Nabis reacted by putting the city under siege. He had some good luck thereafter in besting a poorly executed naval attack and, no longer concerned about further threats from offshore, shifted a third of the men investing Gytheum inland to ward any overland attempt to relieve the port. Philopoemen took advantage of this to sneak a river-borne raiding party down for a nighttime attack upon the resulting Spartan encampment, which lay near the town of Pleiae. His men set the rude wooden huts there on fire to kill nearly everyone within and then spoiled the vicinity before withdrawing. Encouraged by this, the Achaean general next staged at Tegea for a descent upon Sparta in greater force that he might lure Nabis entirely away from Gytheum. But unknown to him, the place had already fallen, freeing the tyrant to reposition troops along the road from

Tegea near a location in the Spartan north known as the Camp of Pyrrhus. Lying in a narrow and heavily wooded valley somewhere south of Sellasia, this otherwise unknown site was apparently associated with a chokepoint that Nabis must have barricaded and manned with hired missilemen if we assume his offensive operations continued to involve only mercenary contingents.[4]

Philopoemen approached having his men and baggage strung out along the narrow roadway with the cavalry and most of the light foot bringing up the rear as a precaution against an attack from behind such as had struck Flamininus' column three years prior. The reported length of this train at nearly 7.5km leads to speculation that the Achaean general might have had something like 14,000 soldiers of all types under his command. This allots half a kilometer for baggage with his men spaced at an average of four abreast and their ranks 2m apart along the remaining line of march. If so, previous Achaean deployments and what little we know about this one combine to suggest complements in the area of 10,000 heavy foot (2,000 hoplite epilektoi and 8,000 conscripted pikemen), 3,000 medium/light infantry (2,000 thorakitai and 1,000 others including Cretan mercenary archers), and 1,000 horsemen (perhaps at least half of them being shield-bearing Tarentines).

Upon seeing the blockade ahead, Philopoemen curtailed his advance and camped fairly close to the enemy position. At the same time, he brought his bowmen and cavalry up to seize ground overlooking a nearby brook on which both his and Nabis' men must depend for water. The competing watering parties came into conflict the next morning. Both sides are said to have deployed their Cretan archers and Tarentine riders, but theurophoroi must have been present as well since the ensuing action involved shock fighting in close formation unsuited to either bowmen or cavalry. Philopoemen's troops eventually fell back; however, that proved to be a trick, serving to draw the opposition into an ambush from a hidden force of Achaean epilektos spearmen.[5] These "were in such order ... that they easily gave passage to their flying friends through openings in their ranks; and then ... in regular order, they briskly attacked the enemy, whose ranks were broken."[6] Those fighting for Sparta fled under hot pursuit until Philopoemen recalled both his skirmishers and hoplites lest the rear bastion being provided by the latter lose cohesion over rough terrain that lay ahead.

Nabis withdrew early the next day, leaving some light foot to hold his barricade along with a few horsemen. When that small rearguard took flight, the Achaeans' spearmen moved to plunder the empty camp while fleeter comrades gave chase, hunting the fleeing men through the surrounding woodlands. Meanwhile, anxious to avoid being caught by a fast-moving pursuit, Nabis and his main body were making their way through the densely forested uplands to the west so as to force any chase on foot to track slowly and prevent horsemen from following at all. However, realizing that this was going to slow Nabis as well, Philopoemen rapidly marched his heavy foot down the now open road and took up position between the tyrant and home. Nabis still somehow managed to regain Sparta, but most of his badly scattered troops were not so fortunate. We are told that "such numbers of them were killed and taken, that of the whole army scarcely a fourth part effected their escape."[7] With Nabis couched behind his walls, Philopoemen wasted the countryside before withdrawing to great acclaim.

Delium (192) and Thermopylae (191)

The Achaean League's ascendency in the Peloponnese following the decline of Macedonian influence there was mirrored by a similar rise for Greece's other major federation, the Aetolian League. In 192, that collective took advantage of the vacuum Philip left in southern Thessaly by seizing the important harbor city of Demetrias on the Pagasaean Gulf and then reached into the Peloponnese to incite a coup in recently humbled Sparta. The latter saw Aetolia send military support to Nabis only for those troops to help murder him upon arrival. That act of treachery promptly backfired, however, as the assassins were themselves attacked with Sparta ultimately being absorbed into the Achaean League to end its long and storied history as an independent state. Alarmed by this and other advancements by their Achaean rivals, the Aetolians petitioned Antiochus III for an alliance.

Antiochus decided to accept the Aetolian League's invitation and made a landing in early winter at Demetrias with an army of 10,000 infantry and 500 cavalry. Based upon past limited Seleucid deployments that were similarly carried out in haste, this was probably the easily assembled 2,000 hoplite peltastai and 8,000 pikemen of the standing Argyraspide strategiai with rather anemic support from only a quarter of the king's mounted bodyguards due to the restrictions that his modest seaborne capacity imposed on horse transport. Wary of this threat to their own position in Greece, the Romans shipped the praetor Marcus Baebius to Apollonia with two legions plus allied forces of 15,000 foot and 500 horse.

When Antiochus invested Chalcis on Euboa, Baebius dispatched a 500-man maniple to its aid. However, this unit came under a surprise attack en route at Delium and was turned back with heavy casualties and the capture of 50 men. The ambush was led by one of the Seleucid guard-unit commanders, Menippus, who must have used 1,000 peltastai and 500 Agrianian javelineers that he is said to have previously led into Boeotia.[8] Chalcis, the rest of Euboa, and all Thessaly save Larissa then fell to Antiochus in short order. The only good news for Baebius in all of this was that Philip V agreed to let a detachment of 2,000 Roman troops march across Macedonian territory to dissuade the Seleucid king from keeping Larissa under siege. He chose instead to retire upon Chalcis for the rest of the winter.

The following spring, a new consul Manius Acilius Glabrio took over the campaign against Antiochus, arriving in Apollonia with 20,000 foot (four legions/alae plus auxiliaries), 2,000 horse (a slight upgrade from the standard 1,800 cavalry assigned to a consular army of this size), and 15 elephants, those last probably accounting for 750 of the auxiliaries (50 per animal) as out-runners with the remaining 2,500 or so being specialist archers, slingers, etc. Glabrio brought this force to bear quickly in reclaiming Thessaly, capturing 3,000 of the Seleucid king's men in the process. Antiochus had received some reinforcements from home since his initial landing, but no more than enough to replace losses to date and maintain his native troops at around their original count. Thus, while 4,000 Aetolians had joined him as well as a modest number of mercenaries (archers, slingers, and javelinmen) and six elephants, he didn't feel strong enough to risk open battle.[9] This led Antiochus to drop back south upon the pass at Thermopylae and set up across its easternmost narrows where he could await reinforcements from Asia that would allow resumption of offensive operations.

Antiochus threw up field works consisting of a trench-fronted wall composed largely of excavated soil and loose stones from the abutting cliffs. We know from Livy that this was of only "moderate height" yet, when combined with a ditch, "afforded to its defenders a higher situation" from which they could still utilize a sarissa even though that weapon required a double underhand grip. Having so hardened his front, the king posted 2,000 Aetolians rearward to the town of Heraclea and sent the rest inland to block various pathways through the mountains, including 600 picked men to hold the narrow track close by that both Persians and Celts had used to circumvent Thermopylae in the past.[10]

Glabrio camped at the Middle Gate where the Spartans had made their legendary stand against Xerxes and advanced on Antiochus. He responded with skirmishers openly deployed at the fore (probably the same Agrianians that had been at Delium), peltastai (one chiliarchy?) in bastion behind them, and a thin phalanx (perhaps no more than a chiliarchy or two) of sarissaphoroi at the rear and just in front of his twinned trench/wall complex. More phalangites manned that barrier with support from artillery (heavy crossbows) placed at intervals along their line. The terrain anchoring Antiochus' left flank was not so rugged as to entirely preclude being enveloped by light foot, and he had warded that danger by stationing archers, slingers, and his remaining javelinmen there, which also allowed them to shoot down on any frontal attack. As for the area along the Euboan Channel on his right, that must have contained a modest opening at wall's end and water's edge for ingress/egress of the defensive works but was otherwise fairly well shielded from wider envelopment by the channel itself. Still, there was some risk that cavalry wading in the nearshore shallows might pose a threat, and to preclude that as well as block the necessary entryway at the strand, Antiochus had stationed his half dozen elephants on that flank. These most likely stood in back of the deliberate beachside opening rather than in front, perhaps extending a bit into the water, and the king personally rode behind them in the company of his small contingent of horse-guards.

The battle opened with dueling between the light-armed vans as Antiochus' men gained at first before being driven back upon their bastion of peltastai. Those spearmen let the skirmishers pass through their ranks and, after briefly repelling the enemy, turned to follow through openings between the phalangite files at the rear as both skirmishers and hoplites moved off via the barrier's channel-side portal. Appian tells us that the Seleucid phalanx then "closed and pushed forward, the long pikes set densely together in order of battle" with Livy adding that "the Macedonians posted before the rampart, for some time, easily withstood the efforts that the Romans made everywhere to force a passage." Given such virtual impenetrability of their foes' serried hedge of sarissai, the only advantage held by the Romans in this fight was that the phalanx's lack of mobility versus their own wider spaced combat formation let them give ground as needed to avoid relatively slow pike thrusts; however, even that was deemphasized here as Antiochus' light foot on the slopes "poured down … a shower of leaden balls from their slings, and of arrows, and javelins" to inflict the casualties that their phalangites could not. In addition, though we are not told anything about the effects that artillery fire from atop the wall might have had, it surely imparted damage as well in its ability to bring men down at great distance and even penetrate shields. Seeing as a practical matter, however, that his pikemen were gaining little from their success and coming under increasing pressure, Antiochus chose to pull them from the field as well and rely entirely on his missilemen and works. Exploiting the next lull in challenges on their front, the phalangites therefore retired in good order, "filing off from the rear" per Livy in yet another savvy mid-combat maneuver by a well-drilled phalanx.

Glabrio's men now threw themselves at the rampart, but that bristled with sarissai and they had even less success than previously against a naked pike array. Livy claims that "many, inconsiderately approaching the work, were run through the body … and they must either have abandoned the attempt and retreated or have lost very great numbers." It was at this pivotal point that things turned dramatically in Rome's favor as 2,000 of its best troops suddenly descended out of the heights behind Antiochus. Taking inspiration from past circumventions of Thermopylae as well as the more recent Roman circuit around Philip V at Aous River (see Chapter 7), Glabrio had sent two such detachments into the mountains the previous night, and the one assigned to the very same track that foiled Leonidas in 480 had managed to get past its several Aetolian-manned outposts. This contingent came against the west-rear of the Seleucids, who were for the most part excess to their wall's manpower needs and thus sat idle well back of it. Taken by surprise and overestimating the number of attackers, Livy says these men "were seized by such a panic that they threw down their arms and fled," first to their camp and then away from the pass.

Antiochus realized what was going on and, being mounted and favorably located rearward along the beach, he and his horsemen made a rapid escape down that still open path. It was much tougher going for his foot soldiers. They initially had help from the frontal barrier as an impediment to swift pursuit even though abandoned, especially as their elephants were able to block its modest seaside gateway. Though but a handful in number, Livy says that those beasts were very difficult for the Roman infantry to get beyond and "the cavalry could by no means do so, their horses being so frightened that they threw each other into greater confusion than when in battle." There was also considerable delay in the chase due to Glabrio's troops stopping to plunder the Seleucid campsite. But ultimately, many of Antiochus' men were run down and either captured or killed, though doubtlessly fewer than our Roman sources claim.[11] Roman casualties are said to have been a mere 150–200 sans another 500 suffered in passing the Aetolians in the mountains, those at Thermopylae falling mostly to missiles and against the pikemen atop the field works. The Seleucid king's defeat was so complete that there was no option left save to sail away and prepare for an attack on his home soil.

Pergamum and Magnesia (190)

Fighting shifted out to sea after Antiochus' retreat from Greece and continued thus with naval battles and small landings through most of the following year. The lone land engagement of note during this period took place at Roman allied Pergamum, which had come under siege from the king's son Seleucus.[12] In addition to its native garrison, the place was defended by a detachment from Achaea, which had managed to sneak into town at night with 100 horsemen and 1,000 foot soldiers. The latter are said to have been veterans and surely would have been drawn from that nation's readily mobilized epilektoi and thus hoplites and/or thorakitai with the latter perhaps making more sense. As for the investing force, we are told that it contained some 4,000 infantry and 600 cavalry, suggesting half of a conscripted strategia numbering 2,000 pikemen and 1,000 organically attached light infantry reinforced by more skirmishers (perhaps the remaining strategia auxiliaries) plus horsemen.[13]

The Achaean commander Diophanes, a talented disciple of Philopoemen, observed that the besiegers had become lax due to a lack of challenges by the garrison. He convinced local authority to let him sally his own picked contingent and exited to array in battle order tight beneath the city wall. There was no attempt by the Seleucids to approach for a fight, which was likely a precaution against drawing unanswerable fire from missilemen atop Pergamum's lofty outer ramparts rather than out of contempt for the Achaeans as our pro–Roman sources would have it.[14] Waiting until his foes had retired for the evening meal, Diophanes sent his horsemen charging at their camp with infantry close behind. This sudden development caught the Seleucids by such great surprise that its effect far exceeded anything reasonable for so modest an attacking force. Diophanes' men scattered all of the enemy troops near to hand, giving hard chase and dealing out casualties for what little remained of the day before returning to the praise of a jubilant and reinvigorated Pergamum.

Seleucus reestablished his camp at a greater distance from Pergamum and deployed the next day to face Diophanes and his men, who had once more taken position along the city's outer works. But the prince was no more willing than before to charge at so well placed a foe and turned about into column for a withdrawal just before sunset. Appian tells us that Diophanes then, having "kept his station under the wall and watched his opportunity ... fell upon his rear and threw it into confusion and, after doing all the damage he could, returned forthwith to his place under the wall." The Achaeans would continue to harass Seleucus at every opportunity until he finally abandoned the siege, short of outright defeat but with no more accomplished than having cast further doubt upon his nation's military prowess.

After joining with Philip and Macedon to overturn all of Antiochus' previous gains on the Greek mainland and force the capitulation of Aetolia, the Romans crossed over into Asia Minor via the Hellespont in 190. Glabrio's army had been reinforced by 12,000 additional men to bring each of its four legions/alae up to 5,400 sans cavalry by raising their counts of velites, hastati, and princepes to 1,600 while keeping the triarii at 600 (all per standard practice for Rome's overstrength deployments).[15] There were also some allied troops, whose infantry included 3,000 from Pergamum and Achaea (likely theurophoroi and Achaean epilektos thorakitai), 500 each in Trallian javelineers and Cretan archers, and 2,000 Thracian and Macedonian auxiliaries. Pergamum also provided 800 horsemen, adding to those with the legions/alae to bring mounted strength up to 2,800. The Roman army thus totaled 30,400 combatants exclusive of any with 16 elephants of the smaller African variety that were also on hand.[16] This host was led by the new consul Cornelius Scipio along with his famous brother Publius (Africanus), who was serving as a subordinate legate.[17]

Having fared badly in his naval efforts and lost control of the Aegean, Antiochus was vulnerable to amphibious landings and therefore elected to retreat into Lydia, moving up the Phyrgius River to fortify a camp well inland on the Plains of Corus to the west of Sardis and near Magnesia-ad-Sipylum.[18] Our primary surviving sources, Livy and Appian, likely draw on the lost work of Polybius and are close in claims for the king's host at 74,000 and 70,000 men respectively and in full agreement that the phalanx of conscripted phalangites at its core numbered 16,000 (four strategiai).[19] Other details regarding Seleucid manpower are available from Livy alone, but offer a sum well short of his preceding statement on the army's overall strength. A best sorting out and supplementation of this data suggests a heavy infantry complement of 26,000 encompassing the two elite Silver Shield strategiai at 5,000 men each plus the draftee phalanx; lighter foot from various sources some 32,000-strong; and additional troops including a little over 13,000 mounted (some on camels), nearly 3,000 attached to 54 large Indian elephants, and 2,000 charioteers/supporting skirmishers.

The processes of gathering allied support and consolidating control in the coastal region vital to securing his lines of supply and communication delayed C. Scipio's march into the interior and it was December before he finally closed against Antiochus. Crossing the Phyrgius just above the entry point of its northwest flowing Hermos tributary, he camped below where the river turned sharply from the east upstream, thereby occupying a pocket channel-bound on three sides and exposed to open attack from his larger and more mobile foe solely along a southeast-facing front a mere 3.2km in width. He could cover 2km of that by anchoring his legionary swordsmen upon the Phyrgius and aligning them southwestward in their usual 2m spacing/15-man depth. That would let his nearly 12,000 in light infantry occupy the remaining distance to the Hermos even in close order (1m spacing) at as much as ten-deep irrespective of any cavalry dispositions. But Antiochus would not agree to a battlefield so favorable to his opposition and refused engagement, knowing that the approaching deep of winter would soon put an end to the present threat if Scipio didn't take a more dangerous stance.

Embracing that greater risk rather than abandon efforts to date and perhaps see a newly elected consul usurp his command in the coming year, Scipio did indeed advance onto less restricted ground. This saw him move out as far as possible and still hug the Phyrgius just downstream of where a bend to the north would eliminate it as a buttress for his left flank. However, the gap from there to the Hermos below was thereby expanded to some 4.7km across, putting it beyond the capability of his troops to fully span at a prudent depth. Accepting this perhaps rashly, Scipio posted the Thracian and Macedonian skirmishers to guard a more vulnerable camp and prepared to fight in the apparent belief that his remaining mobile forces could prevent deadly envelopment of what was now a badly exposed right flank. Given his large advantage in mounted strength, Antiochus must have felt that patience in refusing combat earlier had been well rewarded and eagerly arrayed for action.

To say that the Seleucid battle formation credited in our surviving sources was unusual is an understatement; indeed, bizarre might be a better word for it. These describe the conscripted phalanx as deployed an extraordinary 32-deep and divided into ten segments with each flanked either side by two elephants and their skirmishers. This would have covered a very short front that even in combination with the Argyraspide strategiai filed only half as deep could match no more than half the opposing legionary frontage.[20] Livy claims Antiochus made up the difference by inserting cavalry (500 Galatians, 3,000 cataphracts, and 1,000 elite guard horsemen with the king himself) and 16 elephants between the phalanx and the Argyraspides with 120 mounted Dahae archers on the latter's right followed by 9,000 in light infantry (a multinational mix of archers, slingers, and javelineers) at the end of the line. Dispositions on the other side of the phalanx are then listed (right to left) as 1,500 Galatian horsemen, 4,700 in light foot (2,000 from Cappadocia), more than 6,500 cavalry (3,000 cataphracts, 1,000 guards, an unrecorded number of Tarentines, and 2,500 Galatians), 11,000 skirmishers of various nationalities, and 16 more elephants farthest left. Livy also says that scythed chariots and camel-mounted archers stood in front of these troops off the phalanx's left flank, though he gives no strengths for them. Appian's account offers much less detail but is basically in synch save for identifying no other elephants than the 22 said to be intermingled with the pikemen.

Any such complex arrangements would have been made at a good distance from the Roman position and, once complete, Antiochus advanced toward the opposing front, which held steady so as to keep anchored against the river. Our sources describe what happened next as opening with action between skirmishers plus a few horsemen thrown out by Eumenes of Pergamum on Scipio's right wing and the chariots and camel-archers moving ahead of the Seleucid main array on that part of the field. With their accompanying light foot inadequate to counter and horses vulnerable to a missile barrage, the charioteers were utterly routed, as were the camel-borne troops alongside, all being driven into the line behind to devastating effect. As the camels and chariots dragged by frantic and/or wounded horses bolted among the troops standing left of Antiochus' phalanx, those too panicked and joined in a terrified rush toward the rear. This in turn disrupted and exposed the cataphracts next left, and Eumenes took quick advantage by sending his horsemen

8. An End to the Greek Way of War

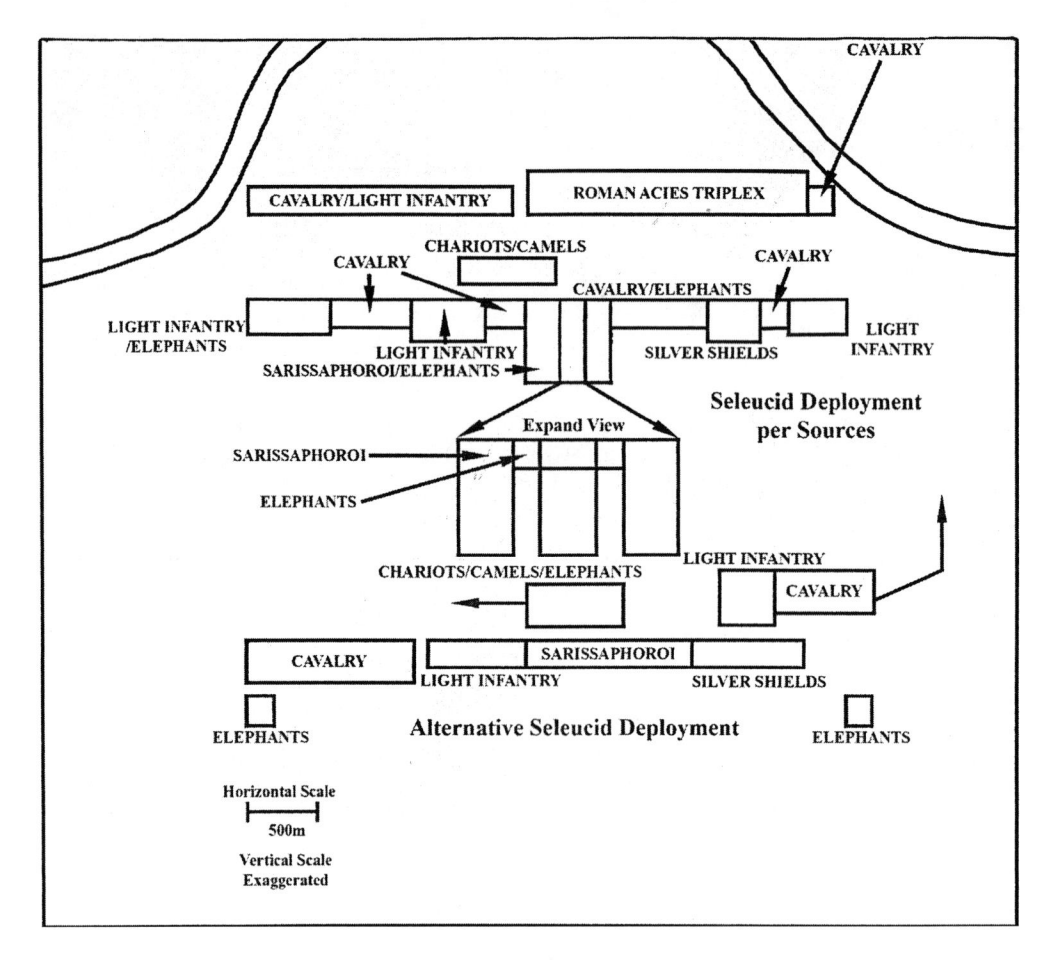

Battle of Magnesia, 190 BCE.

(and perhaps Scipio's modest contingent of elephants that are otherwise absent from either of our battle accounts) against them. Livy says that the Seleucid armored riders "did not sustain their first onset" and any failing to run were "put to the sword." The rest of Antiochus' left wing soon gave way as well, leaving the field abandoned as far down as to where his phalanx of sarissaphoros draftees still held their ground.

Meanwhile, on the other end of the battlefield, it is said that Scipio had placed a small contingent of cavalry on his own far left rather than having his legionaries crowd as close as possible to the edge of the Phyrgius. And when Antiochus saw that those horsemen had clung so tight to their infantry as to create an opening between themselves and the riverbank, he charged some cataphracts with supporting light foot into the break, sending both the enemy horse and the ala of Latin foot adjacent into flight. We are told, however, that the allied auxiliaries guarding the encampment joined then with 200 horsemen arriving from the victorious Roman right under Attalus (brother of Eumenes) to oppose the king's pursuit. And Antiochus, finally aware that his left had been compromised, had no viable course open but to make a general retreat. That was quite a ragged affair for the most part; however, the better-disciplined Seleucid pikemen formed a box-like formation with their long weapons projecting out on all sides and were able to slowly withdraw in good order for a fair distance before they too fell at last into confused flight.[21] Livy reports that Scipio's forces gave chase all the way to Antiochus' camp, ultimately killing 50,000 enemy foot soldiers and 3,000 horsemen while capturing 1,400 more along with 15 elephants.[22] Roman losses are said in contrast to have been astonishingly light at only 300 from the infantry, 24 horsemen, and 25 overall of those with Eumenes.

All of this is quite extraordinary and has raised serious doubt regarding the veracity of parts (if not all) of our surviving accounts due to a perceived pro–Roman bias among their authors. Such criticisms were famously leveled by the highly pragmatic German military historian Hans Delbruck,[23] who summarized the reports of Livy and Appian as "completely fantastic," mocking them as "absurd" and products of "the fantasies of the fiction writer to which we are indebted for the entire battle account." Among the issues here is that a seasoned and reasonably competent Hellenistic commander such as Antiochus would surely not have deepened his phalanx so anomalously in seeking envelopments that a much wider deployment would have facilitated in combination with his huge numerical edge in mobile forces. Likewise, there are problems with the reported admixing of elephant teams within a formation meant to oppose Roman legionaries since those beasts were well-known as more effective against cavalry and such intersperses would inevitably create gaps prone to lethal penetration in any ensuing shock action. And just as odd in presenting an extreme risk to the vital cohesion of Antiochus' heavy infantry array is the placing of horsemen between the phalanx proper and the Argyraspides farther right on that wing. This not only violates the ubiquitous Hellenistic practice of positioning cavalry outboard whenever physically possible but would also leave those heavy-armed contingents perilously split should the horsemen then advance—something they usually did and would indeed do during this very engagement.

Delbruck suggested that such glaring improbabilities within our surviving accounts might reflect misreading by their Latin authors of Polybius' superior Greek text to which we no longer have access. Bar-Kochva in his analysis of Seleucid campaigns offers much the same opinion in noting discrepancies between the two surviving accounts, proposing that "Livy lacked proper understanding in military affairs and may have been misled by vague or ambiguous terms used by Polybius" as well as "carried away by patriotic feelings as he so often was."[24] Taylor arrives at a similar conclusion regarding irregularities between established Hellenistic tactical practices and those described at Magnesia in his study of Antiochus III. He suggests that Polybius was either inaccurately transcribed or that it was Livy that had been miscopied (though the strong parallels between his version and Appian's argue against the latter).[25]

The writings of Livy and Appian on Magnesia ultimately cannot be ignored without intruding into the realm of unacceptable speculation. Still, a reconstruction that assumes their information on the Roman side of the affair is correct in most of its details but recasts key aspects of Seleucid behavior in a more practical light based on commonly observed norms and historical precedent is a worthwhile exercise. This allows for consideration that our surviving depictions of Antiochus' combat array could reflect conflation of engagement and pre-engagement configurations as well as separately deployed elements, suggesting potentially viable alternatives to the battle narrative above.

Exceptionally deep filing of sarissaphoroi in the manner cited here would seem justifiable only when standing stationary on the defensive within a narrows precluding wider deployment. The one recorded exception to this by Alexander the Great at Issus in 333 therefore offers valuable insight into what Antiochus might have been doing at Magnesia.[26] Alexander similarly advanced on a static enemy position with his pikemen marching

32-deep; however, he gradually broadened their ranks by thinning his files, first to sixteen and then eight.[27] This let him honor the universal priority in phalanx tactics of equaling an opponent's width of heavy foot to ward against having a flank overlapped and turned. And a similar approach here appears reasonable as it would let Antiochus' 26,000 pikemen (his peltastai being armed with sarissa as well in keeping with their playing a more defensive role on this occasion) spread across a little over 2km and closely match what Scipio's legionaries were covering in a standard acies triplex. But while Alexander's unusual method of advance had been dictated by terrain, Antiochus more likely would have been disguising his tactical intentions for as long as possible toward reducing exposure to a possible Roman countermove.

If the reported distribution of Antiochus' heavy infantry in our surviving sources might represent its initial rather than final deployment, what then of his other troops? Certainly, the elephant teams interspersed within the phalanx would have moved out in front to be replaced by a like-width of pikemen at the first halving of the latter's files, and most modern analysts have accepted that the other two bodies of elephants probably stood in the rear as reserves. As for the cavalry contingents, the most logical positioning for those on the open-flank left wing would have been outboard with much more of the light foot standing between them and the phalanx on the right than intermingled with the horsemen. But at the other end of the field, where the Roman flank abutted a riverbed, things could have looked quite different. Rather than conflating details of the same array at two different times (as perhaps with the phalangites), reports here might have conflated two different arrays existing at the same time. In a reverse of the proposed posting of the elephant reserves behind the main line of battle, the horsemen and skirmishers on Antiochus' right may thus have been standing in front of it.

The alternate troop distributions suggested above are admittedly speculative; all the same, they comply with a sound (if ambitious) bid to destroy Scipio by simultaneously enclosing him on both flanks. And while it's unknown whether Antiochus' absent advisor Hannibal had any input on the tactical plan at Magnesia, he certainly was a past master of just this sort of deadly double envelopment. The key to success was to be a surprise shift of the mobile forces deployed forward "at the first onset" per Appian. This would laterally redirect the chariots, camel-troopers, and elephant teams near center to join in a mounted assault on the enemy's far right. Meanwhile, the king was to lead most of the cavalry and light foot fronting his heavy array toward his own right to then loop across the Phyrgius against the Roman far left even as the rest of his light forces on that wing struck from the front.[28] But while the latter maneuver proved successful, Eumenes brought the whole scheme to ruin when his forechecking on the other end of the field caught the elephants, chariots, and camels in transit with a flank attack that sent them pell-mell into the Seleucid ranks below with disastrous consequences.[29]

Whether Antiochus was upset due to having a tactical scheme too badly muddled to succeed as our sources might imply or one too clever by far and thus easily foiled by Eumenes' initiatives per the alternative deployments mused upon here, his crushing defeat at Magnesia threw the Seleucid empire into permanent decline. The Roman forces at hand were insufficient to control the interior, and territorial concessions they subsequently obtained were therefore limited to loss of Antiochus' holdings in Asia Minor. Nonetheless, those were among his most valuable assets and never to be recovered. Seleucia would linger for a time as a local power, but its heady days as a major player on the larger Mediterranean stage were over.

The Third Macedonian War

With the specter of Seleucid intrusion gone for good, the Greek mainland fell once more into the sort of disunited squabbling that was ever its normal state of internal affairs. And one such minor conflict was responsible for the only land engagement worthy of mention in Greece over the two decades between Antiochus' expulsion after Thermopylae and the next round of Roman interference. This was quite a small affair, but notable in being Philopoemen's last adventure on behalf of the Achaean League as he tried to prevent the tyrant Dinocrates from leading his city of Messene out of that confederation.[30] Gathering some youthful horsemen from Megalopolis, Philopoemen confronted the dictator at Evander's Hill (perhaps Mount Eva near Messene) only to be repulsed after initial success by the arrival of enemy reinforcements. The elderly general was riding over rough ground helping to cover the subsequent retreat when thrown from his horse and captured. Philopoemen was eventually forced to commit suicide, but that didn't put an end to this latest episode of Grecian intermural mayhem as Athenian-led forces would avenge him by capturing Messene before the year was out.

Callinicus and Phalanna (171)

Perseus, an illegitimate son of Philp V, succeeded to the Macedonian throne in 179. Keen to reverse the nation's decline since Cynoscephalae, he sought to boost his influence through political marriages and other forms of alliance while strengthening the national army.[31] The Romans' rising concern on this resurgence of an old foe was further fueled when Perseus was able to repel an invasion from some of their Thracian allies and began stirring trouble among other Greek states by fomenting pro–Macedonian factionalism. With tensions thus already running high, an assassination attempt upon Rome's primary Asian ally, Eumenes II of Pergamum, then proved a final provocation leading to war in 171.

A Roman army under the consul Publius Licinius Crassus crossed to Illyria to march through Epirus and up into Thessaly, finally camping above the Peneus River near Larissa. This was a typical consular host of four legions/alae reinforced by allied contingents, all the latter being small save for 4,000 foot and 1,000 horse from Pergamum under Eumenes. Perseus claimed that the consul's Latin units each contained 6,000 foot soldiers and 300 horsemen.[32] That fits with his counts of mounted allies, which come to 2,500–2,900 and would thus join the said 1,200 Italian riders for a total consistent with the later note that the opposing cavalries once engaged in force were "nearly equal in numbers."[33] Crassus appears in the end to have fielded something like 30,000 combatants of all classes.

Perseus advanced upon the Roman camp and an inconclusive skirmish between mounted scouting parties ensued. Several days then passed in which the king proved unable to entice his foes from their fortifications into a mounted contest in which he deemed his own forces would prove superior. The king then relocated his base nearer and, having deployed his phalanx in distant bastion, closed at dawn against Crassus with cavalry and light foot. These took position just beyond the Roman ramparts around a hill called Callinicus with 1,000 Macedonian horsemen on the right plus the same in Thracian cavalry to their left and contingents of Companion horse on either wing. Perseus himself rode amid his select agema farthest right. All foot-skirmishers were interspersed throughout these mounted deployments save for 800 picked slingers and javelineers posted in front of the agema.[34] Crassus kept his heavy infantrymen behind their entrenchments but for some unrecorded reason now chose to risk the light-armed duel that he had just spent several days avoiding. This saw him sally the entirety of his mobile elements, forming them up with a select body of cavalry in the middle, the horsemen from Italy on the right, and some of his mounted allies to the left. Like their opposition, all of these had skirmishers seeded within their ranks. Elsewhere, 200 Gallic cavalry supported by 300 light footmen moved out ahead of this main array while 400 Thessalian horse stood by a short distance behind its left wing and the infantry from Pergamum also held station rearward in forming a central reserve under Eumenes.[35]

Opening action saw javelineers leading Perseus' left chase opposing velites and get among the Italian cavalry to throw it into confusion. Meanwhile, with their own front similarly opened up, the king and his agema charged Crassus' allied Greeks and quickly drove them from the other wing. With the Roman primary forces thus almost immediately put to rout, Eumenes and his auxiliaries along with the Thessalians likewise posted in reserve did an outstanding job of providing disciplined cover for their confederates' otherwise disorderly flight. All the same, Crassus lost 200 horsemen and 2,000 skirmishers killed and had 200 more riders captured in claiming only 20 horse and 40 foot among the enemy.[36]

Crassus remained entrenched outside Larissa in the aftermath of his defeat at Callinicus Hill, and Perseus, though having pulled back northward to his previous base, continued to keep him under surveillance. Thus, when informed that the Romans had exhausted forage south of their camp and were now scattered in seeking supplies above it much closer to his own position, the king marched into the vicinity for a surprise attack. Keeping the bulk of his troops hidden, he sent a small force of cavalry and light infantry down against the foragers. These captured nearly a thousand grain-filled wagons along with 600 men and forced a guard of 800 legionaries to form a defensive circle with their shields atop a nearby hill. The Romans suffered there under a fierce shower of missiles until rescued by horsemen and foot-skirmishers arriving from their camp. The Macedonians retreated toward their heavy phalanx, which Perseus was in the process of bringing down in column to create a bastion for his lightly armed advance detachment. However, having been significantly delayed in getting past all the captured wagons crowding his route, the king was still too far away and a good many of the fleeing men were cut down short of his potential safe haven of pikes.

Livy, our sole source for this engagement, casts doubt on propaganda claiming that a general battle took place here in which the Romans gained a great victory costing Perseus many thousands of casualties. The truth would seem to be a much more modest tactical success in which losses inflicted on the defeated Macedonians weren't all that high and perhaps even exceeded by those among the victors.[37] Perseus apparently felt that if Crassus refused pitched battle under these circumstances (a not unreasonable stance given that he faced fighting on open plains with much weakened mobile contingents) then there was nothing more to be gained by lingering further and he retired to Macedonia for the winter.

Minor Actions (170–169) and Pythium (168)

A new consul, Aulus Hostilius Mancinus, landed in Thessaly the next summer to renew the war against Perseus. Sadly, we have no details on his subsequent campaign beyond an all-too-brief summary that "having engaged the king, he was beaten"; however, Livy's tone here implies an action of no greater magnitude nor consequence than that of Crassus the year before.[38] Adding to Rome's frustration was another modest set-back inflicted by Macedon's Illyrian allies. Those heavy-armed barbarians and a few Cretan mercenaries sallied against 3,000 unprepared Romans (apparently a legion sans horsemen and 1,000 men left to guard a distant camp) and 4,000 of their local allies to claim at least 1,000 among the legionaries themselves in heading off an investment at Uscana in the south of Illyria.[39]

Determined to get better results, Rome raised new troops to replace the older men still serving in Greece so as to maintain the infantry within the legions and alae there 1,800 above establishment norms at 6,000 men each and 24,000 overall.[40] Each legion/ala was to again have 300 horsemen with the apparent intent to boost the resulting anemic total of only 1,200 through addition of mounted local allies. The winter of 170/69 saw operations carried out by both sides in Illyria and the northwest of Greece that for the most part seem to have gone better for Perseus but involved no significant pitched battles. The consul Quintus Marcius reached Thessaly that spring via a modestly contested march through the central Greek mountain ranges and delivered the aforementioned fresh reinforcements. However, Marcius' subsequent campaign got no closer to ending the war in Rome's favor than those of his predecessors as both he and Perseus maneuvered for a full season without decisive engagement.

The next year marked the arrival of Lucius Aemilius Paulus to lead the war against Macedon. A veteran aged 60 and brother-in-law of Scipio Africanus, this second-time consul brought 10,000 recently levied men to maintain the two Roman legions in theater at 6,000 foot (and presumably 300 horse) while reforming their associated alae to 5,000 in infantry with 400 cavalrymen. Upgrading his manpower at the same time, he relegated less capable men to static garrisons. With his field force now some 29,000-strong, Paulus confronted Perseus along the king's most southerly line of defense. This was at the Elpeus River, which ran to the sea from Mount Olympus and where defenses had been constructed so as to disadvantage any attempt at crossing its exceedingly stony streambed.

With the intervening rough-rocked surface too uneven for heavy infantry, the following two days witnessed a series of light-armed duels back and forth over the waterway in which Paulus' men took the greater damage in no small part due to missiles raining down from the opposition's field works.[41] Yet, that proved no more than a minor cost for achieving the consul's goal of diverting the enemy's attention from a large body of his troops making an end-run around the mountain. This detachment was slowly working its way through a lone pass the king had left unguarded on the assumption that it would be too difficult to transit in force. When alerted to his error by a deserter from the encircling contingent, Perseus immediately responded by dispatching a strong force of Macedonians and mercenaries to swing around to the north and then climb to block the enemy flankers at Pythium, which was a sanctuary of Apollo sitting on the west side of Olympus near the crest of the involved passage.

Paulus' circling detachment was based around 5,000 infantrymen from the Latin ala regularly positioned on the left wing of his battle array, and he had added 3,000 more foot soldiers said to be non–Roman Italians. Based on the size of the latter contingent and the lack of any mention of auxiliaries having been brought from Italy, these perhaps comprised half of the legion that normally stood next to the ala at hand with the unusual characterization of the legionaries' nationality reflecting their recruitment outside of Rome proper and/or from among the city's non-citizen residents. In addition to the foregoing 8,000 in legion foot, there was enhanced skirmisher support in the form of 200 javelineers and Cretan archers (it was one of the latter that had deserted) plus 120 horsemen. The detachment sent by the king most likely was composed of 2,000 regular peltasts (their hoplite arms best suited among his heavy infantry for this task) along with mercenary javelineers from Thrace.

Plutarch relates two versions of the ensuing confrontation, one now lost from Polybius and one that the Roman commander on the spot wrote to a friend.[42] As Polybius was contemporary and well connected to Roman sources while the other man actually took part in the subject action, it's best to assume that their accounts' key elements are fairly accurate with any seeming conflicts arising from omission of aspects each felt counterproductive to his intended tale. This indicates that Perseus' men gained Pythium after an extremely rapid and exhausting night march only to be hit with a surprise assault at dawn while still recovering from their efforts. Slower daylight ascents would seem to have rendered the Roman attackers not only better rested but also staged close enough below for their advance scouts to have secretly observed the enemy arriving at the sanctuary. Caught unprepared, any among Perseus' blocking force that didn't bolt in a panic put up no more than brief resistance before they too hightailed it back down the pass. And with Paulus' troops now descending to threaten from behind, Perseus quickly decided to abandon the Elpeus and find a better place to make his stand.

Pydna (168)

Perseus took position blocking the narrow plain below the small coastal town of Pydna in southern Macedonia. Paulus, who had reunited with the detachment that had skirted Olympus before following the king's retreat, refused to be lured onto such flat and restricted ground that would favor his foe's fighting style. He therefore swung inland instead and set up within the hills forming the western boundary of Perseus' intended chokepoint. A stream running along the foot of that upland provided a thin mid-summer trickle from which Roman and Greek alike drew water and eventually became the site of incidental contact that escalated into serious skirmishing with a pitched battle developing by late afternoon.

Though Perseus' Thracian auxiliaries and non-royal peltastai had taken at least modest damage at Pythium, the rest of his host remained completely intact to give him 42,000–43,000 combatants. There were around 21,000 heavy footmen (15,000–16,000 phalangites with some reservists present plus 5,000–6,000 peltastai in separate royal and regular contingents that were nominally equal in manpower), 17,000 medium/light foot, and 4,000 horsemen of whom perhaps up to 2,000 were heavier lancers. Our surviving accounts in Livy and Plutarch provide similar descriptions of how these various troop types spread out along a north-south axis to face Paulus' men across the stream in acies triplex on the slope above.[43]

The king employed Thracian theurophoroi along with like-armed Paeonians and a more varied mix of mercenary missilemen to form a large skirmisher screen off the right side of his heavy-armed formation. He tipped that side of the latter with "picked men, the flower of the Macedonians themselves"; these were the newly expanded 3,000 peltastai of his royal foot-guard most likely armed with thrusting spears and the latest version of the aspis shield to judge from their only known physical depiction.[44] Extending to the left of those select troops were the sarissaphoroi that cored the kingdom's military, both of their traditional divisions having also been enlarged during the recent build-up in manpower. This had the lesser regarded Leucaspides (White Shields) at 8,000-strong alongside the guardsmen to complete their phalanx's right wing while the more elite Chalkaspides (Bronze Shields) held post next in line at a similar count to make up the interior of its left wing. Perhaps slightly reduced after Pythium, the normally 3,000-strong peltast regulars then capped that end of the heavy array, all being equipped with pikes to play a more defensive role than their spear-bearing royal counterparts on the opposite flank. Finally, the balance of Perseus' light/medium footmen held his far left even as he personally commanded the cavalry in its entirety to cap the other end of the line.

Paulus had deployed all four legions/alae on his right with lighter armed non–Romans and his Latin cavalry extending out to their left in that order. Battleground mapping suggests that the Roman heavy array fronted across about 2,200m per two 6,000-man legions and two 5,000-man alae in standard acies triplex.[45] That would have been some 450m broader than Perseus' phalanx if it arrayed in typical files of twelve for the spearmen (fronting 1m each) and (as Frontinus perhaps suggests[46]) eight-deep for those with pikes (ranked 2/3m apart). This had forced the king to keep his left wing from being overlapped by assigning a sizeable body of skirmishers (some 5,000 in close order at a probable depth of ten) to that side of the field. The placing of semi-heavy theurophoroi in their front ranks not only let him oppose the facing legionaries with troops of nearly equal weight but also provided increased capacity for missile fire that his heavy infantry lacked. This was necessary in order to counter a combination of allied horsemen and 30-plus elephants that were fronting for the Latin ala occupying the rightmost portion of Paulus' line.[47] With a sizeable number of Macedon's skirmishers diverted thus onto the south lateral and velites in place there as well, both sides' remaining foot and horse on the north end of the field squared off along similar frontages at variable depths.

The tactical challenges presented here to Perseus had strong similarities with those in 279 at Asculum, where Pyrrhus also had an acies triplex (albeit a much larger one) ensconced on sloping ground above his phalanx. The Romans there had descended onto the flat in an attack that ultimately failed, and whether Perseus could have tempted a commander with Paulus' experience into doing the same by showing more patience might be debated, but that was not his choice in any event. Rather than emulating Pyrrhus, he seems to have patterned his approach closer to that taken at Sellasia in 222 by his grandfather (Antigonus III), whose phalanx there had charged upslope to victory on one side the field. So prepared, Perseus gave the signal and his heavy array went into action, crossing through the shallow streambed without much difficulty and flushing any intervening velites back through the wide-spaced ranks of their comrades above to finally close into those waiting swordsmen.

The more tightly ranked Macedonians with their lengthy polearms were able to push back Paulus' legionaries all along the fighting front as most of the Romans took advantage of their acies triplex's loose order to fall back rather than engage the densely serried rows of pikes leading the enemy's slow advance. The inability of the opposing sarissaphoroi to counter that prudent tactic and inflict any real hurt on their foes rendered this stage of the battle relatively bloodless with one glaring exception. That was along the northernmost 120m of the fight where the two maniples of the Pelignians and Marucinians had deployed with some 420 heavy-armed legionaries each.[48] These faced royal peltastai with what appear to have been spears rather than pikes and elected to press the fight, braving strikes from a multiple of those longer weapons for each sword they could bring into play. But despite valiant efforts, neither unit came close to returning the damage it received, and their hastati were "cut to pieces" per Plutarch only to then have the princepes that replaced at least the Pelignians driven back in turn.[49]

As well as this initial action had gone for the Macedonians, a grave problem began to develop as their ranks of sarissaphoroi became increasingly disordered. Perseus might have adopted his grandfather's scheme of attacking uphill but failed to array his troops in the

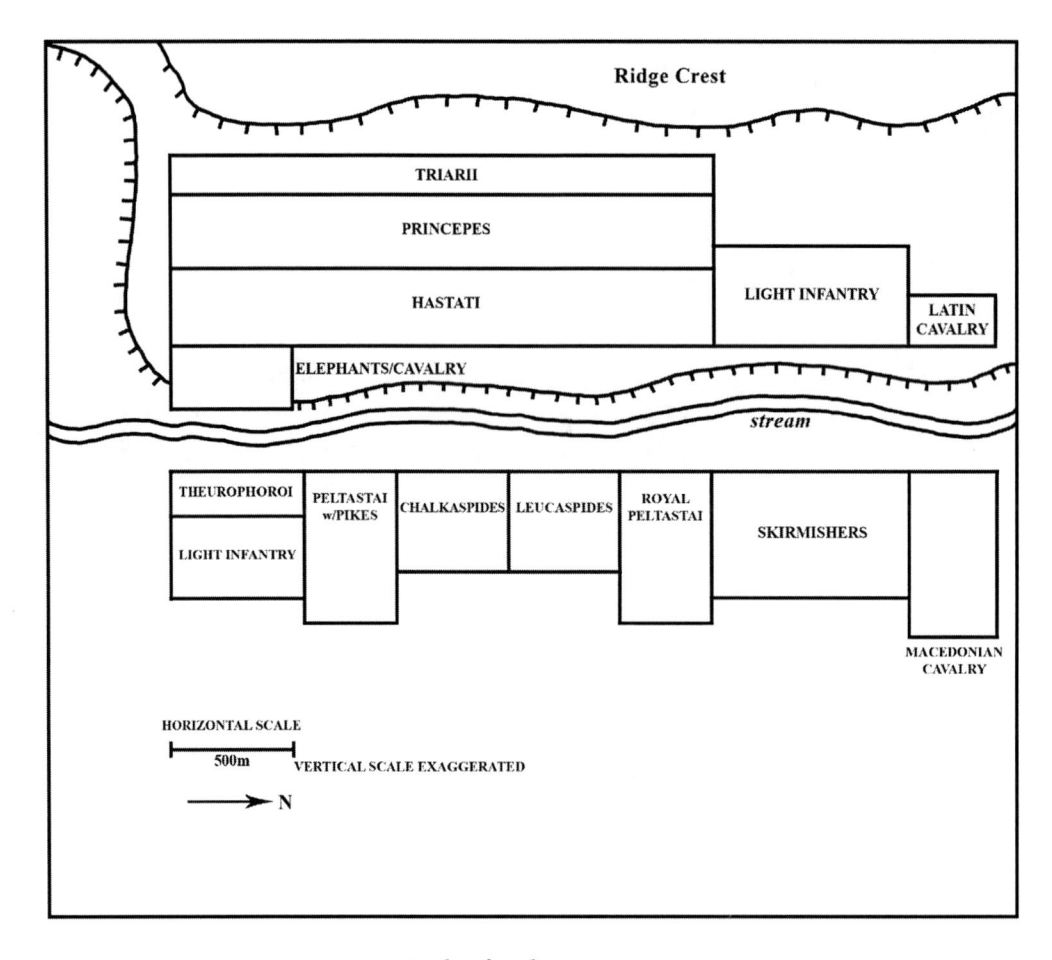

Battle of Pydna, 168 BCE.

mixed arms fashion critical for that to succeed. Whether this was a considered choice on the king's part or the product of an unavoidably rushed deployment, the result was the same.[50] Without the increased flexibility that interspersed bodies of spearmen would have granted his otherwise exceedingly stiff pike formation, segments ended up climbing under variable duress and footing either slower or faster than those alongside, creating a non-linear front that the enemy's agile swordsmen could exploit. This difficulty in moving over steep/broken surfaces was a weakness of the Macedonian phalanx acerbated for the pikemen here by their lack of intense drill.[51] Given the cushion of extended reach that sarissai provided in front of the phalanx, it's not certain that the penetrable gaps thus formed were of sufficient number and depth to completely destroy its cohesion; still, they were more than adequate to stall any further advance and deny a victory. And even the chance to withdraw and fight another day then evaporated as the Romans turned Perseus' left flank.

Rather than along the main line of battle, it was on their far left where Livy says "the retreat of the Macedonians first began." The lighter armed troops fighting for the king there didn't have the task of attacking upslope, but rather were to stand firm and ward the adjacent flank of their phalanx. They were thus holding position reasonably near their heavy infantry and trying to keep the opposition at a distance with missile fire, which could be effective from even their rearmost rank due to its targets being elevated. However, this barrage began to fade as the action dragged on and their supply of projectiles dwindled, and that relief let the opposing elephants and horsemen charge down at last without it being a near suicidal act. Even so, their attack stalled with Livy noting that the elephants were "without the least use." But a renewed effort then followed with likely aid from heavy swordsmen as at Metaurus and Mediolanum that chased their less shock-capable foes to turn and shatter Perseus' left wing.

With the Macedonians' in flight leftward, the remainder of their formation was doomed and its center gave way next as the rout progressed along the line with legionaries now penetrating even more and deeper gaps than they might have earlier to strike from front, side, and rear to laterally roll up the Greeks. Finally, this deadly progression reached the royal peltastai on the far end of the phalanx. Those elites "remained in order and kept on fighting" per Plutarch, but eventually, they too "were all cut to pieces." Still, their steadfast effort wasn't all for naught in that Livy claims the resistance they and a few others put up let Perseus and his horsemen escape "with scarcely any loss" since "the slaughter ... detained the conquerors and made them careless of pursuing the cavalry." This refers to the Roman riders on Paulus' far left who were not only closest to hand but also those best able among his troops there to chase fellow horsemen. They closed instead against the royal peltastai as depicted in several dramatic carvings on the contemporary monument at Delphi celebrating Pydna.

Cut off to north and south and with their backs to the sea, Plutarch allowed that 25,000 Macedonians died at Pydna and Livy put their losses at 20,000 killed and 11,000 captured. As for the victors, Plutarch cites Poseidonius as reporting only a hundred Romans lost their lives while Nacica said that it was fewer still at 80. Livy estimated a hundred Roman dead at most, though noting as well that "a much greater number were wounded." Pydna was a crushing defeat for Macedonia that would end its long history as an independent kingdom when the ensuing peace settlement abolished the Antigonid monarchy and split the land into four lesser states allowed no more than small militias for internal security.

Bactria (167)

An ethnic mix combining elements of Alexander the Great's army and indigenous peoples, the Greco-Bactrians had turned against a weakened Seleucia after Magnesia (probably c. 187) and attached nearby portions of that kingdom to build one of their own. Our source data on what then ensued is extremely vague, but it appears that the Bactrian ruler, Demetrius I, might have died opposing a belated Seleucid counterstrike in 167.[52] Demetrius could probably field a phalanx 10,000-strong drawn from an inherited system of Seleucid military settlements plus mercenaries. These would have formed two divisions of 4,000 pikemen and 1,000 hoplites each, with one unit recruited from Bactria's substantial Greco-Macedonian population and the other from adjoining portions of Seleucia now under Demetrius' control. The resulting heavy infantry tally mirrors that of Molon's revolt over some of the same territory in 220.[53] That analog also suggests that Bactria could have fielded around 20,000 in light foot, while its mounted potential would have been something like the 5,000 riders that fought at Arios River in 209.[54] Demetrius might thus have commanded some 35,000 fighting men.

Barred by Rome from coastal Asia Minor, Seleucia's Antiochus IV had spent the last few years campaigning through Cole Syria into Egypt and in dealing with unrest in Palestine. Though he personally remained in the west with most of his forces, the king put

Eucratides (possibly his cousin) in charge of recovering the rebellious eastern territories. Whether relocating or already on post in Babylon as governor of the "Upper Satrapies" in the old Persian far northeast, Eucratides collected an army and marched on Demetrius. A best guess at his strength assumes that a 4,000-man division of pikemen supported by 1,000 mercenary hoplites must have been provided by Antiochus at minimum, counting on Eucratides to then draw upon local resources in filling out his remaining manpower needs. There were probably at least 3,000 mercenary spearmen already garrisoning the province, but far larger contingents would have been added from the horsemen and skirmishers characteristic of the Upper Satrapies' native musters. These might have supplied up to 12,000 in cavalry and 18,000 light footmen if the region's last recorded potential in those arms still held.[55] Eucratides could therefore have marched into Bactria with something like 38,000 combatants in all.

A meeting on open ground of the above estimated armies would most likely have seen phalanxes of similar width (roughly 1,200m across if their spearmen and sarissaphoroi deployed in short files of four and eight respectively) having cavalry and light infantry divided evenly off either flank. A drawn-out stalemate of heavy-armed arrays must then have quickly developed accompanied by spirited but equally indecisive sparring outboard between well-matched formations of skirmishers. However, depletion of the latter's missiles would inevitably have led to both sides' mounted contingents finally joining the fight to Eucratides' considerable advantage. Ultimately broken on at least one flank, the Bactrian screening forces must then have given way to doom Demetrius and his phalanx to a lethal envelopment in what might well have been the very last battle fought by entirely Grecian phalanxes.

Hybridization of Hellenistic Warfare

In his study of Hellenistic infantry reforms in the wake of Pydna, Sekunda came to the conclusion that "both the Seleucid and Ptolemaic heavy infantry were reorganized and equipped along Roman lines during the 160's."[56] The evidence for this regarding Antiochus IV's Seleucia includes a 5,000-man legion armed in Roman fashion appearing in his parade at Daphne in 166. That event also marks the last mention in our sources of the Argyraspide sarissaphoroi, those elites presumably being disbanded along with the rest of Antiochus' pike units in the ensuing Romanization of his army. Sekunda contends that what modest evidence we have regarding the Seleucid heavy infantry that fought in Palestine at Beth-Zacharia in 162 suggests that it was entirely legionary, while Bar-Kochva sees it as more like the Daphne display with only one division of swordsmen and the rest pike-armed.[57] Either way, Seleucia's army was no longer purely Greek in form, being at the very least a Greco-Roman hybrid if not entirely Roman in its weaponry and tactics. Evidence for Ptolemy VI's Egypt adopting a Roman-styled military at about the same time is even more substantial,[58] and though we know very little about what Punic forces looked like in Carthage's last years of existence, it's almost certain that they too had evolved into an at least partially hybridized form.

Never again would Carthage, Macedonia, Seleucia, or Ptolemaic Egypt take the field with the sort of hosts that had won and maintained their empires for more than 150 years. Admittedly, some elements of those fighting forces of old remained in vogue for a time within these fading realms as well as among lesser states in Greece. And they would persist as well in Asia Minor and on the remote fringes of the Hellenistic world. We thus have Armenia and the Pontic forces of Mithradates the Great deploying combination sword and pike arrays into the early 1st century[59] and evidence from 2nd century Pergamum suggesting its use of compound phalanxes as well.[60] Farther into the hinterlands, the Greeks of Alexandria Eschate at the eastern edge of Alexander the Great's conquests might have deployed hoplites against invaders from China c. 101–102.[61] And more distant still, the Greco-Indian state established by a resurgent Bactria in the mid–2nd century might have kept some Hellenistic military aspects well into the 1st century CE Yet, these were all no more than minor exceptions to a widespread general embrace of Roman gear and practices that put an effective end to phalanx warfare's more than half a millennium of dominance across the Mediterranean world.

Conclusions

The foregoing survey of all significant Hellenistic land battles 300–167 BCE yields some valuable insights into likely combat truths during a period when a greater variety of sophisticated fighting systems saw action than at any other time in ancient history. There is no claim here that anything like absolute certainty can ever be offered when dealing with such severely limited physical data and the further constraints imposed by surviving literature that is habitually incomplete, often a product of second-hand (or worse) interpretation, occasionally conflicted, and sometimes biased to the point of unreliability. But even so, an honest-as-possible evaluation of likelihoods drawn from the unique spectrum of information provided by a comprehensive survey of this era's engagements serves to help understand what might actually have happened on those contested fields as well as yield clues on several broader aspects of ancient warfare toward separating some long-discussed possibilities from more probable realities.

Combat Formations—Revolution or Evolution?

There were a number of meaningfully different combat formations employed in the early 3rd century as well as some notable variations within those several categories of arrays. With the exception of mainland Greece's Epirus and the Italiote colony of Tarentum, the "classical/Doric" phalanx with its heavy-armed element composed entirely of hoplite spearmen remained in use among the host of Greek poleis and confederations independent of the three larger realms derived from Alexander the Great's empire. This saw two of those traditional battle formations square off in the century's first substantial pitched actions during the campaign waged by Demetrius Poliorcetes against Sparta in the Peloponnese. And classical phalanxes of the same sort were still engaging each other in 235 when the Achaean League clashed with Argos more than a century after Philip II had introduced his pike-bearing "Macedonian" phalanx to supposedly make such antique fighting methods obsolete. That it would be another decade yet before the next Greek city-state (Sparta) would adopt pike-armed troops serves to further underscore that Philip's innovations did not break from the fundamentals of past Grecian warfare; rather, they sought to possibly improve upon but at minimum match their optimum execution within his nation's manpower and fiscal limitations.

Nor were the independent Greek states alone in continuing to field spear-based formations well after Macedonian sarissaphoroi began seeing action with considerable success. The Carthaginians too had long deployed hoplite phalanxes essentially identical to those of their contemporaries in Greece and continued to do so; however, they would also modify many of their 3rd century battle arrays to incorporate both foreign swordsmen and spearmen. This created "compound" phalanxes with Punic hoplites usually forming both wings when present in sufficient strength but only the formation center when significantly in the minority. Yet tactical goals remained the same as for all Hellenistic combat formations, seeking a double envelopment if possible or to at least hold firm on one wing and buy time toward achieving a decisive flank-turning of some sort on the other end of the field.

Punic compound phalanxes were a way to integrate foreign troops toward fielding armies of adequate size, and that must also have been a prime motivation in Pyrrhus of Epirus' earlier invention of a different kind of compound formation for his Italian campaigns. While those phalanxes similarly included non-native spearmen (Italiote hoplites as well as tribal theurophoroi), they didn't simply place them at center or on the wing(s) as in Carthage's formulae; rather, Pyrrhus inserted bodies of those allies as well as spear-armed Epirotes either side of his sarissa-bearing contingents. That not only improved flexibility for crossing rough/inclined surfaces but also let him inflict higher ratios of casualties on his legionary opponents (see below re: Hoplites etc.). And it was those enhanced capabilities that would later lead Macedonia's Antigonus III and (likely) Philip V to employ comparable spear/pike arrangements on sloping ground at Sellasia and Cynoscephalae respectively.

Even the phalanxes deployed in main by the three post–Alexander realms of Seleucia, Ptolemaic Egypt, and Macedonia frequently had compound aspects. Unlike Pyrrhus' interspersed arrays, the spear-centered version of Carthage, or even the latter's doubly spear-winged variant, these formations posted elite hypaspists (later called peltastai) armed with dory and aspis on a single "strike wing" (usually far right) with sarissaphoroi making up the rest of the front. Originator Philip II and his son had used this approach to let their defensively superior pikes fix the bulk of an enemy line in place while picked spearmen carried the fight in conjunction with shock-capable cavalry lancers. That last, mounted component in these strike-wing duos proved dominant on expansive plains; therefore, with spears largely impotent against serried hedges of pikes (see below re: Hoplites, etc.), Macedonian phalanxes faced with such terrain in Asia had by the 3rd century come to most often rearm their elite spearmen with sarissai and cede primary offensive responsibilities to horsemen and light foot off their flanks. But back in the more confined terrain of mainland Greece, where many opponents still utilized hoplites and positioning of cavalry and skirmishers outboard could present a challenge, Macedonian commanders continued to find value in a strike-capable wing of spearmen, resorting to all-pike fronts only when purely on defense within narrow chokepoints.

The coexistence of so many variations on the phalanx with each calculated to best fit its deployer's specific needs argues against them demonstrating a teleological progression in combat effectiveness. Rather than a series of "revolutions in military affairs" involving rapid and saturated replacement of older fighting technologies, the process was clearly one of halting evolution. This featured multiple array types of greatly differing vintages operating in parallel over many generations until one might finally fade for one reason or another into general disuse. More revolutionary looking by far is the rapid spread of Roman warfare after Pydna, though even that could fall short in some peoples' eyes (see below re: Phalanx or Legion?).

Hoplites, Sarissaphoroi, Theurophoroi and Legionaries

Examinations of all known engagements between the various Hellenistic battle formations active in the 3rd through early 2nd century and between those and the acies triplex of Rome show that no system could claim universal superiority. What emerges instead is a complex matrix of relative capabilities and vulnerabilities showing that the presence of any competitive advantage in a given combat depended upon the interplay of three key factors: (1) the specific match-up of combatants involved, (2) the nature of the terrain under contest, and (3) the level of offensive aggression on display by either side. To fully comprehend the outcomes of these engagements and any associated broader trends, it is thus necessary to see how the four prime species of shock combatants in the subject era (hoplites, sarissaphoroi, spear or sword-armed theurophoroi, and legionaries) interacted on the field of battle.

Greek and Carthaginian armies at this time deployed hoplites as amateur militiamen, state supplemented elites (epilektoi), and professionals (both native and mercenary) with only modest variation in armor and all sporting a thrusting spear plus aspis shield. Traditionally matched against other hoplites, these troops were at disadvantage against sarissaphoroi, whose long pikes prevented them from getting near to inflict casualties. At the same time, they found it difficult to defend against sarissai even though enjoying good service from their armor and continuous front of large shields to fend strikes coming from but a single opposing rank. That was because their dense array made it hard to give way and avoid pike thrusts. All of this could compel such troops facing sarissaphoroi to awkwardly edge back into their own after-ranks while at risk from the enemy's slow yet powerful polearms should they be applied aggressively. Thus less able to execute the key tactic of turning a wing, hoplites destined to tangle with sarissai were often replaced by pikemen better fit to confront their own kind.

The situation was quite different, however, when hoplites faced foes with weapons shorter than the pike. These included fellow hoplites of equal capability but also theurophoroi armed with spears or (much more commonly) swords against whom they held an edge. Much of that benefit came from theuros shields being wielded separately rather than in the unified system of overlap that let aspides provide superior protection as long as a solid front could be maintained. That last was something facilitated in level settings, making it solely upon rough ground where more flexible theurophoros arrays might be favored. Also of advantage was that theurophoroi plying blades were even less effective against Grecian heavy infantry than those with spears as their swords lacked reach and required wider spacing to reduce strength along the battlefront. It's no wonder then that those engagements in the 270s matching theurophoros Gauls and heavy-armed Greeks saw the barbarians meet defeat on every occasion save against fatally ill-prepared Ptolemy Keraunos on Orestis Plain. Still, the superiority of theurophoroi over difficult footing made them more useful than hoplites for many detached assignments. And while short-comings in pitched combat kept them from supplanting conventional heavy infantry, their success in shock actions against Grecian javelineers would lead to widespread substitution of theuroi for the latter's small bucklers during the 3rd century.

Yet any impact that sword-bearing barbarians had in the subject era is completely overshadowed by that from the swordsmen of Rome. Though themselves carrying a scutum shield much like the theuros, these well-armored troops had been custom-designed to combat theurophoroi of all types and were quite effective at it. That success certainly had elements of superior training and discipline yet stemmed more than anything else from the effectiveness of their acies triplex combat formation. Not only did that array's manipular sub-divisions equal the best of its theuros-equipped opponents in flexibility along the battlefront but it surpassed them in an ability to rotate fresh troops from the after-ranks (principes) to relieve weary lead-fighters (hastati) and prevail in extended actions. Roman legionaries thus usually had a telling advantage against theurophoroi otherwise not all that dissimilar in basic armament.

However, Grecian heavy infantry presented a much greater challenge to Rome's way of war. Our sources show widely spaced legionaries generally unable to get close enough with their much shorter weapons to do more tightly aligned Greeks armed with pikes any real harm—so much so, in fact, that it seems that they rarely even tried. However, the looser order that helped handicap their offensive potential had a contrasting benefit, letting them both dodge laterally and yield ground as needed toward reducing damage from the thrusts of ponderous sarissai. Sparse but solid evidence for this comes from the remarkably low legionary losses against pikemen recorded at Magnesia and Pydna, while the higher costs (real and threatened) when facing sarissaphoroi at Aous River and Thermopylae serve as exceptions that prove the rule. Roman troops in those last simply couldn't employ their tactic of giving way to avoid casualties if they wanted to assault foes standing behind field works.

Combat between Roman swordsmen and spear-armed Hellenistic heavy infantry featured mechanics similar in kind but less extreme in degree than those in play against sarissaphoroi. Much like pikemen, hoplites held advantages in weapon-length and formation density, while the need to maintain close-order hampered them in striking at looser arrayed troops able to step back/aside. The difference was that the lesser reach of spears compared to sarissai neither kept foes at as great a distance nor forced them to cut through multiple layers of weaponry to land a blow. This had a psychological effect in that spear-armed phalanxes simply don't seem to have been as daunting a sight as pike arrays. But there was a real physical impact as well. Working your way past a couple of rows of spear-points wasn't nearly as difficult a task as serially doing so through a deep hedge of sarissai; thus, many a legionary proved willing to give it a try. That led to the sort of vicious struggle seen at Pydna with swordsmen pushing spears aside, slashing at their shafts, and even grabbing them in hand, all while being pummeled and pierced by powerful overhand blows from up to four foes for every legionary in the fight.

This kind of melee usually saw the Romans failing to gain a penetration and, though able to inflict significant harm, taking considerably greater injury in return. Much as per sarissa-related casualties, our hard data on this is quite limited yet fairly compelling. In the three battles for which we have reasonably reliable figures on Roman losses solely against hoplite opposition that are not inflated by subsequent pursuit (at Canusium in 209, Metaurus River in 207, and Mediolanum in 203), deaths range from 20 percent to 40 percent of legionaries actually engaged (with those among individual units possibly running as high as 60 percent). Such numbers are consistent with estimates that Macedonian elite spearmen might have killed up to 10 percent of their legionary opponents at Cynoscephalae and 15 percent at Pydna. They can also be compared to the 13 percent claimed from the Romans at Asculum, who might have fallen to spears rather than pikes and were not extensively pursued, and similar losses at Zama mostly against hoplites. It's interesting to consider such high levels of potential damage in context of the "Pyrrhic" loss of 15 percent at Heraclea having so long been considered something of a disaster.

As a consequence of the foregoing dynamics, legion victories over phalanxes normally involved some sort of envelopment to turn the end of a wing. There are only three engagements in which Roman legionaries likely defeated hoplites via frontal penetration. The first was on Sardinia at Carales in 215, the second a year later along Italy's Calor River, and the last at Zama in 202 when Hannibal's classical "first" phalanx of non-veterans gave way. All followed a similar pattern with spearmen wearing down and then being chased in lengthy actions opposing deeper acies triplex arrays better able to rotate fresh troops into the fight. We have casualty counts for two of those battles, at Calor River and Zama, and they indicate losses well in excess of 10 percent for the hastati and princepes actually engaged. Exceptionally high for otherwise successful combatants, these are very much in line with the sort of extremely steep price seen elsewhere that Roman swordsmen tended to pay for any sustained aggression against formations even partially composed of hoplite spearmen.

Macedonian Cavalry Decline?

The sharp contrast between the widespread pattern of victory achieved by Philip II and Alexander the Great in the 4th century and the lack of similar success by the Successor kingdoms in the 2nd century has led to a good deal of speculation that those later Macedonian armies had degraded, largely due to a reduction in their mounted capability. The strongest support for this idea comes from evidence that Alexander had fielded close to 10,000 horsemen for his last campaign in India to support a heavy infantry force not much larger (24,000 vs. 21,000) than the one Perseus had backed with only 4,000 riders at Pydna. However, a broader examination of all Macedonian deployments under Philip and his son paints a more ambiguous picture. We have only two reliable figures for cavalry ratios under Philip II, with the one at Crocus Plain (353) being much like that at Pydna (both around five in heavy infantry per horseman) and his last at Chaeronea in 338 much weaker in cavalry (fifteen for each mounted man). The latter effort seems to have been aberrantly under-horsed as a way to maximize heavy foot content within logistical limitations in anticipation of fighting inside a relatively narrow valley (Bardunias and Ray 2016, 161–162). Support for the count at Crocus Plain being more the norm comes from Alexander inheriting an army that fielded only eight heavy footmen per rider for his first campaign in 335 and fewer still at 6-to-1 going into Persia a year later.

Alexander did move to boost his cavalry count after engaging a horse-rich Asian army at Granicus River, but only to the extent that his subsequent deployments at Issus and Gaugamela equaled the just under five heavy infantrymen per rider employed by his father more than a decade earlier. Therefore, as far as simple numbers go, the cavalry compositions of Macedonian armies sporting their eponymous phalanx from the formation's introduction in 359 through its famed Persian conquest were pretty much the same as for that final engagement at Pydna almost two centuries later. This reveals Alexander's much higher ratio of horsemen in his closing campaign to have been quite exceptional and probably more a product of having drawn cavalry-heavy reinforcements from his recent acquisitions in Persia's easternmost reaches and India than a fundamental redesign of the Macedonian military system.

Of course, the foregoing doesn't address a possible deterioration in the quality of Macedonia's mounted troops; however, we really have no hard evidence of that being a problem either. To the contrary, though minor mounted skirmishing during the conflicts with Rome had mixed results, the only major engagement saw a smashing Macedonian victory over

Latin and allied Greek horsemen at Callinicus a mere three years before Pydna. It's also worth noting with respect to a decline in mounted prowess potentially leading to Macedonia's downfall that neither of its key defeats at Cynoscephalae and Pydna saw its cavalry play a decisive or even significant role. And elsewhere in the Alexandrian realms, the collapse of the cataphracts that contributed to Antiochus III's disastrous defeat at Magnesia in 190 certainly took place under unusual circumstances that make it difficult to pass judgement on their relative skill versus similar troops in the past. What we can say for sure about the Seleucid Empire at Magnesia in its last battle as a great power is that there was no shortage of mounted strength on display with a massive 13,000 riders (sans chariots and elephants) put into play. This exceeded Alexander's largest ever deployment not only in terms of sheer number but also with regard to ratio at one horseman for each two in heavy infantry. One might find fault in how Macedonian cavalry was utilized during the 2nd century, but the evidence does not support that it had suffered an obvious reduction in either strength or capability.

Phalanx or Legion?

There has been a great deal of learned discussion in modern times pondering the relative merits of Latin and Grecian warfare. A general consensus seems to have emerged therefrom in favor of the manipular legion over phalanxes of any sort; something quite logical in light of Rome's historical conquest of every phalanx-deploying foe from hilly southern Europe to the wider plains of Africa and Asia Minor. However, the exact reason for that documented military dominance has remained in dispute. Was the more flexible legionary battle array that much superior on the field of contention or was it the city on the Tiber's vast pool of manpower that let it wear down opponents whose ways of war were otherwise equal or possibly even superior to its own? The present study includes all 30 pitched engagements that saw manipular legions fight on open ground against Hellenistic phalanxes, allowing us to bring some harder (if unavoidably speculative) data to bear on that question.

The first reality that stands out in looking at these battles is that the Romans came out on top 18 times (60 percent) versus 11 defeats and a lone draw (see Appendix 3). And when one considers the famously amateur nature of many of its commanders, who were often chosen more on the basis of political popularity than tactical savvy, this serves as a strong endorsement of the Roman combat system. However, in the 21 battles that Rome fought against phalanxes from 280 through 209, the legions lost more often than they won with only nine victories, finishing on three straight defeats. It is only in 208 that the record then turns sharply, seeing the legionaries double their victory total without suffering a single loss down through the concluding action against a Hellenistic phalanx at Pydna. What keyed this late run of success that conquered Carthage and Macedonia and sent Seleucia into terminal decline?

The most obvious event associated with Rome's unbroken string of battlefield triumphs after 209 is the promotion of Scipio Africanus to the rank of army commander. He engineered the first of the ensuing victories against Carthaginian phalanxes at Baecula and would be responsible for all but two of the remaining five including the war-winner at Zama. Moreover, the pair of Roman successes in that series sans Scipio were both products of exceptional maneuvers by the other Romans leading those battles. These had Claudius Nero at Metaurus River relocating legionaries from a failed attack on the Carthaginian left to decisively defeat the enemy's mobile screen on the other flank and Marcus Cornelius doing something similar at Mediolanum with a legion that had been standing unengaged behind his acies triplex. A better caliber of generals was therefore a prime reason for improvement in Rome's combat record in the last decade of the 3rd century. But it wasn't the only one.

In addition to the greater skill shown by Roman generals from 208 on, there were significant upgrades in the quality of the soldiers they commanded; and this was broadly spread across all of the three main troop categories: heavy infantry, light infantry, and cavalry. For the heavy-armed legionaries, this was a matter of accumulated combat experience. While Rome's amateur-based military system tended to fill much of its enlistment quota with comparatively raw recruits in the early days of a conflict, a long-running affair like the Second Punic War gradually built up a large pool of seasoned veterans to stiffen the ranks. Thus, Roman legions taking the field in 208 after a decade of active combat against Carthage were significantly better seasoned than those that had gone down to defeat in the war's opening years at Trebia River, Lake Trasimenus, and Cannae. And Rome's skirmisher velites had likewise improved, becoming more shock-capable upon adopting a form of the parma shield c. 211. This had not had a huge immediate impact due to the first battles afterwards denying them much of a role (Himera River easily won after Carthage's Numidian cavalry refused to fight, badly outnumbered Roman screens failing too quickly at Castulo and Herdonia II, and Canusium being fought in a narrows precluding light-armed participation); however, Scipio and his fellow generals thereafter got good service from their upgraded skirmishers that provided time and cover for decisive ad hoc legion maneuvers on the Metaurus and at Mediolanum and carried the day directly at Ilipia, Great Plains, and Zama in tandem with better-quality cavalry contingents. The latter benefited greatly from contributions by the highly skilled Numidian horsemen that joined Rome during the Punic War's final stages. And most of these same improved capabilities would then be decisively brought to bear against Seleucia and Macedonia.

Sekunda (2006, 115) in his review of martial reforms post–Pydna concluded that "[i]t was Rome's capacity to mobilize such huge armies which defeated Macedon, rather than any innate superiority of the Roman military system." If we consider that "system" only in the most restricted sense of its acies triplex battle array, the direct parallel of Hannibal's failure to prevail despite so many crushing victories in the field seemingly offers definitive support for such an assessment. Yet, the tactical picture is demonstrably more favorable to Rome than this would imply. Given reasonably adept leadership, experienced legionaries, and competitive auxiliary forces, Roman manipular formations with their greater flexibility over rugged terrain and capability for independent maneuver by sub-units outperformed all manner of Hellenistic phalanxes with one documented exception and one hypothetical one.

The compound phalanx deployed by Pyrrhus at Heraclea with its interspersing of hoplites and sarissaphoroi might well have been more capable than the acies triplex even at its 2nd century best. Reasonably able to negotiate broken ground, that formation lacked the vulnerable tribal theurophoroi that almost cost Pyrrhus a victory at Asculum; and unlike a classical Doric phalanx, it was nearly "legionary-proof" due to much of its line presenting a pike hedge effectively impenetrable for short Roman weapons. Hoplites could turn a flank (per Cannae, Dertosa, etc., in other circumstances) or drive ahead along an entire front to inflict greater damage than received upon legionaries trying to stand their ground. Barring a preempting failure of outboard screens, such pressure should have been able to combine with the prodding advance of pikemen alongside to push opposing legions from the field. Roman cavalry and light foot gave way too quickly at Heraclea and Asculum to fully confirm this theory, but the uphill drive of just such a compound phalanx at Sellasia is a sound analog and the downhill advance of a likely similar array at Cynoscephalae may actually provide direct proof.

Another formation that potentially could have fared well against the acies triplex is the Macedonian phalanx in its late-4th century form under Alexander the Great. The truth is that Roman legions might never have faced an array like those employed by that famed conqueror or his father. The lone possible opportunity came against the Seleucid formation at Magnesia, but only if the alternative deployments proposed herein are substituted for those in the surviving literature. And even then, the progression of that battle was so unique as to seriously discount its value as a gauge for how contests between legions and phalanxes of the traditional Macedonian sort might normally have played out. The other pitched engagements fought by Rome against Macedonians across open ground involved a compounded deployment most probably of the Pyrrhic type at Cynoscephalae and one at Pydna that replaced Alexander's left wing of pikemen with light infantry fronted by theurophoroi. The older arrangement with hoplites far right and sarissaphoroi along the rest of the line can be seen as having mechanics weaker than yet partially equivalent to those of the interspersed phalanx of Pyrrhus; though less flexible in possessing but a single spear-armed segment, it would still have been practically impervious to attack from short-weaponed legionaries and well able to repel Roman armies via a mixture of spear-thrusts and pike-jabs as long as its cavalry and light foot could match their counterparts off the flanks. Had Alexander lived to turn his ambitions on Magna Graecia and the rest of Italy, he thus might have had tactical success somewhat similar to that of his admirer Hannibal, though it has to be doubted that he could have done any better strategically.

This brings us to the lingering question of whether adoption of elements of the Roman tactical system by Seleucia and Ptolemaic Egypt in the mid–160s constitutes a true military revolution. The rapidity of those moves certainly has a revolutionary appearance. Some might argue that this Romanizing phenomenon falls short of a true revolution in not being universal within the broader Hellenistic military community per the many indicated exceptions among lesser poleis, in Armenia and Pontis, along the Asian frontier, and on the Indian subcontinent. However, such objections seem to go too far in denial of the practical reality that all future conflicts of significance in the civilized western world would now be fought either among or in the deep shadows cast by legionary armies. Therefore, while the verdict may not be beyond all reasonable doubt, the preponderance of evidence favors revolution.

Final Thoughts

Celebrated historian Simon Hornblower has stated that "only an unusually arrogant scholar could claim to know exactly what kind of thing went on in a hoplite battle," and my own work over the last couple of decades confirms this to be no less true for engagements similarly long past involving sarissaphoroi and Roman legionaries. Yet an absence of certainty doesn't preclude squeezing every bit of probability from what little evidence fickle fortune and the ravages of time have left us. And despite the highly conditional nature of the information so deduced, it is vital to understanding key practicalities of ancient warfare. Such everyday verities can't be learned solely from celebrated actions no matter how extensively they were recorded. Study of the full spectrum of any given period's battles makes it obvious that the famous engagements foremost in our preserved literature often reflect circumstances far from commonplace. And that blunt fact severely limits their value as comprehensive guidelines for broader application. It's in that knowledge (and with acute awareness that all is provisional pending new and/or better data) that the foregoing attempt to reconstruct as best able every significant combat in the subject era is offered. It's my most fervent hope that criticism of this work both pro and con will serve to nudge us some small way forward in the quest for an ever clearer vision of what most likely happened on ancient battlegrounds.

Appendix 1

*Roman Defeats at Allia (390 BCE)
and Caudium (321 BCE)*

The engagement at the Allia came about when a hastily assembled Roman army confronted the Gallic Senones as they descended from the north. The consular tribunes in command set up across the closest practical chokepoint along the enemy route of advance down the southeast side of the Tiber Valley. This was at a spot near the river's confluence with its small Allia tributary a mere 16km from Rome. The meandering Tiber channel ran exceptionally close to its steep, northwestern valley wall here to transform what elsewhere was no more than a generous marching path into a broad flat where a phalanx could deploy with flanks anchored against the river on one side and the vale's rising southeastern boundary on the other. This was, however, far from ideal; indeed, it actually constituted a somewhat "make do" site for the tribunes' purposes in that it was 1,800m wide,[1] and covering such an interval seriously taxed available manpower. Due to having only brief notice to gather, there was no allied support, though strength had been boosted by a call-up of elderly and underage reservists plus a crowd of what normally were non-combatants.[2]

Regulars (17–46 years old) that made up the phalanx would have included some 6,000 hoplites with horsemen and skirmishers numbering around 600 each. Even with the latter posted across a likely 600m or so on the far left,[3] the remaining 1,200m front was still too wide for the Roman heavy infantry to span at 1m per man in its preferred six-man files. It was therefore necessary to reduce the central 400m of the phalanx to its practical minimum of three shields, with those 1,200 men then being flanked on either side by 2,400 of their fellows at the normal depth of six.[4] This effectively pinned the entire array in place by rendering its middle too thin to make an orderly advance. With skirmishers holding their left flank against the river, the tribunes then sought to secure the right by stationing their contingent of youth and old age reserves atop a modest height marking that side of the line. At a probable 20 percent of total manpower (a quarter the size of the regular levy), this might have amounted to around 1,500 hoplites and 300 or so light-armed to bring the army's total to 9,000 dedicated troops (exclusive of any poorly trained and equipped draftees from the general population).

The Gauls descended on this blockade, spreading out to form a battle-line of their own that ran from the river to just beyond the height containing the reserve force. Barbarian manpower applied to this was no doubt greater than Rome's in accordance with all our sources, though probably not overwhelmingly so. A reasonable estimate would put 12,000–15,000 Gauls in the field rather than the fantastic 70,000 of Diodorus.[5] Livy claimed only that the barbarians had "superior numbers," and even 12,000 would adequately fit that description, providing a significant advantage with a third more true fighters than Rome. Spread along some 2km at a depth of perhaps ten men at a frontage of 2m or even 3m each, this horde of Gauls crowded "all places in front and on each side" per Livy, and charged with all the wild and noisy fury characteristic of their race.[6] This saw them release a rain of heavy javelins as they swiftly closed into hand-to-hand combat with long swords and spears.

The Senones' leader, Brennus, was concerned that his foe's reserves on the height to the southeast might descend to menace his left flank/rear and took care to bring them under early attack. Diodorus' account of the battle claims that it was these reservists who initially bolted, running down to throw the nearby Roman right wing into fatal confusion. Livy, however, says that their elevated position allowed them to hold out "for some time" and that it was instead the adjacent regulars on the right of the phalanx who balked and first broke. Either way, it appears that the right side of the Roman array failed in rapid fashion and some of the Gauls opposite gave chase, while others turned against the now exposed enemy center to quickly roll it up from right to left. Unable to resist any longer, the remaining Romans took to their heels; however, they couldn't follow their comrades from the right wing in heading straight back for Rome due to the mass of foemen closing over that path. This forced them to flee across the river. Many drowned as a result, though Livy claimed that "the greatest part ... escaped to [allied] Veii" beyond the Tiber's far bank.

The battle near Caudium some 70 years later contrasted in that, rather than rising to the defense as at Allia, it was the Romans instead who were marching aggressively into foreign territory. And despite treaties that would normally have compelled attached Latin states to support such a venture, we have no indications that there were any allied troops whatsoever present at Caudium, suggesting that only the Roman army had taken the field for some reason now lost to history. As such, the consuls' maximum manpower was no more than the nominal estimate for a four-legion army: 12,000 heavy infantrymen (7,200 hoplites and 4,800 hastati) and 5,400 skirmishers (4,800 afoot plus 600 mounted).

The shortest route for the Roman advance ran through a slender divide known as the Caudine Forks (being near the city of that name). This steep-sided vale (the modern Arpaia) was some 4km long and funneled downward onto the flat through a 600m wide narrow near its western entrance to then rise sharply into an exit on the east that was only a few tens of meters across.[7] It soon became clear to the column's van that this eastern gate was guarded by stone and wood works manned by a significant force of enemy warriors. With their troops crowding to a halt behind, the consuls quickly determined that there was no realistic prospect of breaking through so narrow and well-guarded a barrier as that ahead. They therefore sought to retreat the way they had come. But upon approaching the valley's western entry, they found this now blocked as well. An army of Samnites had emerged from hiding to span the slender chokepoint there in a deep array that bristled with spears.

Livy claimed that the Romans assessed their predicament as hopeless and gave up without a fight. This seems highly improbable for several reasons. The valley topography he describes, featuring tight passes on both ends that were too restricted to permit an effective assault, simply does not exist. The location indeed pinches down like that at its eastern extreme; however, its western opening is easily broad enough for deployment of a sizeable attack formation. It's then very difficult to accept that a large army with a recent history of success against the very foes now blocking the path would have discarded even a remote chance to battle its way free. We also have Cicero's comments about Caudium seeming to imply that Rome's defeat there came in a pitched battle.[8]

What then was the most likely course of events on the battlefield? The consuls must have organized their troops in standard fashion, sending their velites swarming ahead to disrupt the Samnites while the hastati followed at a short distance and the hoplite phalanx took station at the toe of the slope. Size of the barbarian host is speculative, but it could easily have equaled if not exceeded what Rome had on hand, and it surely featured more spearmen with some sort of armor.[9] As such, the unarmored velites approaching from downslope would have taken debilitating damage under a javelin barrage from on high, many never even getting close enough to bring their own weapons within range. As the shattered skirmishers fell back, the hastati would then have closed in a relatively tight array. These better-warded troops undoubtedly suffered much less than their velites from a continuing dense fall of missiles. And that, along with the considerable internal flexibility of their ranks, let them move into shock contact across the enemy front.

Deployed maybe eight-deep at around 1m lateral spacing to attack along the entire modest chokepoint ahead, the hastati were well arranged to combat a very similarly equipped foe; nevertheless, both gravity and attendant numbers favored the other side. The Samnites could strike with all the momentum benefit of their uphill position, while taking full advantage of much longer files for shifting fresh fighters to the fore at a better count and rate. That would have inflicted a decisive toll on the Romans during a fierce and grueling melee of extended duration. Therefore, even if able to avoid an outright beating, the hastati ultimately had to abandoned the fight in utter exhaustion.

As so often must have happened in this era, any remaining hope for victory now rested solely with Rome's phalanx. That array of the city's best men had an admirable record in recent years when battling Samnites. This time, though, topography weighed against it. Forced onto the attack, the Roman hoplites had to traverse ground that was not only uneven, but which also rose some 60m along a steep grade before reaching the enemy's position. This sort of terrain was nightmarish for a charging phalanx, virtually insuring that it would suffer serious disorder on the move and develop deadly gaps along its ranks. That phenomenon was well known to the Samnites from the last six years of fighting and had undoubtedly been a prime factor in choosing this site for their ambush. And once the Roman formation became disrupted partway through its negotiation of the slope, those crafty barbarians struck according to plan, launching a furious assault upon their now badly jumbled foes below.

The Samnites' manipular scheme was expressly designed to make just this sort of attack across rough ground and, when it came hard downslope into an already dangerously tattered phalanx front, the tribesmen surely broke through almost at once. Taking casualties from behind for at least a short distance, the routed hoplites fled to join the rest of their army and entrench on high ground at the far eastern end of the valley. It was only then that they judged their plight hopeless and negotiated a surrender that cost them not only their pride, but all their military hardware as well.

Appendix 2
Hellenistic Land Battles/Keys to Victory (300–167 BCE)

Date	Battle	Victor	Defeated	Key to Victory
294	Mantinea IV	Demetrius	Sparta	frontal defeat of left wing
294	Sparta I	Demetrius	Sparta	complete frontal defeat
c. 294	Getae Territory	Getae	Lysimachus	light-armed ambush
290	Pindos Pass	Epirus	Macedonia	frontal defeat of left wing
284	Cyrrhestica	Seleucia	Demetrius	envelopment of left wing
281	Corupedium	Seleucia	Macedonia	envelopment of left wing
c. 280	Hyblaeus R.	Syracuse	Acragas	frontal defeat of left wing
c. 280	Terias R.	Carthage	Syracuse	frontal defeat of left wing
280	Heraclea	Pyrrhus	Rome	envelopment of left wing
279	Asculum	Pyrrhus	Rome	envelopment of left wing
279	Orestis Plain	Gauls	Macedonia	double envelopment
279/8	Thermopylae	Greeks	Gauls	frontal defeat
279/8	N. Aetolia	Aetolia	Gauls	light-armed ambush
279/8	Delphi	Greeks	Gauls	complete frontal defeat
277	Lysimacheia	Seleucia	Gauls	surprise attack on rear
275	Maleventum	Rome	Pyrrhus	defeat of right wing
c. 274	Cyamosorus R.	Messana	Syracuse	frontal defeat due to terrain
c. 273	Elephant Victory	Seleucia	Gauls	envelopment of left wing
273	Haliacmon Pass	Epirus	Macedonia	frontal defeat of both wings
272	Sparta II	Sparta	Epirus	frontal defeat/surprise attack
272	Sparta III	Sparta	Epirus	frontal defeat of both wings
272	Charadrus Pass	Epirus	Sparta	frontal defeat in mounted action
272	Streets of Argos	Argos	Epirus	light-armed ambush
265	Isthmus of Corinth	Macedonia	Sparta	frontal defeat due to field works
265	Longanus R.	Syracuse	Messana	surprise attack on rear
264	Messana III	Syracuse	Rome	envelopment (possibly double)
264	Messana IV	Rome	Carthage	drawn frontal engagement
263	Megalopolis	Megalopolis	Sparta	frontal defeat of left wing
262	Sardis	Pergamum	Seleucia	light-armed engagement
262	Heraclea Minoa	Carthage	Rome	front defeat in mounted action

Hellenistic Land Battles/Keys to Victory (300–167 BCE)

Date	Battle	Victor	Defeated	Key to Victory
262	Agrigentum	Rome	Carthage	frontal defeat on all but center
260	Segesta	Carthage	Rome	surprise attack on column of march?
260	Paropus/Thermae	Carthage	Siciliot Grk.	surprise attack
258	Camarina	Carthage	Rome	drawn engagement/field works
256	Adys	Rome	Carthage	surprise attack/envelopment
255	Tunes	Carthage	Rome	double envelopment
255	Aspis	Rome	Carthage	double envelopment
250	Panormus	Rome	Carthage	surprise attack from gate
245	Chaeronea III	Achaean L.	Aetolia n L.	envelopment of right wing
241	Pellene	Achaean L.	Aetolian L.	surprise attack
240	Bagradas Bridge	Carthage	Mercenaries	complete frontal defeat
240	Naravas Victory	Carthage	Mercenaries	double envelopment
238	Leptis Minor	Carthage	Mercenaries	double envelopment
c. 237	Lydia I	Hierax	Seleucus II	draw or minor engagement
c. 237	Lydia II	Hierax	Seleucus II	draw or minor engagement
c. 237	Ancyra	Hierax	Seleucus II	envelopment of left wing
c. 236	Agadir	Carthage	Iberians	frontal attack/envelopment?
c. 236	Numidia	Carthage	Numidians	complete frontal defeat
235	Chares R.	Argos	Achaean L.	frontal defeat right wing
235	Cleonae	Achaean L.	Argos	frontal defeat/surprise attack
233	Phylacia	Macedonia	Achaean L.	frontal defeat/envelop. of left wing?
231	Medion	Illyrians	Aetolian L.	flank attack
230	Phoenice	Illyrians	Epirus	envelopment
c. 228*	Aphrodision	Pergamum	Hierax	surprise attack
c. 228*	Caicus Spring	Pergamum	Galatians	attack on favorable terrain?
c. 228*	H. Phyrgia	Pergamum	Hierax	surprise attack or envelopment?
c. 228*	Harpassos R.	Pergamum	Hierax	surprise attack or envelopment?
c. 228*	Coloe	Pergamum	Hierax	surprise attack or envelopment?
c. 228*	Royal Road	Pergamum	Seleucia	surprise attack?
227	Mount Lycaeum	Sparta	Achaean L.	surprise attack on column of march
227	Ladoceia	Sparta	Achaean L.	envelopment?
227	Arcad. Orchomenos	Achaean L.	Orchomenos	complete frontal defeat
225	Hecatombaeum	Sparta	Achaean L.	frontal defeat of left wing
222	Sellasia	Macedonia	Sparta	frontal defeat of both wings
220	Caphyae	Aetolian L.	Achaean L.	complete frontal defeat
220	Bab. Apollonia	Seleucia	Molon	frontal defeat of left wing
220	Tagus R.	Carthage	Iberians	complete frontal defeat
219	Saguntum	Carthage	Saguntum	complete frontal defeat
218	Ticinus R.	Carthage	Rome	double envelopment (mounted)
218	Trebia R.	Carthage	Rome	envelopment/surprise attack on rear
218	Cissus	Rome	Carthage	envelopment of right wing
217	Raphia	Egypt	Seleucia	envelopment of left wing
217	L. Trasimenus	Carthage	Rome	flank attack on marching column
217	L. Umber	Carthage	Rome	double envelopment (mounted)
217	Gerunium	Carthage	Rome	surprise attack on flanks and rear

Date	Battle	Victor	Defeated	Key to Victory
216	Cannae	Carthage	Rome	double envelopment
216	Nola I	Rome	Carthage	surprise attack from gate
215	Grumentum	Rome	Carthage	surprise attack?
215	Nola II	Rome	Carthage	surprise attack on foragers
215	Cornus	Rome	Carthage	double envelopment
215	Carales	Rome	Carthage	frontal defeat of left wing
215	Dertosa/Ibera	Rome	Carthage	frontal defeat in center
215	Iliturgi	Rome	Carthage	frontal attack in light-armed action?
215	Intibili	Rome	Carthage	frontal attack in light-armed action?
214	Calor R.	Rome	Carthage	complete frontal defeat
214	Nola III	Rome	Carthage	sally to defeat besiegers
212	Lucania	Carthage	Rome	double envelopment
212	Herdonea I	Carthage	Rome	complete frontal def./dbl. envelop.
211	Himera R. II	Rome	Carthage	complete frontal def./dbl. envelop.
211	Castulo	Carthage	Rome	double envelopment
210	Herdonea II	Carthage	Rome	envelopment of left wing
210	Numistro	Carthage	Rome	light-armed downslope defeat
210	Mount Labos Pass	Seleucia	Parthia	surprise attack on rear
210	Larissa R.	Achaean L.	Elis	frontal defeat in mounted action
209	Canusium	Carthage	Rome	complete frontal defeat in narrows
209	Novo Cartago	Rome	Carthage	frontal defeat of sally by besieged
209	Arios R.	Seleucia	Bactria	frontal defeat in mounted action
208	Petelia H.	Carthage	Rome	ambush of marching column
208	Epizephyrian Locri	Carthage	Rome	frontal defeat of besiegers
208	Baecula	Rome	Carthage	double uphill flank attacks
208	Lamia I	Macedonia	Aetolian L.	envelopment on one flank?
208	Lamia II	Macedonia	Aetolian L.	envelopment on one flank?
207	Metaurus R.	Rome	Carthage	envelopment of left wing/terrain
207	Mantinea V	Achaean L.	Sparta	frontal defeat/envelop. on the right
206	Ilipia	Rome	Carthage	double envelopment
204	Salaeca	Rome	Carthage	nighttime sneak attack
203	Great Plains	Rome	Carthage	double envelopment
203	Mediolanum	Rome	Carthage	envelopment of left wing
202	Zama	Rome	Carthage	double envelopment
201	Scotitas	Achaean L.	Sparta	ambush in wooded terrain
200	Mount Panium	Seleucia	Egypt	envelopment of left wing/terrain
199	Ithacus	Rome	Seleucia	drawn light-armed action
199	Dardanian Frontier	Macedonia	Dardanians	envelopment of one flank
198	Aous R.	Rome	Macedonia	surprise attack on right flank
197	Cynoscephalae	Rome	Macedonia	frontal defeat of left wing
197	Nemea R.	Aetolian L.	Macedonia	envelopment of one wing/terrain
197	Alabanda	Rhodes	Macedonia	envelopment of left wing
195	Eurotas R.	Rome	Sparta	failed rear ambush of column
192	Camp of Pyrrhus	Achaean L.	Sparta	complete frontal defeat/surprise
192	Delium	Seleucia	Rome	surprise attack

Date	Battle	Victor	Defeated	Key to Victory
191	Thermopylae	Rome	Seleucia	envelopment left wing/terrain
190	Pergamum	Pergamum	Seleucia	surprise attack
190	Magnesia	Rome	Seleucia	frontal defeat of left wing
171	Callinicus	Macedonia	Rome	frontal defeat in mounted action
171	Phalanna	Rome	Macedonia	frontal defeat (mounted)
168	Pythium	Rome	Macedonia	surprise attack
168	Pydna	Rome	Macedonia	envelopment of left wing
167	Bactria	Seleucia	Bactria-Sog.	envelopment?

* *Battle took place sometime 237–228.*

Appendix 3

Legion Versus Phlanx (280–168 BCE)

Pitched Battles on Open Ground*

Date	Battle	Victor	Defeated Element(s)	Victorious Element(s)
280	Heraclea	phalanx	cavalry/light foot flank	cavalry/elephants
279	Asculum	phalanx	cavalry/light foot flank	cavalry/elephants
264	Messana III	phalanx	cavalry/light foot flank?	cavalry/light foot?
262	Agrigentum	legion	theurophoroi both wings	legionaries
255	Tunes	phalanx	mounted/lt. foot both flanks	cavalry/elephants
255	Aspis	legion	cavalry/lt. foot both flanks?	mounted/light foot?
250	Panormus	legion	theurophoroi right flank	legionaries
218	Trebia R.	phalanx	mounted/lt. foot both flanks	mounted/light foot
218	Cissus	legion	hoplites left wing?	legionaries
216	Cannae	phalanx	legionaries both wings	hoplites/cavalry
215	Grumentum	legion	?	?
215	Cornus	legion	hoplites both wings	legionaries
215	Carales	legion	hoplites left wing	legionaries
215	Dertosa	drawn	legionaries-Theurophoroi	hoplites-legionaries
214	Calor R.	legion	hoplites at center	legionaries
212	Lucania	phalanx	legionaries both wings	hoplites/cavalry
212	Herdonea I	phalanx	legionaries both wings	hoplites
211	Himera R. II	legion	mounted troops/hoplites	cavalry/legionaries
211	Castulo	phalanx	legionaries both wings	hoplites
210	Herdonea II	phalanx	cavalry/light foot left flank	cavalry/light foot
209	Canusium	phalanx	legionaries both wings	hoplites
208	Baecula	legion	theurophoroi both flanks	legionaries
207	Metaurus R.	legion	mounted/light foot left flank	legionaries
206	Ilipia	legion	mounted/lt. foot both flanks	cavalry/light foot
203	Great Plains	legion	cavalry/lt. foot both flanks	cavalry/light foot
203	Mediolanum	legion	mounted/light foot	legionaries
202	Zama	legion	cavalry/elephants/lt. foot	cavalry/light foot
197	Cynosceph.	legion	hoplites/pikemen left wing	legionaries
190	Magnesia	legion	mounted troops/light foot	cavalry/light foot
168	Pydna	legion	theurophoroi left wing	legionaries

* Battles exclude those lacking pitched frontal engagement (Segesta, Adys, L. Trasimenus, Petelia H.) and those on ground not open due to field works (Maleventum, Aous R., Thermopylae).

Chapter Notes

Chapter 1

1. These original Successors respected Alexander publicly in all things; however, their personal tactics were informed by past direct observation of his shortcomings in the field. Beyond many a recovered misstep, they had seen rash decisions lead to at least three outright defeats in 335 at Peuce (Pine) Island (Arian 1.3.3–5), in the winter of 331/30 at the Persian (Susian) Gates (Diodorus 17.68.1–4; Polyaenus 4.3.27; Curtius 5.3.17–23; Arian 3.18.1–3), and in 329 across the Jaxartes River in the far Persian northeast (Curtius 7.6.1–7).

2. These poets include Mimnermnus, Callinus, Alcaeus of Mytilene, and Tyrtaeus (Millett 2013, 48–50).

3. It is likely that the slang term *hoplon* for the Greek heavy infantry shield derived from its use by hoplites (hoplitai) rather than the name for those warriors having come from that for the shield.

4. Owning a horse with its attached grazing land in this era might be compared to modern ownership of a costly luxury like an exotic sports car or private yacht. Such ultra-wealthy aristocrats probably represented no more than 1 percent of the adult citizens within a typical ancient Greek state with hoplites making up around 10 percent.

5. Much of this design was geared toward allowing hoplites to survive the great pressure generated while pressing ahead in concert (*othismos*). Each hoplite aligned his forearm parallel across the body to shelter his chest within the shield's broad hollow and avoid asphyxiation from compression. The reinforced rim aided this not only by helping to prevent the aspis from splitting, but also by letting it rest securely against the collar and upper thighs.

6. Argos may have been an early adopter of the aspis rather than creator in that the ancient Greeks themselves credited its invention to the Carians of Asia Minor, though this might refer only to the shield's porpax and antilabe suspension system rather than to its final, overall design (Herodotus 1.171.4).

7. Bardunias and Ray 2016, 109–112.

8. Advancing offensively or otherwise maneuvering at a depth of anything below six men was impractical for poorly drilled militia due to the high risk of becoming greatly disordered and creating fatal frontal gaps (Goldsworthy 1996, 196–197), thus depths of four were usually used only to receive attacks in place. Eight-man files were most common in line with experimental data showing them to be most cost-efficient for concerted pushing in othismos (Bardunias and Ray 2016, 132–136). Depths above sixteen added mass, but probably had the primary purpose of either fitting into a limited battle-space or crowding the path of retreat for reluctant fore-rankers.

9. Thucydides 5.71.1; however, modern field tests suggest that twisting of the body to keep one's shield in front while marching and a natural contraction of ranks during advance were probably greater contributors to rightward drift than the apprehensive hedging noted by Thucydides (Bardunias and Ray 2016, 129).

10. The exception here is that phalanxes from Thebes would occasionally strike with their left wing as a counter to cyclosis; something recorded at the battles of Leuctra (371) and Mantinea II (362).

11. Heckel 2013, 162–166, 168–169; Ray 2012, 88–91.

12. Sekunda and Chow 1992, 26–27.

13. Relative to spear-armed fronts, sarissai had less striking power in terms of both frequency (only the leading rank could make contact versus at least the front two ranks of spearmen) and power (several studies have shown the sort of underhand thrusting required by a pike is much less forceful than the overhand blows deliverable by a spear) and were more limited in their range of targets (only being able to hit those straight ahead—Heckel et al. 2010, 105). All of this added to even lower formation flexibility than that of the classical phalanx (by no means itself very flexible) to restrict the offensive potential of sarissa arrays (see discussion: Ray 2012, 91).

14. These picked hoplites appear to have originally been called *pezhetairoi* (foot-companions), perhaps that title dating back to an origin as royal guards. Becoming a larger contingent in the new phalanx, they then took up the name "hypaspists" (aspis/shield-carriers) and the old term pezhetairoi fell to those armed with sarissai (Heckel 2004, 24; Heckel and Jones 2006, 31; Bosworth 2010, 98–99).

15. Philip was clearly aware that months of intense drilling was critical to the success and maintenance of his new-style phalanx, and this was simply not possible for part-time militiamen. In converting to a full-time army, he compensated his troops for their resulting loss of civilian employment by putting them on a gen-

erous salary by no later than spring 357 (Bardunias and Ray 2016, 201).

16. The Macedonians might already have been intimately intermixing light-armed footmen among their horsemen; however, even if not, Philip would have observed it among the Boeotians during his hostage stay in Thebes as a youth. The noted cavalry expert Xenophon (*Hellenica* 7.5.23–25) praised this technique in contrast to the inferior custom at Athens and elsewhere of fielding cavalry and its supporting light infantry in separate bodies.

17. The most notable upgrades given to the Macedonian phalanx during two centuries or so of deployment were adjustments to its sarissai, which became much longer than the originals, with Philip himself probably instituting the first such extension sometime after 354 (Ray 2012, 110; Bardunias and Ray 2016, 150, 214, note 62).

18. This followed in the steps of an earlier occasion when Alexander equipped his hypaspists with pikes rather than their usual spears; however, that was in India at Hydaspes River (326) and appears to have been a "one-off" tactic to counter an exceptional threat of elephants from a foe lacking in the sort of heavy foot best met by hoplites.

19. Bardunias 2018.

20. There is dispute on Antigonus' early career. A minority view makes him a peasant farmer, but the majority holds he came from nobility (Billows 1990, 15–22). If a commoner, his best route to command would have been through the ranks of the king's elite hoplite contingent, the hypaspists. If noble, his rise would have been much swifter via appointment to a post of authority within the hypaspists. Nobility would also imply previous service in the picked heavy cavalry (*hetairoi*), which comports with Antigonos riding among his own select horsemen in all the battles he led in Asia prior to Ipsus (where he was too old at 82 for such athletics). Either way, he would have had outstanding experience in heavy infantry warfare, applying it effectively in using a residual infantry force to repel a hoplite sortie at the siege of Perinthos in 340 (Billows 1990, 28–29) and in commanding Alexander's allied hoplites in the major battles of his Persian conquest (Bardunias and Ray, 2016, 146).

21. Diodorus 19.80.3–84; this rash action by his son lost Antigonus some 13,000 men and the city of Gaza.

22. Diodorus 20.47.1–3, 49–52; Plutarch *Demetrius*, Vol. II, 448, 454.

23. Plutarch *Demetrius*, Vol. II, 467.

24. Spartan manpower here is based upon the spartiate hoplite levy being well along in a decline that would reduce it to a mere 1,000 men at the time of Cleomenes' reforms in the later 3rd century (see Chapter 4). This is also compatible with likely Spartan strength for the subsequent engagement a few days later (see below).

25. At 300 ships of all types (perhaps 165 warships [55 percent] and the remaining 135 being troop carriers and supply transports as in a past ratio cited by Diodorus [20.82.4]) and previous indications of averaging around 80 combatants per gross vessel for amphibious operations (Grainger 2011, 33–34).

26. Note that the force that fled with Demetrius from Ipsus is not informative here. Those escapees represented Antigonus' right-wing cavalry (4,000 horsemen) plus attached foot-skirmishers (typically deployed in a ratio of close to 1-to-1 with the mounted troops). The landing party at Athens would have had a substantially different mix of arms out of simple tactical necessity, which required it to be dominant in heavy infantry with only a small cavalry content as per known ratios for some of Demetrius' previous amphibious operations.

27. Frederick the Great (1747, 314); the presence of firearms in Frederick's armies versus the Hellenistic period did not fundamentally change combat dynamics due to three key factors. The first is that the use of un-aimed musket fire in Frederick's day (his orders forbade aiming that would slow the rate of fire) put his combats in the same modeling category as ancient warfare with both direction of ranged weaponry to an area (rather than at individual targets) and the use of ancient hand-weapons subject to the mathematics of Lanchester's Linear Law. Second is the notorious ineffectiveness of the period's musket fire, with only the first volley generally considered capable of doing any significant harm (like an opening flight of javelins or arrows). It was axiomatic that "*to kill a man required an expenditure of lead equal to his weight*" (Rothenberg 1980, 14, going on to say that "this *might appear exaggerated, but it was true*"). Calculations of combats in the Napoleonic era suggest that it took between 200 and 500 rounds to hit a single enemy soldier, killing about one out of five (Muir, 1998, 46, 82). Lastly, due to these and other limitations of gunfire, the doctrine of Frederick's (and nearly every other) army called for the carrying of battlefields by bayonet charges in column; indeed, in Frederick's early campaigns, advances were made solely using bayonets. These mechanically resembled hoplite attacks, though sans aspis shield and thus lacking rightward drift. A typical Napoleonic battalion in "column" contained 600 men filed 12-deep along a front of 50yds at 1yd/man (Rothenberg 1980, 68). With bayoneted muskets analogous to spears, this was virtually identical to the array in phalanx of a similarly sized battalion (*lochos*) of Spartan hoplites in the early 4th century.

28. Such tactics applicable here would have been either an unexpected mobilization or surprise attack and neither is mentioned in Plutarch's account. The former clearly could not have happened under the circumstances at hand, while the latter seems nearly impossible at the apparent site of the engagement.

29. See Pritchett (1969, 37–72) for a description of the topography in this region.

30. The Spartan victory at Dipaea c.471 is of note here as a phalanx of Spartans likely standing at a similar depth of four shields (later exaggerated in the retelling to a single rank) defeated an Arcadian formation there that was filed much deeper. However, this famed action varied significantly from Mantinea IV due to the Spartans having executed a surprise mobilization that caught their foes short of full assembly and unprepared to fight (Herodotus 9.35; Pausanius 3.11.7; Ray 2009, 121–122).

31. Bardunias and Ray 2016, 206.

32. Both tactical logic and the lessons of history would have dictated the Spartans' use of restricted terrain here. They had faced similar threats on home

soil in the 360's from large Boeotian armies and took advantage of familiar tight passages and elevated positions to mount a successful defense on those occasions. Lacking identification of an exact battle site, it's unknown just how narrow the chosen ground was in 294, thus the wide range offered for the Spartan depth of file. As for the proposed upper end of that range, the subsequent defeat suggests failure to stand more than eight-deep, which would have forced Demetrius to file inefficiently above sixteen as Boeotian offensives had likely been forced to do in those past failures.

33. At about 7 percent killed among the hoplites engaged for Sparta, this would be toward the lower end of normal loss for a beaten phalanx, indicating that most of those defeated were allowed to get away. Similarly, the victors captured 500 men rather than killing them, which also suggests that Demetrius had probably ordered restraint toward seeking better relations with a famously proud people he desired to now bring under his sway.

34. Arian 1.3.2; Webber 2001, 10.
35. Arian 1.3.5.
36. Ray 2012, 205–206.
37. Pausanius 1.9.6; Polyaenus 7.25; Diodorus 21.11.1, 12.1–3; the confusion here comes from Diodorus splitting the Getae campaign into two segments with suspiciously similar outcomes. The first invasion in 297 is led by Agathocles and results in his capture, while the second is by Lysimachus sometime 294–292 in which he suffers the same fate. Pausanius' tale of a single campaign seems the more likely version.
38. The state of Epirus' army upon the return of Pyrrhus 35 years after Alexander's death is unreported. The Epiriote military had been modestly engaged in the interim, fighting four recorded battles. Epirus' Aeacides lost two actions and his life fighting Macedonia on home soil in 313, but his army then recovered quickly to deal a defeat to the Macedonians the following year near Eurymenae only to come up short against that same force after it had been heavily reinforced. The Epiriotes probably waged the first and last of these clashes at significant disadvantages in manpower (a third to half again more Macedonians, respectively); however, the middle two likely involved well-matched forces, showing a positive trend suggestive of an army on the upswing after 19 years or so of inaction. It's reasonable then to assume that major remnants of his uncle's past military strength were present upon which Pyrrhus could base a restoration. And the two years he had for that project prior to his first foreign campaign were ample to make considerable headway; after all, Philip had created his own phalanx from scratch in a single fall/winter season even though saddled with native troops lacking any experience of heavy infantry fighting whatsoever. It's also notable that Pyrrhus had a great deal of credibility and prestige going for him toward gaining strong local support for such an ambitious undertaking, being the alleged descendent of Greece's most legendary warriors (Achilles and his son Pyrrhus of Trojan War fame), a cousin of the greatest commander in Greek history (Alexander the Great), and having fought at the side of highly regarded Demetrius the Besieger.
39. Diodorus (18.9.5) and Pausanius (see below) indicate 7,000-man Aetolian deployments for foreign expeditions with Diodorus (18.24.2, 38.1) citing a nationwide potential of 12,000 infantry plus 400 in cavalry. An expanded Aetolia fielded 7,000 hoplites and perhaps 9,000 light foot a decade later (Pausanius 10.20.3–5; Scholten 2000, 36), suggesting a likely nominal figure of around 5,000 hoplites, 7,000 light footmen, and 400 horsemen in 290, though deployable parade strength might have been no more than 80 percent of that.

40. Less flexible Macedonian pikemen would have been a poor choice for operating in the oft rugged terrain of Aetolia and much better employed with Demetrius' column.

41. Garofaulius 1979, 274, note 60.
42. Plutarch *Demetrius*, Vol. II, 471.
43. See Chapter 2 re: *Heraclea*.
44. The more than 15,000 Molossian casualties reported in a battle against Illyrian invaders in 385 (Diodorus 15.13.3) is clearly far too high to be a realistic death count or even a reasonable size for that tribe's army. This much more likely reflects the entire force put into the field (those defeated rather than killed) from all the tribes, though the Molossians might have contributed more due to having a larger population and being the primary focus of the attack. Had the Molossians made up half the army at an 80 percent rate of mobilization and the other tribes contributed about two-thirds of their totals (as common for allies throughout Greece), this would indicate a roughly 20,000-man nominal potential for the entire coalition. Garoufalias (2000, 268, note 50) has suggested that the army Pyrrhus deployed in a 291 feint toward Macedonia had a similar tribal strength (his 13,000 equating to a two-thirds muster from all three tribes), making for a total of 15,000 after adding 2,000 more men from the attached Greek region of Ambracia.
45. Plutarch *Pyrrhus*, Vol. I, 523–24.
46. Plutarch describes Pantouches as *"Demetrius' most experienced commander"*; and likely being over the age of 60, it has been suggested (though much disputed) that he might have served as an officer under Alexander the Great during his Indian campaign in 327–325 (Garoufalias 1969, 274 note-60).
47. While the exact number of men in opposing files was dependent upon the unknown width forced onto Pantouches' line in spanning the mountain passage at hand, the ratio would have been constant. Had he filed eight-deep across a 750m front (at 1m for each hoplite in rank), then Pyrrhus could have filed twelve-deep (at the same 1m per hoplite and two-thirds that for his pikemen standing side-on) to gain a 1.5-to-1 edge in depth across the entire line, including the 250m manned by spearmen on his right wing. And this favorable ratio would have applied along any other front whether wider (6 vs 4 across 1,500m) or narrower (18 vs 12 over 500m). It must be noted here that spacing for phalangites likely varied with regard to the situation attaining, with Polybius (18.29.2) citing an interval of around 1m and Asclepiodotus (4.1) putting it as tight as half that when standing purely on the defensive, the latter having a close analog in similar spacing used by 15th-16th century CE Swiss pikemen (Schneider 1893, 70). Apparent formation widths observed in the 4th century (Ray 2012) indicate that something between those extremes on

the order of 2/3m might have been more the norm. That matches Asclepiodotus' optimum recommended width for phalangite shields (5.1) as well as measurements on surviving examples (Sekunda 2012, 18). This 2/3m interval is generally applied throughout the reconstructions that follow with the proviso that wider or narrower spacings are always possible and accommodating them require adjustment of the proposed depths of file (from eight to twelve men in going from 2/3m to 1m for example).

48. Plutarch *Pyrrhus*, Vol. II, 524.

49. If reconstructed here within reasonable bounds, Pindos Pass serves as an excellent exemplar for the logic in retaining Philip II's hoplite/hypaspist-manned attack wing where it was devised and perfected in a region with rugged topography and spear-armed threats rather than going to the pike-dominated Macedonian phalanx model then ascendant in Asia's more open, cavalry-friendly terrain. It would have been much more difficult for pikemen to have cleared the pass by frontal attack as done by Pyrrhus' hoplites.

50. The size of the enemy armament was modest, but its losses were equivalent to those inflicted on a much larger host in a conventional victory. A thoroughly routed and pursued phalanx might expect to lose a crippling 20 percent of its troops; therefore, with Pantouches' men being entirely put out of action between those giving up and those killed (both in battle and while trying to escape through Aetolian occupied territory), Pyrrhus' triumph here was effectively like having badly beaten a force of 50,000 at very little cost.

51. Plutarch *Demetrius*, Vol. II, 479.

52. Plutarch *Demetrius*, Vol. II, 476.

53. There are several fairly clear instances in the ancient literature in which the total strength of a defeated army gleaned from some source appears to have been erroneously reported as a count of its casualties (i.e., those killed rather than those engaged). This seems a likely variant on that phenomenon outside of a battle setting, with a known figure for those remaining having been mistaken for those dying or otherwise lost. Like Plutarch's tally on the original landing force, this might comprise only the foot soldiers.

54. These would have been cross-trained in both the dory and sarissa. The latter was probably by far the more frequently used weapon in a land where enemy pikemen and cavalry were common opponents; however, it's likely that spear and aspis were employed here against an army of mercenary hoplites. This finds further support in Seleucus detaching a select hypaspist unit in the stratagem that ended the battle; a role that would have been typical for elite spearmen (Alexander the Great had so utilized his own hypaspists on several occasions), but completely inappropriate for pike-armed troops of any sort.

55. The projected numbers here are largely informed by forces from the same region recorded at Ipsus in 301 with some reduction in native Macedonians lost/re-patriated in connection with that battle.

56. Bar-Kochva 1976, 114.

57. This interpretation of the battle's final phase is a synthesis that resolves potential conflicts in our two ancient accounts. Plutarch (*Demetrius*, Vol. II, 478) tells of Seleucus bringing the enemy over solely with an appeal from behind his own lines, while Polyaenus (4.9.3) has him do so from their rear at the head of his flanking contingent. It is unlikely that Seleucus took himself off the field as in the latter version or could have won over a foe on the brink of victory per the former.

58. Justin (17.1.10) lists Lysimachus as 74 in 281, though this was still younger than Seleucus at 77.

59. Justin 17.1–3; Orosius 3.23.58–62; Pausanius 1.10.5; Strabo 13.4–5.

60. Montagu (2000, 115) offers a good review of consensus opinion on this location.

61. *The Babylonian Chronicles* (BCHP 9.1) attest that Lysimachus ("*the king*") gathered troops from the land of Sardis (Lydia), though the capital city itself would fall to Seleucus' forces before his arrival.

62. This assumes a ratio of one hypaspist for every three native Macedonian phalangites per past practice under Philip II and Alexander with the pantodapoi pikemen serving in regiments of 3,000 (representing three *chiliarchies* or battalions of 1,000 men each) like their European counterparts and a 4,000-man mixed-arms combination via attachment of a fourth chiliarchy of spearmen then forming the most basic operational unit (a *strategia*). Note that some of the Macedonian natives at this time might still have been carrying a unique shield associated with the late Demetrius Poliorcetes. Instead of the pelte's usual 66cm across, shields linked to Demetrius have been found that average 74cm (Sekunda 2012, 18–19). These were not concave and would not have been suitable for spearmen in a tight press; however, being barely compatible with a two-hand pike, they could have provided front-rankers better warding from opposing sarissai. Awkward when paired with a hefty pike, such shields apparently did not see widespread or lasting use.

63. This assumes that the Seleucid ratio of one hypaspist for every four Macedonian colonial phalangites (see discussion in Chapter 3 re: *The Elephant Victory*) came into use when the colonies were established and that the pantodapoi pikemen filled 4,000-man regiments like those of their colonial comrades (the smallest Seleucid operational unit or strategia thus comprising 5,000 men versus the 4,000 used in Macedonia proper).

64. *The Babylonian Chronicles* (BCHP 9.8) indicate that Seleucus deployed elephants from Bactria (modern Afghanistan), which was the gateway for animals obtained from India.

65. Memnon of Heraclea via the <I>Extract of Photius.

Chapter 2

1. This upside estimate derives from forces fielded by Syracuse's Agathocles at his zenith in 310–307. These included 10,000 hoplites (6,500 mercenaries, including 1,000 elite bodyguards and 1,000 Etruscans, plus 3,500 citizen militiamen) under the tyrant's personal command in North Africa (Diodorus 20.11.5) and another 6,000 or so spearmen back on Sicily as projected from a reported 8,200-man infantry total (Diodorus 20.56.1). The latter contingent also had 1,200 horsemen and a likely 2,000 foot-skirmishers.

2. Diodorus 20.56.1.

3. Some (perhaps most) of the mercenaries serving Syracuse under Agathocles had abandoned the city after his death brought an end to their contracted income.

4. This is based on deployments in past campaigns (Bardunias and Ray 2016, 177, 218, notes 12, 13) and data for a division at Crimisus River in 341. Diodorus (16.80.4) cited the latter at 2,500 men (likely nominal less a detached 500-man sub-unit), while Plutarch (*Timoleon*, Vol. I, 348) implied 3,000 men (full nominal). This division size also sometimes applied to allied/mercenary contingents (Polybius 2.7.6–10, Livy 21.21.10–13. 23–4–6). Contemporary Roman legions likewise boasted 3,000 heavies (see below), suggesting a common practical component of logistics and/or command and control limiting the size of these largest tactical elements. Similarly, if 500-man sub-units existed, this would be much like the most common size for Greek militia *lochoi* (battalions).

5. Funerary steles, coins, and various decorative artworks dating from the 5th into the 2nd century (Head 1982, 140–142, 143–144; Salimbeti and D'Amato 2014, 21–22, 33–39) show this hoplite gear to have been standard for all categories of Carthaginian heavy foot, including non-citizen conscripts per its depiction on stele of Libyan origin. Unlike the practice in Grecian communities, the Carthaginian state appears to have supplied this equipment in uniform fashion as indicated by Polybius' report (36.6) of a staggering 200,000 panoplies being recovered from storage in the city after its fall in the Third Punic War (though this is perhaps an order of magnitude error in transcription of the historian's actual number). It's notable that Carthage was unique in its ability to afford this kind of thing due to controlling trade from Iberia and Britain that supplied the Mediterranean world with most of its tin ore. That rare metal was essential to making bronze for these armaments and its wholesale abundance at Carthage allowed for fashioning and distribution in bulk of this otherwise prohibitively expensive gear at a sustainable cost. One other significant variation versus Grecian norms was that Punic marines used javelins and a small, round, center-grip shield (Nelson 1975, 20–21; Salimbeti and D'Amato, 2014, 13) rather than the long spears and aspides of their Greek counterparts (*epibatai*), though this limited their use in landed operations to missile support versus the shock fighting capability of true hoplite epibatai.

6. Diodorus 20.10.6; in the 5th and 4th centuries these elite spearmen were city residents of a division known to the Greeks as the "Sacred Band" and distinguished by their hoplite aspides being painted white.

7. Head 1982, 142–143; Salimbeti and D'Amato 2014, 23, 36, 39.

8. The area now under attack by Hicetas had been ceded to Carthage's sphere of influence by Agathocles, and alliance to the Carthaginians was a hedge by the local population against Syracusan aggression. For example, the Mamertine mercenaries that had recently left Syracuse to settle on the island's northeast coast (see Chapter 3 re: *Messana III*) would likely have joined the effort against Hicetas.

9. Diodorus 22.2.1.

10. Concise primers on this stage of Roman warfare (mid–8th–6th century) can be found in Sekunda and Northwood (1995), Fields (2011), and Southern (2014, 33–44). Armstrong (2016a, 1–128; 2016b, 1–56) offers useful 6th century detail along with some dissenting interpretations of the sparse data available on this subject.

11. The tendency to embrace foreign technologies, especially from Greece, has long been recognized as an Etruscan trait. A good example of this is that so many Greek-style pots were found in excavations of Etruscan archaeological sites that they were initially mistaken for Greek settlements (Armstrong 2016a, 81).

12. Armstrong 2016a, 55.

13. Though arms could be purchased from the state, Republican Rome supplied no equipment at public cost save in the most exceptional of emergencies. The short-term call-up of normal non-combatants for the battle of Allia in 387 is a likely instance of such a crisis-driven deployment (see Appendix 1). Gear was provided In the early 3rd century for the poorest auxiliaries. This practice probably wasn't extended to legionaries until 216, when men from the lower classes formed new legions during the 2nd Punic War (Penrose 2005, 25–26).

14. Sekunda and Northwood 1995, 16–17.

15. Fields 2011, 49; Sekunda and Northwood 1995, 16; Bardunias (2017, personal communication) has also pointed out several art works from Paestum showing 4th century hoplites with multiple javelins, though these would date from that city's pre–Roman, Graeco-Lucanian period.

16. Sekunda and Northwood (1995, 18–21) estimate Roman cavalry strength at only 600 horsemen until near the end of the 4th century. Foot skirmisher numbers are not attested prior to the mid–3rd century but were perhaps at this earlier date comparable to those of the cavalry. At one skirmisher and horseman per ten hoplites, manpower for Roman auxiliaries would have closely paralleled 5th century Greek standards. The exact terminology applied to Roman light infantry is uncertain, with "rorarii" persisting in some capacity to the end of the 2nd century, when it was universally replaced by "*velites*" (Lazenby 1996, 178, note 8); however, "*leves*" also applied to skirmishers and it's possible that both that term and rorarii came to identify specialized assignments within the velites (see below).

17. Head 1982, 136; Armstrong 2016a, 103.

18. Some Greek phalanxes might have initially used a similar system based on threes. Chrimes (1949, 394–395) has proposed that this was the norm at Sparta with its tripartite Dorian tribal system prior to reorganizing into multiple geographic districts (*obai*). If so, other Dorian militaries could also have filed by threes in their early days.

19. Livy (8.8.2) noted battles that were like those of a civil war "*so little did the Latins differ from the Romans.*"

20. Livy 5.37.6; Diodorus 14.114–115.2; Plutarch *Camillus*, Vol. I, 180–182; Polybios 2.18; Festus 119; see also: Kroymayer and Veith 2016, 49–50.

21. Armstrong 2016b, 244–248.

22. Armstrong 2016a, 103, 152; 2016b, 257, 264.

23. Greeks identified the large and ovular scutum

with their very similar *theuros*, and those using them as *theurophoroi*.

24. Livy (8.9.7) anachronistically called these spearmen *triarii* (see below) but their ability to move up and launch an extended assault upon a similar array of Latins (also misidentified as triarii) marks them in this era of amateur militiamen as more likely having been hoplites ranked six or more deep and thus better able to maintain cohesion during such an aggressive advance.

25. Southern 2014, 64–65.

26. Livy 9.1–12; Appian *Samnitica* 4; Zonaras 7.26.

27. Head 1982, 41–42, 162–167; Sekunda and Northwood 1995, 36–39.

28. A shorter spear was less cumbersome and perhaps better suited to the more mobile Samnite combat style.

29. Cowan 2009, 48–49.

30. Fields (2012, 14) makes strong arguments for this. Such a conclusion fits well with known circumstances post–Caudium and is supported by several ancient sources that explicitly cite Samnite inspiration for Rome taking up both the scutum and javelin. An earlier borrowing from Gallic practice has also been proposed, which better matches Livy's outlier claim that the manipular legion using these devices dates from c.400. A strong consensus on this issue is lacking, though it's widely held that Livy's timing is premature.

31. In fact, changing gear cut reequipment costs in that substitution of a less expensive scutum for the clipeus among the triarii and *principes* (see below) generated considerable savings.

32. Sekunda and Northwood (1995, 41) posit that the principes used spears well into the 3rd century due to Dionysius (22.11.2) describing them plying cavalry spears with both hands at the battle of Maleventum in 275. Alternatively, it's been suggested that he simply misidentified principes with triarii, since the latter are known to have retained the hasta into the mid–2nd century. However, his unusual designation of the spears as cavalry devices and their use in two hands without a scutum clearly look like a one-time improvisational repurposing to counter Pyrrhus' elephants, those beasts having given the Romans fits in two recent defeats. This also much resembles a report that hastati took up hastae under similarly unusual circumstances against Gallic foes at Telamon in 225 (Polybius 2.27–31.2). It's likely that the principes and hastati had become javelin-bearing swordsmen by no later than the end of the Samnite Wars.

33. Armstrong (2016b, 265–269) has posed that Rome's manipular system, though likely drawn in detail from a Samnite model, might have some roots in traditional warbands/kin groups. Independent maneuvering by these could have given at least the hastati a sort of "pre-manipular" flexibility even in the phalanx era.

34. Polybius' description (6.20.8–9) of the manipular legion is preferred over those of Livy (1.42.5–43.8) and Dionysius (4.16.1–18.2) in that his work was compiled much closer in time to the organization of concern here as well as by an experienced military man quite familiar with Rome's legions. The major conflict Polybius has with later writers is that Livy indicates a slightly larger infantry component in his legions at 5,000 men. This perhaps either reflected an early transitional organization or inclusion of armed baggage handlers (*asccensi*).

35. Data on the allied legions is relatively scanty and besides the larger cavalry attachment (per Polybius) they might originally have had slightly more foot-soldiers than their later Roman counterparts at 5,000 organized in 500-man sub-units (Southern 2014, 76). However, by 280, the allies' infantry organization had probably been standardized to essentially match that of the Roman troops fighting alongside.

36. Plutarch *Pyrrhus*, Vol. I, 530.

37. Dionysius 20.1; Justin 17.2.14; Griffith 1935, 62; Griffith's numbers on horsemen and elephants are followed here and above as being more reliable than Justin's 4,000 and 50, respectively. Justin also claimed that the elephants came with the men loaned by Ptolemy; however, Pausanius (1.12.3) said that they were spoils gained by Pyrrhus from Demetrius. That he still had these animals well after the Macedonian troops returned at the end of their allotted term of service strongly supports Pausanius' version.

38. This picked Chaosian contingent is recorded later in Greece (Plutarch *Pyrrhus*, Vol. I, 543).

39. Head (1982, 19–20) provides excellent background on likely Epiriote manpower and Sekunda (2019) offers some relevant alternative estimates with implications for Pyrrhus' initial strength in Italy as suggested by a projection of his possible deployments just a year later at the battle of Asculum.

40. Livy 46.41.

41. Dionysius 20.1; the alternative of Pyrrhus totally re-arming and training Tarentine citizen soldiers in a short period of time seems rather less reasonable. While our sources indicate Pyrrhus extensively drilled the Tarentines in the company of his own men, there is no mention that he re-equipped them in any way.

42. Strabo (6.3.4) indicates 1,000 citizen horsemen at Tarentum in the mid–4th century (see Fields 2008, 9). These were members of the upper economic class in the polis and a force of similar size in 280 would fit with a ratio of about one horseman for each ten in the income group making up the infantry militia. As for those foot-soldiers, Tarentum might have fielded a force of twice this size in the 4th century; however, that likely included mercenary contingents no longer present that probably equaled the somewhat larger citizen militia of that time (many militiamen had deserted in 280 to avoid conscripted service under Pyrrhus).

43. Plutarch *Pyrrhus*, Vol. I, 531, 533; the lowest and most reliable number here for Roman losses at Heraclea is 7,000 (see below). Casualties for even a hard-pursued victim in this era would not normally exceed 20–25 percent, and anything much above that for an army that had not been doubly enveloped or otherwise encircled and cut off from retreat (clearly not the case in this battle) is simply not realistic. The smallest possible Roman force consistent with the reported losses would thus be around 28,000. A regular consular army of two Roman and two allied legions would have amounted to only 16,800 in infantry and 2,400 horsemen nominal; thus, a six-legion force (three Roman and three allied) of 25,200 foot-soldiers and 3,600 in cavalry (28,800 men in all exclusive of armed camp-followers) seems to be indicated. This

would have left one Roman and one allied legion either as a defensive reserve or for the second consul's operations in addition to any special levies raised in this time of crisis. These detached legions might have been the two said to have reinforced Laevinus at Capua after Heraclea (see *Asculum* below for an alternative view on the identity of those units).

44. Plutarch *Pyrrhus*, Vol. I, 532.

45. Justin 8.1.5; Plutarch *Pyrrhus*, Vol. I, 533.

46. This speculation on Pyrrhus' deployments is based upon him having less manpower than that of six legions. However, should Laevinus have commanded all four of the regular Roman legions plus four of allies for a total of around 38,400 regulars, then most of the troops projected here as assigned to garrisons must have been included in Pyrrhus' field force, leaving those rear posts manned solely by modest contingents of light infantry.

47. Zonaras 8.3.

48. We have a detailed description of this tactic at Asculum, and Polybios said that Pyrrhus placed his differently-armed contingents "*in alternate order in his battles with the Romans*" (18.28.10), use of the plural indicating this same tactical device was applied at Heraclea and Maleventum as well.

49. Scullard 1974, 104; such use of elephants in reserve is also documented at Asculum.

50. This assumes that the hoplites were arrayed at a depth of four shields (probable minimum for these professionals to maneuver in good order) at 1m spacing and the phalangites eight men deep at 2/3m apart. Regarding the latter, Smith (2011, 41–42) in studying the physical practicality of phalangite spacing found approximately 1/2m adequate for the soldier himself and that another 1/2m was necessary to employ his weaponry; however, other sources cite alternative spacing for pikemen down to just above that for Smith's unarmed man at 1/2m. See discussion on the use of 2/3m in Chapter 1 (note 47 re: *Pindos Pass*).

51. The three levels of hastati, principes, and triarii at six, six, and three deep , respectively, with 2m/man (as per Polybius 18.30.3–8) would have aligned along a front of around 2,400m in a six-legion formation. An investigation of the physical practicalities of Polybius' spacing claims by Smith (2011, 42–45) lends considerable support to the legionaries' need for a frontage of approximately 2m in width. Taylor (2014a, 110, fig. 17) similarly cites 2m/legionary spacing, adding the key observation that men in each succeeding rank were offset so as to put a shield-bearing comrade into the 1m gap between each two legionaries in the rank immediately in front of him.

52. Livy Epitome 13.

53. Polybius (18.30.9–10) details the similar plight of Roman swordsmen at Pydna in 168, where they faced the points of even longer pikes five-deep held at half their spacing to put them at a ten-to-one disadvantage.

54. This was at Thermopylae in 480, where one Spartan wit predicted only a favorably shady battlefield should the enemy's flight of arrows prove so thick as to blot out the sun. And those higher-velocity arrows had more penetrating potential than a javelin along with greater numbers (thousands every few seconds versus thousands in total) to seek out any unprotected flesh.

55. See Garoufalias (1979, 341–343, notes 99–101) for a discussion of tactical considerations re: the elephants.

56. Dionysius (20.1.3–4) reports that the elephant teams were so placed on both wings at Asculum, though perhaps only those on the right (where the Thessalians probably stood) were critical at Heraclea.

57. This is the first reliable reference to elephant towers, which may have been an invention of either Pyrrhus himself or Demetrius from whom he apparently obtained the animals (Head 1982, 184–186).

58. Zonaras 8.3.

59. Plutarch *Pyrrhus*, Vol. I, 533; these numbers come from Hieronymus, who was contemporary to the battle, while the later Dionysius is cited as claiming losses of 15,000 for Rome and 13,000 for Pyrrhus, an incredible 52 percent for each if the manpower estimates preferred here are correct (and a similarly unlikely 40 percent for a double-consular army and 34 percent for Pyrrhus had he fielded every man brought from Greece plus 10,000 from Tarentum). Orosius (4.1) also gives fantastic figures for Roman losses and in even greater detail, listing 14,880 in infantry and 246 in cavalry slain for Rome along with 1,310 foot-soldiers and 802 horsemen taken prisoner.

60. Estimated fatalities for 5th-4th century victorious phalanxes run a mean 5 percent (Bardunias and Ray, 2016, 85).

61. Plutarch noted that the Romans had "*filled up their legions and enlisted fresh men with all speed*" (*Pyrrhus*, Vol. I, 533). Garoufalias (1979, 78) has proposed that the two legions sent to reinforce Laevinus at Capua were formed of new volunteers. If this is correct, the citizen force had been expanded to at least six legions; something that had precedent in that six legions had been raised in 295 during a like time of crisis (Southern 2014, 82). We are not told by Plutarch of any corresponding increase in allied contributions, though Dionysius (20.3.2; also, Zonaras 8.5) recorded a fifth legion of allies that arrived late to Asculum and attacked Pyrrhus' camp instead of joining the battle. And while Dionysius put that detached unit near legion standards at 4,000 in infantry plus 400 horsemen, he boosted the other four alae to nearly three times their normal manpower (see discussion below).

62. Accounts for Asculum include: Plutarch *Pyrrhus* Vol. I, 536–537; Dionysus 20.1–3 (in excerpted form); Zonaras 8.5; Orosius 4.1.19–23; and Livy epitome 13. Plutarch cites sources contemporary to the battle, while sources for the others are uncertain (see discussion: Garoufalias 1979, 368, note 183).

63. Dionysius 20.1.1–4.

64. Assumptions: (1) Pyrrhus' losses at Heraclea ran about 5 percent for his pikemen, 20 percent among the foot-skirmishers and cavalry, with the hoplites taking the remainder (25–30 percent) to total around 15 percent; (2) the rates of loss cited for foot-skirmishers and hoplites brought from Greece also reflect post-battle redistribution as well as some promotion of the former to the latter using panoplies recovered from the dead; (3) Tarentine losses (both citizen and mercenary) were replaced by new draftees/hires.

65. Estimates of tribal manpower in Pyrrhus' alliance are based on evidence that combined peak strength for the Lucanians and Bruttians was about

equal to that of the Samnites at around 40,000 (Champion 2009, 81; Livy 7.37, 10.38, 24.2; Polybios 2.26) and that all these tribes contributed around a quarter of their entire nominal complement to Pyrrhus' campaign. Cavalry and light foot are each put at 20 percent of the heavy infantry count.

66. This width is based upon the pikemen standing 2/3m apart at eight deep, the hoplites at 1m and eight shields in depth, and the theurophoros tribesmen spaced at 1m with an average depth of ten. Alternative to this battle order, Dionysius (22.1.8) put Pyrrhus' infantry at 70,000; however, his numbers elsewhere appear much inflated compared to what should be reliable writing contemporary to the battle (from Hieronymus and Pyrrhus himself). Plutarch records Dionysius' otherwise lost figure for fatalities at Asculum to be 15,000 versus 9,550 from those other sources. Applying that as a correction to his Pyrrhic infantry count produces less than 46,500. This is more consistent with Frontinus' 40,000 (2.3.21) as well as just over the heavy infantry estimate suggested here.

67. Dionysius cites only four legions of 5,000 men each plus four alae sociorum harboring an extraordinary 50,000 soldiers for a 70,000-man total; however, those tallies (much as noted above for his casualties at Heraclea and losses plus Pyrrhus' manpower in this battle) are suspect. Taking the same reduction ratio used earlier to reconcile his casualties at Asculum with those reported contemporaneously to that engagement reduces his count to a round 47,000—essentially equal to the Roman manpower projected here and not much above the 40,000 claimed by Frontinus. Dionysius also records 8,000 Roman and allied horsemen, which might be prorated on the same basis to 5,100 and thus much more consistent with a normal deployment.

68. Plutarch *Pyrrhus*, Vol. I, 536.

69. This event is not mentioned in the accounts of Asculum by Plutarch and Orosius despite its seeming significance. There are also some puzzling logistical issues associated with it. First, that a breach 1.25km across (width of the Lucanian/Bruttian and Tarentine sectors) could be blown in the middle of Pyrrhus' phalanx without routing it is hard to imagine. And it seems equally improbable that the flight of more than 10,000 men and several thousand pursuers then carried through the described position of Pyrrhus' cavalry reserve without disrupting its subsequently documented offensive ability. Finally, it's somewhat unusual that Dionysius' account has the successful legionaries ending up cowering on a hill down on the outwash plain when that sort of rugged topography would be expected to lay toward the uplands in the opposite direction. The most logical solution for these conundrums that accommodates a breakthrough is that the cavalry reserve had already left for its flank attack and the Romans were fleeing rather than pursuing (later seeking refuge atop a remnant outlier at some distance in front of the foothills). Such timing for the cavalry action explains the Romans' flight (the horseman had turned the battle behind their breach). And while "forward retreats" are extremely rare, they are not unknown (Theban hoplites broke through a Spartan phalanx to escape at Coronea in 394 and Roman contingents fled at *Trebia* and *L. Trasimenus* by cutting through frontal opposition [see Chapter 5]). However, a couple of simpler answers are also possible. One is that the Roman force trapped atop a hill was the detached allied legion said to have attacked Pyrrhus' camp. The other is that a breakthrough of Pyrrhus' line was merely threatened; and when that triggered his decisive commitment of reserves, the Romans involved fled back into the hills. Either of these alternative scenarios might have come to Dionysius from old accounts in vague and/or disjointed form, causing him to misinterpret and place the incident within a narrative with no clear winner.

70. Applying other manpower figures from the literature yields loss rates for Pyrrhus ranging from 5 percent to 9 percent—significant, but far from spectacular. If we assume that Plutarch could have mistakenly cited a number for total casualties from Pyrrhus' memoirs that applied only to the men brought from Greece, his rate of loss can be run up to around 18 percent. That would indeed be "Pyrrhic" as we understand it. However, beyond being quite a gaff for Plutarch to have let pass, such an interpretation runs counter to surviving descriptions of the battle. Those clearly imply that any pursuit relatable to such hefty losses, if it occurred at all, was inflicted solely upon the Italian allies. Perhaps the best explanation as to why Pyrrhus might have taken a dire view of his losses at Asculum as reported lies in the actual word applied to the victory there in ancient times, which was "*Cadmean*" (Diodorus 22.5.6). That term did not necessarily imply calamitous casualties for the victor; rather, it meant that the battle's result was as great or even greater a threat to the winner's cause as it was to that of the loser. As such, Asculum was indeed Cadmean in that, though bloodied, the Romans had emerged unconquered, while the campaign of Pyrrhus was now in doubt.

71. Based on apparent casualties to date and his likely Sicilian armament (see below), the garrison probably came to no more than 4,500 infantrymen (maybe 2,000 pikemen, 1,000 hoplites, and 1,500 javelineers).

72. Appian (*Samnite Wars*, 28) reports a landing of only 8,000 horsemen, clearly an error for 8,000 either total or sans mounted support. Based on normal organizational patterns for a Philippian phalanx, the most likely deployment would have been 8,000 in heavy infantry not counting auxiliaries. The latter can be put at 3,000 horsemen (per those later said to have returned from Sicily) with a matching number of foot-skirmishers.

73. Plutarch *Pyrrhus*, Vol. I, 538.

74. Plutarch *Pyrrhus*, Vol. I, 539; the infantry count here exceeds that of Pyrrhus' original landing on Sicily and must include Sicilian mercenaries (possibly 8,000 hoplites and up to 2,000 javelineers).

75. Plutarch *Pyrrhus*, Vol. I, 539.

76. This assumes that it was the polis' phalangites that Pyrrhus took on in "*reinforcing himself with the choicest troops of the Tarentines*" (Plutarch *Pyrrhus*, Vol. I, 539).

77. The mounted contingent would have included 1,000 Tarentines in addition to the riders brought from Sicily.

78. Plutarch cites both combat losses and discontent with Pyrrhus among the Samnites as being such

that "*not many came in to join him*" (*Pyrrhus*, Vol. I, 542), perhaps only 1,000–2,000.

79. This honors Dionysius' note that Pyrrhus had the larger army at Maleventum (22.10.1), though his claim that it was three times the size of his opposition is grossly exaggerated by any reasonable calculation.

80. Six legions deployed in the normal acies triplex would cover a front of 2,400m at 2m per man and be fifteen men deep. Equaling that expanse would have required every one of Pyrrhus' pikemen (at 2/3m spacing and a depth of eight) and 6,000 of his hoplites (at 1m spacing and four shields deep) plus nearly all (1,500) of the available Samnites (at 1m spacing and files of ten).

81. See Arian (1.3.6; 1.6.9; 3.17.2). Invariably involving night marches, these detached-squad offensives featured different troop mixes depending on the terrain and foes to be overcome; however, Alexander always included contingents from his hypaspist elites (3,000 strong in three chiliarchies) and Agrianian peltasts (some 1,600 in all).

82. Plutarch *Pyrrhus*, Vol. I, 540.

83. Dionysius (22.11.1) notes in explaining their subsequent poor performance "*that hoplites burdened with helmets, breastplates and shields and advancing against hilly positions by long trails that were not even used by people but were mere goat-paths through woods and crags, would keep no order and, even before the enemy came in sight would be weakened in body by thirst and fatigue.*"

84. Dionysius (20.11.2) has principes using spears two-handed, likely confusing them with the retooled equites. This special tactic against elephants would be repeated in 215 during the Second Punic War (see Chapter 5 re: *Nola II*).

85. Dionysius 20.12.3.

86. We have no record of the Greek formation for this engagement but can reasonably assume it to have been much like those used previously against Rome. That would have called for spearmen on each end (apparently these were the Samnites on the right side) with contingents of pikemen and hoplites alternating along the rest of the line plus the few remaining elephants (six or seven) concentrated behind what must have been the right wing. The cavalry, being denied a flanking opportunity, was probably sitting far back in a central reserve.

87. Orosius (4.2.5–6) makes the claim that Pyrrhus suffered 33,000 killed and 30,000 captured out of an 86,000-man complement. None of these numbers appears to be even remotely realistic.

Chapter 3

1. Biologists recognize a behavior known as "stotting/pronging" that males display in defiance of danger as a signal of their superior reproductive fitness. This can be seen in a tendency of male gazelles to stand behind as their herd flees a lion, daring the predator to charge so as to display its mate-desirable superiority by escaping unharmed. Among humans this can be seen in men "dressing down" to show themselves as still attractive despite eschewing enhancing attire. Closer yet to our animal roots are smoking rituals in which a male signals potency through ostentatiously casual use of dangerous tobacco products; a phenomenon well illustrated by overtly macho avatars like past advertising's "Marlboro Man" and others. The custom of Gauls fighting naked very much seems to be an institutionalized behavior grown out of this genetic instinct, and their most distinguished warrior castes continued the death-defying practice long after the wearing of armor became widespread.

2. See discussion in Head (1982, 57–58).

3. Typical of these kudos was that of Xenophon, an ex-cavalryman and expert on horsemanship, who gave high marks to Gallic horsemen serving Sparta as mercenaries in the 4th century (*Hellenica* 7.1.21). Indeed, it's likely that the lone recorded victory of Sparta's Gallic hirelings over a hoplite phalanx was due to their cavalry and supporting footmen turning a flank (Xenophon *Hellenica* 7.1.22; Ray 2012, 72; Bardunias and Ray 2016, 152–153).

4. Justin 24.4.1; this, of course, would be a coalition grouping in that Diodorus put Gallic tribes at 50,000 to 200,000 each, which suggests that they had 12,500–50,000 combatants (see note 18 below for methodology). The bottom of that range seems most probable, with Ellis (see Appendix I) opining that a single tribal army "*could scarcely have been more than 12,000 fighting men even by a conservative estimate based on a populous tribe.*" Navarro (1928, 101) similarly noted in this respect that the Gallic migrations' "*actual fighting men cannot have been numerous*" but suggested that they had gained from inclusion of "*contingents from conquered Illyrian and Thracian tribes.*"

5. See below re: *Lysimacheia* plus Memnon 11.2–3 and Livy 38.16.

6. See discussion below regarding the Gallic order of battle at Thermopylae.

7. Pausanius records a Gallic infantry-to-cavalry ratio in this same year of 7.5-to-1 (see below re: *Thermopylae*); however, both smaller and larger ratios have been indicated elsewhere in the same general era.

8. Ptolemy's insulting reply to this proposal caused the Dardanian king in the words of Justin (24.4.9–10) to predict that "*the renowned kingdom of Macedonia would fall because of the foolhardiness of a callow youth.*"

9. Justin 24.4.8.

10. These estimates derive from an assessment of Macedon's nation-wide manpower a generation earlier via Diodorus (17.17.3–5; see discussion Ray 2012, 143). We don't know if Ptolemy had elephants in his company, but he is unlikely to have left behind so valuable an asset had it been close to hand. Likely few at most, any elephants Ptolemy might have taken along would probably have stood in reserve behind the mounted contingent off his right wing. That would have paralleled what Pyrrhus had done the previous year at Heraclea and a few months earlier at Asculum. If so, the great beasts, even if some were present, likely never came to action, but simply joined defeated cavalry remnants fleeing the ensuing battle.

11. Based upon the manpower proposed here as most likely, some 1,500 Gallic theurophoroi could have stood with the cavalry. That is, of course, highly speculative; however, the next best guesses on orders of battle for this engagement all trend toward higher

numbers for the Gauls and lower ones for Ptolemy with any combination putting even more swordsmen at Bolgios' disposal.

12. Justin 24.5.5–7; failure of the phalanx off both flanks rather than a single flank or along its interior is strongly indicated by the taking of prisoners. Rearward flight in the latter cases would have lost men to pursuit but given little chance for capture of such scattered prey in significant numbers. Men trapped in a double envelopment, on the other hand, stood together, allowing them to resist and surrender in mass. Similarly, Ptolemy's likely post with his royal guard and behind a large force of fronting peltasts off the right flank would have let him ride to safety had it not been for his formation giving way off the wings and plunging him into the fight.

13. "Brennus" was a kingly title common among the Gauls, thus this man's similarity in name to the Gallic chieftain that had bested Rome at Allia just over a century earlier (see Appendix 1).

14. The current wealth of Delphi was probably more myth than fact after extensive pillaging of its treasures by the Phocians to finance their mercenary hires during the 3rd Sacred War.

15. Detached Aetolian peltasts (1,500–6,500) might also have held post in the mountains (Scholten 2000, 36).

16. Greece's leading naval power for more than two centuries, Athens had the Greek world's largest collection of triremes (fighting galleys with three levels of oars).

17. Pausanius 20.6; this coalition army was significantly larger than the one deployed to block Xerxes in 480, that having probably been the largest Greek host gathered to that point in time at 8,000 hoplites—see Ray (2009, 71) for discussion on why the Athenian-led force at Marathon a decade earlier was probably smaller.

18. There are several calculations suggesting this scope of Gallic manpower. The first is that a proportional share for the two warlords at Thermopylae of all fighters among the migration of 279 comes to an upside of 40,000 (see above re: *Orestis Plain*). The second is that Justin's tally of 165,000 and Diodorus' 160,000 (22.9.1) for the invading bands reduces to just 41,000 and 40,000 when considering that they probably included three times as many non-combatants (as per reasonable population modeling). And Pausanius' claim (10.19.9) of 172,400 can plausibly be reduced to some 43,000 using the same methodology. Finally, Pausanius lists separate forces of 40,000 infantry on three occasions (10.21.2; 10.,22.7; 10.22.10) and Diodorus (22.9.3) cites 40,000 casualties. These are all more likely to be surviving traces of contemporary estimates for total strength than either deployments for those more modest, detached operations or a true accounting of those killed.

19. Pausanius (10.21.1–22.11) provides the details on the ensuing battle quoted below.

20. It was not possible to effectively target individuals from behind an array greater than four deep nor even see the head of the opposing formation when hidden beyond the backs of one's own fronting troops.

21. Pausanius' comment on Gauls suffering up to four times the losses of Greeks might seem hyperbolic; however, hoplites could strike with four spears for each opponent brandishing a sword since the latter were at twice the lateral spacing and had no help from behind (see Chapter 2 re: *Heraclea*).

22. Pausanius numbers the Gallic infantry in this expedition at 40,000, which appears to be far too many men for such a diversionary action. The 75 percent reduction applied elsewhere to his manpower claims is probably relevant here as well, with the resulting 10,000-man figure matching the detachment used earlier in crossing the Spercheius. These teams might have had 8,000–8,500 theurophoroi, 500–1,000 javelineers, and 1,000 horsemen.

23. Pausanius 10.22.6–7; however, Gallic losses could not have reached the more than "*half*" claimed here.

24. Justin (24.6.9) cites Brennus' host at 65,000. In establishing a realistic range for Gallic manpower, this might be reduced to just over 16,000 in line with four-fold exaggerations seen elsewhere. With that at the low end, Pausanius' report of 26,000 Gallic casualties during this campaign (10.23.10) offers a high-end, should it, like so many other accountings of this sort, be an echo of the total force defeated rather than just its body count.

25. Justin 24.6.9; Pausanius 10.23.1–10.

26. It's worth noting that Pausanius' count of 6,000 Gallic dead falls within the upper bounds of historic norms if it is taken in context of the highest estimate for Gallic manpower proposed above. At 23 percent of that 26,000-man maximum, this would be consistent with the 20–25 percent losses common for a defeated army in this era that had suffered the sort of heavily damaging pursuit that our sources indicate at Delphi.

27. Pausanius 10.23.11.

28. Justin (25.8.12) says that Acichorios retreated with 10,000 men sans his wounded. Combat losses at Thermopylae might have reached 500, in Northern Aetolia perhaps 2,500 (25 percent), and at Delphi a reported 6,000, with the latter perhaps then doubled during the subsequent retreat for a total of 15,000 killed out of a probable 40,000 to start. Justin's figure for escapees (10,000) thus indicates that 15,000 wounded were then left behind. This is plausible in that having those disabled by wounds equal those killed in battle was frequently the historical ratio for defeated armies in ancient times (see Bardunias and Ray 2016, 205, note 76).

29. Some secondary sources have repeated Roman legends that treasure stolen from Delphi was carried into Asia by these Gauls. However, there is no support for this in the primary literature, which clearly states that Brennus met fatal defeat without ever having breached the shrine's defenses.

30. The death of Ptolemy Keraunos had set off a scramble for his throne over the intervening two years, with candidates laying claim to the crown for brief periods (one for as short a time as forty-five days).

31. Pausanius (10.19.9–11) claimed that Gallic cavalry practice was based on "*trimarcisia*," which he said involved each horseman having two servants near the battlefield riding re-mounts. This allowed one of them to bring up a replacement should a horse go down. However, these "*slaves*" were also good enough equestrians to replace any master that might fall. This seems

quite improbable, not least in holding two-thirds of all available armed riders with mounts out of an initial battlefield deployment that was highly dependent on its opening charge. It therefore seems logical that Pausanius might well have confused two poorly known aspects of cavalry recruitment and organization among the Gauls in attempting to interpret a curious foreign term he had encountered. The first is that each wealthy aristocrat joining the cavalry was probably expected to finance (or help finance) two aristocratic companions to ride at his side, thus forming a three-man basic unit of organization called a "trimarcisia." Second, the pair of "servants" or "slaves" mentioned were likely foot-skirmishing peasants in the primary rider's employ, who provided screening support in a ratio of two for every trio of horsemen. This would have been much like the servants in classical Greece that accompanied armies into the field at one per hoplite, the non-slaves among these personal aides also being expected to become skirmishers (*psiloi*) should a battle arise.

32. See Chapter 1 for discussion of Demetrius' amphibious potential re: *Mantinea IV*.

33. Each trireme would have had 170 oarsmen (*nautae*) and sixteen crewmen (*hyperesiai*), with even the modest number that had been converted into transports still having 60 rowers with the same number of sailors.

34. Justin 25.2.6–7; historical precedent suggests that an army surrounded in this manner could well have suffered 60 percent or even more killed.

35. Livy 38.16.

36. Dates have been proposed ranging from 277 to 269, though the earliest seems highly unlikely.

37. Lucian *Zeuxis* 8–11.

38. Bar-Kochva provides discussions regarding these different Seleucid contingents (1976, 64–65, 75, 82). The Argyraspides consisted of two 4,000-man units of pikemen and two 1,000-man units (chiliarchies) of cross-trained hypaspists. These could form two 5,000-man strategiai with attached skirmishers recruited from the same base communities to allow for detached operations on short notice (see Chapter 4 re: *Raphia*). One cavalry chiliarchy was called the Agema and the other the Hetairoi (Companions). The fifty skirmishers cited per elephant by Diodorus (19.82.3) applied only when they were thus widely spaced.

39. There was perhaps some confusion here in that the term "peltast" might have been applied to the heavy infantry (as was sometimes the case in late Hellenistic accounts) and then misinterpreted by either Lucian or his source as referring to the light-armed javelineer peltasts of the Hellenic and early Hellenistic eras.

40. Antiochus' father, Seleucus I, deployed a much larger number of elephants ahead of his infantry line at Ipsus in 301; however, that was only a ruse, and he shifted them onto his left flank when the fighting started (Tarn 1930, 68–69; Ray 2012, 208). It's reasonable to think that the son might have followed his father's lead in this tactic.

41. There are many questions regarding Lucian's details on chariot usage here. He cites an exceptionally large size for the chariot contingent relative to the total force engaged, makes a third of those vehicles of the Persian scythed type, and has the chariots leading the main battle line as per past Persian practice. Those claims all seem to conflict with better documented Gallic norms. A sounder view in context of those standards is that the action likely involved much fewer chariots, scythed vehicles were not present, and participation by chariots of any type probably took place off just one wing.

42. Our sources fail to provide an accounting of Pyrrhus' forces at this time, but figures for the subsequent campaign in Sparta (see below) minus its reinforcements out of Macedonia suggest some 20,000 foot-soldiers (possibly 4,000 hoplites, 12,000 phalangites, 2,000 in Greek light infantry, and 2,000 Gallic theurophoroi) plus 2,000 in cavalry (perhaps evenly split between lancers and javelineers).

43. Plutarch *Pyrrhus* Vol. I, 541.

44. Pausanius 1.13.2.

45. Pausanius (1.13.2–5) provides the preceding quotes.

46. Plutarch *Pyrrhus* Vol. I, 542; this armament reflects the troops Pyrrhus had deployed a year earlier plus 5,000 or so Macedonians now added to his cause. The latter were perhaps a Philippic-style strategia of 1,000 hypaspists and 3,000 pikemen supported by 1,000 foot-skirmishers (probably some of the Gallic mercenaries of Antigonus). Most (if not all) of the elephants would have been those captured at Haliacmon Pass.

47. Plutarch (*Pyrrhus* Vol. I, 542) cites ambition to seize the Peloponnese as Pyrrhus' prime motivation in aiding Cleonymus. He lied about this to Spartan representatives who met with him at Megalopolis, saying he was there to protect them from Antigonus' attentions, even going so far in extolling his regard for their polis and its traditions that he pledged to have his own sons educated there.

48. Plutarch has the Spartan defensive preparations carried out over just a few hours in the dark after Pyrrhus scorned a nighttime assault and waited for dawn encamped before the city. It is more likely that the significant works described (*Pyrrhus* Vol. I, 543) reflect a much lengthier effort well prior to arrival of the Epirotes. Famously unwalled at its height in the 5th and 4th centuries, Sparta had been ringed with defenses of various types during the war with Demetrius in 294 (Pausanius 1.13.6).

49. Pyrrhus is unlikely to have deployed his phalangites in this situation, undoubtedly being aware of the past poor performance of his cousin's pikemen against an even less well-entrenched foe at Issus (Arrian 2.10.1; Bardunias and Ray 2016, 150–151).

50. Plutarch *Pyrrhus* Vol. I, 543.

51. This is an example of Bardunias' "barricade" mode of linear combat. The Spartan phalanx stood perhaps four shields deep (if reservists and others equaled prime-age spartiates in the array) but was effectively twice that stout thanks to the significant force-multiplying effect of its fronting field-works. Spartan skirmishers could therefore shelter behind their barricade of spearmen and lob all sorts of missiles (javelins, arrows, sling bullets, and even loose stones) into an enemy stalled in place before the trench.

52. Plutarch *Pyrrhus* Vol. I, 544.

53. Plutarch *Pyrrhus* Vol. I, 545.

54. Plutarch *Pyrrhus* Vol. I, 546.

55. Plutarch *Agis* Vol. II, 319.

56. This is an estimate based on manpower employed on the Dema Wall (Munn 1993, 38, 47), a fortification system of roughly similar scope, though differing in being of a sturdier, more permanent design. The 4.38km length of that Athenian barrier was manned by some 5,000 troops (Diodorus 15.38.2), which would scale up to nearly 7,000 to service the wider interval involved here. We might thus imagine half a dozen posts spaced a kilometer apart along this line with around 1,000 mercenary hoplites and 150 javelineers in each.

57. Sparta had won a famous victory between the Long Walls of Corinth back in 392 using such a ditch and piled-earth arrangement (Xenophon *Hellenica* 4.4.9–12; Bardunias and Ray 2016, 48–51), and similar works almost surely figured in his polis' successful defenses against Boeotian invaders after its defeat at Leuctra.

58. Pausanius (3.6.4–6) claimed that, while Areus advanced on the Macedonian position, he then declined to attack under such unfavorable conditions. However, this conflicts with Plutarch asserting that a battle did take place, and that seems to more plausibly explain the Spartan king's demise at just this crucial juncture than Pausanius' version of him coincidentally dying from natural causes.

59. Pausanius 8.27.11.

60. Strabo 13.4.2.

61. Head (1982, 26) notes that Pergamum had no military colonies from which it could draw heavy infantrymen of Macedonian descent until 189, and the largest army it ever deployed (in 171) totaled only 7,000 combatants consisting of 6,000 foot-soldiers and 1,000 horsemen. Had that many men even been available nearly a century earlier, the infantry would have been solely light-armed, and the entire force would have been no match for Antiochus' royal guards alone. There is evidence for hired troops at Pergamum as early as 263 (Austin 2006, 402–405), with Griffith (1935, 171) stating that *"there is no doubt at all that Pergamum employed mercenaries in the standing army at a very early date,"* but what details can be gleaned confirm only light-armed contingents.

62. Surviving artworks of similar Campanian warriors of the era show them using typical hoplite gear, which would have been standard to allow tactical integration with Syracuse's classical phalanx. See below re: *Longanus* on Mamertine manpower c.265. Agathocles fielded some 10,000 mercenary infantrymen in the late 4th century (Diodorus 19.17.2), which might represent the practical limit of Syracuse's finances at this time as well. Given that the Campanians are unlikely to have made up over half those hirelings, 4,000 is perhaps a reasonable upside for their early strength at Messana. Local skirmishers would have been recruited to replace the professional light infantry support previously enjoyed in Agathocles' employ.

63. This was no idle concern as the city had suffered in the past from mercenary uprisings (see Ray 2013).

64. Syracuse normally fielded some 5,000 citizen hoplites and, in reduced condition after Agathocles' time, the mercenary force would have been no more than equal to that and more likely only half (forming one wing of the phalanx at a third of the army with citizen militia at center and on the other wing).

65. Polybius 1.9.1–6.

66. Diodorus 22.13.2; the number of Mamertine horsemen here is unclear, perhaps 40 in the text, but more reasonably 400, with even that being only half a common mounted proportion in this era. The increase in Mamertine strength since Cyamosorus River probably in part reflects absorbing of survivors from those abandoned by Hiero in that battle. Syracuse's heavy infantry would likely have been 5,000 militiamen, 3,000 hired hoplites, and 2,000 professional missilemen. Hiero had acquired new mercenaries, perhaps doubling what he had fielded a decade earlier, but still only half what Agathocles could afford at his peak.

67. Diodorus 22.13.4 here and above; this implies (and Diodorus goes on to indicate) that there were few Mamertine survivors. However, given the modest size of the attacking force at their rear and that the river stood between them and the main body of their pursuers, many if not most of those defeated here must have escaped to later man Messana's defenses (see below re: *Messana III*).

68. Though Polybius says small boats (*pentekonters*) were among the vessels loaned to Claudius by allies at Tarentum and Locri, he must have used triremes for the most part, those being the standard warships of the day (Polybius indicates that some larger types of galleys were borrowed as well, but these were present in only very small numbers solely among the most well-heeled navies at this time). And transportation of a consular army's normal cavalry in one go at the usual five riders and mounts per trireme (Rodgers 1937, 15–16) would have required 360 ships in addition to those carrying the infantry. Claudius could have employed a smaller number of vessels on multiple crossings; however, carrying out so time-consuming an operation without greater interference than our sources report from the large Carthaginian naval force present seems quite a stretch.

69. Polybius 1.11.10–15, 1.15.1–5; Diodorus 23.3; Dio (11.11–15), Zonaras (8.9), and Orosius (4.7.2–3) mirror Polybius.

70. Lazenby 1996, 49–50.

71. Had they lost around 40 percent of their spearmen and 20 percent of their light infantry at Longanus River, the Mamertines likely would have fielded some 3,500 hoplites plus 1,000 skirmishers (out of 1,500) for this diversion.

72. Zonaras 8.9; this assumes Hiero had 1,500 horsemen as at Longanus River, while survivors from the 400 Mamertine riders in that battle plus some mounted Romans came to only around 500.

73. Note that these battles are labeled Messana III and IV in recognition of previous actions there in 425 and 394.

74. Dio 11.2.

75. Carthage had reinforced Sicily with mercenaries, most of them Iberian, but including Ligurians and Gauls as well (Polybius 1.17.4–6). Diodorus (23.8.1) quotes a credible Philinos in saying that island-wide manpower for Carthage might have reached 50,000 foot-soldiers, 6,000 cavalrymen, and 60 elephants. Subsequent Infantry casualties (see below re: *Agrigentum*) at an estimated 10 percent of total deployment

indicate Hanno had some 30,000 foot-soldiers, suggesting he also had 30 elephants (with 1,500 of the infantrymen in support at fifty each) and roughly 3,500 horsemen should those elements have been present at a similar percentage (60 percent) of their totals. Per Frontinus (4.1.19), at least 4,000 of the hirelings were Gauls. Had the Ligurians provided similar numbers, then the Iberians could have come to 19,000 even with a division of Liby-Phoenicians in play (see note 77 below). The Iberian troops would have been a mix of types with shielded swordsmen dominant (maybe 15,000), the rest being javelineers called *caetrati* after the small leather buckler (*caetra*) they carried.

76. A double consular army of eight legions would normally deploy 38,400 men (24,000 heavy infantrymen, 9,600 foot-skirmishers, and 4,800 horsemen), but disease plus combat losses among the cavalry would have reduced them closer to Hanno's strength.

77. Something over 5,000 Liby-Phoenician hoplites had probably been dispersed around Sicily after their defeat at Messana IV and it's quite possible that Hanno, who had commanded in that battle, deployed a reconstituted 3,000-man division of these at Agrigentum.

78. Iberian shields at this time were round; later, these would be replaced by an elongate scutum-type device.

79. Roman legionaries in the 3rd century were mostly conscripted farmers with some urban workers. The term of service for draftees (at least those filling standing legions in regular consular armies) allowed for extensive drill critical to formation maneuvering and fundamental weapons-use; however, it would not have put them on a par in single combat against better seasoned, career mercenaries.

80. Polybius 1.19.5–11; Diodorus 23.8.1; Zonaras (8.10) records a less likely variant on what happened in this battle, with the Romans engineering the victory despite a sally against their rear from Agrigentum, doing so by means of an ambush of their own that sent a small contingent into Hanno from behind.

81. Lazenby (1996, 72, citing Zonaras, Polybius, and Naevius); Zonaras 8.12; Orosius 4.9.1–3; Livy *epitome* 17.

82. Polybius (1.24.3–4) gives the number for Greek casualties, while Diodorus' claim (23.9.4) that a loss of 6,000 represented "*nearly the whole army*" provides a strong clue as to the total force defeated.

83. Zonaras 8.12; Livy epitome 17; Orosius 4.8.1–3.

84. Polybius 1.29.8; this was apparently two under-strength Roman legions with a pair of alae sociorum. If the allies were at full nominal complement, then the native Romans were 900 infantrymen short per legion, possibly all light infantry of lesser value for filling limited fleet billets. And the cavalry was weaker still at just over 20 percent of the norm for a consular army. This suggests that the shortage/lack of horse-transports noted as likely for the landing at Messana in 264 was still a problem for Rome.

85. These numbers are projected along the lines of Carthaginian norms from the killed and captured reported in the ensuing battle (Orosius [4.8.16] and Eutropius [2.21.3] probably tallying the total force defeated) as well as the army later fielded at Tunes (see below). The strength of skirmishers supporting so many elephants was probably well less than the fifty-each used for smaller numbers more widely dispersed.

86. Diodorus describes Xanthippus as a full Spartan citizen or "*spartiate*" (23.14.1), though some lesser ranking men were also among those trained in the agoge.

87. Bardunias 2009, 29–31.

88. The proposal by Gabriel (2011, 22) that Xanthippus introduced hoplite spears as replacements for pikes runs counter to abundant evidence for Carthaginian use of hoplite gear with thrusting spears of moderate length well before Xanthippus' time. There is no evidence for Carthage employing pikes at any point in its history. Head (1982, 144) suggests that mistake crept into modern literature via Loeb's Volume II of Polybius, which wrongly translates "longchophorai" (skirmishers with a short throwing spear or longche) as "pikemen."

89. Polybius 1.32.9.

90. A consular army normally deployed 4,800 hastati at 2m/man and six-deep across 1,600m. Having taken a few casualties at Adys, that span would have shrunk to better match the phalanx proposed above. See Bardunias (2009) for an alternative Roman deployment in close-order per a different take on Polybius' comments on Regulus' formation width/depth. Given a deeper Carthaginian phalanx as well, the opposing formation lengths would still have matched, creating a dynamic essentially identical to the one presented here.

91. The forest species of elephant native to North Africa used by the Carthaginians was up to 2.5m tall and a weight of 4.5 tons versus the more massive Indian elephants of Pyrrhus and the Successors that had 3.5m and 5-ton upsides (Nossov 2008, 5; Beer 1956, 93–94).

92. The lone example of Pyrrhus using elephants against infantry (at Maleventum in 275) was still a flanking action, it's just that there were no mounted Romans on the field that day; and, of course, it failed when met unexpectedly by a close-ordered defense.

93. Diodorus 17.87.1–89.3; Plutarch *Alexander* Vol. II, 187–188; Curtius 8.13.5–8.14; Arian 5.8.4–5.19.

94. Standard spacing of elephants were 12–15m, fitting with them covering 1,500m here. Polybius' account with none apparent in front of the Punic right wing probably reflects a relocation rather than initial absence.

95. Zonaras 8.13.

96. Polybius indicates that the native Carthaginian portion of the phalanx endured due to the Romans having fought through the elephant screen so that they were then beset by it from behind; however, this would have required a seemingly impossible feat of tactical gymnastics. Any such rear attack would surely have been a result of the elephants having circled around against the back of the acies triplex after enveloping its flank(s).

97. Failure of the veteran mercenaries on Carthage's right rather than the leftward-standing militia is quite a curious feature of Tunes. Two answers for this seem most plausible within the scenario presented here. The first is that Regulus exceeded the hired men's capability by sending his best legion against them. However, this is unconvincing in that it pits draftees (albeit some

perhaps with previous tours of duty) against generally more savvy pros operating within the phalanx system, which had proven to be highly durable for as long as formation integrity could be maintained. It's also important to note that recent service among Regulus' troops did not include exposure to actual combat outside of Adys, where one legion probably did not engage, two were bested by Carthage's mercenaries, and the fourth gained its success only via a surprise attack that did not have to face an intact enemy formation. None of this boded well for either a physical advantage or superior esprit de corps against seasoned professional hoplites standing in good order. (Even the native Carthaginians at Tunes might have been as well-trained as some of their opposition after six months of hard drilling under Xanthippus, and their classical phalanx was famously effective in accommodating just such amateurs.) This all combines to strongly suggest that a better solution to the failure of Carthage's mercenaries lies in a flank-turning that destroyed their formational cohesion. A nominal strength consular army had enough men to extend its front some 100m beyond the phalanx width posed here, and it would have taken a loss of 300 hastati at Adys to have eliminated that potential. Given that a smaller loss there is highly likely, it might well have been an overlapping lateral attack on an ineptly screened mercenary right flank lacking in shield protection that caused its associated wing to fail—something that simply did not happen in parallel on the militia-held left side.

98. A loss of 60 percent would better match the historical upside in double envelopments, where it was common for large sub-groups to gain surrender terms from victors eager to avoid needless further casualties among their own men. Low-side and perhaps more accurate estimates of Roman losses due to the double envelopment at Cannae in 216 (see Chapter 5) run close to this 60 percent standard, though less likely high-sides there also reach the mid–80s.

99. Zonaras 8.14; Orosius 4.9.7.

100. Orosius 4.9.15; Eutropius 2.24; Diodorus 23.21; having perhaps 2,000 horsemen, Hasdrubal's army might also have included some 6,000 missile-armed skirmishers and 12,000 heavier infantrymen. Most of the latter must have been shield-bearing Gallic and Iberian swordsmen, though it's quite possible that he retained a 3,000-man Liby-Phoenician division as well.

101. Polybius 1.67.13; this strength likely had dropped at least a couple of thousand by the time of the revolt.

102. Polybius (1.72.3) claims 70,000 Libyans joined, this more likely being the rebellion's total strength at its peak.

103. Sometimes referred to as "The Great" (a title given to at least two others named Hanno in Carthaginian history), this man had opposed the First Punic War and was an outspoken critic of Hamilcar Barca. Hoyos (2007, 92–93) reasonably estimates his army at 8,000–10,000 and the opposing rebels at some 15,000.

104. Polybius 1.75.2.

105. Polybius 1.76.1–2; see Hoyos' discussion (2007, 117–118) of this issue and his variant translation indicating that the two rebel forces might have joined in a single formation operating like a hinge that would allow its northern arm to close around Hamilcar's right flank and trap him against the river. The scenario presented here seems both simpler and more consistent with contemporary tactical practice, posing that the rebel formation was a conventional phalanx and the "hinged arm" meant to enclose the Carthaginians merely the left wing of Spendius' array set to carry out a typical envelopment of the shorter enemy line.

106. Polybius 1.76.7.

107. Polybius 1.76.9.

108. Polybius numbers the original force (1.77.4–5) and tallies of the rebels' casualties provide another measure of their manpower (1.78.12). The Libyans might have been two 3,000-man heavy divisions plus maybe a thousand or more skirmishers of some sort while the Numidian horsemen were 2,000 strong (1.78.9). Bringing Hamilcar's probable two divisions of citizen hoplites up to 3,000-man establishment would have given him at least 12,000 men overall with further additions of light foot also being possible.

109. Hoyos (2007, 137) gives a good review of the possibilities for this location, suggesting a couple of sound alternatives of which a small plain about 40km southwest of Tunes may be the most promising.

110. Polybius 1.84.9–85.7; debilitated by starvation, the rebels were slaughtered with ease in the final attack.

111. Hoyos 2007, 240.

112. Based on Carthage's various previous deployments, a supreme effort here might have fielded some 18,000 hoplites (six divisions: three of Carthaginian citizens, two of Liby-Phoenicians, and one of Libyans gained from Naravas' Victory), 8,000 skirmishers (3,000 supporting the phalanx and cavalry with 5,000 attached to 100 or so elephants at 50 per animal), and 4,000 horsemen (2,000 citizens and an equal number of Numidians).

Chapter 4

1. Achaea in the 4th century had long been second only to neighboring Arcadia as a source for mercenary hoplites. Our best documented example of this was the hired legion that Xenophon helped lead out of Persia in 400. This originally contained 10,400 hoplites (80 percent of its total manpower) with an estimated 2,000 (19 percent) of them being Achaean to form its second largest ethnic contingent (after Arcadia's 4,000—Lee 2007, 61). Achaea continued to supply such hired spearmen throughout the 4th century, notably to Phocis in the Third Sacred War (356–346) as well as the anti–Macedonian effort at Chaeronea in 338 (English 2012, 119, 122), and there is no evidence to support any change in this pattern of widespread mercenary service by Achaean hoplites prior to the reforms of Philopoemen very late in the 3rd century.

2. Ethnic Achaean forces at this time "*did not equal the strength of one ordinary city*" (Plutarch *Aratus*, Vol. II, 616, no doubt referencing hoplites alone), which has led to speculation that 10,000 or so was a complete turnout (Head 1982, 9) and might even have included mercenary support (Griffith 1935, 100). Later establishment of a standing force of 3,000 picked infantry and 300 horsemen (see discussion at *Sellasia* re: Achaean epilektoi) marks likely numbers of wealthier combatants. As for poorer men, they would have provided

light infantry, which probably in Aratus' day adopted theuros shields (Anderson 1967, 105) and perhaps added a short spear to their javelins as well toward improving shock potential. This all suggests that the League levy on this occasion might have included up to 3,000 hoplites from Sicyon (past maximum strength attributed to that polis being 3,200 in 479 at Plataea and Mycale on the same day) plus a mix of Sicyonian light foot and mercenary missile-specialists (archers, slingers, and expert javelineers).

3. See Polybius (20.4) and Scholten (2000, 258–259) on the role played by that long-standing enmity.

4. This site on the Boeotian Plain had hosted so many past battles that the famed Theban commander Epaminondas once called it *"the dancing floor of War"* (Plutarch *Marcellus*, Vol. I, 423).

5. Plutarch *Aratus* Vol. II, 620; Polybius 20.4.4–5.2.

6. Pausanius 10.20.4.

7. Pausanius implies that the Aetolians exceeded 10,000 men at Thermopylae, and modern estimates of their potential strength at that time run up to some 15,000 (Scholten 2000, 36) for a range of 1,500–6,500 peltasts being potentially available above the listed manpower in the pass. These detached troops were responsible for defeating the first Gallic attempt to circumvent Thermopylae across Mount Oeta.

8. The Achaeans likely deployed a significant if not full-force effort for a threat this close to their holdings, while Sparta sent a smaller contingent of *"auxiliaries"* drawn from poorer and mostly young men whose debts were to be forgiven under a pending decree pushed by Agis to boost citizen numbers (Plutarch *Agis*, Vol. II, 326). Agis was dethroned and executed before this reform ever came to pass and the Aetolians would invade c.241 to ravage the territory of a weak and divided Sparta (Scholten 2000, 127–130).

9. See discussion of this incident in Scholten (2000, 123–127).

10. Plutarch *Aratus*, Vol. II, 631.

11. Plutarch *Aratus*, Vol. II, 628.

12. Aratus would have had a force comparable to the one fielded at Chares River, with his small loses there replaced by Cleonae, which could have supplied a 500-man lochos of spearmen at minimum. Aristippus, meanwhile, had taken the greater harm in that recent battle and could probably now turn out fewer men.

13. Plutarch *Aratus*, Vol. II, 629.

14. See Plutarch (*Aratus*, Vol. II, 632) on this battle. It's possible that the native Achaeans had been becoming steadily more specialized as a source of theurophoros skirmishers under Aratus, which would have lowered hoplite counts and phalanx widths somewhat to put League armies at greater hazard for envelopment.

15. Polybius 2.2–3.

16. Head 1982, 29–30, 129–130.

17. Illyrian dispositions are extremely speculative. However, if actually around 5,000-strong, they might have lined 3,500 spearmen against the Aetolian phalanx in four-man files, posted all their skirmishers (likely 500) to contain the cavalry holding the enemy's flank on the flat, and sent the remaining 1,000 or so spearmen (perhaps four speirai tactical units) up to clear the low rise on the other flank.

18. Polybius 2.5.

19. Grainger 2014, 195; Seleucus I had perhaps commanded close to 40,000 men in 281 at Corupedium, including 15,000 ethnic Macedonians out of 27,000 in heavy infantry, while Antiochus II took the field for the Elephant Victory c.273 with maybe only 16,000 men, including 10,000 in Macedonian-colonial heavy foot.

20. Mayor 2010, 113; the hoplites used to seed Mithradates IV's military expansion in the late 2nd century were Greek mercenaries; however, that role would have been filled at this time by conscripted militiamen from Pontus' rich and populous Grecian settlements along the Black Sea coast. The light-footmen were javelineers traditional in the region and mostly from the rural inland to the south, while the cavalry was descended from the nation's past Persian aristocracy and would have been javelin-armed as well.

21. Trogus *Prologues* 27; Polyaenus 8.61.

22. Polyaenus 4.9.6.

23. *ibid*.

24. Justin 27.6.11.

25. Justin 27.3.2; these Galatians appear to have pressured Hierax into this largely predatory expedition.

26. Austin 2006, 405; these statuary remnants are dated sometime c.238–227. The chronological sequence of the listed actions is uncertain, with the one used here being that proposed by Grainger (2014, 203–205).

27. Pausanius 1.8.1, 10.15.3.

28. See discussion of Pergamum's military in Chapter 3 re: *Sardis*.

29. Grainger 2014, 205; even if Hierax's first two losses post–Aphrodision had been small, maybe involving mere detachments defeated in detail, Coloe seems to have been a full engagement of his forces with rather more negative results. Hierax would later attempt a return only to be chased out by Seleucus, with this second exile ending in death at the hands of his Gallic hosts in Thrace (Green 1990, 264–265).

30. Seleucus II had died falling from a horse in 226, with his son ruling briefly as Seleucus III before being assassinated and replaced by his younger brother as Antiochus III (later "the Great"). Antiochus' cousin and general, Achaeus, then expelled Attalus from Seleucid territory (Green 1993, 265).

31. Sparta still technically had a dual-monarchy with two kings from different family lines serving subject to a council of elders (the "ephors"). However, this system had declined as single rulers came to contest the ephors for dominance (Cleomenes' co-king would later be murdered without consequence for the crime's perpetrators).

32. Plutarch *Cleomenes*, Vol. II, 333; apparently not counting any Argive input, the League's 20,000 footmen here represent an apparent doubling of its manpower under Aratus due in large part to the addition of Corinth in 243 and Megalopolis a decade later. It's also clear that this force included some mercenaries (Griffith 1935, 100), most likely specialist missilemen among the light infantry.

33. This estimate of Achaean manpower is suggested both by the relatively modest opposition that would have been expected from Elis and that Aratus

was still able to take the field in substantial strength shortly after his troops here were largely killed or captured.

34. Spartiate families were down to around 700 by the mid–3rd century per Plutarch, and Aristotle (*Politics* 1270a.29–32) claims they could raise less than 1,000 hoplites, though residents of lesser standing must have provided some spearmen as well. Agis' failed land redistribution scheme suggests that the perioeci formed nearly 77 percent of the population in this era (Michalopoulos 2016, 6–7); and having refused their past obligation to join Spartan levies in the wake of Leuctra in 371 (Xenophon *Hellenica* 6.5.23, 32; 7.2.2), they seem to have been acting much more like privileged allies than a subject population.

35. This is based on Tegean manpower being about equal to that for pre–3rd century all-out deployments, which ran around 1,500-strong when it was similarly second among Arcadian cities after Mantinea.

36. Plutarch *Aratus*, Vol. II, 633–634.

37. Plutarch *Cleomenes*, Vol. II, 334 and *Aratus*, Vol. II, 634; Polybius 2.51.3.

38. If subsequent Orchomenian losses ran 15 percent or so (typical of a hard defeat near a refuge), then it would indicate an original deployment of around 2,000 heavy spearmen plus perhaps a quarter that in supporting light foot. Given that Aratus' preceding setback in Messenia had involved only a modest League deployment, he could easily have fielded twice that many here.

39. Plutarch *Aratus*, Vol. II, 634.

40. Around 2,000 of these new spartiates came from a pool of "inferiors" (*hypomeiones*), most of whose families had lost spartiate status due to poverty (Michalopoulos 2016, 6). The remaining 1,000 or so probably were select resident aliens (equivalent to the *metoikos* of Athens) and well-placed perioeci.

41. Plutarch *Cleomenes*, Vol. II, 337; it is important to note here that Plutarch does not state that the new pikemen drawn from "*the best and most promising of the country people*" constituted the whole of Cleomenes' army, but rather that he raised them in the course of "*completing the number of citizens*" such that it then made up a "*body of four thousand men*" in total. The pre-existing contingent of some 1,000 hoplites consisted of spartiates in good standing, *mothakes* (native-born non-citizens including illegitimate sons financially backed by spartiate sponsors), and others whose loss of spartiate rank had not been related to impoverishment.

42. Plutarch *Cleomenes*, Vol. II, 339.

43. Cleomenes was inspired to recruit helots as a counter to word that Antigonus was bringing his less celebrated Leucaspides pikemen (see note below) toward ensuring an all-out effort (Plutarch *Cleomenes*, Vol. II, 345). Some 6,000 helots were emancipated, the most fit becoming phalangites and some of the others serving as skirmishers (Michalopoulos 2016, 56). The sum of 500 talents at an equivalency of 26kg of sliver each would be worth approximately $7,500,000 in modern terms, enough to afford relatively inexpensive arms for the helots as well as to cover the meager salaries of sizeable mercenary contingents for a few seasons.

44. Per Plutarch (*Cleomenes*, Vol. II, 348), Polybius concurring (2.65.1–5) with a detailed tally of 29,200.

45. See Pritchett (1965, 59–70), Morgan (1981), and the topographic map in Walbank (1970, 276) for this terrain.

46. Michalopoulos (2016, 63, 210–11 note 233) suggests 3,500–4,000 perioeci and 1,500–2,000 allies.

47. Macedonian operations in Greece since the days of Philip II indicate use of 3,000-man pike regiments paired with elite hoplites (hypaspists) 1,000-strong. The 3,000 hypaspists at Sellasia (see note 48 below re: "peltasts") thus suggest three regiments were probably present at 3,000 men each plus an additional 1,000 veteran reservists to run the phalangite total to 10,000 in a maximum deployment. Macedon's pikemen were split into the select Chalkaspides and lesser Leucaspides (White Shields), with the latter perhaps forming two of the three regiments at Sellasia. That ratio would parallel past hypaspist deployments where two less renowned units accompanied a single "agema" of elites. The Chalkaspides are sometimes misidentified with the peltasts, but Asclepiodotus notes that "[peltasts'] *spears are much shorter than those of the* [phalangites]" (1.2) and Polybius takes care at both Sellasia (2.65.2) and Raphia (5.82.4) to distinguish them from pikemen standing immediately alongside.

48. Polybius identifies Macedon's elite hoplites (hypaspists) here as peltastai, a word previously used solely for the javelin-armed light infantry that had by now largely been superseded across Greece by theurophoros javelineers. Polybius' peltasts were clearly not light-armed, but rather stratiotai of the regular phalanx even though equipped per literature and contemporary artwork with much shorter spears plied with one hand versus the two-handed sarissai of their phalangite line-mates. Polybius was apparently employing anachronistic terminology from his own day (early 2nd century) when use of such a diminutive word for heavy infantry might have arisen from adoption by that era's hypaspist equivalents of the sort of shields shown on the monument commemorating Pydna in 168 (see Chapter 8 note 43). These devices had the classical aspis' central porpax and rim antelabe suspension and covered the entire upper body but lacked offset rims for which they compensated through a marked increase in concavity. This made them a bit smaller (around 80cm across versus 90–100cm for the classical aspis), but by no means as small as the old skirmisher pelte. That such "neo-hoplite" aspides were already in use at Sellasia is highly doubtful due to a monument honoring Alexander son of Akmetos, who was one of the phalanx commanders below Evas in that battle (Polybius 2.66.5). Erected sometime shortly thereafter under Philip V, who succeeded Antigonus Doson in 221, this features a carving of an aspis with a narrow rim of adequate offset as to remain deeply shadowed when the adjacent face-edge is brightly lit (Sekunda 2012, 36–37). The hypaspists/peltasts at Sellasia must thus have been using aspides compatible with a one-handed spear (either the classical dory or a shorter, dual-purpose longche) that were at most no more than in transition to the rimless shields of the 2nd century's elite neo-hoplites.

49. Previous Epirote infantry deployments included skirmishers, pikemen, and traditional hoplites, while

the Acarnanians are thought in the past to have provided hired hoplites to Pyrrhus at 1,000 strong (see Chapter 2 re: *Heraclea*) and were otherwise well known for their slingers. A unified contingent from these close neighbors in northwestern Greece could well have provided a mixed-arms force in accordance with reported manpower to the tune of 100 horsemen, 1,000 phalangites (all from Epirus, where this was the most common troop type), and 800 spearmen plus 200 slingers from Acarnania.

50. See discussion below on probable Achaean troop types present. It is unlikely that Antigonus here was emulating the use of a reserve phalanx as per Alexander the Great's custom in Persia (Bardunias and Ray 2016, 146) given that the tactical situations there (facing larger, cavalry-dominated foes across flat, open ground) were dramatically different from those at Sellasia. There simply wasn't room to put every contingent in the front line.

51. The rearward position of the 2,000 Achaeans on Antigonus' right and their problems dealing with more mobile theurophoroi half as numerous indicates they were hoplites; indeed, what must have been the same 2,000 troops are later described as "*hoplites*" with heavy arms by Polybius (4.11.3, 7; 14.6). Past restriction of the term to picked spearmen suggests that these were probably the only true Achaean "epilektoi" present. Participation of 300 Achaean horsemen as well implies that this hoplite contingent was likely at the core of a special mixed arms force of 3,300 that had one mounted man per ten foot-soldiers in line with common ratios in ancient Greek armies. And since no other skirmishers are mentioned supporting Antigonus' cavalry, the other 1,000 Achaean foot-soldiers down in the pass must have been light-armed troops filling that role. At a third of the complement of foot, those would have exceeded the 10–20 percent norm for skirmisher content in Greek infantry musters, indicating that theurophoroi had already become more prominent in Achaea than elsewhere.

52. A final note on Antigonus' army at Sellasia is that he is said to have had 2,000 in Boeotian infantry that are not mentioned in the battle. These men might have either formed some sort of reserve or provided a guard for the Macedonian camp. The latter is more probable, and the attachment of 200 horsemen suggests that the foot-soldiers were perhaps 800 hoplites (phalangites appear rather less likely) and 200 skirmishers as per previously documented Boeotian infantry deployments at the kind of 10-to-1 ratio with cavalry seen here.

53. See Polybius (2.66.11–67.1) on this preliminary attack and Plutarch (*Cleomenes*, Vol. II, 348) on its purpose.

54. The Spartan works on the Dagla Ridge were substantial. Pritchett (1965, 62, plate 58a) has described their surviving westernmost portion as a "*low rubble wall extending along the top contour of the ridge for more than a hundred meters*" with a ditch running alongside part of its extent.

55. Polybius 2.68.3–7.

56. Pritchett observed that this ravine presented "*a formidable natural barrier*" (1965, 65), while Morgan (1981, 328) noted that its walls angle at 45-degrees. An incline greater than 30-degrees can neither be descended upright nor scaled without going to hands-and-knees by even an unburdened man. For a phalanx looking to retain its heavy weapons and other gear, this would quite literally have been impossible.

57. Morgan 1981, 329.

58. Plutarch *Cleomenes*, Vol. II, 348; Polybius 2.69.8.

59. Morgan 1981, 330.

60. Polyaenus 4.2.2, 7; Frontinus 2.1.9; Onasander 21.9; Bardunias and Ray 2016, 160–165, 172.

61. Polybius 2.69.9.

62. Plutarch *Cleomenes*, Vol. II, 348.

63. Any detailed reconstruction of Sellasia (as for most ancient battles) requires speculation on key elements. Some well-considered recent alternatives to what is presented here as most probable can be found in Sabin (2007, 154–157); Pietrykowski (2009, 170–180); Park (2010); McDonnell-Staff (2011), and Michalopoulos (2016, 60–73).

64. Polybius 2.70.6.

65. Polybius 4.4.11–12, 4.14.6; the men physically bested were thus but a portion of the 1,300 Achaean cavalry and foot-skirmishers on hand while the hoplites must have been approximately 2,000-strong.

66. Bar-Kochva's analysis of Seleucid manpower in this period (1976, 20–53) indicates roughly 44,000 citizen pikemen, which suggests in light of consistent manpower counts in multiples of 5,000 and what is known about the Argyraspides (see Chapter 3 re: *Lysimacheia*) that there might have been nine 5,000-man divisions in all. With one of these from the north Syrian settlement at Cyrrhos in revolt (Polybius 5.50.7), Antiochus likely led six divisions here with 30,000 phalangites from other western region bases. The last two divisions came from settlements in Media established around Ecbatana (Polybius 5.54.8; Bar-Kochva 1976, 32, 121) and had sided with their rebellious satrap to give him some 10,000 pikemen. Antigonus' Greek mercenary hoplites seem to have played a key offensive role in contemporary Seleucid tactics that had formerly fallen to the hypaspists (see below and in context of the positioning and likely use of such troops by both sides at Raphia). The cavalry and lighter infantry numbers proposed for the royal army are a little less than a third of Seleucid totals in 217, a few such men being in revolt with the Cyrrhos contingent, but the great majority beyond those attached directly to Antiochus' phalangite divisions standing with Molon, who controlled their most important recruiting districts.

67. Bar-Kochva makes a detailed case for Molon being blocked from the area's main pass and forced to deploy across a ridge some 4km long and 500m wide (1976, 119–120), which fits the troop set-ups offered here. Alternatively, Grainger (2015, 17) puts him in the valley of the Diyala River just southeast of that plateau.

68. This assumes frontages for the phalangites of 2/3m and 16-man files, 1m for the Gauls (standing purely on the defensive in close-order rather than the 2m/man they usually assumed for offensive purposes) in 10-man files, and the horsemen four-deep at 2m/mount.

69. Bar-Kochva 1976, 122–123.

70. Polybius 5.52.12–14.

71. The notable naval battles were at Cos in 261 (Seleucid victory) and Andros in 246 (Seleucid defeat).

72. It's interesting to note that the Seleucids were most successful on the field of battle against Egypt in the late 240's during the Third Syrian War. It's probable that their armies were led at that time by Xanthippus, the same Spartan mercenary that had authored Carthage's victory over the invading Romans at Tunes in 255.

73. There had been two issues to deal with prior to refocusing on Syria: securing Media from any remaining rebels and a new uprising in Asia Minor led by Antiochus' cousin and general Achaeus. The first was resolved with a brief campaign into that satrapy and the second was reduced in scope when most of Achaeus' army revolted.

74. Polybius provides manpower for Antiochus (5.79.3–13) and Ptolemy (5.65.2–10), though he fails to list skirmishers with the latter's elephants (about 3,650 at 50 each). The heavy infantry counts include pikemen and Greek mercenaries on both sides plus some elite Ptolemaic troops (peltastai and royal foot guards). Other Seleucid spearmen with shields suitable for "line" work were part of a levy of "Iranians" (Medes, Cissians, Hyrkanians, etc.). This included men so equipped as to be compared by past Greek observers to their own heavy spearmen, with Arian repeating claims that these troops (up to half of "*kardakes*" contingents that also included missilemen) "*were also hoplites*" (2.8.6). Late 4th century artwork suggests that this heavier fraction of the kardakes had in times past carried hoplite aspides; however, they are likely by this date to have adopted the popular theuros in that it was both cheaper to acquire and more tactically versatile. Generally being less robustly armored than traditional hoplites (sans helmet for example), these might best be classified as "medium" infantry.

75. Bar-Kochva 1976, 129–131.

76. Polybius 5.82.8–13.

77. The Seleucid military had inherited Philip II's tradition of deploying elite troops called hypaspists on the right/strike wing of its phalanxes. Originally spear-armed hoplites, these were probably cross-trained/equipped as pikemen in Asian theatres beginning with Alexander III's Indian campaign. And while hypaspists well suited to Greece's rugged terrain continued to serve there as picked hoplites against enemy spearmen, fighting across the wide plains of Asia favored mounted offensive action. This largely recast phalanxes as defensive devices to lock foes in place while horsemen and elephants sought decisions off their flanks, which led by the late 3rd century to Seleucid heavy arrays arming almost solely with the defensively superior sarissa. It seems that whenever more hypaspists than still resided within the Argyraspide elite divisions were desired, the Seleucids might resort to using mercenaries as here. Savvy and self-equipped, these could be contracted for short-terms and thereby eliminate the cost of cross-training citizen soldiers and providing them with expensive hoplite gear. While Polybius does not specify the equipage of Antiochus' Greek hirelings, he notes (5.82.10) that they occupied the spear-armed hypaspists' old post on the right wing of their phalanx and distinguishes them from the phalangites standing alongside who are contrastingly "*armed in the Macedonian fashion*" (i.e., with pikes).

78. Having to fire over forward ranks in excess of four-deep hindered the effectiveness of missilemen.

79. Polybius has this Arab/tribal light infantry form the left wing of Antiochus' phalanx, but the choice of such extremely unsuitable troops for that role is unconscionable for so experienced a commander, suggesting that Polybius must have this wrong. The Medes and other Iranians he puts next in line would clearly have been the vastly better choice as proposed here. And strong support for this comes from the battle description he later repeats in which the Greeks on Ptolemy's right wing defeat not only Arabs but Medes as well (5.85.4–5). This is something that those contingents' disproportionate sizes would have rendered physically possible only if the smaller Median/Iranian levy had been standing on the inside immediately next to the pike array.

80. It's probable that each of the six pike divisions (strategiai) present had a nominal 1,000 skirmishers from the same recruiting district organically attached. These men would have made up this contingent with the remainder (perhaps one 500-man unit from each heavy division) detached to provide security for the army's camp/baggage.

81. Daae, Carmanian, and Cilician skirmishers (Polybius 5.79.3) supported the elephants at 50 per animal.

82. Polybius 5.82.2–7.

83. It has been proposed that Polybius somehow double-counted a portion of the Graeco-Macedonian pike contingent and that Ptolemy had only some 25,000 phalangites on hand from the Egyptian territories with a mere 5,000 of them being Graeco-Macedonian (Walbank 1970, 590). This is perhaps plausible yet seems improbable within the parameters of Polybius' clear statements on overall infantry counts. Certainly, Walbank's assumption that "*a phalanx of 45,000* [Polybius' phalangite count sans Libyans] *must surely have broken Antiochus' phalanx of 20,000* [less the two 5,000-man divisions of Argyraspides] *at the first clash*" is not valid. Unlike classical/Doric phalanxes, whose hoplites could exert othismos from their after-ranks, greater depth of file (per that imposed on Ptolemy in the confined setting at Raphia) would give no advantage along the battle-front to a pike-array since it had no similar pushing capability and could only bring a single row of sarissai into offensive play. However, even should this lesser manpower have been the case, it would have resulted in no significant change to the combat's dynamics since Ptolemy could then have simply deployed in files of 16 rather than 24.

84. Gear for the peltastai and royal guards (formerly hypaspists and royal hypaspists) is not described but probably included traditional hoplite spear and aspis in contrast to the Libyans alongside who were differently equipped with sarissa and pelte "*in the Macedonian manner*" (Polybius 5.85.3–4). This explains why Polybius lists the peltastai/guardsmen elites as being on the "*left wing*" rather than within the "*phalanx*" proper per his own highly restricted definition of that last as being solely pike-armed.

85. Xenophon *Hellenica* 6.4.8–15.

86. Polybius 5.65.3–4; 5.82.5–6.

87. The sudden offensive said to have been executed on command by Ptolemy's Greek mercenaries at

Raphia (see below) would not have been practical for a pike array limited to applying no more than a single rank in thrusting. However, such action was quite possible for traditional hoplites able to individually strike with greater force and do so in concert using twice the weaponry (from two ranks) as well as push with files more than double those trying to resist with theuros shields inferior for that purpose.

88. Polybius 5.84.10.
89. Interestingly, this initial passivity by Ptolemy's right wing harks back once more to Leuctra, where the Theban right had held back while its left wing attacked in a tactic often called "oblique order" by modern writers.
90. Polybius 5.86.5–6.

Chapter 5

1. Caven (1980, 78) draws from Polybius to infer that Hamilcar's army "*included no fewer than 100 elephants,*" but otherwise was "*merely ... adequate for the conquest of Spain,.*"
2. Polybius 25.10.1.
3. Head 1982, 36.
4. Diodorus 25.10.3; maximum Libyan potential in the late 3rd century was some 50,000 foot and 10,000 horsemen (Head 1982, 36); however, only half that might have been in revolt at this time. Higher Numidian cavalry contents (up to 40 percent) are known but represent smaller infantry turnouts rather than larger mounted ones.
5. Polybius 3.35.1; Diodorus 25.12.1; assessing these numbers, it's likely the Carthaginians were now drawing from recent colonies like Acra Leuce and Novo Cartago (founded by Hamilcar and Hasdrubal, respectively) to boost their heavy "African" infantry to some 30,000 with the other foot-soldiers being 20,000 Iberians (including Balearic slingers) and 10,000 Celts. The figure for cavalry seems valid, but that for elephants might be inflated by a factor of two (see note 6 below). All these troops would have been exclusive of numerous static garrison contingents.
6. Polybius (3.15.8) and Livy (21.5.11) cite 100,000 tribesmen; likely full population tallies, only a quarter of these would have been combatants. Hannibal is said to have had some 40 elephants on the Tagus out of the 200 claimed to be in stable. Such numbers are suspect, but their ratio could be valid, and its application to troop counts implies that some 12,000 foot-soldiers (9,000 heavy-armed) and 1,600 horsemen might have been with Hannibal at the Tagus. Only 58 elephants in total are attested at the time of the march to Italy in 218 (37 with Hannibal per Appian plus 21 with Hasdrubal), fitting with Hamilcar's 100 in 237 after reasonable interim losses. This is also consistent with as few as 20–25 being at Tagus River if we cut Diodorus' and Polybius' reports there to match the reduction needed to bring the former's 200-count down to the better documented figures for 218.
7. Polybius 3.14.2–8; Livy 21.5.8–16.
8. Diodorus 25.15.1; the versions of Polybius and Livy do not mention this sortie, only a lengthy siege.
9. Polybius 3.33.14–15; "African" refers to hoplites whether local colonial or African citizenry/conscripts.
10. Polybius 3.33.8–11, 13.
11. Polybius 3.35.8; the noted presence of an Iberian general here suggests that these were mostly of his nationality with a lesser content of "Africans" plus a few Celts (see discussion below re: *Cissus*).
12. Polybius (3.56.4) cites here a monument inscribed by Hannibal himself. Reports that he had first marched with 90,000 foot and 12,000 horse (Polybius 3.35.1; Appian 7.1.4) must reflect total Punic manpower in Iberia. The field army seems to have included 61,000 in infantry plus all the cavalry with the remaining 29,000 being garrison troops (if the 19,000 foot and 1,200 horse recently sent to Africa were newly raised, otherwise there were only 10,000 in the garrisons). After equipping Hasdrubal and Hanno, Hannibal set out for Italy with 38,000 foot (likely 15,000 African heavies, 8,000 scutarii, 4,000 caetrati, 2,000 other Iberians, and 9,000 Celts) plus around 8,500 in cavalry (Polybius 3.60.5). His losses in the Alps thus came to roughly 3,000 Africans (20 percent), 6,000 Iberians (43 percent), all the Celts (more by desertion than casualty), and 2,500 horsemen (29 percent) for a total of 20,500 (44 percent).
13. Livy 21.17.9.
14. Polybius 3.45.1–2; Scipio's Roman and Celtic riders are said to have killed over 200 Numidians at a cost of 140 of their own; however, these numbers appear exaggerated for what was little more than a skirmish.
15. Polybius (3.65.5–6) records dispositions, but sadly with no numerical details. It is notable that the Loeb version of these lines misinterprets Scipio's Roman and other allied cavalry as standing "*behind*" the Gallic horse. A more accurate translation is that they were "*in line facing the front*" (Walbank 1970, 399); thus, the consul's cavalry was ordered along the ranks in fully filed ethnic contingents.
16. Livy 21.17.5; unfortunately, here as so often elsewhere, Livy provides no break-down of troop types, perhaps thinking that such details would be common knowledge among his target audience.
17. Polybius 3.71.1, 5–7; needing good mobility/flexibility plus shock capability, Mago's infantrymen likely were scutarii that apparently had about half of the Numidian horse in support. The Trebia flowed down a very low gradient and thus formed what geomorphologists call a "braided" stream, spreading out along a fairly straight course with multiple intertwining channels. Mago's hide was behind one such channel that had steep banks topped by dense growths of thorny plants that provided good cover.
18. Polybius 3.72.11–13; this claims there were 4,000 horsemen deployed for Rome, which was the count prior to Ticinus (Sempronius' 2,400 and the 1,600 of Manlius). With the loss of some 200 Gauls plus a probable 20 percent or so of the other riders having been either killed or debilitated by wounds (as per Scipio), surviving cavalry from Ticinus active at Trebia would have come to no more than 1,200. That gives Sempronius a maximum of 3,600 horsemen and quite possibly less, making it likely that loyal Gauls made up the difference to reach 4,000. The Gallic infantry later reported off the Roman right flank (maybe matching or slightly exceeding their cavalry count) must be considered separately (Livy [21.55.4]

sets these "*auxiliaries*" apart from the 20,000 "*allies of the Latin name*"). All the light foot indicated here came with Sempronius (including velites attached to his heavy units), suggesting that whatever remained of Scipio's skirmishers from Ticinus were detached to guard the camp.

19. Our sources vary in describing Hannibal's elephant deployments. Polybius says that he set the beasts "*in front of his wings*" (3.72.9), Livy that they took post "*on the outer extremities of the wings*" (21.55.7), and Appian that they stood "*opposite the Roman horse*" (7.2.7). There have been arguments that Polybius' use of the term "wings" indicates a position in front of the phalanx's heavy foot that is consistent with them then engaging legionaries directly across the field (Walbank 1970, 406). However, the considerable and unavoidable ambiguity in any such language aside, it's clear that the Roman infantry opposing the elephants was light-armed (Livy 21.55.11) and would have held post outboard of their legions and the Punic phalanx. As a great admirer, Hannibal would surely have employed his few elephants much like Pyrrhus had when facing Roman opposition with a similarly small complement, using them as anti-cavalry devices in support of his own horsemen. That seems to have been the overwhelmingly dominant practice among other elephant-savvy ancients as well. And accounts of past battles in which pachyderms spooked horses unfamiliar with their strange sight and smell are echoed at Trebia, where both Livy (21.55.7) and Appian (7.2.7) detail how they terrified Roman mounts.

20. Polybius 3.76.5; Livy 21.59.5–7, 60.1; Walbank (1970, 409) opines that Punic losses may be overstated.

21. Frontinus 2.3.1.

22. A maximum 60 percent rate of infantry loss for Hanno is consistent with past double envelopments, which also often saw large bodies of surrounded men agreeing to lay down arms.

23. Walbank (1970, 419–420) and Lazenby (1978, 65) project Flaminius had 25,000 men per reports of 15,000 having been slain (Polybius 3.84.7, 85.2; Livy 22.7.1–2; though Appian [7.2.10] says 20,000) and 10,000 surviving (per Livy and Appian versus Polybius' 15,000). This fits the force Sempronius brought back from Sicily (24,000 foot and a tenth that in cavalry) if we accept a modest reduction of around 2,000 irregular auxiliaries.

24. Some of Hannibal's men adopted Roman gear after Trasimenus (see notes 30 and 32 below), but that began post Trebia (Livy 22.46.4), probably involving superior scutum shields and highly valued chainmail common among that battle's fallen Romans with some of it likely used to convert caetrati into scutarius swordsmen.

25. Fields (2017, 69) puts 25,000 Gauls with Hannibal at Trasimenus similar to Polybius' figures on his army a year later at Cannae (3.114.5). Though that is perhaps a bit high, there must surely have been a substantial increase from the 14,000 or so Gauls likely present at Trebia.

26. Modern analyses have fixed on two stretches bordering Lake Trasimenus for the site of this engagement, one to the west thought to better match Livy and one on the east seen as closer to Polybius, with both running along the shore for about 7km (Walbank 1970; Lazenby 1978, 62–64; Caven 1980, 122–125; Bagnall 1990, 180–181; Fields 2017, 69). The last is significant in that fitting Flaminius' column of march (*agmen*) within would take more than 4km for the regular (legion/ala sociorum) infantry alone at the usual six-abreast and then one must add space for intermingled cavalry, irregular auxiliaries, and the baggage train. Either site would have been narrow in 217 given that the current broader expanse of the westerly locale results from later outbuilding of river sediments and greater recession of the shoreline due to a lowering of the water level across its more gently inclined surface. The eastern option was favored in the past as better accommodating popular views on how Flaminius' vanguard fled the battle; however, the western site has since gained credibility. Bagnall's observation that cremation pits have been found there with arrow and spearheads among human skeletal remains certainly adds strong support, and there are compatible alternatives for the vanguard's escape route.

27. Polybius 6.40.4; the normal position Flaminius' irregular skirmishers would have had in this standard marching order is not specified, but a few were presumably scouting ahead and outboard while most accompanied and looked after the army's baggage.

28. Fields 2017, 81; Polybius 3.84.3; Livy 22.5.5.

29. Polybius 3.86.7–4–5; Livy 22.8.1; Appian's version of this engagement (7.2.9,11) is completely different. He has, Centenius, who was a private citizen, holding position in a narrow passage through a mountainside swampland with an 8,000-man militia sent from Rome that had been gathered in haste prior to Trasimenus from the leftovers of previous drafts. Attacked by Hannibal in front and Maharbal down the mountain on one flank, the Romans are defeated with the loss of 3,000 killed and 800 captured. Walbank (1970, 420–421) repeats a viable theory that Appian confused this action with that of another Centenius in 212 (see below re: *Lucania*).

30. Polybius 3.87.3, 18.29.9; Livy (22.46.4) implies the same, though the nature of these "*select*" adoptions is not detailed by either author. It's most likely that we are dealing here with captured equipment other than weapons. Significantly supporting this is Polybius' lone specific note on the Roman gear used by Hannibal's men at Cannae (3.114), which clarifies that "*the armor of the Libyans was Roman, for Hannibal had armed them with a selection of the spoils taken in previous battles.*" A further indication that Hannibal adopted only defensive items from his fallen foes can be seen in Polybius' sole identifying reference to the Africans' weaponry. This was his report at Cannae (3.116.9–10) that "*the Libyan heavy-armed troops*" stationed on the Punic left wing turned "*spear-side*" (rightward) as they enveloped the opposing Roman right flank (see that battle below). As the technical term "spear-side" was classically used in reference to the Doric phalanx, its seemingly intentional application here in marked contrast to Polybius' simple "left" and "right" elsewhere at Cannae strongly suggests his recognition that the subject Libyan heavy foot was indeed spear-armed.

31. Lazenby 1978, 14.

32. One is tempted to turn Polybius' statement on its head and propose that when it came to actual weapons Hannibal might have re-equipped all *except*

the Africans. His scutarii and Gallic swordsmen were much better suited to Roman weaponry. Yet, Iberian blades (including a prototype of the *gladius Hispanicus* later adopted by the Romans themselves) were superior and the Gauls didn't abandon their longswords if we are to believe Polybius' description of their using them at Cannae (3.114). The Roman scutum, however, apparently improved upon some Iberian and Gallic shield designs and Appian (7.4.23) indicates that they were used at Cannae by some of Hannibal's Celtiberians. Clean of identifying devices (Field 2017, 21,25), these could easily be re-decorated and would fit with the "select" distributions of captured material (whether to Africans or anyone else) being entirely defensive in nature (save possibly for swords used to upgrade light infantry).

33. Polybius 3.92.1–94.6; Livy 22.15.1–18.4; known as Ager Falernus, this was not a pitched battle but rather a disorderly affair over rugged upland terrain in which Hannibal's lighter Iberians (presumably caetrati) had an advantage over heavier-equipped Romans better suited to fighting in formation across flatter ground.

34. The dictatorship's army had four legions (Livy 22.27.10, 34.6) plus the same in alae sociorum and perhaps another 3,200 auxiliaries (400/legion) for a total of about 40,000 combatants.

35. Polybius (3.104.4) gives the hidden force 5,000 light foot and 500 cavalry, Livy (22.3.6) says 5,000 in total.

36. See Kromayer and Veith (2016, 66) for a map of the likely battle site; Walbank (1970, 432) does not dispute this proposal, yet maintains that the engagement's exact location remains uncertain.

37. Livy 22.28.14.

38. Polybius 3.105.6.

39. A similar problem arose at Sparta as to which of its two kings would control the army on campaign. The Spartans sensibly resolved this by simply not allowing both to take the field at the same time. Athens solved a comparable conflict differently. Though the generals from each of its army's tribal divisions were of equal status, only one was given supreme authority in the field as polemarch (*polemarchos*). Herodotus famously got this wrong in his reporting on the battle of Marathon in 490, claiming that the Athenians rotated command there among all ten generals on a daily schedule; however, this practice did not apply to field leadership, but rather only to administrative affairs and did not actually go into effect until sometime post–Marathon.

40. Polybius 3.113.5.

41. Polybius 6.21.9–10; a similar overstrength deployment would be used in 190 (see Chapter 8 re: *Magnesia*).

42. Polybius 3.113.5.

43. Hannibal's initial 12,000 African heavy foot had been engaged at Trebia and Trasimenus with only the former seeing them take any appreciable casualties (likely around 5 percent and certainly well less than 10 percent). Losses among the 4,000 or so scutarii would have been more significant but they had been more than replaced through upgrading a portion of the 4,000 caetrati and other Iberian light foot with captured arms. How many of the allied Gauls also sported heavier Roman equipment at Cannae is speculative; however, many must have acquired chainmail and other useful items on the basis of individual merit with those now better-armed warriors making up the leading ranks in their battle array.

44. See Walbank (1970, 444) and Lazenby (1978, 80) for the logic supporting an average depth of 50 for the Roman heavy array (hastati, principes, and triarii) at Cannae in light of Polybius' implication (3.113.3) that its maniples were deeper than they were wide. The oversized legions in this case covered a slightly broader front than the alae alongside; however, the entire deployment of Roman and allied line-troops would have stretched across a frontage that closely matched that of Hannibal's phalanx.

45. Polybius 3.113.8–9; the curved nature of the formation outlined here is widely accepted (see Walbank 1970, 445), but may be a misunderstanding in that its mechanics are highly improbable. A step-like arrangement of component units as per Kroymayer and Veith (2016, 67) seems the only practical way to have done this.

46. This wheeling maneuver by elite troops (cyclosis) had been perfected at Sparta. Though requiring much drill for maximum efficiency, it was not complex and had originated inadvertently from the inherent dynamics of phalanx warfare; indeed, the most famous example of its use for double envelopment prior to Cannae was just such a natural action by undrilled Athenians at Marathon in 490. With specific regard to Carthage, cyclosis must have been part of the intense drill imposed upon its phalanx by Sparta's Xanthippus during the First Punic War, though rout of his right wing at Tunes likely precluded it from enhancing his mounted envelopment there. Hannibal's father would have been familiar with the tactic as a colleague of Xanthippus, as would the Spartan Sosylos, who was Hannibal's tutor in Greek, personal historian, and military advisor. Popular alternatives to cyclosis at Cannae call for the Romans to either have deliberately invited envelopment by attacking a much broader battle array than their own (certainly possible had Hannibal filed his European swordsmen thinner than proposed here even if the African spearmen were virtually in column) or have compacted tremendously in the course of driving back the Gauls and Iberians at field-center. The latter would seem physically impossible for an array of such great depth that would have been urged toward no more than minor compaction (legionaries lacking room to swing a sword would have been rather less effective than these appear to have been) solely among its first few ranks. And as to throwing themselves at a much wider opposing formation, such normally suicidal behavior under the practical realities of linear combat in this era must be considered unlikely even for a relatively inexperienced general like Varo given the kind of advice that Paulus and other veterans on the command staff would surely have given him in abundance had he contemplated such a thing.

47. Livy 22.49.15, 49.13, 49.18, 50.3, 54.1, 54.4; and Appian reinforces part of Livy's claims by citing a round 50,000 Roman deaths. Polybius' alternative account of the losses runs much higher with 70,000 being slain (not counting cavalry), 10,000 captured, and only 3,000 escaping (3.117.1–4). Given the latter numbers' overtly generalized appearance and internal

conflicts, Lazenby has reasonably suggested that *"Livy's more convincing and detailed figures are ... to be preferred"* (1978, 84).

48. Livy 23.16; Plutarch Vol. I *Marcellus*, 415; Livy notes that *"for my own part, I would not take upon me to assert what some authors have declared* [regarding casualties] ... [but] *whether the victory was great or small ... not to be vanquished by Hannibal was then a more difficult task ... than to conquer him afterwards."*

49. Livy 23.37.10-11; while Livy doesn't directly disavow the Roman casualty claims here, the extreme brevity of his remarks on what should by all measures have been quite a momentous victory is remarkably dismissive.

50. Livy 23.41.10, 43.5-6; the officer Bomilcar had landed at Locri with the reinforcements plus supplies. We have no details on these men beyond being infantry; however, it's likely they included a 3,000-strong division of African heavy foot. That was not only the most likely troop type available direct from Carthage, but such men had figured prominently in Mago's report given there on the recent smashing success at Cannae (Livy 23.11). The remaining troops must have been light-armed with many attached to the elephants.

51. Plutarch Vol. I *Marcellus*, 416; Zonaras 9.3; Livy alternatively describes this action as a set battle before the city in which Hannibal was heavily defeated (23.44), yet even he puts the action in context of an initial threat to the foraging detachments and notes that *"all the forces of the enemy were not in the field ... they were rambling about the country in plundering parties."* Significantly, though Polybius' record regarding Nola II has been lost, it clearly did not contain an account of Hannibal being beaten, since he categorically states later that the Carthaginian was never defeated prior to Zama in 202 (15.16.5).

52. Livy (23.40) cites 3,000 Sardinians killed, 800 captured, and an unspecified number escaping for a minimum total of around 4,000. This fits speculative projections of rebel strength for the later battle at Carales as follows: (1) four of the dozen major Punic settlements on Sardinia (Cornus, Tharros, Othoca, and Neapolis) were clustered in Hampsicora's vicinity and probably provided the rebel army at Cornus; (2) If those four cities accounted for about a third of available Punic colonials, then the remaining settlements might have yielded twice as many (8,000) at Carales; (3) had the interior tribes contributed about a third of the rebel army at Carales with 3,600 infantry and 400 (10 percent) horsemen, it would have come to 12,000; (4) reinforcing the Sardinians with 8,000 foot-soldiers from Africa (see below) would then have produced a combined host approximately 20,000-strong.

53. Livy 23.40; the Romans operated quinqueremes (galleys with a single bank of 15 oars on each side manned by up to five rowers per oar but only three each when serving as transports—Rodgers 1937, 272, 306). Having capacity for around 250 men, transport configurations could carry 125 passengers, which would require a 40-ship fleet to move the infantry from a single legion. That means that two trips would have been needed to deliver both a legion and its paired ala sociorum sans cavalry. At 125 sailors and oarsmen per quinquereme, the crews of a 40-ship fleet numbered 5,000 and adding these to the nearly 17,000 foot of two legions plus their associated alae would then bring total manpower up to Livy's infantry figure of 22,000. As for the 1,200 horsemen of Livy, that was the normal allotment for only one legion/ala pair and must represent cavalry previously transferred to the island in a more leisurely fashion as part of the original garrison.

54. This assumes that the landing operation involved the same quinqueremes that had previously been operating off Sardinia in raids against the mainland. These 70 Carthaginian ships were slightly smaller than their Roman counterparts with a 235-man capacity that could carry some 110-115 passengers each in 3-men/oar transport mode for a total of around 8,000 (Rodgers 1937, 273, 323). These troops coming straight from Carthage likely composed two 3,000-man divisions of heavy spearmen plus 2,000 supporting light missilemen at 25 percent of the total.

55. Livy 23.40.1-41.4.

56. Polybius 3.33.14-15; Livy 21.17.5, 23.28.7-29; projections of Hasdrubal's contingents reflect those assigned by Polybius plus additions of Iberian troops indicated by Livy with his comments that (1) the Iberians were the largest faction, likely composing a plurality rather than majority with 9,000 foot soldiers at their usual 2-to1 ratio of scutarii versus caetrati against 5,000 each for the other large contingents of Punic colonial and Libyan/African hoplites and providing some significant share of the horsemen as well; and (2) that the Roman foot (presumably the heavier fraction alone) outnumbered its Carthaginian counterpart once the Iberians were removed from the equation (12,000 versus 10,000 as proposed here). This requires recruiting all of Hasdrubal's Iberian infantry after Hannibal's departure and reducing his original muster by some 2,000 African-style heavy footmen, who were perhaps transferred to the replacement army recently arrived under Himilco for seeding within the new troops as a training/stiffening measure. As for the Roman numbers here, they reflect nominal legion/ala infantry counts as well as Livy's specifics on cavalry and overall allied strengths.

57. Bardunias and Ray 2016, 165-166, 172-173.

58. Livy 23.49.5-11.

59. An estimate on Hasdrubal's likely losses at Dertosa/Ibera under the alternative scenario advanced here suggests about 1,200 Iberians (20 percent) in their rout and pursuit along with 1,000 colonials/Africans in heavy action prior to their withdrawal, all being consistent with him still having about 20,000 combatants at Iliturgi.

60. Livy 23.49,12-14.

61. Lazenby 1997, 129.

62. Livy 23.13.8-11 and 23.17.

63. Livy 24.41.8-10, 42.1-8; here we see claims of Roman victories at Iliturgi, Munda, and Aurinx that took over 12,000, 12,000, and 8,000 Carthaginian lives, respectively. The first is probably a false doublet of the lesser action at the same site in 215 (see above), while the latter two are of much exaggerated scope at very best. Lazenby has evaluated these events (1997, 129), warning that *"it is doubtful how far they can be accepted as historical."*

64. Livy 25.14, 15, 18.1-19.5.

65. Livy 25.19.

66. The manpower estimate here reflects Hannibal's

strength at Cannae with the Gallic allied foot still at least 2,000-strong (per Livy 25.9) and reinforcements from Carthage plus perhaps some local recruiting having offset losses in heavy infantry over that time frame. This assumes that 2,000 horsemen deployed to Capua (Livy 25.15) were about half of the entire Punic mounted force in line with having been a minority of the 10,000 riders at Cannae.

67. Livy 25.20–21; assuming near-nominal strength for Fulvius' infantry divisions, his 18,000-man total leaves room for only some 1,200 horsemen, which was but half the norm for a four legion/ala deployment.

68. Here as elsewhere, Hannibal seems to have gotten excellent data from a highly efficient intelligence operation, using it along with keen appreciation of the terrain to again devise a tactical deployment and plan of action finely tuned to the specific conditions at hand.

69. Fulvius could have extended his line the necessary length by shifting men out of each file in his regular acies triplex to form new files. A reasonably practical method for accomplishing this would have been to deploy as usual and then move five or six men from either side into the inter-file spaces between each pair of files to form a new one. Once those new files were properly ordered front-to-back, the entire formation could then dress ranks and reestablish 2m spacing while increasing its frontage by up to half again.

70. This was the second major battle fought along the Himera River located in southeastern Sicily (not to be confused with the more famous waterway of that same name in the island's north), the first occurring in 446 between the Sicilian city-states of Syracuse and Acragas.

71. Livy 24.35.1–3; the Punic troops had come direct from Carthage under Himilco. Strength for the Syracusan cavalry is based upon its detachment from an army of 8,000 (Livy 24.36.6–36.1) at around 10 percent of that force.

72. Lazenby 1978, 107–108.

73. Marcellus' siege force included two legions of Cannae survivors, some of whom (besides all being war-weary) were past prime age after an additional five years of service. It's likely that one of those units was left at Syracuse after exchanging/transferring enough younger men to bring the other up to full strength.

74. Livy 25.40.5–41.7; Carthaginian casualties above 5,000 would be quite reasonable under this scenario with large additional numbers cut off from retreat and surrendering in groups.

75. Estimates on the Punic armies in Iberia at this time can be drawn from dispositions at the beginning of the war plus Livy's comments on the same three armies at Dertosa/Ibera and Iliturgi in 215 (see above). Making allotments for prior casualties and recruitment, reasonable projections might be: (1) Hasdrubal Barca with 20,000 men (9,000 heavy spearmen, 5,000 scutarii, 2,500 caetrati, 1,000 missilemen, 2,500 horsemen, and 15–20 elephants); (2) Hasdrubal Gisco with 21,000 men (12,000 heavy spearmen, 4,000 scutarii, 2,000 caetrati, 3,000 Numidian horsemen, and 15–20 elephants); and (3) Mago Barca with 19,500 men (9,000 heavy spearmen, 4,000 scutarii, 2,000 caetrati, 3,000 missilemen, 1,500 horsemen, and 20 elephants).

76. Livy 25.34; proposed Roman manpower reflects reported strength at the time of Dertosa/Ibera (see above) affected by only minor casualties and recruitment in the interim. The size cited for Publius Scipio's command represents 66 percent of the brothers' entire original army per Livy's "*two-thirds*" comment.

77. *ibid.*; these 7,500 men likely broke down along the lines of common Iberian practice into some 4,000–4,500 scutarii, 2,000–2,250 caetrati, and 750–1,000 horsemen.

78. Livy 25.32.3–33; Pliny (3.9) mentions Scipio's tomb at "*Ilorcum*" to give us a name for this location.

79. Lazenby 1978, 109.

Chapter 6

1. Livy's account of the battle mentions two legions (the "*fifth*" and "*sixth*") with "*the left wing of the allied infantry*" confirming the presence of one ala sociorum and implying another on the right. He says the Romans were "*inferior in strength*" and four legions/alae with 19,200 nominal would indeed have been smaller than the army of 27,000 that the Carthaginian had last taken into action two years earlier (an estimated 23,000 infantry including 11,000 heavy spearmen and 4,000 scutarii plus 4,000 horsemen and 15 elephants—see Chapter 5 re: *Lucania*).

2. Livy 27.1.

3. Livy indicates that one legion formed a "*second line*" and was taken in the rear; however, this is highly unlikely since all four legions/alae had to make a common front if Fulvius was to avoid being dangerously overlapped by Hannibal's phalanx. This legion must thus have been standing right of its paired ala and was struck from behind due to the mounted envelopment coming on that wing. Livy notes that half of Hannibal's cavalry moved against the camp while the rest attacked the Roman rear. Such an even split of manpower in the midst of action must have been the result of pre-assigning a different follow-up target to each mounted contingent.

4. Appian 7.48.

5. While Livy (27.2) and Plutarch (Vol. I *Marcellus*, 426) report this battle as inconclusive, Frontinus (2.2.6) rates it with some justification as a victory for Hannibal. The contested ground remained in his hands at the end of the day and the longer range at higher elevation of his javelineers plus superior firepower from his slingers surely inflicted disproportionately heavier damage on Marcellus. The latter's skirmishers also had to advance and retreat without benefit of the kind of shield barricade protecting their counterparts up the hill and couldn't take cover until all the way back down among their legionary bastion on the flat below.

6. Livy 27.12; Plutarch Vol. I *Marcellus*, 427.

7. Lazenby 1998, 131.

8. Polybius 10.12; Livy 27.2; Appian (7.20–23) contradicts Polybius and Livy in claiming that 10,000 men took part in the failed defensive sortie at Novo Cartago, but this seems to have been a modest affair targeted narrowly on Scipio's siege engines and the other authors' figure of 2,000 is undoubtedly correct.

9. Livy 27.26.5–6; Plutarch Vol. I *Marcellus*, 429–430.

10. Livy 27.26–27; Plutarch Vol. I *Marcellus*, 430–431.

11. Livy 27.28; see Lazenby (1998, 177) on size of the Roman fleet.

12. Beyond any Carthaginian-supplied troops on hand, Epizephrian Locri had in the past fielded a militia phalanx of some 3,000 spearmen plus light-armed support (Ray 2009, 164–165, 172–173) and would at a minimum have had similar manpower for its present defense. It's unknown if the hoplite equipment traditionally passed down within families was still in use; but if not, abundant captured Roman gear was available for rearming.

13. Polybius 10.38.6–10.59; Livy 27.18.

14. Walbank (1967, 247, citing an estimate from Kahrstedt)

15. *ibid.*; Scipio initially fielded around 31,000 men, his ships could then have provided another 3,000–4,000 from their crews, and there must now have been somewhere between 4,000 and 12,000 allied Iberians on hand.

16. Montagu 2000, 189.

17. Walbank 1967, 252; Bagnall 1990, 211.

18. See Scullard's map of the probable battle site (1970, 72, also plate 29).

19. It's quite possible that Hasdrubal's phalanx was prepared to again reverse front and attack any disordered close pursuit the Romans might have made as per his father's equally well-drilled maneuver in 240 during the Mercenary War (see Chapter 3 re: *Bagradas River*).

20. Livy 27.20.3–8.

21. Appian 6.25–27.

22. Livy 27.41–42; Polybius 15.16.5; Walbank (1967, 267) notes the overblown nature of these reports and that Scullard typified their subject actions as "*skirmishes which Roman tradition magnified into victories.*"

23. Appian (7.52) cites an impossible 48,000 foot and 8,000 horse in line with Livy's 56,000 casualties (27.49), and even that inflated number falls short of the 58,000 dead and 5,400 captured claimed by Orosius (4.18.14).

24. See Walbank (1967, 273) for further discussion in favor of Hasdrubal having 30,000–35,000 men.

25. The site of the ensuing battle of has never been firmly identified, even as to on which side of the river it occupied (Walbank 1967, 270). However, the evidence leans toward south of the Metaurus (Lazenby 1978, 188).

26. Polybius (11.1–3), Livy (27.43–49), and Zonaras (9.9) provide accounts of the battle.

27. Polybius lists Hasdrubal's better than 10,000 casualties as coming among "*the Carthaginians and Celts together.*" Though this makes no mention of Iberians, Lazenby (1998, 190) is surely correct in assuming they were lumped in with the African troops as "Carthaginians." Losses among the Celts would have been low due to their having an escape route downslope to the rear with no enemy skirmishers to pursue. Even with a few drunks killed abed, Celtic losses probably didn't exceed 5 percent (250–300 men). Damage to Punic mobile forces outboard must have been steeper, but still modest at about 10 percent (700) in light of their ability to flee at speed into open ground behind. That puts most of the losses among heavy footmen forming the phalanx. Perhaps half the scutarii present had been shut in on three sides on the far right and taken down at a rate approaching the 60 percent typical in near or full envelopments. Many of the remaining scutarii leftward probably fled, reducing their losses to something more like the 20 percent that an intense battle and pursuit commonly inflicted. That puts the complete scutarius death count at 3,000. The African spearmen enclosed on all sides (enemy troops on three fronts and the hill on the fourth) must therefore have taken the lion's share of Punic casualties at Metaurus River. A few of them might have escaped from their last couple of ranks, but the rest remained penned in to be slain at a rate in the 60 percent range similar to that suffered by their almost as badly surrounded scutarius line-mates farthest right. This suggests a loss of around 7,000 African heavy foot to run their army's body count to 10,000–11,000 in agreement with Polybius' "*not less than 10,000.*" The estimate of approximately 10,000 captives being taken derives from money collected for their sale in context of going prices (Walbank 1067, 252). Africans and Iberians trapped on the field (and thus positioned to give up in mass) likely comprised at least 6,000 of the prisoners. Most of the remaining 4,000 or so would have been caught in small groups at a distance from the battlefield.

28. If we consider Polybius' 2,000 to be only the ethnic Romans killed at Metaurus River as Walbank (1967, 274) seems to suggest, then reasonable assumption of some 1,000 men lost among the flanking light forces would require that around 5,000 heavy-armed Roman allies died in order to preserve Livy's overall casualty count. That would be more than 55 percent of those engaged, which is an astounding level of damage for victorious contingents among which none had suffered individual defeat. Even upping the non-citizen contribution by making Licinus' two legions a legion/ala pair would result in a stunning loss among allied legionaries of over 40 percent.

29. In terms of percentage fatalities, Pyrrhus' costliest victory came at Heraclea, where about 15 percent of his troops died, making the Roman death rate in this battle better than half again more grievous. Pyrrhus lost only 6 percent in triumphing at Asculum for a mere quarter the rate of fatalities suffered by Nero et al. at Metaurus River.

30. This lopsided relative loss is suggested by an analysis that conservatively assumes a clear majority (75 percent) of an estimated 10,000 Punic heavy foot killed at Metaurus River went down after their formation broke apart (as was normally the case when a phalanx collapsed) in contrast to a like majority (75 percent) of the 7,000 Roman line-infantry projected to have died succumbing prior to that (relatively few then being lost in polishing off a broken foe).

31. Polybius 11.20.24; Livy 28.12–15; Appian's tally adds only 1,000 horsemen and four elephants to Polybius while retaining his 70,000 foot.

32. This assumes that the Celtiberians here from the Turdetani were roughly equivalent to a force of similar ethnicity under Hanno that had just recently been defeated before being able to join Gisco (Livy 28.1). This boasted 4,000 javelineers and 200 horsemen among a contingent that was "*in number above nine*

thousand" to imply there were at least 5,000 scutarii as well.

33. Our descriptions of the battle come from Polybius (11.20–24) and Livy (28.12–13).

34. Campbell (2018), 70.

35. See Bardunias and Ray (2016, 168–172); this technique seems to have been developed at Sparta sometime before the end of the 6th century and would have been a commonly practiced drill in Xanthippus' day. Being employed for actual as well as false retreats, use of the latter by Xanthippus' contemporary Hamilcar Barca at Bagradas Bridge in 255 strongly suggests that this was now an integral part of the Carthaginian tactical toolbox.

36. Our sources provide no casualty counts for Ilipia, but Roman losses must have been light in that the legionaries and many of their scutarii faced less dangerous foes on the wings with similar arms and spacing, while those Iberian swordsmen opposite the hoplites did not press the fight. We might thus project something like 1,500–2,000 dead with over half likely being light-armed men outboard and a majority of the rest Iberian scutarii. Gisco's losses probably ran around 24,000–28,000 killed plus 5,000–10,000 captured and saw the elimination of more than 80 percent of his spear-armed African infantry.

37. Livy 28.46.10, 29.4.6; there is no breakdown of Mago's host, but the original landing party might have contained 6,000 heavy spearmen with the later infantry reinforcement entirely composed of hoplites. Roman forces remaining in Italy were a hefty 16 legions; however, this was down from as many as 25 legions in the past (Lazenby 1998, 195) and it was probably to compensate for a stressed and somewhat depleted draft pool that Scipio's newly added troops had to be volunteers.

38. Livy 29.28.10; Appian 7.14.

39. Lazenby (1998, 208) rejects Livy's 40,000 killed and 5,000 captured as well as Appian's 30,000 dead and 2,400 prisoners (any numbers from Polybius have been lost, but he describes the damage done in dire terms), suggesting they were designed in response to gross overestimates of Gisco's and Syphax's combined strength (93,000 per Livy and Polybius). Leaving such dubious specifics aside, Livy's 48 percent lost might be reasonable; yet, should we also accept his claim that less than 2,000 infantrymen and 500 horsemen fled with Gisco, it would imply that he had no more than 4,000 infantry and 1,000 cavalry in his camp, which is surely far too few even sans any mercenaries that might have been present.

40. Lazenby (1998, 209) provides an analysis of the battle's most likely location.

41. Polybius (14.7) says that the Punic army numbered 30,000 men while Livy (30.7) gives it 35,000.

42. Inaccurate reports of 2,000 Numidian riders at Salaeca (Livy 29.29.4) likely record this later deployment.

43. The citizen legions that Scipio had inherited on Sicily were largely composed of survivors from Cannae plus Rome's two later defeats at Herdonia. Known collectively as the *Cannensis Exercitus*, these men had put in anywhere from seven up to 13 years of continuous service.

44. Livy (30.18) is our sole source for this battle.

45. Appian 8.40.

46. Hannibal's army when last seen in action (at Herdonia II) probably consisted of at least 10,000 spearmen, up to 4,000 scutarii, 7,000 light foot, and 3,000 horsemen plus a dozen elephants. Had he retained around 80 percent of the non–Iberian heavy infantry (many of these were now Bruttians and some refused to go to Africa per Appian 7.59), he would have landed with around 8,000 spearmen, 4,000 scutarii, and all the mobile troops of African and Iberian origin (perhaps 1,500 foot and 1,500 horse) plus 10 elephants. Mediolanum had cost Mago 5,000 men at most from his army of 12,000 hoplites, 6,000 in light infantry, and 2,800 cavalry. Having lost all his elephants, he therefore probably retained 8,000 heavy spearmen and would also have brought back all the African light foot and horse (maybe 1,500 each) as well as 8,000 Ligurian mercenaries (probably 6,000 heavier swordsmen and 2,000 skirmishers). Gisco at Great Plains had about 6,000 horsemen, 6,000 Celtiberians (4,000 scutarii and 2,000 caetrati), and 6,000 additional light foot in support of at least 12,000 African hoplites. A worst-case scenario (losing all the scutarii, two-thirds of his hoplites, and 25 percent of the rest) suggests that he kept around 4,000 heavy spearmen, 1,500 Celtiberian caetrati, and 4,500 other skirmishers, but perhaps ended up with only 2,000 or so horsemen due to widespread Numidian defections.

47. See Bahmanyar (2016, 47–48) for a discussion on the most likely locations for the camps and battle.

48. Appian (8.41) notes that the Numidians contributed greatly to the security of Scipio's wings "*because they were accustomed to the sight and smell of elephants.*"

49. Arrian 1.13.1, 2.9.3, 3.12.1; Bardunias and Ray 2016, 146, 213 n31.

50. See Bardunias and Ray (2016, 92–94) on the deleterious effects of negative training and combat experience.

51. All of the hoplites in Hannibal's front phalanx were Africans (Carthaginians, Punic colonials, Liby-Phoenicians, and Libyan conscripts) and so were a majority of the spearmen in his rear phalanx. The latter included troops who had crossed the Alps in 218 and arrived as reinforcements in 215 plus perhaps a few survivors of Metaurus River in 207. The majority of these were by no means geriatric in that phalanx fighters required discipline and stamina rather than youthful agility, commonly manning field armies up to the age of 50 and reserve units until 60. Still, 15 years' worth of disease and misadventure had added to modest combat losses in slowly thinning Hannibal's ranks and he had compensated with local Bruttians. These Oscan spearmen carried scutum-style shields and could stand alongside Punic hoplites in the close order of a phalanx. Livy (30.35) says that the rear phalanx consisted "*principally of Bruttians*," but that was surely not the case since most of Hannibal's Africans must have lived to repatriate with him. There more likely were only 2,000 or so Bruttians at Zama, representing perhaps half their count in Italy. It's also possible these men carried aspis shields rather than scuti. Hannibal had occupied Bruttia for more than a decade and, suffering only minor and very gradual attrition largely outside of combat, he may have been adding locals all

along as individuals or in small batches and providing them with recycled gear identical to that of the rest of his troops. This would have had some parallels to what other Hellenistic armies were doing at this same time in recruiting Asians and Africans and equipping them as Macedonian-style pikemen (pantodapoi), as well as to Rome's similar rearming of its alae sociorum in legionary fashion (later accepting provincial barbarians directly into its legions) and Carthage itself transforming subject Libyans into hoplite spearmen.

52. Again, this resembles a concept Hannibal might have drawn from Alexander the Great, who had designed but never instituted a scheme calling for three ranks of Macedonian phalangites to head files in a revised type of phalanx that incorporated Asian missile troops in all of its after-ranks save the last (Arian 7.23.3).

53. Appian 8.43; this tactic of pitting cavalry spears against elephants had first been employed by dismounted riders at Maleventum in 275 (see Chapter 2) and more recently by velites at Nola II in 215 (see Chapter 5).

54. It's often assumed that these elephants were channeled by design down the openings between the hastati in Scipio's checker-boarded maniples per passing commentary to that effect from Polybius (15.12) and Livy (30.33), though Livy does not say this actually happened during the battle and Appian asserts instead that it was Latin cavalrymen that transited those pathways. Elephants moving down the alleys between hastati contingents was not physically practical as these were not "*vacant*" as Polybius claims but rather occupied by velites at a density at least equal that of the hastati and perhaps greater had dismounted horsemen been present as well.

55. Livy 30.34.

56. Polybius 15.14; equality in numbers here must refer to the first phalanx versus Scipio's surviving swordsmen.

57. The Carthaginians do not appear to ever have equipped the modestly sized African elephants they employed with towers containing several soldiers as the Greeks did with their larger Indian animals (Scullard 1974, 232); instead, their elephants probably carried no more than mahout/driver and a single javelineer riding bareback.

58. Assuming 5 percent losses among Scipio's Roman horse and light foot, we might project that something like 15 percent of the hastati and 12 percent of the principes on the field could have fallen in the battle.

59. Nepos 23.6.4.

Chapter 7

1. Polybius 10.29.4–31.3, 49.1–15; Grainger (2015, 62) estimates that Antiochus had about 35,000 fighting men including 15,000 in heavy foot, which appears more reasonable than Justin's claim of 100,000 infantry and 20,000 cavalry (41.5.7). The two elite Argyraspide units would have accompanied the king at 10,000-strong along with at least one more such heavy division of militiamen. Cavalry was critical to campaigning in the horse-rich east and a full levy of 6,000 as at Raphia is also a logical assumption. If the light infantry count was equal to that of the horsemen plus a like number supporting the phalanx in addition to the Cretans listed separately, then those 14,000 skirmishers bring the total to 35,000 combatants in line with Grainger's estimate. Antiochus' remaining, militia-based military would have stayed behind to secure the core kingdom in his absence.

2. Polybius 10.29.30; heavy infantry here was likely the two Argyraspide chiliarchies of peltastai.

3. Polybius 10.31.

4. While Philip II and his son Alexander famously utilized their heavy cavalry as the most mobile element in this pin and envelop technique, the latter had substituted infantry as here on a couple of occasions when similarly operating within mountainous terrain (Ray 2012, 158–159). A basic version of that tactical variant is first described in the celebrated Spartan defeat on Sphacteria in 425 (Thucydides 4.36.1–2).

5. Polybius 10.49.

6. Alexander the Great had set a precedent for use of such specialized detachments of mobile troops (Ray 2012, 143, 147, 160) and often fielded a similar mix of select horsemen ("companion" cavalry), expert javelineers (Agrianian tribesmen), and elite hoplites (hypaspists). One of Alexander's successors, Eumenes of Cardia, also used such a rapid response contingent at a river crossing in 317 (Diodorus 19.18.4–6).

7. Taylor 2013, 90.

8. This honors the 30,000 native phalanx fighters at Rapha as a minimum; however, there were also 8,000 hired hoplites there and it's at least possible that some mercenary spearmen were present here as well.

9. Polybius 16.18–19; Polybius here is critical of certain elements from his contemporary Zeno's otherwise lost work; however, Walbank (1967, 523) suggests that Polybius "*might have read Zeno carelessly.*"

10. Bar-Kochva 1976, 146–157.

11. Zeno puts the lancers on the left in error, later impossibly reporting both they and the opposing enemy right were victorious. Their posting on the plain to the right versus rough terrain leftward is not only practical, but also fits with them returning from pursuit to envelop Scopus' rear after flight of his left-side mobile screen.

12. There is no assurance that Antiochus had mercenary spearmen to reinforce his left wing; and lacking that sort of like-armed help, his peltastai would probably have been forced to file only four-deep, leaving them highly vulnerable to being driven back in any extended action by some combination of spear-thrust and shield-push (othismos) from opposing Aetolian hoplites likely standing at thrice that depth.

13. Taylor (2013, 92), citing Jerome (*Commentary on Daniel*, 11.15).

14. Plutarch Vol. I *Philopoemen*, 488; Pausanius 8.49.7; Polyaenus 6.4.3.

15. Plutarch (Vol. I *Philopoemen*, 489) cites the adoption of pikes, but also notes introduction of "*heavy shields*" as opposed to the smaller/lighter pelte-like devices compatible with sarissai. It is his near contemporary Pausanius (8.50.1) who provides us with the clarification that these shields were "*Argive*" (i.e., hoplite aspides). Achaea had deployed a 2,000-man contingent of elite epilektos spearmen at Sellasia fif-

teen years earlier and that unit was apparently reinstituted at the time of Philopoemen's reforms. This is directly indicated by the use of Argive shields as well as strongly implied by execution of a type of envelopment maneuver in 207 never ascribed at any time to less flexible sarissaphoroi arrays (see below re: *Mantinea V*).

16. Livy 27.30.

17. Livy's report (*ibid.*) of Philip V later posting a 4,000-man strategia at Achaea reflects just such a combination of 3,000 phalangites and 1,000 hypaspists per a standard deployment practice dating from Philip II. In terms of overall manpower, Antigonus III had brought the same strength of peltastai (3,000) as proposed here to Sellasia in 222 as part of what was likely a very similar total muster in terms of native Macedonians.

18. Walbank (1967, 282–283) opines that Achaea in 207 could have fielded no more than 15,000–20,000 troops, about half of its documented capability some 40 years later when drawing from the entire Peloponnese. He estimates that 12,000–14,000 of these would have been League residents and the rest mercenaries and also notes that Sparta's army had been below 20,000 earlier under Cleomenes and only 18,000 later under Nabis. This supports it being around 20,000-strong here with mercenaries included.

19. Polybius 11.11; see Walbank (1967, 239, 285; 1970, 460–461) for evaluations of the thorakitai in support of their being "*neither light-armed proper nor phalangites*" and thus medium infantry between those types. Krason (2019), making the same observation discussed above regarding the "heavy shields" of Philopoemen's reforms being incompatible with sarissai, has proposed that these devices were employed by the thorakitai. He poses that such shields were akin to the wider of the two types associated much earlier with Demetrius Poliorcetes (see Chapter 1 note 63 re: *Corupedium*). Yet, that flat shield variety employed on some unknown scale (and perhaps only briefly) by Demetrius is quite distinct from the broader, concave Argive aspis that Pausanius says was adopted by Philopoemen. One would expect that, if thorakitai were essentially hoplites using a one-handed spear (albeit one longer than the classical dory to create a kind of hoplite/phalangite hybrid), then they would have served in the phalanx as heavy infantry. But their only well-detailed deployment was detached from the phalanx at a good distance outboard in a support role (see below re: *Mantinea V*). Finally, the way in which these men are consistently identified solely by the term "cuirass-wearers" implies that particular aspect was what distinguished them from otherwise similar troops (theurophoroi) lacking such costly gear.

20. Walbank cites past evaluations suggesting these Illyrians were "*auxiliaries*" (1967, 285) and points out (1970, 461) that Polybius classed them with the thorakitai, who were skirmishers, albeit heavier equipped than the norm.

21. Polybius (11.13.3) notes that Machanidas' mercenaries had an advantage in numbers as well as experience.

22. Walbank 1967, 286.

23. Even had Philopoemen followed Pyrrhus's lead by alternating his differently equipped heavy contingents, he would not have derived similar benefit. The advantage that tactic imparted lay in the ability of the spear-armed sections to press ahead under protection on either flank from near-impenetrable hedges of pikes; however, by taking position behind a frontal barrier here, Philopoemen had effectively denied any potential for such forward projection of force not only to his foes, but to his own men as well.

24. Pritchett (1969, 67) cites a study putting the still existing drainage pathway below Mantinea at 1,400m in length; however, Walbank (1967, 284–286) notes evidence within the described troop deployments that favors the field-work stretching between the temple of Poseidon farther east and a sinkhole (*katavothra*) some 2,000m to the west. (The valley containing Mantinea famously lacks external stream drainage and such sinkholes or "ponors" serve as its only outlets for rain and meltwater.) The natural drainage channel into the katavothra cited by Pritchett had therefore probably been artificially extended for military purposes.

25. There was a bridge on this western end of the depression (Polybius 11.17) that later allowed Achaean cavalrymen and skirmishers to cross over and exploit their mobility in pursuit.

26. The artillery comprised large cross-bows for which the Spartans had brought a supply of bolts (Polybius 11.11).

27. Plutarch's short account of Mantinea V (Vol I *Philopoemen*, 289–90) and the even briefer one of Pausanius (8.50.2) derive from Polybius' detailed description (11.11–18) with all in agreement on the severity of Sparta's casualties. They provide no numbers for the victors, but Achaean losses would have been almost entirely confined to mobile troops routed off Philopoemen's left wing and thus relatively modest.

28. Polybius 16.36.

29. See Walbank (1940, 317–323) for a chronologic review of the Second Macedonian War.

30. Livy provides the Macedonian manpower total and is our sole authority on this engagement (31.34.5–36.6).

31. Livy is our lone source on this action (31.35–36), reporting that the Macedonians lost 200 horsemen with another 100 being captured. These figures suggest that the battle was not all that large and might actually have been of higher cost to Sulpicius even though it was Philip who withdrew.

32. Livy (31.43) provides our only account of this action and the sparse data on its participants. It seems odd that the Dardanians would have been utterly bereft of light-armed men for a self-contained campaign and we might suspect that such troops were merely in short supply rather than completely absent.

33. See Kromayer and Veith (2016, 80, Sheet 9) for maps and a discussion of this terrain.

34. Livy 32.5.8–6.4, 6.10–12; Plutarch Vol. I *Flamininus*, 501–502.

35. Livy (32.5) records Philip's claim that his phalanx "*had stood firm*" at Aous River and withdrew voluntarily.

36. Polybius 18.20.

37. Plutarch Vol. I *Flamininus*, 504; this manpower total suggests that the consul had replaced losses at the Aous and since with troops either from Italy or drawn from the Roman fleet. Livy (33.3) describes the Aetolian footmen here as "*auxiliaries*," likely reflect-

ing both the difficulty of combining hoplite spearmen and legionaries in the same formation and depletion of Aetolia's pool of heavy infantry due to Scopus on a couple of recent occasions having drawn most of his nation's troops of that type into mercenary service overseas (see above re: *Mount Panium*).

38. Livy 33.3; the "regular" peltastai here were below their maximum of 3,000 due to 500 (two speirai), and perhaps as many as 1,500, being at Corinth and 500 in Asia (see below re: *Nemea R. and Alabanda*).

39. Polybius 18.25; as seen previously, the advantages that the first two closely ordered ranks of spearmen held in weapon-reach and strike-frequency could be devastating against a single rank of widely spaced swordsmen, with the peltastai here being further aided by the slope as well as pikes securing their flanks.

40. That the Macedonians did this without serious disruption to close order offers strong support for their use of a flexible array with interspersed arms. It not only compares favorably to the previous experience at Sellasia when employing such intermingling, but also contrasts with Pydna, where they became disordered while charging upslope without so mixing their array (see Chapter 8).

41. Polybius 18.25.

42. Polybius 18.27; Roman losses would largely have been among the heavy infantry battered downslope by Philip's right wing, with those legions' fatalities exceeding 5 percent and running perhaps as high as 10 percent.

43. Livy 33.14.

44. Mounted reinforcements were needed due to Androsthenes having taken Corinth's horsemen hostage. Livy describes the Acarnanians, Boeotians, and Thessalians as carrying small shields, possibly implying that all were light infantry; however, most contemporary Greek cavalry also bore shields in the Tarentine manner.

45. Livy 33.14; with no Roman witness present, this account must ultimately derive from a lost Grecian source.

46. Livy 33.15; this describes the Achaean phalanx as composed of "*cilpeati caetratique*" (shield-bearers and targeteers) indicating that both types of Grecian heavy infantry (pikemen and spearmen) were present.

47. It's likely that the Achaean League financially supported 2,000 hoplites and a like number of theurophoros javelinmen with body armor (thorakitai) as semi-professional epilektoi. A thousand of the spearmen and 800 of the javelineers were probably in Asia at this time (see below re: *Alabanda*), thus limiting the number of either of those elite troop types available here.

48. Livy (33.18) provides the only surviving account of Alabanda and the forces engaged there.

49. Livy's detailed strengths for the Rhodians establish this 3,800 total in contrast to his later claim that "*the numbers engaged ... were no more than 3,000 infantry on each side and about 100 horse.*" The simplest solution to this potential conflict is that his figure for foot-soldiers tallies only heavy infantry at 3,000 for Dinocrates and nearly as many for Rhodes. As at Nemea River, Livy's account here is second-hand or worse from an original Grecian source and that remove is evident in these kinds of seeming inconsistencies.

Chapter 8

1. Livy (34.25–28) is our sole source on this campaign and provides all relevant quotes herein.

2. At a strength of 5,000–6,000, Sparta's mercenaries would have been fewer than Flamininus' possible overall count of 7,400 auxiliaries but equal to (or even slightly more numerous than) their allied segment. It's notable that this strategy of largely passive defense on the tyrant's part was historically rooted in that Sparta's king Agesilaus had employed a somewhat similar approach in foiling a Theban incursion in 369 during a time of weakness after the Spartan defeat at Leuctra (Diodorus 14.65.4; Plutarch Vol. II *Agesilaus*, 63).

3. We are given no insight on just how Flamininus' subordinate Appius Claudius brought his rearguard about in this way that Livy's sources clearly found quite exceptional; however, it might well have been Achaea's epilektoi that provided the necessary expertise. Being the product of significant drilling at state expense, it's highly likely that forming either a thin barrier of hoplites from behind which the thorakitai could fire or an array interspersing those same armored/shielded javelineers and spearmen along a common front was a well-practiced routine they could rapidly execute on command.

4. A maximum for Nabis' mercenaries per his Eurotas River deployment would be around 6,000. Reduced by a third at Pleiae, he might now have had 4,000 at most. Notably, even if he did field some Spartan citizens within a larger force, they did not engage here, though they would certainly have suffered in the subsequent retreat.

5. Contingents available for this action were the Achaeans' phalangites, who were not at all fit for such a role, and their two types of epilektoi: hoplites and thorakitai. There are two indications that it was the heavy spearmen that carried out the surprise attack. First, Philopoemen would recall his ambushers from pursuit lest they have to traverse broken ground, something that was problematic for hoplites but not javelineers. And second, the same men said by Livy to have executed the ambush are named later as taking Nabis' campsite at the very time that more mobile troops pursued his rearguard. With pikemen inappropriate for either task and the thorakitai vastly better suited to give chase, it must have been hoplites at both camp and ambush.

6. Livy 35.29; Plutarch I *Philopoemen*, 493.

7. Livy 35.30.

8. Livy 35.5; 36.13, 50–51; the peltastai were one of two such Argyraspide chiliarchies and, combined with the Agrianians, formed a type of classic Macedonian "flying column" dating back to Alexander the Great's time.

9. None of our three sources on these events (Livy 36.15–19; Appian *Syrian Wars*, 17–20; and Plutarch Vol. I *Marcus Cato*, 466–468) record the disposition of the more than 20,000 Roman and allied troops previously on hand under Baebius, but it's possible that some (if not all) were incorporated into Glabrio's command to further fuel Antiochus' reluctance to openly engage. Reasonable doubts about the reliability of his Aetolian allies might well have been a factor in that calculation as well.

10. See Kromayer and Veith (2016, 82 and Sheet 9) and Bar-Kochva (1976, 158–162) on various aspects of the terrain relevant to this engagement.

11. Livy says that of the infantry brought from Asia only "*a very trifling number got off,*" while Appian claims its losses were 10,000 including prisoners. Grainger (2015, 169) opines that the idea only 500 of Antiochus' men escaped is "*ludicrous*" and "*it does not seem that his battle casualties were very numerous*"; and difficulties cited for the pursuit as well as proximity of a Seleucid refuge on Euboa appear to lend some weight to this criticism.

12. Sources on this action are Livy (37.20–21) and Appian (*Syrian Wars*, 27).

13. With the two Argyraspide strategiai still recovering from Thermopylae, the core of Seleucus' force probably consisted of draftees from the kingdom's pool of military settlements. Still, their organization would have mirrored that of those elite units (see notes in Chapter 3 on the Argyraspides re: *The Elephant Victory* and Chapter 4 on auxiliaries re: *Raphia*) save for lacking a fifth chiliarchy alternatively armed as peltastai.

14. The danger inherent in getting within the height-enhanced range of missilemen atop a barrier wall was widely known in this period, most famously through Xenophon's account (*Hellenica* 5.3.3–5) of the Spartan general Teleutias' defeat and death in 381 when he impulsively pursued some skirmishers too near Olynthus and his arguably much superior army was mortally disrupted by missile fire from its city wall. There were also many recorded examples of other commanders avoiding such dangerous approaches to manned barriers and thereby refusing to engage inferior opponents (Bardunias and Ray 2016, 54–55).

15. See Polybius (6.21.9–10) on these above-nominal musters. This unit size had precedent in the same 5,400-man infantry counts for the legions and alae deployed at Cannae in 216 (see Chapter 5).

16. Livy (26.39); the elephants would normally have had 800 out-runners (50 each) and 32 men aboard.

17. Hannibal was now serving Antiochus but being underutilized in naval operations. That would combine with an illness keeping Scipio Africanus out of the field to prevent the two old foes from again doing battle.

18. This was near the site of the battle of Corupedium in 281 (see Chapter 1). Kroymayer and Veith (2016, 82–83 and Sheet 9) provide an analysis of the relevant terrain and address questions raised by Delbruck regarding the validity of our extant sources on what took place here (see discussion below).

19. Livy (37.37–44) and Appian (*Syrian Wars* 30–36) provide the fullest accounts of Magnesia.

20. This assumes lateral spacing of 2/3m for heavy infantrymen entirely armed with pikes (including the Argyraspide peltastai in alternate defensive mode) and 15m for each elephant team.

21. Diodorus (19.43.4–5) describes this same Macedonian maneuver at Gabene in 317/16.

22. Appian cites 50,000 killed and captured with Justin (31.8.7) claiming 50,000 killed and 11,000 prisoners.

23. Delbruck 1990, 398–401.

24. Bar-Kochva 1976, 167; Evans (2011, 114) has expressed similar concerns on Livy's competence regarding such vital details of military affairs, noting that the historian "*does not have a fine appreciation of tactics or logistics when describing campaigns or battles.*"

25. Taylor 2013, 137–138.

26. Polybios 12.19.6.

27. See Asclepiodotus (10.17–22) for a description of how this maneuver might have been performed.

28. Both these maneuvers would have had precedents known to Antiochus. The shifting of elephants by Seleucid commanders onto flanking attacks dates back all the way to the very first at Ipsus in 301 (see Chapter 3 note 40 re: *The Elephant Victory*). And Alexander the Great had led a cavalry charge across Lydia's Granicus River in 334 to envelop an enemy left flank in near identical fashion (Arrian 1.14.6–7). The main difference here versus what Alexander faced was having to cross the river twice; however, this was quite doable during the dry winter season. It's possible that the small body of Roman horse reported next to the riverbank might actually have been posted across it to guard (inadequately as it turned out) against just such a threat. That makes rather more sense than Scipio needlessly invalidating his flank anchor by placing cavalry between his legionaries and the waterway. In the same vein, a pre-planned advance in force across the river better justifies Antiochus' significant deployment of mounted troops on his right than him doing so in the oddly prescient expectation that his foes would choose to carelessly provide the sort of anchor-busting opening that our surviving ancient accounts have him exploiting.

29. The attack of Eumenes' men would have sent both panicked beasts shorn of mahouts and chariots with wounded horses and whirling scythes to trample and cut swaths through the Seleucid ranks. As for the camels, they were long-notorious for being unendurable to horses (Xenophon *Cyropaedia* 6.2.18; 7.1.27).

30. Plutarch Vol. I *Philopoemen*, 496–497.

31. Livy (42.51) numbers Perseus' expanded host at 43,000, saying that "*since the army which Alexander the Great led into Asia, no Macedonian king had ever been at the head of so powerful a force.* In fact, that expedition into Persia was a bit smaller at only 40,000-strong (Diodorus 17.17.3–5), but adding troops that Alexander left behind in Greece would bring the overall strength of his military in line with Livy's claim.

32. Livy 37.52; it's notable that this strength is the same as for the legions sent to Greece in 169 (see below).

33. Livy 42.59; the range for allied cavalry reflects that 400 Gallic horsemen cited might have come with Eumenes.

34. The intimate mixing of foot-skirmishers within mounted deployments rather than as separate bodies had been recognized in the early 4th century as most effective for close support of cavalry (Xenophon *Hellenica* 7.5.23–24; Diodorus 15.85.4–5). This became standard procedure for horse-savvy armies (Spence 1993, 19–23, 30–32, 58–60) including those of Macedonia as documented by Arrian at Granicus River in 334 (1.16.1).

35. Livy (42.57–60) provides these details on dispositions and our only surviving engagement description.

36. These are Livy's figures. Plutarch (Vol. I *Aemilius Paulus*, 381) puts Roman losses higher at 2,500 dead and another 600 taken prisoner.

37. Livy (42.66) lists losses for Perseus of 300 skirmishers and 24 from his agema, saying that Crassus, having relieved his trapped legionaries, "*was content with that moderate share of success*" and "*led his troops to camp*." He follows this with a seemingly dismissive comment that "*there are writers who state that ... eight thousand of the enemy were killed ... and about two-thousand-eight hundred taken,*" also noting that the same sources report a loss of more than 4,300 for Crassus. As these Latin authors would seem unlikely to exaggerate their side's damage, we could be looking at either a mutually costly draw or a disguised Roman defeat; however, Livy's version with a smaller action looks to be the better-documented and more likely alternative.

38. Livy 43.3.

39. Livy 43.9–10.

40. Livy 43.12; judging from past overstrength deployments, this increased the number of velites, hastati, and princepes by 50 percent, allowing for their acies triplex to span 600m at 2m spacing. The legion's 600 triarii could stand bastion for that width using a single rank in 1m spacing. Other legions organized at this time show a range of manpower with those under the second consul having 5,200 foot and 300 horse and those sent to Spain at 5,000 foot plus 330 horse as well as an attached ala of only 4,000 foot and 300 horse. All were much like Paulus' units in being short on Latin cavalry as best illustrated by the aforementioned ala having only a third of the mounted strength common for its ilk. Simultaneous commitments in multiple theatres were clearly outstripping Rome's capacity to raise/outfit horsemen in contrast to a nearly unlimited ability to recruit much less costly foot-soldiers from its huge population base.

41. Livy 44.35.9–24.

42. Plutarch Vol. I *Aemilius Paulus*, 365–366.

43. Plutarch Vol. I *Aemilius Paulus*, 367–370; Livy 44.40–42; Polybius' lost work was a key common source. Other surviving information on Pydna is contained in Frontinus (2.3.20), Justin (33.1–2), and Zonaras (9.23).

44. Plutarch Vol. I *Aemilius Paulus*, 368; Livy makes these a select portion of the Leucaspide pikemen; however, Plutarch sets them apart as elites clearly distinguished from the less highly regarded Leucaspides on their left. It's notable that Livy fails to otherwise mention the royal foot-guards, while Plutarch's positioning echoes their most frequent post on the phalanx's extreme right. As to equipment, our sole illustrations (on the monument erected at Delphi to commemorate this battle) show what must be the royal peltastai with large, round shields that cover their entire torso suspended by the central porpax and rim antelabe of a hoplite aspis and having distinctive Macedonian blazons. These devices lack a recessed reinforcing rim per the classic version of the aspis, but the lateral view of one laying atop a fallen peltast shows it to be highly concave toward providing similar service at both a lower cost in material and lighter burden of weight (see discussion of these "neo-hoplite" shields in Chapter 4 note 48 re: *Sellasia*). All polearms shown are plied overhead with one hand and either a typical hoplite dory or shorter longche also suitable as a missile. This conflicts with Livy and Plutarch (possibly via Polybius) describing pikes held in two hands yet seems the higher probability view in being more surely derived from contemporary eyewitness testimony as well as highly likely to have been modeled upon captured gear.

45. Kromayer and Veith 2016, Plate 10; the entire battlefront is projected to have spanned some 3.7km.

46. Frontinus (2.3.20) confirms Paulus' use of an acies triplex against Perseus, who had "*drawn up a double phalanx of his own troops and placed them in the center of his forces.*" Phalanx depths were constructed in increments of four; therefore, a "double" allotment might have called for no more than eight men. That is highly speculative but logical in terms of spreading thinly in pursuit of the common tactical goal of precluding envelopment by matching or exceeding an opponent's heavy-armed front. Such eight-deep files are both explicitly recorded as well as reasonably inferred for many past Macedonian phalanxes under similar circumstances.

47. Scullard (1974,182) estimates that the Romans had at least 34 elephants in Greece two years earlier and it's likely most if not all were still available here. These would have had support from teams of light infantry out-runners up to 50-strong.

48. This assumes that a maniple represented a tenth of a legion. In the case of these 6,000-man legions, each maniple would have had 180 hastati with the same in princeps plus 60 triarii for a heavy-armed total of 420.

49. Livy (44.42) says that among the Romans "*there fell not more than one hundred, the greater part of whom were Pelignians.*" Based on the latter engaging with only 360 hastati and principes, the loss of more than 50 of them as implied here would produce a fatality rate approaching 15 percent to mirror those of a typical defeat in this era. That they took over half Rome's losses despite holding less than 3 percent of its active front indicates there was something much more going on than the mere excess of enthusiasm our sources describe. And the Marucinians standing next right, who were likewise "*hurled headlong back,*" could have suffered at a similar rate if their principes did not see action. The low Roman death toll elsewhere at Pydna combines with a fair probability that most of these loses came against spear-armed peltastai rather than sarissaphoroi to cast doubt on extravagant claims for the lethality of pikes in a few of our ancient sources. Sarissai simply couldn't have inflicted damage anything like that if such casualty reports are accurate. Though the defensive value of pikes is well documented, the indications of their seeming impotence on the attack against Roman swordsmen here and elsewhere suggest that the offensive value of sarissaphoroi outside the limited realm of phalanx versus phalanx warfare lay much more in their psychological impact than in the ability to inflict physical harm. This view is, of course, quite controversial as per the much higher opinion of the sarissa's versatility on offense argued by Matthew (2015, 167–236).

50. Perseus was well aware of the valuable increase in flexibility that interspersing spearmen among his pike units would lend on sloped and/or broken ground from the experiences of his grandfather at Sellasia and (most probably) his father as well at Cynoscephalae. His failure to deploy that way here is therefore less

likely to have stemmed from ignorance than out of a shortage of both time and adequately drilled troops. He must have maximized his capacity to defend the narrow coastal plain below Pydna by outfitting the peltast regulars with pikes and would have needed a fair amount of time for rearming them to have enough spearmen to compose a properly intermixed array. And more time yet would have been required to then compose a complex formation of a type to which his under-drilled men (see note 51 below) had no field or even exercise exposure. Whether or not Perseus' focus was diverted by feints as at the Elpeus, the threat that developed uphill to the west therefore seems to have come as enough of a surprise to have deprived him of adequate time for an optimum response.

51. Livy (42.52) had noted in regard to the expanded military that Perseus created upon taking the throne that the Macedonians themselves, though professionals "*in continual practice of military service … performed some few movements, but not the regular course of exercise.*"

52. Tarn (1938, 129–182) has proposed that this episode followed upon a campaign by Demetrius I in India; however, it is now generally accepted that Bactria's Indian conquests came later (c.150) under Demetrius II (Stoneman 2019, 375–404). Nonetheless, Tarn's conjecture that Antiochus IV's triumphal parade at Daphne in spring 166 (Athenaeus 5.194–195; Polybius fragment 30) could have been in celebration of his subordinate Eucratides' military victory in Bactria remains a strong possibility and forms the basis for the reconstruction proposed here.

53. See Chapter 4 re: *Babylonian Apollonia*.

54. See Chapter 7 re: *Arios R.*

55. This was under Seleucus I (then governor of the Upper Satrapies) at Ipsus back in 301 (Diodorus 20.113.4).

56. Sekunda 2006, 115.

57. Sekunda 2006, 98–100; Bar-Kochva 1976, 180–181.

58. Sekunda (2006, 21–83) summarizes the various data to conclude that "*the maniple was introduced into the Ptolemaic infantry … certainly before 163/62 …* [and presumably] *Roman tactics and equipment were adopted on this same occasion as well as Roman organization.*"

59. Sekunda 2006, 176–178.

60. An engraved 2nd century belt from Pergamum shows what might be a pikeman fighting in line alongside an apparent neo-hoplite spearman (Sekunda 2012, 5).

61. Morales 2013; Tarn 1938, 309–310.

Appendix 1

1. Kromayer and Veith 2016, map Sheet 1 (post-p. 54).

2. Diodorus claimed that there were 24,000 in the Roman force, perhaps mistakenly based on the presence of an army of four legions, which did not exist in 390 (his contemporary, Dionysius of Halicarnassus, made this same anachronistic error in a passing reference to Allia). A force of that size does not appear to have come into being until later in the 4th century and the Roman army at Allia likely had only two legions of 3,000 hoplites each with modest numbers of attached auxiliaries and available age-reservists. Contributions from the reported muster of untrained men can only be speculated upon yet seem probable to have been much smaller than what would be needed to produce a host to match Diodorus' claim; most likely, these were not combat effective and had little or no impact on the battle beyond adding to those that fled in panic.

3. There were several spacing options here, but the cavalry probably stood four-deep at half the practical maximum (Polybios 12.18.2) across 300m at 2m/file with the skirmishers covering 300m at 3m per file of six.

4. Livy said Rome's commanders sought to avoid being flanked by stretching their line "*so thin that the center was weakened*" and that it "*hardly held*" in the subsequent action.

5. Beresford Ellis (1998, p. 10) has opined that even the low end of the likely range suggested would at 12,000 be quite a large deployment for a single Celtic tribe.

6. Livy described the Gauls as having "*a natural turn for* [instilling in their foes] *causeless confusion*," and at Allia "*their harsh music and discordant clamors filled all places with a horrible din.*"

7. Kroymayer and Veith 2016, 50–51, map Sheet 1 (post-p. 54).

8. Cicero *On Duty* 3.109; Cowan 2009, 49; Fields 2011, 56.

Note 9: Ancient estimates of Samnite manpower in this period indicate an upside potential of 70,000–80,000 in infantry and 7,000–8,000 in cavalry (Cowan 2009, 33); and even though these numbers are likely much exaggerated, a gathering for the sort of pre-planned ambush sprung at Caudium could easily have run to 20,000 or more combatants. The Samnite foot would have exclusively been scutum-bearing spearmen with secondary javelins, though the level of armor for any one of them undoubtedly varied with personal wealth.

Bibliography

Ancient References

Aelian: *The Tactics of Aelian, Revised,* translated and edited by Christopher Matthew. Barnsley: Pen & Sword, 2012.

Aeneas: *Aeneas Tacticus, Asclepiodotus, Onasander, Loeb Classical Library,* translated by Illinois Greek Club., Cambridge: Harvard Univ. Press, 1928.

Appian: *Appian's Roman History, Loeb Classical Library.* Cambridge: Harvard Univ. Press, various translators and dates; *Complete Works of Appian.* Hastings: Delphi Classics, 2017.

Arrian: *The Landmark Arrian: The Campaigns of Alexander,* translated by Pamela Mensch. New York: Pantheon Books, 2010.

Asclepiodotus: See **Aeneas** above.

Athenaeus: *The Complete Works of Athenaeus.* Hastings: Delphi Classics, 2017.

Cicero: *The Complete Works of Cicero.* Hastings: Delphi Classics, 2014.

Curtius: *Quintus Curtius Rufus: The History of Alexander,* translated by John Yardley. London: Penguin, 1984.

Dio: *Dio's Roman History, Loeb Classical Library.* Cambridge: Harvard Univ. Press, various translators and dates; see also **Zonaras** below.

Diodorus: *Diodorus Siculus, Loeb Classical Library.* Cambridge: Harvard Univ. Press, various translators and dates.

Diogenes: *The Complete Works of Diogenes Laertius.* Hastings: Delphi Classics, 2015.

Dionysius: *Dionysius of Halicarnassus, Roman Antiquities, Loeb Classical Library.* Cambridge: Harvard Univ. Press, various translators and dates; *The Complete Works of Dionysius of Halicarnassus.* Hastings: Delphi Classics, 2017.

Eutropius: *Eutropius, Abridgement of Roman History.* translated by the Reverend John Selby Watson, London: George Bell and Sons, 1886.

Florus: *Florus, Epitome of Roman History, Loeb Classical Library.* translated by Edward Seymour Forster. Cambridge: Harvard Univ. Press, 1984.

Frontinus: *Frontinus, Stratagems, Aqueducts of Rome.* Loeb Classical Library, translated by Charles E. Bennett. Cambridge: Harvard Univ. Press, 1925.

Herodotus: *The Landmark Herodotus: The Histories.* translated by Andrea I. Purvis. New York: Pantheon Books, 2007.

Justin: *Justin, Epitome of the Philippic History of Pompeius Trogus.* translated by J.C. Yardley with and introduction and explanatory notes by R. Develin. Atlanta: Scholars Press, 1994.

Livy: *Livy—Books I-XLV,* translated by Aubrey De Selincourt (I-V, XXI-XXX), Betty Radice (VI-X), and Henry Bettenson (XXXI-XLV). New York: Penguin Books, 1960-1982; *The History of Rome (Books I-VIII)* by Titus Livius, translated by D. Spillan. Digireads.com Publishing, 2009; *Livy, Rome's Mediterranean Empire, Books Forty-One to Forty-Five and the Periochae,* translated with an introduction and notes by Jane D. Chaplin. Oxford: Oxford Univ. Press, 2007; *The Complete Works of Livy.* Hastings: Delphi Classics, 2014.

Lucian: *The Complete Works of Lucian of Samosata.* Hastings: Delphi Classics, 2016.

Nepos: *Cornelius Nepos, Loeb Classical Library,* translated by J.C. Rolfe. Cambridge: Harvard Univ. Press, 1984.

Onasander: See **Aeneas** above.

Orosius: *Orosius, History Against the Pagans; The Apology of Paulus Orosius,* translated with introduction and notes by Irving Woodworth Raymond. New York: Columbia Univ. Press, 1936.

Pausanius: *Pausanius, Description of Greece, Loeb Classical Library.* Cambridge: Harvard Univ. Press, various translators and dates; *The Complete Works of Pausanius.* Hastings: Delphi Classics, 2014.

Plutarch: *Plutarch's Lives,* Vol. I/II: The Dryden Translation with Preface by Arthur Hugh Clough. New York: Random House, 2001.

Polyaenus: *Polyaenus, Stratagems of War,* Vol. I/II (Books I-VII, Excerpts and Leo the Emperor), edited and translated by Peter Krentz and Everett L. Wheeler. Chicago: Ares, 1994.

Polybius: *Polybus: The Histories, Loeb Classical Library.* Cambridge: Harvard Univ. Press, various translators and dates; *The Complete Works of Polybius,* Hastings: Delphi Classics, 2014.

Silius: *Silius Italicus, Punica, Loeb Classical Library.* translated by J.D. Duff, Cambridge: Harvard Univ. Press, 1934.

Strabo: *Geography, Loeb Classical Library.* Cambridge: Harvard Univ. Press, various translators and dates; *The Complete Works of Strabo.* Hastings: Delphi Classics, 2016.

Thucydides: *The Landmark Thucydides: A Comprehensive Guide to the Peloponnesian War, edited by Robert B. Strassler, New York: The Free Press, 1996.

Xenophon: *Xenophon Hellenica, Loeb Classical Library*. Cambridge: Harvard Univ. Press, 1918–1921; *The Landmark Xenophon's Hellenika*, translation by John Marincola, New York: Pantheon Books, 2009.

Zonaras: *Dio's Rome, Gleanings from the Lost Books. I. The Epitome of Books 1–21 Arranged by Ioannes Zonaras, Soldier and Secretary in the Monastary of Mt. Athos, About 1130 A.D. II. Fragments of Books, 22–35, V. 2. Extant Books 36–44 (B.C. 69–44), V. 3 Exta*. Troy: Pafraets Book Company, 1908.

Modern References

Anderson, E.B. 2017:"Renowned Horsemen: Italic Cavalry During the Roman Conquests," in *Ancient Warfare*, Vol. XI, Issue 2, p. 14–18.

Anderson, J.K. 1967: "Philopoemen's Reform of the Achaean Army," in *Classical Philology*, Vol. 62, No. 2, p. 104–106.

Anderson, J.K. 1976: "Shields of Eight Palms Width," in *California Studies in Classical Antiquity*, Vol. 9, p. 1–6.

Armstrong, D. 1966: *The Reluctant Warriors: The Decline and Fall of the Carthaginian Empire*. New York: Thomas Y. Crowell Co.

Armstrong, J. 2016a: *Early Roman Warfare, from the Regal Period to the First Punic War*. Barnsley: Pen & Sword Military.

Armstrong, J. 2016b: *War and Society in Early Rome, from Warlords to Generals*. Cambridge: Cambridge Univ. Press.

Armstrong, J. 2016c: "The Ties That Bind: Military Cohesion in Archaic Rome," in *Circum Mare: Themes in Ancient Warfare* (Mnemosyne Supplements, History and Archaeology of Classical Antiquity, Vol. 388), J. Armstrong (ed.), Boston: Brill, p. 101–119.

Austin, M. (ed.) 2006: *The Hellenistic World from Alexander to the Roman Conquest: A Selection of Ancient Sources in Translation, Second Augmented Edition*. Cambridge: Cambridge Univ. Press.

Bagnall, N. 1990: *The Punic Wars: Rome, Carthage, and the Struggle for the Mediterranean*. London: Random House.

Bagnall, R.S., and P. Derow. 1981: *The Hellenistic Period: Historical Sources in Translation*. Oxford: Blackwell.

Bahmanyar, M. 2016: *Zama 202 BC: Scipio Crushes Hannibal in North Africa*. London: Osprey.

Bardunias, P.M. 2009: "Mercenary Rescues Carthage: The Battle of Bagradas River," in *Ancient Warfare*, Vol. III, Issue 1, p. 29–35.

Bardunias, P.M. 2018: "Shifting the Shield Wall: The Greek Phalanx in Context," in *Ancient Warfare*, Vol. XI, Issue 6, p. 36–42.

Bardunias, P.M., and F.E. Ray 2016: *Hoplites at War: A Comprehensive Analysis of Heavy Infantry Combat in the Greek World, 750–100 BCE*. Jefferson: McFarland.

Bar-Kochva, B. 1976: *The Seleucid Army: Organization and Tactics in the Great Campaigns*. Cambridge: Cambridge Univ. Press.

Bath, T. 1981: *Hannibal's Campaigns: The Story of One of the Greatest Military Commanders of All Time*. New York: Barnes & Noble, 1992.

Beazley, M. 2013: "Rome's Rise to Dominance: The First Samite War," in *Ancient Warfare*, Vol. 7, No. 3, p. 33.

Beek, A. 2017: "Developing the Legion: Sword, Spear, or Javelin?," in *Ancient Warfare*, Vol. 11, No. 2, p. 35–43.

Beer, G. De. 1956: *Alps and Elephants: Hannibal's March*. New York:.E.P. Dutton and Co.

Bennett, B., and M. Roberts 2008: *The Wars of Alexander's Successors 323–281, Volume I: Commanders and Campaigns*. Barnsley: Pen & Sword.

Bennett, B., and M. Roberts 2009: *The Wars of Alexander's Successors 323–281, Volume II: Battles and Tactics*. Barnsley: Pen & Sword.

Billows, R.A. 1997: *Antigonos the One-Eyed and the Creation of the Hellenistic State*. Berkeley: Univ. California Press.

Bingen, J. 2007: *Hellenistic Egypt: Monarchy, Society, Economy, Culture*. Berkeley: Univ. California Press.

Blumberg, A. 2015: "Rome's Disastrous North African Interlude: The Battle of Tunis, 255 BC," in *Ancient Warfare*, Vol. 9, No. 4, p. 47–51.

Bosworth, A.B. 2010: "The Argeads and the Phalanx," in E. Carney and D. Ogden, eds, *Philip II and Alexander the Great: Father and Son, Lives and After Lives*. Oxford: Oxford Univ. Press, 91–102.

Bradford, A.S. 2001: *With Arrow, Sword, and Spear: A History of Warfare in the Ancient World*. New York: Barnes & Noble, 2007.

Bradford, E. 1981: *Hannibal*. New York: Dorset Press.

Campbell, D. 2014: "How Long Was the Macedonian Sarissa?" in *Ancient Warfare*, Vol. 8, No. 3, p. 48–52.

Canales, C. 2005: *Hannibal's Army*. Madrid: Andrea Press.

Carey, B.T. 2008: *Hannibal's Last Battle: Zama and the Fall of Carthage*. Barnsley: Pen & Sword.

Caven, B. 1980: *The Punic Wars*. New York: Barnes & Noble.

Champion, J. 2009: *Pyrrhus of Epirus*. Barnsley: Pen & Sword.

Chrystal, P. 2015a: *The Wars and Battles of the Roman Republic, 753 BC –100 BC: The Bloody Road to Empire*. Oxford: Fonthill Media.

Chrystal, P. 2015b: *Roman Military Disasters: Dark Days and Lost Legions*. P Barnsley: Pen & Sword.

Connolly, P. 2000: "Experiments with the Sarissa—The Macedonian Pike and Cavalry Lance—A Functional View," in *Journal of Roman Military Equipment Studies* 11, 103–112.

Cook, S.A., F.E. Adcock, and M.F. Charlesworth (eds.) 1930: *The Cambridge Ancient History, Volume VIII: Rome and the Mediterranean 218–133 B.C.* Cambridge: Cambridge Univ. Press.

Cornell, T.J. 1995: *The Beginnings of Rome: Italy and Rome from the Bronze Age to the Punic Wars (c.1000–264 BC)*. London: Routledge.

Cowan, R. 2007: *For the Glory of Rome: A History of Warriors and Warfare*. Greenhill, London.
Cowan, R. 2008: "Grinding Pyrrhus Down: How Romans Recovered from Defeat," in *Ancient Warfare*, Vol. 2, No. 2.
Cowan, R. 2009: *Roman Conquests: Italy*. Barnsley: Pen & Sword.
Daly, G. 2002: Cannae, *The Experience of Battle in the Second Punic War*. London: Routledge.
Dean, S.E. 2012: "How Brave a Field of War: Pyrrhus' Campaigns in Sicily," in *Ancient Warfare*, Vol. 6, No. 4, p. 34–38.
Dean, S.E. 2014: "Pilum Vs Pike: Equipment of the Roman Macedonian Wars," in *Ancient Warfare*, Vol. 8, No. 6, p. 37–42.
Dean, S.E. 2015: "Besiegers Besieged: Agrigentum, 262–281 BC," in *Ancient Warfare*, Vol. 9, No. 4, p. 27–31.
Dodge, T.A. 1891: *Hannibal: A History of the Art of War Among the Carthaginians and Romans Down to the Battle of Pydna, 168 B.C., with a Detailed Account of the Second Punic War*. New York: Barnes & Noble.
Dougherty, M.J., M. Haskew, P.G. Jestice, and R.S. Rice 2008: *Battles of the Bible 1400 BC—AD 73: From Ai to Masada*. London: Amber Books.
Ducrey, P. 1985: *Warfare in Ancient Greece*. New York: Schocken Books.
Ellis, P.B. 1997: *Celt and Greek: Celts in the Hellenic World*. London: Constable.
Ellis, P.B. 1998: *Celt and Roman: The Celts of Italy*. New York: St. Martin's Press.
Esposito, G. 2014: "The Army of Antiochus IV: Organization and Structure of the Late Seleucid Army," in *Ancient Warfare*, Vol. 8, No. 4, p. 38–43.
Evans, R. 2011: *Roman Conquests: Asia Minor, Syria, and Armenia*. Barnsley: Pen & Sword.
Evers, R. 2012: "A One-Man Army: The Forces of Epirus," in *Ancient Warfare*, Vol. 6, No. 4, p. 22–27.
Fields, N. 2007: *The Roman Army of the Punic Wars, 264–14 BC*. London: Osprey.
Fields, N. 2008: *Tarentine Horseman of Magna Graecia, 430–190 BC*. London: Osprey.
Fields, N. 2010a: *Carthaginian Warrior, 264–146 BC*. London: Osprey.
Fields, N. 2010b: *Roman Conquests: North Africa*. Barnsley: Pen & Sword.
Fields, N. 2011: *Early Roman Warrior, 753–321 BC*. London: Osprey.
Fields, N. 2012: *Roman Republican Legionary, 298–105 BC*. London: Osprey.
Fields, N. 2017: *Lake Trasimene, 217 BC*. London: Osprey.
Fischer-Bovet, C. 2014: *Army and Society in Ptolemaic Egypt*. Cambridge: Cambridge Univ. Press.
Gabriel, R.A. 2011: *Hannibal: The Military Biography of Rome's Greatest Enemy*. Washington, D.C.: Potomac Books.
Garoufalias, P. 1979: *Pyrrhus, King of Epirus*. London: Stacy International.
Goldsworthy, A. 2001: *Cannae: Hannibal's Greatest Victory*. London: Cassell.
Goldsworthy, A. 2003: *The Fall of Carthage: The Punic Wars 265–146 BC*. London: Cassell.

Grainger, J.D. 1990: *Seleukos Nikator: Constructing a Hellenistic Kingdom*. Oxon: Routledge.
Grainger, J.D. 2011: *Hellenistic and Roman Naval Wars, 336–31 BC*. Barnsley: Pen & Sword Maritime.
Grainger, J.D. 2012: *The Wars of the Maccabees*. Barnsley: Pen & Sword.
Grainger, J.D. 2014: *The Rise of the Seleucid Empire, 323–223 BC*. Barnsley: Pen & Sword.
Grainger, J.D. 2015a: *The Seleukid Empire of Antiochus III, 223–187 BC*. Barnsley: Pen & Sword.
Grainger, J.D. 2015b: *The Fall of the Seleucid Empire, 187–75 BC*. Barnsley: Pen & Sword.
Green, P. 1990: *Alexander to Actium: The Historical Evolution of the Hellenistic Age*. Berkeley: Univ. of California Press.
Griffith, G.T. 1935: *The Mercenaries of the Hellenistic World*. Chicago: Ares.
Hammond, N.G.L. 1984: "The Battle of Pydna," in *Journal of Hellenic Studies*, Vol. 104, p. 31–47.
Hammond, N.G.L. 1988: "The Campaign and the Battle of Cynoscephalae in 197 BC," in *Journal of Hellenic Studies* Vol. 108, p. 60–82.
Harris, W.V. 1979: *War and Imperialism in Republican Rome, 327–70 BC*. Oxford: Clarendon Press.
Hart, B.H. Lidell 1926: *Scipio Africanus: Greater than Napoleon*. Cambridge: Da Capo Press, 1994.
Healy, M. 1994: *Cannae 216 BC: Hannibal Smashes Rome's Army*. London: Osprey.
Heckel, W. 2002: *The Wars of Alexander the Great*. Oxford: Osprey.
Heckel, W. 2009: *Who's Who in the Age of Alexander the Great*. Malden: Wiley-Blackwell.
Heckel, W. 2013: "The Three Thousand: Alexander's Infantry Guard," in *The Oxford Handbook of Warfare in the Classical World*. p. 162–178, Oxford: Oxford Univ. Press.
Heckel, W., and R. Jones 2006: *Macedonian Warrior: Alexander's Elite Infantryman*. Oxford: Osprey.
Heckel, W., C. Willekes, and G.C. Wrightson 2010: "Scythed Chariots at Gaugamela: A Case Study," in E. Carney and D. Ogden (ed.) *Philip II and Alexander the Great: Father and Son, Lives and Afterlives*. Oxford: Oxford Univ. Press.
Herzog, C., and M. Gichon 2002: *Battles of the Bible*. London: Greenhill.
Hillen, A. 2017: "Divisions Among the Greeks of Italy: Under Pressure," in *Ancient Warfare*, Vol. XI, Issue 2, p. 19–23.
Holbl, G. 2001: *A History of the Ptolemaic Empire*. Oxon: Routledge.
Holt, F.L. 2012: *Lost World of the Golden King: In Search of Ancient Afghanistan*. Berkeley: Univ. California Press.
Hornblower, S. and A. Spawforth 1996: *The Oxford Classical Dictionary*. Oxford: Oxford Univ. Press.
Hoyos, D. 2015: *Mastering the West: Rome and Carthage at War*. Oxford: Oxford Univ. Press.
James, S. 2011: *Rome & the Sword: How Warriors & Weapons Shaped Roman History*. London: Thames & Hudson.
Jarva, E. 2013: "Arms and Armor, Part I: Arming Greeks for Battle," in *The Oxford Handbook of*

Warfare in the Classical World, p. 395–418, Oxford: Oxford Univ. Press.

Juhel, P., and N.V. Sekunda 2009: "The Agema and 'the Other Peltasts' in the Late Antigonid Army, and in the Drama/Cassandreia Conscription *Diagramma*," in *Zeitschrift fur Papyrologie und Epigrafik*, Bd 170.

Keppie, L. 1984: *The Making of the Roman Army: From Republic to Empire*. New York: Barnes & Noble.

Krason, M. 2019: "Achaean Armored Fist: Philopoemen's Heavy Hoplites," in *Ancient Warfare*, Vol. XII, Issue 6, p. 44–47.

Kromayer, J., and G. Veith 2016: *The Atlas of Ancient Battlefields*. Oswiecim: Napoleon V.

Lancel, S. 1995: *Carthage: A History*. Oxford: Blackwell.

Lazenby, J.F. 1996: *The First Punic War: A Military History*. Stanford: Stanford Univ. Press.

Lazenby, J.F. 1998: *Hannibal's War: A Military History of the Second Punic War*. Norman: Univ. Oklahoma Press.

Lobacz, M. 2010: "At the Edge of Hellenism: Armies of the Greeks in Bactria and India," in *Ancient Warfare*, Vol. 4, No. 6, p. 20–24.

Matthew, C. 2015: *An Invincible Beast: Understanding the Hellenistic Pike-Phalanx at War*. Barnsley: Pen & Sword.

Mayor, A. 2010: *The Poison King: The Life and Legend of Mithradates, Rome's Deadliest Enemy*. Princeton: Princeton Univ. Press.

McDonnell-Staff, P. 2008: "Sparta's Last Hurrah: The Battle of Sellasia (222 BC)," in *Ancient Warfare*, Vol. 2, No. 2, p. 23–25.

McDonnell-Staff, P. 2010: "Macedon's Last Hurrah: The Third Macedonian War and Pydna," in *Ancient Warfare*, Vol. 4, No. 6, p. 33–37.

McDonnell-Staff, P. 2011: "Hypaspists to Peltasts: The Elite Guard Infantry of the Antigonid Macedonian Army," in *Ancient Warfare*, Vol. 5, No. 6, p. 20–25.

Michalopoulos, M. 2016: *In the Name of Lykourgos: The Rise and Fall of the Spartan Revolutionary Movement 243-146 BC*. Barnsley: Pen & Sword.

Miles R. 2010: *Carthage Must Be Destroyed: The Rise and Fall of an Ancient Civilization*. New York: Penguin.

Millet, P.C. 2013: "Writers on War, Part I, Greece: Winning Ways in Warfare," in *The Oxford Handbook of Warfare in the Classical World*, p. 46–73, Oxford: Oxford Univ. Press.

Montagu, J.D. 2000: *Battles of the Greek & Roman Worlds: A Chronological Compendium of 667 Battles to 31BC from the Historians of the Ancient World*. Mechanicsburg: Stackpole Books.

Morgan, J.D. 1981: "Sellasia Revisited," in *American Journal of Archaeology*, Vol. 85, No. 3.

Muir, R. 1998: *Tactics and the Experience of Battle in the Age of Napoleon*. New Haven: Yale Univ. Press.

Munn, M.H. 1993: *The Defense of Attica: The Dema Wall and the Boiotian War of 378-375 B.C.* Berkeley: Univ. California Press.

Navarro, J.M. de 1928: "The Coming of the Celts," in *The Cambridge Ancient History, Volume VII: The Hellenistic Monarchies and the Rise of Rome*; S.A. Cook, F.E. Adcock, and M.P. Charlesworth, eds; Chapter II, p. 41–248. Cambridge: Cambridge Univ. Press.

Nossov, K. 2008: *War Elephants*. Oxford: Osprey.

Park, M. 2010a: "Sparta, Macedon and Achaea: The Politics and Battle of Sellasia," in *Sparta*, Vol. 6, No. 1, p. 12–20.

Park, M. 2010b: "Climax of the Syrian Wars: The Battle of Raphia, 217 BC," in *Ancient Warfare*, Vol. 4, No. 6, p. 25–32.

Park, M. 2014: "The Dogs' Heads: The Battle of Cynoscephalae, 197 BC," in *Ancient Warfare*, Vol. 8, No. 6, p. 25–32.

Penrose, J. (ed.) 2005: *Rome and Her Enemies: An Empire Created and Destroyed by War*. London: Osprey.

Pietrykowski, J. 2009: *Great Battles of the Hellenistic World*. Barnsley: Pen & Sword Military.

Prevas, J. 1998: *Hannibal Crosses the Alps: The Invasion of Italy and the Punic Wars*. Cambridge: Da Capo Press.

Pritchett, W.K. 1965: *Studies in Ancient Greek Topography, Part I*. Berkeley: Univ. California Press.

Rawlings, L. 2016: "The Significance of Insignificant Engagements: Irregular Warfare during the Punic Wars," in *Circum Mare: Themes in Ancient Warfare* (Mnemosyne Supplements, History and Archaeology of Classical Antiquity, Vol. 388), J. Armstrong (ed.), Boston: Brill, p. 204–236.

Rawlinson, H.G. 1889: *History of Phoenicia*. First Rate Publishers.

Rawlinson, H.G. 1912: *Bactria: The History of a Forgotten Empire*. Yardley: Westholme, 2013.

Ray, F.E. 2009: *Land Battles in 5th Century B.C. Greece: A History and Analysis of 173 Engagements*. Jefferson, NC: McFarland.

Ray, F.E. 2012: *Greek and Macedonian Land Battles of the 4th Century B.C.: A History and Analysis of 187 Engagements*. Jefferson, NC: McFarland.

Ray, F.E. 2013: "Revolutionary Episodes at Syracuse in the 5th Century BCE: Some Political and Military Aspects of Ancient Greek Insurgency," in *The Ancient World*, 45:1, 30–43.

Rees, O. 2014: "Philopoemen, Last of the Greeks," in *Ancient Warfare*, Vol. 8, No. 6, p. 20–24.

Roberts, M., and B. Bennett 2012: *Twilight of the Hellenistic World*. Barnsley: Sword & Pen.

Rodgers, W.L. 1937: *Greek and Roman Naval Warfare: A Study of Strategy, Tactics and Ship Design from Salamis (480 B.C.) to Actium (31 B.C.)*. Annapolis: Naval Institute Press.

Roisman, J., and I. Worthington 2010: *A Companion to Ancient Macedonia*. Oxford: Blackwell.

Roth, J.P. 2009: *Roman Warfare*. Cambridge: Cambridge Univ. Press.

Rothenberg, G.E. 1978: *The Art of Warfare in the Age of Napoleon*. Bloomington: Indiana Univ. Press.

Sabin, P. 2007: *Lost Battles: Reconstructing the Great Clashes of the Ancient World*. New York: Hambeldon Continuum.

Salimbeti, A., and R. D'Amato 2014: *The Carthaginians, 6th-2nd Century BC*. Oxford: Osprey.

Schneider, R. 1893: *Legion und Phalanx: Taktische Untersuchungen*. Berlin: Weidmann.

Scholten, J.B. 2000: *The Politics of Plunder: Aitolians and Their Koinon in the Early Hellenistic Era. 279–217 B.C.*, Berkeley: Univ. California Press.

Scullard, H.H. 1935: *A History of the Roman World, 753 to 146 BC*. London: Routledge, 1980.

Scullard, H.H. 1967: *The Etruscan Cities and Rome*. Ithaca: Cornell Univ. Press.

Scullard, H.H. 1970: *Scipio Africanus: Soldier and Politician*. Ithaca: Cornell Univ. Press.

Scullard, H.H. 1974: *The Elephant in the Greek and Roman World*. Ithaca: Cornell Univ. Press.

Sekunda, N. 1995: *The Ptolemaic Army, Under Ptolemy VI Philometor*. Stockport: Montvert.

Sekunda, N. 1996: *Republican Roman Army, 200–104 BC*. London: Osprey.

Sekunda, N. 2006: *Hellenistic Infantry Reform in the 160's BC*. Gdansk: Gdansk Univ.

Sekunda, N. 2012: *Macedonian Armies After Alexander, 323–168 BC*. Oxford: Osprey.

Sekunda, N. 2013: *The Antigonid Army*. Gdansk: Gdansk Univ.

Sekunda, N. 2019: "The Army of Pyrrhus: The Deployment at Asculum," in *Ancient Warfare*, Vol. XIII, Issue 1, p. 40–47.

Sekunda, N., and S. Chow 1992: *The Persian Army, 560–330 BC*. Oxford: Osprey.

Sekunda, N., and S. Northwood 1995: *Early Roman Armies*. London: Osprey.

Skarmintzos, S. 2008: "Phalanx Versus Legion: Greco-Roman Conflict in the Hellenistic Era," in *Ancient Warfare*, Vol. 2, No. 2, p. 30–34.

Smith, A. IV 2011: "The Anatomy of Battle: Testing Polybius' Formations," in *Ancient Warfare*, Vol. V, Issue 5.

Snodgrass, A.M. 1967: *Arms and Armour of the Greeks*. Ithaca: Cornell Univ. Press.

Soren, D., A. Ben Abed Ben Khader, and H. Slim 1990: Carthage, *Uncovering the Mysteries and Spender of Ancient Tunisia*. New York: Simon & Schuster.

Southern, P. 2014: *The Roman Army: A History 753 BC–AD 476*. Stroud: Amberly.

Stephenson, I. 2011: *Hannibal's Army*. Brinscombe Port Stroud: The History Press.

Stoneman, R. 2019: *The Greek Experience of India: From Alexander to the Indo-Greeks*. Princeton: Princeton Univ. Press.

Strauss, B. 2012: *Masters of Command: Alexander, Hannibal, Caesar, and the Genius of Leadership*. New York: Simon & Schuster.

Tarn, W.W. 1913: *Antigonos Gonatas*. Oxford: Clarendon Press.

Tarn, W.W. 1930: *Hellenistic Military and Navel Developments*. Chicago: Ares.

Tarn, W.W. 1951: *The Greeks in Bactria and India*. Cambridge: Cambridge Univ. Press.

Taylor, D. 2017: *Roman Republic at War: A Compendium of Battles from 502 to 31 B.C.* Barnsley: Pen & Sword.

Taylor, M.J. 2012: "The Rise of a Superpower: The Roman Army in the Age of Pyrrhus," in *Ancient Warfare*, No. 6, Vol. 4, p. 24–29.

Taylor, M.J. 2013: *Antiochus the Great*. Barnsley: Pen & Sword.

Taylor, M.J. 2014a: "Visual Evidence for Roman Infantry Tactics," in *Memoirs of the American Military Academy in Rome (MAAR)*, 59/60, p. 103–120.

Taylor, M.J. 2014b: "Set in Stone: The Pydna Monument at Delphi," in *Ancient Warfare*, Vol. 8, No. 6, p. 10–12.

Tomlinson, R.A. 1972: *Argos and the Argolid: From the End of the Bronze Age to the Roman Occupation*. Ithaca: Cornell Univ. Press.

Toynbee, A. 1969: *Some Problems of Greek History*. London: Oxford Univ. Press.

Trevino, R. 1986: *Rome's Enemies 4: Spanish Armies*. London: Osprey.

Venning, T. 2015: *A Chronology of Ancient Greece*. Barnsley: Pen & Sword Military.

Vries, E. de. 2013: "The Roman Army Defeated: Livy and the Claudine Forks," in *Ancient Warfare*, Vol. 7, No. 3, p. 34–38.

Walbank, F.W. 1940: *Philip V of Macedon*. Cambridge: Cambridge Univ. Press.

Walbank, F.W. 1967: *A Historical Commentary on Polybius, Volume II: Commentary on Books VII–XVIII*. Oxford: Oxford Univ. Press.

Walbank, F.W. 1970: *A Historical Commentary on Polybius, Volume I: Commentary on Books I–VI*. Oxford: Oxford Univ. Press.

Walbank, F.W. 1979: *A Historical Commentary on Polybius, Volume III: Commentary on Books XIX–XL*. Oxford: Oxford Univ. Press.

Warmington, B.H. 1960: *Carthage*. London: Robert Hale.

Waterfield, R. 2011: *Dividing the Spoils: The War for Alexander the Great's Empire*. Oxford: Oxford Univ. Press.

Waterfield, R. 2014: *Taken at the Flood: The Roman Conquest of Greece*. Oxford: Oxford Univ. Press.

Webber, C. 2010: "Fighting on All Sides: Thracian Mercenaries of the Hellenistic Era," in *Ancient Warfare*, Vol. 4, No. 6, p. 38–43.

Wise, T. 1982: *Armies of the Carthaginian Wars, 265–146 BC*. London: Osprey.

Yalichev, S. 1997: *Mercenaries of the Ancient World*. London: Constable.

Index

Achaean League 67
Acichorios 40, 42, 44, 46, 47, 196
acies triplex 27, 171, 175–176
Acra Leuce 205
Adys (256) 58–59
Aetolian League 151
Agadir (c. 236) 88
Agathocles, Syracuse 21, 54, 190–191, 198
Agathocles, Thrace 15, 18–19, 37
agema 29, 197
Ager Falernus (217) 207
Agesilaus 214
agmen 206
agoge 60, 199
Agrianians 146–147, 152, 214
Agron 70
Alabanda (197) 146–147
alae sociorum 28, 212
Alexander, Epirus 15, 29
Alexander III, Great 1, 10, 173–174, 176, 187
Alexander V 14–15
Alexandria Eschate 167
Allia (390) 26, 179–180
Alps 91, 116, 205
anabasis 131
Ancyra (c. 237) 72–73
Androsthenes 145–146, 214
Antaritus 65
Antigonus Gonatus 17, 47, 69
Antigonus Monophthalmos 10–11
Antigonus III, Doson 78, 82
antilabe 6, 87, 202, 216
Antiochus Hierax 71, 201
Antiochus I (Sotor) 48–49
Antiochus III, Great 74, 201
Antiochus IV 165
Aous River (198) 141–142
Aphrodision (c.238) 73
Apollonia 83, 151
Appius Claudius 55, 214
Apulia 33, 97, 99, 108, 113–114
Aratus 67–70, 74–77, 82–83, 201–202
Arcadian Orchomenos (227) 76
Archidamus IV 11–14
Areus 51–54, 60, 198
Argive shield 7–8

Argolid 69, 74, 77–78
Argos, Streets of (272) 52–53
Argyraspides 48, 85–86, 132, 155, 157, 197, 203–204, 215
Arios River (209) 132–133
Aristippus 64, 201
Armenia 167, 176
Arno River 95
artillery 137–138, 252, 213
Asculum (279) 33–35
Aspis (255) 62
Attalus I 73–74, 83, 201
Aufidus River 99
Aurinx (213) 208

Babylonian Apollonia (220) 83–84
Bactria 132, 167, 190, 217
Bactria (167) 165–166
Baebius, Marcus 151, 214
Baecula (208) 115–116
Bagradas Bridge (240) 63–65
Bagradas River 122
barricade 10
bastion 10
Beth-Zacharia (162) 166
bludgeon 10
Bolgios 40–44, 47, 196
Brennus, Senones 180, 196
Brennus, Thermopylae 40, 42, 44–47, 196
Bruttians 35, 106, 193, 211

caetra 199
Caicus Spring (c.238) 73
Callinicus (171) 159–160
Calor River (214) 106–107, 173
Camarina (258) 58
camels 154–155, 158, 215
Camp of Pyrrhus (192) 149–150
Campanians 33, 54, 61, 198
Cannae (216) 99–101
Cannensis Exercitus 211
Canusium (209) 113–114, 172, 175
Cape Hermaeum 62
Caphyae (220) 82–83
Capua 108–109, 111, 193, 209
Carales (220) 103–104
Carpetani 90

Cassander 10, 40, 43
Castulo (211) 110–111
cataphracts 134, 155–156, 174
Caudium/Caudine Forks (321) 27, 180–181, 217
Celtiberian 89
Centenius, Marcus 108
Cerethrios 40, 47
Chaeronea I (338) 10, 82, 173, 200
Chaeronea III (245) 67–68
chainmail 41, 49, 96, 206–207
Chalkaspides 79, 81, 162, 202
Charadrus Pass (235) 52
Chares River (235) 69
chariots 6, 24, 48–49, 83–84, 154–155, 158, 174, 197, 215
Chersonese 47
chiliarchy 145, 152, 190, 197, 215
China 167
chokepoint 14, 19, 40, 42, 53, 63, 78, 85, 150, 162, 170, 179–181
Cincius, Lucius 114–115
Cisalpine Gauls 91
Cissus (218) 94, 205
Cleomenes III 74–78, 80–82, 135, 188, 201–203, 213
Cleomenes' reforms 76, 188
Cleonae (235) 69
Coloe (c.238) 73, 201
Corinth, Isthmus of (285) 53
Cornelius, Marcus 123–124
Cornus (215) 102–103
Corupedium (281) 19–20, 201, 214–215
Crassus, Publius Licinius 159–160, 216
Cretan archers 51, 75–76, 80, 84–86, 131, 140, 145–146, 149–150, 154, 160–161, 212
Crocus Plain (353) 173
Cyamosorus River (c.274) 54–55
cyclosis 8, 138, 187, 207
Cynoscephalae (197) 3, 142–144, 170, 172, 174, 176, 216
Cyrrhestica (284) 17–19
Cyrrhos 17, 203

Dagla Ridge 78–80, 203
Damascus 133

225

Daphne parade 166, 217
Dardanian Frontier (199) 141
Delium (192) 151
Delphi (279/278) 46
Dema Wall 198
Demetrias 151
Demetrius, Poliorcetes 10–19, 28, 37, 47, 67, 169, 188–190, 192–193, 197, 213
Demetrius I 165–166, 217
Demetrius II 69–70, 77, 82, 217
Dertosa/Ibera (215) 104–105
Dinocrates 146–147, 215
Dinocrates, tyrant 159
Diophanes 153–154
Dipaea (c.471) 188
dory/doru 6, 190, 202
double envelopment 62, 65, 72, 94, 101, 105, 158, 170, 196, 200, 206–207
double phalanx 216
Dyme 77

Ebro River 90–91, 94, 104–105, 110
Egypt 9, 11, 14–15, 53–54, 60, 72, 74–76, 82, 84–87, 131, 133, 139–140, 165–166, 170, 176, 204
elephant 24, 193, 197, 199, 211–212
The Elephant Victory (273) 48–49, 191, 201, 215
Elimeia 50, 141
Elpeus River 161
Epicydes 109–110
epilektoi 8
Epizephyrian Locri (208) 114–115, 210
equites 25, 38, 195
Euboa 151–152, 215
Eucratides 166, 217
Eukleidas 78, 80–81
Eumenes of Cardia 212
Eumenes I 54
Eumenes II 155–160, 215
Eurotas River (195) 148–149, 214
Evas 78, 80–82, 202
extraordinarii 95–96, 110

Fabius Maximus 113–114
Fabius Verrucosis, Quintus 97–98
field-works 37–38, 51, 53, 56–58, 63, 77–78
file, depth 7, 25
file, spacing 189–190, 194, 199
Flamininus, Titus Quintus 141, 143
Flaminius, Gaius 94–96, 206
flying column 132, 139, 214
Frederick the Great 13, 188
Fulvius Flaccus, Gneius 108–109, 112, 209

Gabene (317/316) 215
Galatia 48–49, 72–73, 83–84, 155
Gauls/Celts 40–41, 217

Gaza 11, 85, 133–134, 188
Gerunium (217) 97–98
Getae Territory (c.294) 14–15
Glabrio, Manius Acilius 151–154, 214
gladius 25, 207
Golan Heights 133–134
Gorgylos River 78–80
Granicus River (334) 173, 215
Great Plains (203) 122–123
Grumentum (215) 103
Gytheum 149

Haemus Mountains 40
Haliacmon Pass (273) 50
Hamilcar, son of Bomilcar 105
Hamilcar Barca 58–59, 63–66, 88–90, 100, 165, 211
hammer and anvil tactic 132
Hampsicora 102–104, 208
Hannibal Barca 3, 90–102, 104–105, 107–109, 111–117, 119, 121, 125, 129, 158, 173, 175–176, 205–209, 211–212, 215
Hanno, 1st Punic War in Africa 57–58, 199
Hanno, 1st Punic War on Sicily 109–110, 200
Hanno, 2nd Punic War in Iberia 63, 66
Hanno, 2nd Punic War on Sicily 91, 94
Hanno, subordinate of Hannibal Barca 102, 106–107
Harpassos River (c.238) 73
Hasdrubal, 1st Punic War on Sicily 63
Hasdrubal (son-in-law of Hamilcar Barca) 89–90, 205
Hasdrubal Barca 91, 104–107, 110–111, 115–119, 121, 205, 208–210
Hasdrubal Gisco 110, 116, 119–123, 125–128, 209–211
Hasdrubal the Bald 103–104
hasta 25
hastati 26
Hecatombaeum (225) 77, 137
Helenus 38–39, 52–53
Hellespontine Phyrgia (c.238) 73
helots 77–78, 82, 137, 202
Heraclea (280) 3, 29–30, 33–37, 103, 172, 175–176, 189–190, 192–196, 203, 210
Heraclea Minoa (262) 57
Herdonea I (212) 108–109
Herdonea II (210) 112–113, 175, 211
Hermon, Mount 133
Hermos River 154–155
hetairoi (Hetairoi) 188, 197
Hicetas 21–22, 24, 191
Hiero 55–56, 193, 198
Himera River II (211) 109, 175, 209

Himilco 2080209
Hindu Kush 3, 132
Hiostus 102–103
Hippo/Hippacra 63
hoplite, Grecian 6
hoplite, neo 202, 217
Hyblaeus River (c.280) 22, 24
Hydaspes River (326) 61, 188
hypaspists 9

Ilipia (206) 119–121
Iliturgi (215) 105–106
Illyrians 42, 70–71, 80, 82, 137–138, 140–142, 145, 213
Intibili (215) 106
Ipsus (301) 10–11, 14–15, 61, 84, 188, 190, 197, 215, 217
Iranians 85, 204
Issus (333) 157, 173, 197
Isthmus of Corinth (265) 53
Italiotes 33, 36
Ithacus (199) 140

Jaxartes River 187
jinetes 89, 92

kardakes 204
koinon 6
kopis/machaira 6

Ladoceia (227) 75–76
Laevinus 29–30, 193
Lamia I/II (208) 136–137
Lanchester's Linear Law 188
Larissa River (210) 135
Latium 95
Leonidas 46, 153
Leonorios 48
Leptis Minor (238) 66
Leucaspides 162, 202, 216
Leuctra (371) 84, 94, 187, 198, 202, 205, 214
leves 28, 191
Liby-Phoenicians 22
Licinus, L. Porcius 117, 210
Ligurians 97, 117, 121, 129, 198–199
Lilybaeum 36, 91
Longanus River (265) 55
longche 23
lophoi 78
Lucania (212) 107–108, 205
Lucious Manlius Vulso 91–92
Luturios 48
Lydia I/II (c.237) 72
Lydiades 75–76
Lysimacheia (277) 10–11, 14–15, 17–20, 28, 43, 54, 189–190
Lysimachus 47–48

Machanidas 137–139
Magna Graecia 21
Magnesia (190) 154, 156–158, 165, 172, 174, 176, 207, 215
Mago Barca 93–94, 105, 110–111,

115–116, 119, 121, 123–127, 205, 208–209, 211
mahout 118, 129, 133, 212, 215
Maleventum/Beneventum (275) 35, 37, 39, 102, 106, 192–193, 195, 199, 212
Mamers 54
Mamertine War 55
Mancinus, Aulus Hostilius 160
maniples 28
Manlius Torquatus, Titus 102–104
Mantinea II (362) 187
Mantinea IV (294) 11–13, 188
Mantinea V (207) 137, 189
Marathon (490) 196, 207
Marcellus, Marcus Claudius 101–102, 107, 109–110, 113–115, 201, 209
Marcius, Quintus 161
Marucinians 163, 216
Masinissa 110–111, 116, 121–122, 126, 129
Massilia 91
Mathos 65–66
Maximus, Quintus Fabius 113
Medes 204
Mediolanum (203) 123, 125–126, 172, 175, 211
Medion (231) 70–71
Megalopolis (263) 53–54, 201
Megara 44, 69
Megistonus 76–77
Memnon of Heraclea 190, 195
Menippus 151
Messana III/IV (264) 55–56, 198–199
Metaurus River (207) 116–120, 125, 172, 174–175, 210–211
Metellus 63
Milon 39
Minucius Rufus, Marcus 97–98, 101
Mithradates the Great 167, 201
Mixellenes 64
Molon 83–85, 165, 203
Mount Labos Pass (210) 132
Mount Lycaeum (227) 74–75
Mount Oeta 45–46, 201
Mount Panium (200) 133–134
Mount Provatares 78, 81–82
Munda (213) 208
Mutines 109

Nabis 139, 148–150, 213–214
Naravas' Victory (240) 65, 200
Nemea River (197) 145–146, 214
Nero, C. Claudius 117–118, 125, 174, 210
Nicanor 143–144
Nola I (216) 101
Nola II (215) 102, 195, 208, 212
Nola III (216) 107
Northern Aetolia (279/278) 45–46, 196
Novo Cartago 114, 205

Numidia (c.236) 89–90
Numistro (210) 113–115

oarsmen/nautai 47, 197, 208
Oinous River 78
Olympia 115
Olympos 78, 81
Olynthus 215
Orchomenus (227) 76
Orestis Plain (279) 42–43, 171, 196

Paeonians 162
palta 25
Pandosia 30
panoply, Grecian 7
panoply, Roman 25, 28
Panormus (250) 62–63
pantodapoi 18–20, 190, 212
Pantouches 15–16, 189–190
parma 25
Paropus/Thermae (260) 58
Parthia 131–132
Paulus, Lucius Aemilius 98–99, 101, 161–163, 165, 216
Pelignians 163, 216
Pellene (241) 68–69
Pelops 137, 139
peltastai 202
pelte 9
penteconter 70, 198
Pera, Marcus Iunius 101
Pergamum 54
Pergamum (190) 153–154
perioeci 12
Perseus 159–165, 173, 215–217
Persian/Susian Gates 187
Petelia Hill (208) 114
Peuce Island 187
pezhetairoi 187
phalangites 9
Phalanna (171) 160
Phalanx, classical/Doric 7, 169
Phalanx, compound 31, 170
Phalanx, Macedonian 8–10, 170, 176, 188
Pharsalus 142
Pherae 77, 142
Philinos 56, 198
Philip II 82, 5, 8, 10, 15–16, 29, 82, 169–170, 173, 190, 202, 204, 212–213
Philip V 82, 135–136, 148, 151–152, 170, 202, 213
Philopoemen 78, 81, 135–139, 149–150, 153, 159, 200, 213–215
Philopoemen's reforms 135
Phintias 24
Phoenice (230) 71
Phoenice, Treaty of 139
Phylacia (233) 69–70
Pillars of Hercules 3, 88
Pindos Pass (290) 15–17
Placentia 92, 94
Po River 91–92

polemarch 207
polis 6
Pontus 72, 201
porpax 6
Porus 61
principes 28
promachoi 54
psiloi 197
Ptolemy Keraunos 20, 28–30, 35, 42–43, 171, 196
Ptolemy I 11, 14–15, 19–20, 84
Ptolemy II 53–54
Ptolemy III 72, 74, 85
Ptolemy IV 85, 131, 204
Ptolemy V 139
Ptolemy VI 166
Punic War, Third 130
Pydna (168) 162, 164–166, 170, 172–176, 193, 202, 214, 216–217
Pyrrhic/Cadmean victory 33, 118, 194
Pyrrhus 3, 10, 15–17, 19, 24, 28–39, 43, 49–53, 55, 57, 60–61, 71, 80, 90, 102–104, 118, 137, 144, 163, 170, 175–176, 189–190, 192–195, 197, 199, 203, 206, 210, 213
Pythium (168) 161–162

quincunx 126, 128, 138
quinquereme 208

Raphia (217) 84–87, 197, 202–205
Regulus 58–62, 115, 199–200
Rhegium 30, 33, 36, 54–55
rhevma 78
Rhodes 146–147, 214
rightward drift 8
rorarii 25, 28, 191
Royal Road (c. 238) 73

Sacred War, 3rd 196
Saguntum (219) 90
sailors/hyperesiai 47, 197, 208
Salaeca (204) 204
Salinator, M. Livius 117–118
Samnites 27–28, 35–38, 180–181, 194–195
Sardinia 66, 88, 102–103, 173, 208
Sardis (262) 54, 201
sarissa 9
sarissaphoroi 171–172, 217
sauroter 6
Scipio, Cornelius 154–156, 158, 215
Scipio, Gnaeus 94, 104–107, 110–112, 209
Scipio, Publius Cornelius, Africanis 114–116, 119–123, 125–126, 128–129, 154, 161, 174–175, 205, 209–212, 215
Scipio, Publius Cornelius, the elder 91–92, 94, 104–107, 110, 112, 205–206, 209
Scopus 133–134
Scotitas (201) 139

Index

scutarii 89
scutum 26
Segesta (260) 58
Seleucus, son of Antiochus III 153–154, 215
Seleucus I 10–11, 17–20, 37, 43, 84, 190, 197, 201, 217
Seleucus II 71–74, 201
Sellasia (222) 78–82, 144, 163, 170, 176, 200, 202–203, 212–214, 216
Sempronius, Gnaeus 91–96, 102, 106, 205–206
Senones 20, 179–180
sibina (70)
Sicyon 67–69, 74, 77, 145, 201
Sosthenes 43–44
Sparta I (294) 13–14
Sparta II/III (272) 50–52
spartiates 12
speira 70
Spendius 63–65, 200
Stotting/pronging 195
strategia 190
stratiotai 48
Successors of Alexander 5
Sulpicius Galba 136, 140–141, 213
Syphax 122–123, 211
Syrian Wars 84

Tagus River (220) 90
Tarentine horsemen 75, 134, 150, 202
Tartessians 88–89
Tauron 82–83
Taurus Mountains 73
Tegea 75, 78, 139, 149–150
Teleutias 215
Terias River (c.280) 24
Teuta 70–71
Thermopylae (191) 151–153, 172, 215
Thermopylae (279/278) 44–45, 151, 195–196, 201
Thermopylae (480) 46, 151, 193
theurophoroi 41, 171–172, 175, 192
theuros 41, 192, 204–205
thorakitai 137, 213–214
Tiberius Sempronius Gracchus 106
Tiberius Sempronius Longus 91, 102
Ticinus River (218) 91–92
tower, elephant 32, 52, 193, 212
Trasimenus, Lake (217) 92–96, 99, 102, 175, 194, 206–207
triarii 28, 192
trimarcisia 146–147

trireme 196–198
Troezen 69
Trojan War 189
Tunes (255) 60–62, 128, 199–200, 204, 207
Turdetani 119, 210
tyrants 21

Umber, Lake (217) 96
Upper Satrapies 166, 217
Utica 63–64, 121–122

Varo, Gaius Terentius 98–99, 101, 105, 207
Varus, Publius Quinctius 124
velites 191

wagons 34, 51, 160

Xanthippus 3, 59–61, 120, 128, 199–200, 204, 207, 211
Xerxes 44, 152, 196
xiphos 6
xyston 9

Zama (202) 125–129, 172–175, 208, 211